BUDGETING
and
GOVERNING

BUDGETING
and
GOVERNING

Aaron Wildavsky

Edited with a postscript by Brendon Swedlow
and an introduction by Joseph White

Transaction Publishers
New Brunswick (U.S.A.) and London (U.K.)

Library of Congress Catalog Number: 00-062883
ISBN: 0-7658-0033-0
Printed in the United States of America

Library of Congress Cataloging-in-Publication Data

Wildavsky, Aaron B.
   Budgeting and governing / Aaron Wildavsky ; edited by Brendon Swedlow, with an introduction by Joseph White.
     p. cm.
   Includes bibliographical references and index.
   ISBN 0-7658-0033-0 (alk. paper)
   1. Budget. 2. Finance, Public. 3. Budget—United States 4. Finance, Public—United States. I. Swedlow, Brendon II. Title.

HJ2005 .W378 2000
336—dc21
                                                             00-062883

Contents

Acknowledgments

Chapter 1 first appeared in *Public Administration Review* 38, 6(November/ December 1978): 501-9; also in B. Geist, ed., *State Audit:Developments in Public Accountability* (London: Macmillan, 1981): 253-68.

Chapter 2 first appeared in *Public Administration Review* 26, 4 (December 1966):292-310.

Chapter 3 first appeared in *Public Administration Review* 29, 2 (March/April 1969): 189-202.

Chapter 4 first appeared in *Congress: The First Branch of Government: Twelve Studies of the Organization of Congress* (Washington, DC: American Enterprise Institute, 1966): 115-65.

Chapter 5 first appeared in *The Public Interest* 33 (Fall 1973): 84-108; also cited as Working Papers on House Committee Organization and Operation, Select Committee on Committees, U.S. House of Representatives (Washington, DC: GPO,1973).

Chapter 6 first appeared in Thomas Vocino and Jack Rabin, eds., *Contemporary Public Administration* (New York: Harcourt, Brace, Jovanovich, 1981): 261-91.

Chapter 7 first appeared in C. Lowell Harris, ed., *Control of Federal Spending, Proceedings of the Academy of Political Science* 35, 4 (1985): 59-71.

Chapter 8 first appeared in Budgeting: A Comparative Theory of Budgetary Processes, 2nd edition (New Brunswick, NJ: Transaction Publishers, 1986): 7-27.

Chapter 9 first appeared in *Planning and Budgeting in Poor Countries* (New York: John Wiley and Sons, 1974).

Chapter 10 first appeared in *Canadian Public Administration* 26, 2 (Summer 1983): 163-81.

Chapter 11 first appeared *Australian Journal of Public Administration* 42, 4 (December 1983): 421-32.

Chapter 12 first appeared *Journal of Public Economics* 28 (1985): 349-57.

Chapter 13 first appeared in *Journal of Contemporary Studies* 5, 2 (Spring 1982): 3-20.

Chapter 14 first appeared in Ralph Clark Chandler, ed., *A Centennial History of the American Administrative State* (New York: Free Press, 1987): 379-413.

Chapter 16 first appeared in Annelise Anderson and Dennis L. Bark, eds., *Thinking About America: The United States in the 1990s* (Stanford, CA: Hoover Institution Press, 1988): 265-75.

Editor's Preface

This is the third title in a series of Aaron Wildavsky's writings being published posthumously by Transaction.[1] Perhaps two months before his death in September 1993, he went through his vita with me, his research assistant, selecting articles he wished to include in several collections of his papers. He also asked me to search for additional suitable material, including book chapters. We discussed this collection just once more, and then only to the limited extent of agreeing that it should begin with his retrospective on his first budgeting article, the precursor of his path-breaking *Politics of the Budgetary Process*. With three exceptions, then, the articles in this collection include all of the pieces Aaron selected,[2] as well as seven additional papers, two of which were suggested by Joe White,[3] the last student to write a budgeting dissertation and book with Aaron. Joe and I also worked together to sequence and group these pieces into the present arrangement. With one exception, all of the papers here were published previously.

The organization of the collection runs from an introductory section that provides an overview of Aaron's early and final ideas about the political and cultural context of budgeting, including some theoretical discussion, to the incremental theory of budgeting with which he began, to empirical support for the theory, to analysis and criticism of non-incremental reform attempts, and from there to advocacy of incremental reforms—all within the context of American national government. From there, the collection moves to comparisons with budgeting in cities and other countries, beginning with what is perhaps his most comprehensive theoretical statement, encompassing not only culture, but the structural conditions of wealth and certainty, to predict budgetary practices and outcomes all over the world. Following this is a section given over entirely to his cultural analysis of budgeting, where the theory is invoked to explain the causes of budgetary growth, imbalance, and content, as well as the history of American budgeting from colonial to contemporary times. The collection concludes with what was Aaron's primary political, as opposed to scholarly, concern: articles that are as much analysis as advocacy of the (here budgetary) requisites of democratic self-government. Indeed, as he asks in the last piece here, "If you can't budget, how can you govern?"

This collection distinguishes itself from Aaron's many other budgetary books in at least four significant ways. First, it gathers in one place his important collaboration with Otto Davis and M.A.H. Dempster, which allowed a rigorous test of the behavioral regularities he thought he had discovered in the *Politics of the Budgetary Process*. Second, it collects his side of the debate with those who would try to take the politics out of the budgetary process. To the extent this debate centers on particular reform proposals, it may appear dated, but such a reading is misleading for similar proposals with similar flaws are almost a perennial occurrence. If present and future budgetary reformers can survive the concentrated blast found in these pages, they may with some justification conclude that their proposals have merit. Third, since this collection is organized largely chronologically, it allows readers to trace the development of Aaron's thinking about budgeting. Fourth, and he would say most importantly, it gathers in one place the papers that represent the most significant single shift in his conceptualization and analysis of the subject: his "cultural theory" of budgeting. In a postscript, I survey his efforts to apply this theory in this context, suggest how it might be extended to budgetary topics he had previously analyzed in other terms, try to answer criticism, and offer some illustrations of how this anthropological approach might improve future budgetary theorizing.

The scanning or digitalization of Aaron's papers was done by several hardworking Berkeley undergraduates at the Odin Corporation, headed by Sasha Dolbrovsky and assisted by Elise Knowles, Janna Israel, and Jamie Molden. Aaron's long-serving administrative assistant, the late Doris Patton, who, with another research assistant, David Schleicher, also worked to put the notes in a common format, painstakingly removed the considerable errors introduced by this still imperfect process. Aaron's colleagues at the Survey Research Center, Henry Brady and Percy Tannenbaum, took turns monitoring our progress and offered advice and assistance to keep things moving along. Aaron's widow, Mary Wildavsky, and his publisher and longtime friend, Irving Louis Horowitz, did the same from afar. John Elwood read a draft of Joe White's introduction, and Joe, Percy, Naomi Caiden, Richard Coughlin, Margarita Decierdo, Mary Douglas, Richard Ellis, Richard Gunther, Chandra Hunter, Charles Lockhart, Rob Pirro, James Savage, Allen Schick, Michael Thompson, and the late Marcia Whicker commented on my postscript. The Bradley and Smith-Richardson foundations generously supported this large and extended undertaking, while the director of the Survey Research Center, Michael Hout, allowed us the continued use of Aaron's offices.

This collection would not be here in its present form without the contributions of all of these people and organizations. But it would not be here at all without Aaron, who in this multimedia age stands out as a resolute "content provider." Not that he took himself that seriously. He thought that our academic scribblings were only optimistically called knowledge. But he wrote this stuff, while all we have to do is read it. And he hoped that we would. He wanted his collected papers "to say things of interest to contemporary readers," to "stand on their own," to include only things of "lasting significance." He intended to update old material, provide retrospectives on predictions, "however badly the world [had] treated [them]," and add new pieces, "so as to keep faith with [his] conception of collected essays as a living and growing organism, not gray with dust, but green with life."[4] Unfortunately, he did not live long enough to shape this collection in exactly the way he would have liked. But we hope any shortcomings do not hide the green sprouting amid any grays. In fact, Aaron's absence from the final composition of this collection testifies to the power of his original analyses. With this work, he is with us still.

Brendon Swedlow
Oakland, California

Notes

1. The first posthumous title, *Culture and Social Theory*, edited by Sun-Ki Chai and me, contains essays on the social construction of the concepts of public goods, externalities, and national productivity that should also be of interest to readers of this collection. The second posthumous title, *Federalism and Political Culture*, edited by David Schleicher and me, contains essays on the proper character of public administration in a truly federal system, which may also be of interest to readers of this collection. Both were published by Transaction in 1998.
2. Aaron had wanted to include his earliest budgeting article, "Political Implications of Budget Reform," but I felt that it was already adequately represented since his included retrospective on that piece consists of adding italicized paragraphs to it. Another piece he selected, but which I did not include, is his introduction to a volume he co-edited with Michael J. Boskin, "Toward a New Budgetary Order." Most of the text of this piece is reprinted in the "The Budget as New Social Contract," which he also wanted to include, and which is more comprehensive, so I kept it and dropped the other. Finally, I substituted the 1988 "A Cultural Theory of Budgeting" for the 1985 "Budgets as Social Orders" he selected because the more recent piece is a clear attempt to expand the earlier one.
3. In addition to "A Cultural Theory of Budgeting," I added "The Political Economy of Efficiency" because Aaron's included retrospective on that piece, "The Political Economy of Efficiency Has Not Changed But the World Has and So Have I," does not contain enough of the original to make sense without it. I also added "Rescuing Policy Analysis from PPBS" because when read together with the other articles in the section, it should give readers a fuller sense of what Aaron did not like about proposed budgeting reforms and, as importantly, an explanation for why he felt the way that he did. Chapter 1 of *Budgeting*, "Toward a Comparative Theory of Budgetary Processes," and the prologue and introduction to *Planning and Budgeting in Poor Countries* are reprinted here on Joe White's suggestion for the reasons he gives in his introduction. I added "A Cultural Theory of Expenditure Growth and (Un)balanced Budgets" because it is Aaron's best exposition of

the theory in a budgeting context. Finally, I added a copy of a speech Aaron gave to Maastricht officials, "Securing Budgetary Convergence in the European Community Without Central Direction," because it shows the master at work, mobilizing his budgetary knowledge with vigor and humor on behalf of an emerging European governmental structure.

4. *Craftways: On the Organization of Scholarly Work* (New Brunswick, NJ: Transaction Publishers,1989, 1993), p. xi.

Introduction

Aaron Wildavsky wrote about budgeting because, "when a process involves power, authority, culture, consensus and conflict, it captures a great deal of national political life."[1] In the course of his long and yet too short career, Wildavsky's scholarship detailed and explained much of politics besides what can be seen from the study of budgeting. Yet his analyses of budgeting were what established him as, in Richard Rose's words, "the world's leading scholar in public administration."[2]

This book gathers in one place articles that otherwise would be scattered over a world of journals and edited volumes, so that future scholars will have easier access to the work of budgeting's most eminent scholar. They surely justify his claim that the study of budgeting would capture a great deal of political life. Not only does he address budgeting in many different polities, but the concepts that he developed and/or elaborated can be and have been copiously applied elsewhere. Thus many students and practitioners first encountered the concept of "incrementalism" in Aaron's work; his formulation of the unreasonableness of applying common notions of rationality to politics applies to much of both policy-making and administration; and the cultural theory that he applied to budgeting in later work has sweeping implications for the study of political preferences.

The articles collected in this volume are only a part of a rich lifetime of work. Before he passed away, Aaron selected a larger group of articles for consideration. In order to create a more physically and financially manageable volume, the series editor, Professor Irving Louis Horowitz, and I pared the list a bit. We chose to forego those that addressed a more tangential theme (e.g., Social Security reform), or articles that covered ground that also was covered well in articles that are included here. But we also added two chapters to Aaron's original list. Although Wildavsky thought any idea worth publishing once was worth publishing thrice, and duplication and redundancy were sources of certainty rather than waste, he did not publish everything in multiple forms. So we have included chapters from two major works whose contributions would otherwise be missed: *Budgeting: A Comparative Theory of Budgetary Processes*, and *Planning and Budgeting in Poor Countries* (written with Naomi Caiden).

The selections here do not include all of Wildavsky's intellectual contribution. They cannot provide the vibrancy and liveliness, the sense of discovery that one can get from reading the original, *Politics of the Budgetary Process*. It was this book above all that, when published in 1964, made Aaron's reputation.[3] The articles here provide some sense of how their author's understanding changed, such that in 1988 he published *The New Politics of the Budgetary Process*, but they cannot show readers the breadth of that work. Nor does this collection introduce the marvelous account of British budgeting and government that Wildavsky and Hugh Heclo published as, *The Private Government of Public Money*.

But that would be asking too much. In the balance of this introduction I will provide an overview of what is inside, not what is missing. Readers interested in an even broader assessment of Wildavsky's contributions might consult the essays in *Budgeting, Policy, Politics: An Appreciation of Aaron Wildavsky*, especially the bibliographic review by L.R. Jones and Jerry McCaffery.[4] But no one should imagine that any scholar could summarize all that Aaron had to say: the best source by far is Aaron himself.

*   *   *

What Aaron Wildavsky wrote about budgeting changed (and grew) over time because both his data and his questions changed. His studies moved from decision-making in the American federal government, through investigation of budgeting in other contexts, and on to placing budgeting within a broader theory of political culture. The development reflected not just looking at different situations, but asking different questions.

At the end of his career, Aaron's focus was on the origin of the political preferences that drive macrobudgetary trends: the size of government and the broad purposes it serves. Yet his journey through budgeting began with very different questions. At Berkeley, his graduate seminar began with V.O. Key's classic lament about "The Lack of a Budgetary Theory." "On what basis," Key asked, "shall it be decided to allocate X dollars to Activity A instead of Activity B?" And before he did any research, Wildavsky knew that this is the wrong question, "for the excellent reason that the task, as posed, is impossible to fulfill." No answer can be obtained, because it would amount to a normative theory of all of politics.

Aaron's very first work on budgeting, "Political Implications of Budget Reform," makes this point. The introductory section of this collection, "Budgeting, Politics, and the Mirage of "Rationality," begins not with that article but with a retrospective in which Wildavsky considered how his argument had stood up over thirty years.[5] Calls for budget reform, Aaron insists, are often unacceptably vague about what reform should accomplish. He says the point of reform must be to change outputs, and so the preferred change in outputs must be clear from the start. Wildavsky's own preferences about outputs would vary somewhat over time because, as he would say, "what you want depends on what you can get." But he was always explicit about his goals.

Instead of asking what people should do, Aaron began his research on budgeting by asking what the people who made the federal budget did, and why. *The Politics of the Budgetary Process* brilliantly described what we might call the daily life of the federal budget process (then conceived as the making of domestic appropriations): how people managed the task and conflict of budgeting. Its review of strategies did not allow prediction of when specific strategies would either be adopted or succeed, as Aaron's great friend Nelson Polsby reminded him. But explaining the behavior of budgetary actors must be at least a component of any explanation of outputs, so Aaron was willing to begin with the answer that he could obtain first.[6]

How was the budget made? Incrementally. There would be a great deal of later criticism of this answer, but much of it concedes the most useful point.[7] Aaron was criticizing an alternative position that was and remains central to most reform proposals: the idea that budgets can be constructed in a synoptically rational manner.

Aaron taught and wrote and lived on behalf of rationality in the sense of linking means to ends and selecting ends in a way that best exploits the human capacity to reason. Unfortunately, budget reforms usually involve a more limited and limiting version of rationality: deductive logic, quantification for comparison, and ultimately the elimination from budgeting of all political conflict about values. Such an approach could only lose truth by ignoring power—and human nature.

The second, third and fourth chapters of this book hence address the question of where rationality fits into budget processes. "The Political Economy of Efficiency," first published in 1966, describes the limits of a focus on efficiency in compelling terms. Studies of efficiency were, however, one of the main points at which, historically, rational, rigorous analysis entered the political process. In critiquing that limited form of analysis, Wildavsky had to provide a replacement. He did so by helping to define a broader field of policy analysis, both in his writings and as the founding Dean of the Graduate School of Public Policy at Berkeley.[8]

Policy analysis, however, turns out to have an uncomfortable relationship to budgeting. Many practitioners of both were tempted to say that the new form of analysis should drive budget decisions. In "Rescuing Policy Analysis from PPBS," Wildavsky explains why the routines of budgeting should not be allowed to drive analysis (a subject to which we will return). In the fourth chapter of this book, Aaron revisits, in 1989, the argument of "The Political Economy of Efficiency."[9]

These articles show, in varied ways, why common notions of rationality are not reasonable normative standards for a budget process. In *The Politics*, Aaron also showed that decision-making in the federal budget process of the early

1960s did not meet the prerequisites of synoptic rationality. Clearly, no actors had the necessary comprehensive view of the budget; decisions were made by a division of labor and aids to calculation that much better fit the theory of incrementalism. But were decisions, in fact, "incremental," as opposed to fitting some other pattern?

Talk in terms of a base and fair shares, for example, might have been justificatory rhetoric that was not followed in practice. In the original book, Wildavsky therefore provided some summary statistics and tables that supported his argument. But that clearly was not methodologically sufficient, and he soon found colleagues, Otto Davis and M.A.H. Dempster, with whom to embark on much more ambitious analyses. These efforts to build models of federal appropriations became the focus of a long academic dispute.[10]

As a person who came late to this debate, I was never sure what people were arguing about. What, exactly, would one do with a precise specification of the variance explained by incrementalism? Nobody, least of all Aaron Wildavsky, would seriously maintain that all budgeting was totally predictable from a combination of last year's spending and some economic and political summary variables. He could never believe that because it would remove human volition and choice from politics—and if people were not considering and choosing in politics, there would be no reason to write and talk about it. To represent Aaron's side of the controversy, therefore, we have selected only one of the attempts to model budget results, Aaron's essay with M.A.H. Dempster, "On Change: Or, There Is No Magic Size for an Increment," first published in 1979.[11] This essay provides a particularly good discussion of the issues involved in attempting to quantify incrementalism.

Those issues include not just measurement difficulties, but the relationship between policy-making and budgeting. One of the reasons that policy analysis had to be protected from budgeting is that budgeting has goals (such as enforcing legislative dominance of the government, or providing a framework for control of agencies, or pursuit of microefficiencies in management) that are independent of the drift of policy disputes. It is these goals that justify routine budgeting at routine intervals. Policy choice cannot be put on a regular schedule. It depends on an unscheduled development of ideas (such as the delegitimation of counter-cyclical public works spending in the 1970s), or on changes in the world situation (the USSR invades Afghanistan; the USSR disintegrates), or on a change in the composition of the decision-making group (a new subcommittee chairman, or the 1994 election). The modeling work demonstrates this distinction between the rhythms of budgeting and policy-making. Agency budgets tend to be on a fairly stable trend year-to-year, but there are occasional "shift points" in which the trend changes. These shift points are determined exogenously, not by the budget routines; indeed, part of the authors' efforts is to explain the shifts, not to deny them or to consider them "incremental."

As descriptive theory of a decision-making process, then, the case for incrementalism was and remains strong.[12] The logical next question is, "given what they do, how does it come out?" In the early 1960s, Aaron thought the results looked pretty good. So his next question was, "why does it come out okay?" After all, if the "rational," "right" way of making a budget was impossible, how came the results to seem acceptable?

Aaron concluded that the federal budget system was in large measure self-equilibrating, because the participants had adopted a stable pattern of roles. He understood quite clearly that actual outputs depended on many forces outside of the budgeting arena. Even in "Political Implications" he emphasized that the best way to change results would be "to introduce basic political changes (or to wait for secular changes like the growing industrialization of the South)." But, given some stability outside the budget process, budgeting itself could be coordinated without a coordinator: without a central, controlling mind.

That analysis had at least two implications. First, "rationalizing" reforms, by disrupting the pattern of roles, would be more likely to make policy worse than to improve it. Second, Congress was legitimate. Throughout his career Aaron Wildavsky was almost always on the side of the legislature against the executive in disputes about budget procedure.

By the late 1970s, results, in Aaron's view, had changed dramatically. He became an advocate of limits on government spending. But his work on *Forces for Spending and Reforms to Limit It*, as represented in the second section of this collection, was analytically consistent over time. Wildavsky continually sought not discretion for an executive to impose order on the legislature, but limits on legislative discretion that would allow the representative body to control itself.

Aaron's position thus was quite different from the great mass of conservative opponents of "big government," who tend to see Congress as bad and the executive as good. That perspective was reinforced in part by his comparative work. The section on *Budgeting in Comparative Perspective* provides instances of the comparisons that gave Aaron a way to think and test ideas about the background variables of budgeting: not just the strategies, but the overarching norms, or resource contraints, or values that shaped both process and product. From a comparative standpoint, these other things seem to matter much more than the relative strengths of the executive and legislature.

When Wildavsky looked at budgeting outside the federal government—from Oakland to Nepal—he found much the same set of roles, and much the same problems of calculation and consent.[13] He also found that other systems did not seem to equilibrate so easily, that overall outcomes differed so much that one could not even pretend that the budget procedures explained them, and that patterns of budgeting and allocation changed over time. Comparison did not contradict his earlier work. Nothing in his earlier work required that all systems look like the U.S. circa 1962. Instead, comparison provided perspective on the aspects of the U.S. in 1962 that were hard to see from inside that time and place.

The comparative studies in the third section of this volume still represent the same type of analysis as in the original discussion of the United States. In that beginning, budgeting was a decision problem for actors facing a series of constraints (such as each other!). Poor countries and a city like Oakland faced nastier constraints than the federal government had when Aaron did his first research. *Budgeting: A Comparative Theory of Budgetary Processes* defines the variables that structure system behavior in a way that parallels "strategies" and "calculations": namely, amount of and certainty about the available resources. The "norms" of annualarity, comprehensiveness, and balance are another level of the "roles" in the original work. Roles structure disagreement; norms, shared by all participants, are supposed to contain that disagreement within bounds.

"The Transformation of Budgetary Norms" meant, Wildavsky argued, that the only way to make peace among all participants was to spend more: essentially, the spending role had to win. His arguments for various forms of spending limits were presented as ways to recreate the effects of the vanished norms. Comparative work confirmed for Aaron that those norms were not unique to the United States. It also suggested that they had broken down elsewhere as well—at least, if their success were measured by control of the deficit.

But an argument about norms begs the obvious question: why do they change? Somebody must have wanted them to change. Why? Whence do preferences come?

That preferences were important had been clear all along, as shown by the discussion of "shift points" in the modeling efforts. Wildavsky's evolving sense of how preferences matter, and which preferences matter, was also evident in the work on spending control. But when he finally confronted this question head on, Aaron had traveled a long way, only to reach a much more difficult path than the one on which he began. Incrementalism is, after all, a theory of how decisions are made, not what they will be. It is a theory of constrained choice: ultimately, decisions are made incrementally because the supposed alternative, comprehensive calculation, is impossible. But many preferences are possible—aren't they?

Aaron's answer, bold and complex, was that preferences also are constrained. They are constrained by the need to rationalize ways of life. A theory that relates beliefs to ways of life must address far more than budgeting, and what Aaron called "cultural theory" certainly did so.[14] Developing the approach through applications, in collaborations with colleagues such as Richard Ellis, Michael Thompson, and the theory's originator, Mary Douglas, Wildavsky addressed phenomena as diverse as environmental politics, presidential leadership, and Moses. "Cultural theory" became the dominant theme of the last decade of Aaron's work, with only rare exceptions.[15]

Why a theory of culture? Wildavsky rejected economic determinism, such as that it was easy to follow the old budgetary norms while the economy provided regular increments of extra growth, because he did not think those arguments could explain what he saw as growth in good times as well as bad. Nor could they explain the forms of spending that grew (what he called redistributive). Nor could they explain the differences among countries. Was the economic need for government greater in Sweden than in the United States? Although Aaron did argue that the collapse of budgetary norms in the United States might be repaired by an amendment to the constitution, whether people would choose such an amendment had to depend on something.

Unfortunately, Aaron never fully explained the basic theory within his budget papers, so a reader might feel he or she has dropped into the middle of a particularly obscure movie. "Cultural theory's" place in Aaron's work deserves, so has received, a separate compilation of articles.[16] I could not do the theory justice in this space, so I will just offer a few guideposts.

The most basic notion is that ways of life involve choices about with whom to live (the boundaries of one's Group) and the degree of restrictions on one's transactions (which he calls Grid). Group involves both the boundaries among groups and having a sense of place in some group. Grid includes not just notions of what is forbidden and permitted, but who can deal with whom. In some societies group boundaries are quite weak; in others they are quite strong. In some societies there are many limits; in others few. A society with strong senses of group membership (which may mean divided into many groups) and a lot of regulation is called a hierarchy. A society with a strong distinction between insiders, and outsiders, positive view of being inside, but little internal restriction would be a sect (i.e., an egalitarian collective). A society in which group membership matters little and there are few restrictions on transactions is individualistic (e.g., a market form of organization). And, when people are heavily regulated but have little sense of membership in a group (except through shared oppression), they are part of a slavery.

Aaron and his colleagues in cultural theory argued that a preference for any of these ways of life, or even habituation to it (assuming few people actually want to be slaves), can generate or is supported by a wide range of cultural attitudes. Gardens look different in Berkeley than in the English countryside, or at Versailles, because they are the products of different organizational lives. Sectarians see threats from within; hierarchs see threats from outside; and thus, in the America of the 1980s, the former worried more about pollution and the latter more about the Russians. More generally, in the long run cultural attitudes must support organizational life, because people have to justify their lives to themselves and others. So attitudes will come to fit organization (position on a grid/group matrix), or vice versa.

Culture, then, is a set of attitudes that cohere with a way of life. If the balance of cultures changed, so must the balance of budgetary preferences, and conflict would follow. In particular, a set of arrangements that was stable and seemingly self-equilibrating at one time could be destabilized. Incrementalism needed little extra help in the 1950s and early 1960s because the balance of cultures, a mix of individualism and hierarchy with a dash of egalitarianism, was stable. When the 1960s saw a rise in egalitarianism (more or less around the world), the balance was upset and the budget spun out of control. Political conflict then followed cultural lines: hierarchs focusing on balanced budgets above all, though with some preference for defense against outsiders; individualists seeking to restrain taxes (so they would have more with which to make deals) and willing to spend for defense against threats to individualism; and egalitarians demanding more spending and, preferably, higher taxes on the successful (so unfairly unequal) individualists and hierarchs.

Such an ambitious theory is likely to have holes, and this one certainly does.[17] It also was a work in progress, and the applications of the analysis to budgeting should be viewed as steps along a path that was particularly difficult, but that Aaron thought could also have an especially rewarding end. Both the form and the contents of budgeting, he argues in chapters 13 through 15, represent an agreement (perhaps quite temporary) among proponents of different ways of life. Put that way, it may seem a truism; what Wildavsky did, though, was put a tremendous amount of argument and theoretical backbone into that perception. Budgets are not just about allocations of goods, but about how people live together. "Cultural theory" provides a way to discuss the basic terms of shared life, and so relate budgeting to society and polities as a whole.

Aaron was interested in budgeting because of what it could tell us about the classic questions of politics, who gets what and how and why. The progression towards cultural theory followed from a redefinition of the interesting "output": from the budgets of agencies to the budget in total. But it also follows from the understanding that budgeters are not just budgeters: "A Cultural Theory of Budgeting" is about preferences, not roles. It is about society as much as government: budgeting as a conflict among groups about totals rather than among agencies about details. Indeed, budgeting here is a conflict of cultures: of ways of life.

How people choose to live may seem a long way from a discussion of what they cannot do within a routinized governmental process. Yet they may not be further apart than two sides of the same coin. This collection's final section, on "Budgeting and Governing," brings them together.

Budgeting is both routine and fundamental. If you cannot budget, as Wildavsky argues in the first article of this collection, you cannot govern. Indeed, if a group cannot budget, they will have a very hard time living together. Perhaps the budget process is the canary in the political coal mine.

Although Aaron wanted to limit government, he also wanted it to be able to function. He wanted a world of competition among spenders so as to maintain stability of the totals. But when he saw how conflict actually played out, in the American budget battles since 1980, he sought ways to dampen, not intensify, the struggle.[18] If he had an overriding goal as a budget reformer, it was to get expectations in line with possibility in a given jurisdiction. That above all is the point of his suggestions for the EC in the penultimate article. Yet again he seeks to avoid coercive hierarchy (thus, "without central direction"). He seeks rules that he hopes will become norms. As a skeptical policy analyst he recognizes that the Maastricht standards may not make a whole lot of sense, but at least they are more moderate than the American demand for a balanced budget. (What would he say of the new world of budget surpluses that, nonetheless, has not reduced conflict? Would that he were around to tell us!) Aaron saw entitlements as a fundamental problem, but believed they needed to be addressed not by new structures but by political persuasion that would allow government to redefine its promises, by convincing citizens to change what they expect.

This collection, and Aaron's work on budgeting, began with a discussion of budget reform. As Aaron emphasized, it is pointless to discuss reforms without a sense of the society and government one is trying to create. Yet it is equally senseless to ask more of a process than it could possibly give. Reformers need to understand not just the forces that affect, but the limits on, budgeting.

We have chosen to end this collection, therefore, with Aaron's most powerful and synthetic statement about budget reform. In "A Budget for All Seasons?" Aaron reminds us of the frequently forgotten purposes of budgeting. He reminds us that the budgeting that we study and hope to reform is budgeting by governments whose citizenry can demand some sort of accountability. He reminds us that, precisely because it is a basic process of governing, budgeting must be flexible, its procedures usable by factions with very different purposes. He reminds us that budgeting is a process of management as well as policymaking, of operation as well as direction, and that ignoring the former is as unwise as ignoring the implementation of government programs. These goals must be combined with the more standard subjects of dispute, such as economic management and setting national priorities. All must be met, to some extent, for budgeting to serve the needs of governance.

Others might be paralyzed by recognition of such complexity. Aaron cuts through it with insight. "What is it," he asks, "that is inferior for most purposes and yet superior over all?" He elaborates that,

> The ability of a process to score high on one criterion may increase the likelihood of its scoring low on another. Planning requires predictability and economic management requires reversibility. Thus, there may well be no ideal mode of budgeting. If so, this is the question: Do we choose a budgetary process that does splendidly on one criterion but terribly on oth-

ers, or a process that satisfies all these demands even though it does not score brilliantly on any single one?

It's the right question for reformers, and Aaron's answer follows from his sense not just of the legitimacy of many goals, but that the world is unpredictable, so the relative importance of goals will change over time. "Because budgets are contracts within governments signifying agreed understandings, and signals outside of government informing others of what government is likely to do so they can adapt to it, budgets must be good (though not necessarily great) for all seasons."

We could say the same for governments. Aaron Wildavsky was acutely aware that life was hard, that living together was an endless process of compromise and adjustment, that conflict was necessary for progress but also had to be dampened to maintain the prerequisites of society. The study of budgeting captures not only "a great deal of national political life," but also a great deal of what is possible through politics. Incrementalism helps to manage otherwise impossible tasks of calculation and bargaining. Analysis should serve politics, not try to displace it. Expectations should be adjusted to resources, such as levels of wealth or certainty. Decision-making procedures should make it easier for contrary cultures to negotiate the terms of coexistence.

In a world that demands simple reforms and easy answers, the wisdom of Aaron Wildavsky's analyses of budgeting will often be forgotten. Yet it will remain good for all seasons.

Notes

1. Aaron Wildavsky, *Budgeting* (Boston: Little, Brown and Co., 1975), p. xiii.
2. Richard Rose, "Professor Aaron Wildavsky," *The Independent* (London) September 10, 1993.
3. A quarter century later, it was judged the third most influential book published about public administration from 1941 through 1990. See Frank P. Sherwood, "The Half-Century's 'Great Books'" in *Public Administration Review* 50 (March/April 1990).
4. Naomi Caiden and Joseph White, eds., *Budgeting, Policy, Politics: An Appreciation of Aaron Wildavsky* (New Brunswick, NJ: Transaction Publishers, 1995).
5. Readers might also be interested in the other portions of the retrospective, both in *Public Administration Review* 52:6 (Nov/Dec 1992): Glenn Deck, "A Practitioner's Reaction: Reform is Not Politically Neutral," p. 600, and Marcia Lynn Whicker, "An Academician's Response: Toward a Grander Budget Theory," pp. 601-03.
6. For Polsby's critique and Aaron's reply, see L.R. Jones and Jerry McCaffery, "Budgeting According to Wildavsky: A Bibliographic Essay," in Caiden and White, *Budgeting*, fn. 30.
7. For criticism from a variety of angles, see the chapters by Lance T. LeLoup, Irene S. Rubin, Allen Schick, and Jeffrey S. Straussman in *New Directions in Budget Theory*, ed. Irene S. Rubin (Albany: SUNY Press, 1988). Also see Roy T. Meyers, *Strategic Budgeting* (Ann Arbor: The University of Michigan Press, 1996).

8.   Much of his contribution is collected in Aaron Wildavsky, *Speaking Truth to Power: The Art and Craft of Policy Analysis* (Boston: Little, Brown & Co., 1979).
9.   Another article on similar themes, the proper and improper uses of analytic techniques in budgeting, is "The Shifting Sands of Cost-Benefit Analysis," in *Scritti in onore di Alberto Mortara*, Vol. 2, eds. G. Bognetti, G. Muraro, and M. Pinchera (Milano: Franco Angeli, 1990), pp. 1003-1017.
10. Among the best examples of articles that offered alternatives to Wildavsky et al.'s incremental theory, or identified difficulties in the whole enterprise, see William D. Berry, "Testing Budgetary Theories with Budgetary Data: Assessing the Risks," *American Journal of Political Science* 30:3 (August 1986), pp. 597-627; John F. Padgett, "Bounded Rationality in Budgetary Research," *American Political Science Review* 74 (1980), pp. 354-372; and John Wanat, "Bases of Budgetary Incrementalism," *American Political Science Review* 68 (September 1974), pp. 1221-28.
11. Others include Otto A. Davis, M.A.H. Dempster, and Aaron Wildavsky, "A Theory of the Budgetary Process," *American Political Science Review* Vol. 60, No. 3 (September 1966), pp. 529-47; Davis, Dempster, and Wildavsky, "On the Process of Budgeting: An Empirical Study of Congressional Appropriations," in *Papers in Non-Market Decision-Making, ed.* Gordon Tullock (Charlottesville: Thomas Jefferson Center for Political Economy, University of Virginia, 1966), pp. 63-132; Davis, Dempster and Wildavsky, "On the Process of Budgeting II: An Empirical Study of Congressional Appropriations," in *Studies in Budgeting*, ed. R. F. Byrne et al.(Amsterdam: North-Holland, 1971), pp. 292-392; Davis, Dempster, and Wildavsky, "Towards a Predictive Theory of Government Expenditure: U.S. Domestic Appropriations," *British Journal of Political Science* Vol. 4 (1974), pp. 419-452; and Dempster and Wildavsky, "Modeling the U.S. Federal Spending Process: Overview and Implications," in *The Grants Economy and Collective Consumption, eds.* R.C.O. Matthews and G.B. Stafford (London: Macmillan, 1983), pp. 267-309.
12. For further elaboration of this point see Joseph White, "(Almost) Nothing New Under the Sun: Why the Work of Budgeting Remains Incremental" in *Budgeting, Policy, Politics: An Appreciation of Aaron Wildavsky, eds.* Naomi Caiden and Joseph White (New Brunswick, NJ: Transaction Publishers, 1995), pp. 111-132.
13. In addition to the three chapters included here, readers might be interested in Arnold J. Meltsner and Aaron Wildavsky, "Leave City Budgeting Alone! A Survey, Case Study, and Recommendations for Reform," in *Financing the Metropolis: The Role of Public Policy in Urban Economics*,eds. John P. Crecine and Louis H. Masotti, Vol. 4(Beverly Hills, CA: Sage Publications, 1970), pp. 311-358.
14. I put the term in quotes because its use otherwise suggests that the line of argument Wildavsky and many others have followed is the only possible form of cultural theory, which I rather doubt.
15. The only exception, in his later budgeting work, was our own collaborations on *The Deficit and the Public Interest: The Search for Responsible Budgeting in the 1980s* (Berkeley and New York: The University of California Press and The Russell Sage Foundation, 1989 and 1991), and related articles. That is one reason that the publisher and I chose to exclude articles that Aaron and I co-authored and that Aaron at first selected for this volume. The most sweeping and challenging of those pieces is "Public Authority and the Public Interest: What the 1980s Budget Battles Tell Us About the American State," *Journal of Theoretical Politics* Vol. 1, No. 1 (1989), pp. 7-31. I think Aaron would argue, if he were here, that the phe-

nomena that we identified and critiqued could be explained in terms of cultural theory. For example, he could say that the phenomenon of centrist politicians sowing panic about the deficit can be explained in terms of the usual concerns of people with hierarchical values. But we didn't say that, because I'm not sure I agree!

16. Aaron Wildavsky, *Culture and Social Theory*, eds.Sun-Ki Chai and Brendon Swedlow (New Brunswick, NJ: Transaction Publishers, 1998). For other introductions to the work, see Michael Thompson, Richard Ellis, and Aaron Wildavsky, *Cultural Theory* (Boulder,CO: Westview Press, 1990), and Mary Douglas and Aaron Wildavsky, *Risk and Culture: An Essay on the Selection of Environmental and Technological Dangers* (Berkeley: University of California Press, 1983).

17. A whole raft-full of challenges are possible. It is not so easy to distinguish group from grid, nor even to classify any individual's organizational life, since in modern society we often live in many different types of organizations. Nor is it so easy to distinguish among types of group boundaries: when does a hierarchy with substantial inequalities become a slavery, and is a slavery a slavery for just the slaves, or the masters as well? Most important, while cultural theory may make sense for certain kinds of budgetary studies, such as the evolution of budget processes over the history of the Western world, its logic may not be appropriate for the kinds of questions Aaron addresses in the chapters in this volume. The logic of change in the theory is essentially evolutionary: over time, certain attitudes should fit best with certain organizational forms. Aaron then could argue that environmentalism in the long run challenges individualistic organization, so that an individualistic society must eventually either downplay environmental concerns or become more egalitarian or hierarchical. But environmentalism could nevertheless arise due to stresses within individualistic society, or even plain old entrepreneurial politics (some individualist selling environmental soft soap). To say that the environmental movement arose because of an increase in egalitarianism could be either dead wrong or get the direction of causation backwards, even if the basic insights of "cultural theory" were correct. Using the theory to explain short-term budgetary developments may be equally inappropriate.

18. See Joseph White and Aaron Wildavsky, "How to Fix the Deficit—Really" *The Public Interest* no. 94 (Winter 1989), pp. 3-24.

Part 1

Making Budgets

1

A Budget for All Seasons?
Why the Traditional Budget Lasts

Almost from the time the caterpillar of budgetary evolution became the butterfly of budgetary reform, the line-item budget has been condemned as a reactionary throwback to its primitive larva. Budgeting, its critics claim, has been metamorphosed in reverse, an example of retrogression instead of progress. Over the last century, the traditional annual cash budget has been condemned as mindless, because its lines do not match programs, irrational, because they deal with inputs instead of outputs, shortsighted, because they cover one year instead of many, fragmented, because as a rule only changes are reviewed, conservative, because these changes tend to be small, and worse. Yet despite these faults, real and alleged, the traditional budget reigns supreme virtually everywhere, in practice if not in theory. Why?

The usual answer, if it can be dignified as such, is bureaucratic inertia. The forces of conservatism within government resist change. Presumably the same explanation fits all cases past and present. How, then, explain why countries like Britain departed from tradition in recent years only to return to it? It is hard to credit institutional inertia in virtually all countries for a century. Has nothing happened over time to entrench the line-item budget?

The line-item budget is a product of history, not of logic. It was not so much created as evolved. Its procedures and its purposes represent accretions over time rather than propositions postulated at a moment in time. Hence we should not expect to find them either consistent or complementary.

Control over public money and accountability to public authority were among the earliest purposes of budgeting. Predictability and planning—knowing what there will be to spend over time—was not far behind. From the beginning, relating expenditure to revenue was of prime importance. In our day we have added macro-economic management to moderate inflation and unemployment.

3

Spending is varied to suit the economy. In time the need for money came to be used as a lever to enhance the efficiency or effectiveness of policies. He who pays the piper hopes to call the tune. Here we have it: Budgeting is supposed to contribute to continuity (for planning), to change (for policy evaluation), to flexibility (for the economy), and to provide rigidity (for limiting spending).

These different and (to some extent) opposed purposes contain a clue to the perennial dissatisfaction with budgeting. Obviously, no process can simultaneously provide continuity and change, rigidity and flexibility. And no one should be surprised that those who concentrate on one purpose or the other should find budgeting unsatisfactory or that, as purposes change, these criticisms should become constant. The real surprise is that traditional budgeting has not been replaced by any of its outstanding competitors in this century.

If traditional budgeting is so bad, why are there no better alternatives? Appropriate answers are unobtainable, I believe, so long as we proceed on this high level of aggregation. So far as I know, the traditional budget has never been compared systematically, characteristic for characteristic, with the leading alternatives.[1] By doing so we can see better which characteristics of budgetary processes suit different purposes under a variety of conditions. Why, again, if traditional budgeting does have defects, which I do not doubt, has it not been replaced? Perhaps the complaints are the clue: What is it that is inferior for most purposes and yet superior over all?

The ability of a process to score high on one criterion may increase the likelihood of its scoring low on another. Planning requires predictability and economic management requires reversibility. Thus, there may well be no ideal mode of budgeting. If so, this is the question: Do we choose a budgetary process that does splendidly on one criterion but terribly on others, or a process that satisfies all these demands even though it does not score brilliantly on any single one?

The Traditional Budget

Traditional budgeting is annual (repeated yearly) and incremental (departing marginally from the year before). It is conducted on a cash basis (in current dollars). Its content comes in the form of line-items (such as personnel or maintenance). Alternatives to all these characteristics have been developed and tried, though never, so far as I know, with success. Why this should be so, despite the obvious and admitted defects of tradition, will emerge if we consider the criteria each type of budgetary process has to meet.

What purpose is a public sector budget supposed to serve? Certainly one purpose is accountability. By associating government publicly with certain expenditures, opponents can ask questions or contribute criticisms. Here the clarity of the budget presentation in linking expenditures to activities and to responsible officials is crucial. Close to accountability is control: Are the funds which are authorized and appropriated being spent for the designated activities? Control (or its antonym "out of control") can be used in several senses. Are expenditures within the limits (a) stipulated or (b) desired? While a budget (or item) might be "out of control" to a critic who desires it to be different, in our terms "control" is lacking only when limits are stipulated and exceeded.

Budgets may be mechanisms of efficiency—doing whatever is done at least cost or getting the most out of a given level of expenditure—and/or of effectiveness—achieving certain results in public policy like improving the health of children or reducing crime.

In modern times, budgeting has also become an instrument of economic management and of planning. With the advent of Keynesian economics efforts have been made to vary the rate of spending so as to increase employment in slack times or to reduce inflation when prices are deemed to be rising too quickly. Here (leaving out alternative tax policies), the ability to increase and decrease spending in the short run is of paramount importance. For budgeting to serve planning, however, predictability (not variability) is critical. The ability to maintain a course of behavior over time is essential.

Now, as everyone knows, budgeting is not only an economic but a political instrument. Since inability to implement decisions nullifies them, the ability to mobilize support is as important as making the right choice. So is the capacity to figure out what to do—that is, to make choices. Thus, the effect of budgeting on conflict and calculation—the capacity to make and support decisions—has to be considered.

Unit of Measurement: Cash or Volume

Budgeting can be done not only in cash but by volume. Instead of promising to pay so much in the next year or years, the commitment can be made in terms of operations performed or services provided. Why might anyone want to budget in volume (or constant currency) terms? One reason, obviously, is to aid planning. If public agencies know they can count not on variable currency but on what the currency can buy, that is, on a volume of activity, they can plan ahead as far as the budget runs. Indeed, if one wishes to make decisions now that could be made at future periods, so as to help assure consistency over time, stability in the unit of effort—so many applications processed or such a level of services provided—is the very consideration to be desired.

So long as purchasing power remains constant, budgeting in cash or by volume remains a distinction without a difference. However, should the value of money fluctuate (and, in our time, this means inflation), the public budget must absorb additional amounts so as to provide the designated volume of activity. Budgeters lose control of money because they have to supply whatever is needed. Evidently, given large and unexpected changes in prices, the size of the budget in cash terms would fluctuate wildly. Evidently, also, no government could permit itself to be so far out of control. Hence, the very stability budgeting by volume is designed to achieve turns out to be its major unarticulated premise.

Who pays the price for budgeting by volume? The private sector and the central controller. Budgeting by volume is, first of all, an effort by elements of the public sector to invade the private sector. What budgeting by volume says, in effect, is that the public sector will be protected against inflation by getting its agreed level of services before other needs are met. The real resources necessary to make up the gap between projected and current prices must come from the private sector in the form of taxation or interest for borrowing. In other words, for the public sector volume budgeting is a form of indexing against inflation.

Given an irreducible amount of uncertainty in the system, not every element can be stabilized at one and the same time. Who, then, will be kept stable and who will bear the costs of change? Within the government the obvious answer is that spending by agencies will be kept whole. The central budget office (the Treasury, Ministry of Finance or the Office of Management and Budget, as it is variously called) bears the brunt of covering larger expenditures and takes the blame when the budget goes out of control, i.e., rises faster and in different directions than predicted. In Britain, where budgeting by volume went under the name of the Public Expenditure Survey, the Treasury finally responded to years of severe inflation by imposing cash limits, otherwise known as the traditional cold-cash budget. Of course, departmental cash limits include an amount for price changes, but this is not necessarily what the Treasury expects but the amount it desires. The point is that the spending departments have to make up deficits caused by inflation. Instead of the Treasury forking over the money automatically, as in the volume budget, departments have to ask and may be denied. The local spenders, not the central controllers, have to pay the price of monetary instability.[2]

Inflation has become not only an evil to be avoided but a (perhaps *the*) major instrument of modern public policy. Taxes are hard to increase and benefits are virtually impossible to decrease. Similar results may be obtained through inflation, which artificially elevates the tax brackets in which people find themselves and decreases their purchasing power. Wage increases that cannot be directly contested may be indirectly nullified (and the real burden of the national debt reduced) without changing the ostensible amount, all by inflation. The sensitivity of budgetary forms to inflation is a crucial consideration.

From all this, it follows that budgeting by volume is counterproductive in fighting inflation because it accommodates price increases rather than strug-

gling against them. Volume budgeting may maintain public sector employment at the expense of taking resources from the private sector, thus possibly
reducing employment there. There can be no doubt, however, that volume budgeting is for counter-cyclical purposes because the whole point is that the amount
and quality of service do not vary over time; if they go up or down to suit short-
run economic needs they are bound to be out of kilter over the long run.

How does volume budgeting stack up as a source of policy information? It
should enable departments to understand better what they are doing, since they
are presumably doing the same thing over the period of the budget, but volume
budgeting does poorly as a method of instigating change. For one thing, the
money is guaranteed against price changes, so there is less need to please outsiders. For another, volume budgeting necessarily leads to interest in internal
affairs—how to do what one wishes—not to external advice—whether there
are better things one might be doing. British departments that are unwilling to
let outsiders evaluate their activities are hardly going to be motivated by guarantees against price fluctuations.

Time Span: Months, One Year, Many Years

Multiyear budgeting has long been proposed as a reform to enhance rational choice by viewing resource allocation in a long-term perspective. Considering one year, it has been argued, leads to shortsightedness—only the next
year's expenditures are reviewed; overspending—because huge disbursements
in future years are hidden; conservatism—incremental changes do not open up
larger future vistas; and parochialism—programs tend to be viewed in isolation rather than in comparison to their future costs in relation to expected revenue. Extending the time-span of budgeting to three or five years, it is argued,
would enable long-range planning to overtake short-term reaction and substitute financial control for merely muddling through. Moreover, it is argued, the
practice of rushing spending to use up resources by the end of the year would
decline in frequency.

Much depends, to be sure, on how long budgetary commitments last. The
seemingly arcane question of whether budgeting should be done on a cash or a
volume basis will assume importance if a nation adopts multiyear budgeting.
The longer the term of the budget, the more important inflation becomes. To
the degree that price changes are automatically absorbed into budgets, a certain volume of activity is guaranteed. To the degree agencies have to absorb
inflation, their real level of activity declines. Multiyear budgeting in cash terms
diminishes the relative size of the public sector, leaving the private sector larger.
Behind discussions of the span of the budget, the real debate is over the relative shares of the public and private sectors—which one will be asked to absorb inflation and which one will be allowed to expand into the other.

A similar issue of relative shares is created within government by proposals to budget in some sectors for several years, and, in others, for only one. Which sectors of policy will be free from the vicissitudes of life in the short term, the question becomes, and which will be protected from them? Like any other device, multiyear budgeting is not neutral but distributes indulgences differently among the affected interests.

Of course, multiyear budgeting has its positive parts. If control of expenditure is desired, for instance, a multiyear budget makes it necessary to estimate expenditures far into the future. The old tactic of the camel's nose—beginning with small expenditures while hiding larger ones later on—is rendered more difficult. Still, hard-in, as the British learned, often implies harder-out. Once an expenditure gets in a multiyear projection it is likely to stay in because it has become part of an interrelated set of proposals that could be expensive to disrupt. Besides, part of the bargain struck when agencies are persuaded to estimate as accurately as they can, is that they will gain stability, i.e., not be subject to sudden reductions according to the needs of the moment. Thus, control in a single year may have to be sacrificed to maintaining limits over the multiyear period; and, should the call come for cuts to meet a particular problem, British experience shows that reductions in future years, (which are always "iffy") are easily traded for maintenance of spending in the all-important present. By making prices more prominent due to the larger time period involved, moreover, large sums may have to be supplied in order to meet commitments for a given volume of services in a volatile world.[3]

Suppose, however, that it were deemed desirable to reduce significantly some expenditures in order to increase others. Due to the built-in pressure of continuing commitments, what can be done in a single year is extremely limited. Making arrangements over a three-to-five-year period (with constant prices, five percent a year for five years compounded would bring about a one-third change in the budget) would permit larger changes in amount in a more orderly way. This may be true, of course, but other things—prices, priorities, politicians—seldom remain equal. While the British were working under a five-year budget projection, prices and production could hardly be predicted for five months at a time.

As Robert Hartman put it, "there is no absolutely right way to devise a long-run budget strategy."[4] No one knows how the private economy will be doing or what the consequences will be of a fairly wide range of targets for budget totals. There is no political or economic agreement on whether budget targets should be expressed in terms of levels required for full employment, for price stability, or for budget balancing. Nor is it self-evidently desirable either to estimate where the economy is going and devise a governmental spending target to complement that estimate or to decide what the economy should be doing and get the government to encourage that direction.

In any event, given economic volatility and theoretical poverty, the ability to outguess the future is extremely limited. Responsiveness to changing economic conditions, therefore, if that were the main purpose of budgeting, would be facilitated best with a budget calculated in months or weeks rather than years. Such budgets do exist in poor and uncertain countries. Naomi Caiden and I have called the process "repetitive budgeting to signify that the budget may be made and remade several times during the year.[5] Because finance ministries often do not know how much is actually in the nation's treasury or what they will have to spend, they hold off making decisions until the last possible moment. The repetitive budget is not a reliable guide to proposed expenditure, but an invitation to agencies to "get it if they can." When economic or political conditions change, which is often, the budget is renegotiated. Adaptiveness is maximized but predictability is minimized. Conflict increases because the same decision is remade several times each year. Agencies must be wary of each other because they do not know when next they will have to compete. Control declines, partly because frequent changes make the audit trail difficult to follow, and partly because departments seek to escape from control so as to reestablish a modicum of predictability. Hence, they obfuscate their activities, thus reducing accountability, and actively seek funds of their own in the form of earmarked revenues, thus diminishing control. Both efficiency and effectiveness suffer. The former is either unnecessary (if separate funds exist) or impossible (without continuity), and the latter is obscured by the lack of relationship between what is in the budget and what happens in the world. Drastically shortening the time frame wreaks havoc with efficiency, effectiveness, conflict, and calculation. However, if it is immediate responsiveness that is desired, as in economic management, the shorter the span the better.

Just as the annual budget on a cash basis is integral to the traditional process, so is the budgetary base—the expectation that most expenditures will be continued. Normally, only increases or decreases to the existing base are considered in any one period. If budgetary practices may be described as incremental, the main alternative to the traditional budget is one that emphasizes comprehensive calculation. So it is not surprising that the main modern alternatives are planning, programming and budgeting (PPB) and zero-base budgeting (ZBB).

Calculation: Incremental or Comprehensive

Let us think of PPB as embodying horizontal comprehensiveness—comparing alternative expenditure packages to decide which best contributes to larger programmatic objectives. ZBB, by contrast, might be thought of as manifesting vertical comprehensiveness—every year alternative expenditures from base zero are considered for all governmental activities or objectives treated as discrete entities. In a word, PPB compares programs and ZBB compares alternative funding.

The strength of PPB lies in its emphasis on policy analysis to increase effectiveness. Programs are evaluated, found wanting, and presumably replaced with alternatives designed to produce superior results. Unfortunately, PPB engenders a conflict between error recognition and error correction. There is little point in designing better policies so as to minimize their prospects of implementation. But why should a process devoted to policy evaluation end up stultifying policy execution? Because PPB's policy rationality is countered by its organizational irrationality.

If error is to be altered, it must be relatively easy to correct,[6] but PPB makes it hard. The "systems" in PPB are characterized by their proponents as highly differentiated and tightly linked. The rationale for program budgeting lies in its connectedness—like-programs are grouped together. Program structures are meant to replace the confused concatenations of line-items with clearly differentiated, non-overlapping boundaries; only one set of programs to a structure. This means that a change in one element or structure must result in change reverberating throughout every element in the same system. Instead of alerting only neighboring units or central control units, which would make change feasible, all are, so to speak, wired together so the choice is effectively all or none.

Imagine one of us deciding whether to buy a tie or a kerchief. A simple task, one might think. Suppose, however, that organizational rules require us to keep our entire wardrobe as a unit. If everything must be rearranged when one item is altered, the probability we will do anything is low. The more tightly linked the elements, and the more highly differentiated they are, the greater the probability of error (because the tolerances are so small), and the less likelihood the error will be corrected (because with change, every element has to be recalibrated with every other one that was previously adjusted). Being caught between revolution (change in everything) and resignation (change in nothing) has little to recommend it.

Program budgeting increases rather than decreases the cost of correcting error. The great complaint about bureaucracies is their rigidity. As things stand, the object of organizational affection is the bureau as serviced by the usual line-item categories from which people, money, and facilities flow. Viewed from the standpoint of bureau interests, programs, to some extent, are negotiable; some can be increased and others decreased while keeping the agency on an even keel or, if necessary, adjusting it to less happy times without calling into question its very existence. Line-item budgeting, precisely because its categories (personnel, maintenance, supplies) do not relate directly to programs, is easier to change. Budgeting by programs, precisely because money flows to objectives, makes it difficult to abandon objectives without abandoning the organization that gets its money for them. It is better that non-programmatic rubrics be used as formal budget categories, thus permitting a diversity of analytical perspectives, than that a temporary analytic insight be made the permanent perspective through which money is funneled.

The good organization is interested in discovering and correcting its own mistakes. The higher the cost of error—not only in terms of money but also in personnel, programs, and prerogatives—the less the chance anything will be done about them. Organizations should be designed, therefore, to make errors visible and correctable—that is, noticeable and reversible—which, in turn, is to say, cheap and affordable.

The ideal, ahistorical information system is zero-base budgeting. The past, as reflected in the budgetary base (common expectations as to amounts and types of funding), is explicitly rejected. There is no yesterday. Nothing is to be taken for granted. Everything at every period is subject to searching scrutiny. As a result, calculations become unmanageable. The same is true of PPB, which requires comparisons of all or most programs that might contribute to common objectives. To say that a budgetary process is ahistorical is to conclude that it increases the sources of error while decreasing the chances of correcting mistakes. If history is abolished, nothing is settled. Old quarrels become new conflicts. Both calculation and conflict increase exponentially, the former worsening selection, and the latter, correction of error. As the number of independent variables grows, because the past is assumed not to limit the future, ability to control the future declines. As mistrust grows with conflict, willingness to admit and, hence, to correct error diminishes. Doing without history is a little like abolishing memory—momentarily convenient, perhaps, but ultimately embarrassing.

Only poor countries come close to zero-base budgeting, not because they wish to do so but because their uncertain financial position continually causes them to go back on old commitments. Because past disputes are part of present conflicts, their budgets lack predictive value; little stated in them is likely to occur. Ahistorical practices, which are a dire consequence of extreme instability and from which all who experience them devoutly desire to escape, should not be considered normative.

ZBB and PPB share an emphasis on the virtue of objectives. Program budgeting is designed to relate larger to smaller objectives among different programs, and zero-base budgeting promises to do the same within a single program. The policy implications of these methods of budgeting, which distinguish them from existing approaches, derive from their overwhelming concern with ranking objectives. Thinking about objectives is one thing, however, and making budget categories out of them is quite another. Of course, if one wants the objectives of today to be the objectives of tomorrow, which is to say if one wants no change in objectives, then building the budget around objectives is a brilliant idea. However, if one wants flexibility in objectives (sometimes known as learning from experience) it must be possible to change them without simultaneously destroying the organization by withdrawing financial support.

Both PPB and ZBB are expressions of the prevailing paradigm of rationality in which reason is rendered equivalent to ranking objectives. Alas, an efficient mode of presenting results in research papers—find objectives, order them, choose the highest valued—has been confused with proper processes of social inquiry. For purposes of resource allocation, which is what budgeting is about, ranking objectives without consideration of resources is irrational. The question can not be "what do you want?" as if there were no limits, but should be "what do you want compared to what you can get?" (Ignoring resources is as bad as neglecting objectives as if one were not interested in the question "what do I want to do this for?"). After all, an agency with a billion dollars would not only do more than it would with a million dollars but might well wish to do different things. Resources affect objectives as well as the other way around, and budgeting should not separate what reason tells us belongs together.

For purposes of economic management, comprehensive calculations stressing efficiency (ZBB) and effectiveness (PPB) leave much to be desired. For one thing, comprehensiveness takes time and this is no asset in responding to fast-moving events. For another, devices that stress the intrinsic merits of their methods—this is (in)efficient and that is (in)effective—rub raw when good cannot be done for external reasons, i.e., the state of the economy. Cooperation will be compromised when virtue in passing one test becomes vice in failing another.

I have already said that conflict is increased by ahistorical methods of budgeting. Here I wish to observe that efforts to reduce conflict only make things worse by vitiating the essential character of comprehensiveness. The cutting edge of competition among programs lies in postulating a range of policy objectives small enough to be encompassed and large enough to overlap so there are choices (trade-offs in the jargon of the trade) among them. Instead, PPB generated a tendency either to have only a few objectives, so anything and everything fit under them, or a multitude of objectives, so that each organizational unit had its own home and did not have to compete with any other.[7] ZBB worked it this way: since a zero base was too threatening or too absurd, zero moved up until it reached, say, 80 percent of the base. To be sure, the burden of conflict and calculation declined, but so did any real difference with traditional incremental budgeting.

Insofar as financial control is concerned, ZBB and PBB raise the question of control over what? Is it control over the content of programs or the efficiency of a given program or the total costs of government or just the legality of expenditures? In theory, ZBB would be better for efficiency, PPB for effectiveness, and traditional budgeting for legality. Whether control extends to total costs, however, depends on the form of financing, a matter to which we now turn.

Appropriations or Treasury Budgeting

A traditional budget, without saying much about it, depends on traditional practice—authorization and appropriation followed by expenditure post-audited by external authorities. In many countries traditional budgeting is not, in fact, the main form of public spending. Close to half of public spending in the United States as well as in other countries does not take the form of appropriations budgeting, but what I shall call treasury budgeting. I find this nomenclature useful in avoiding the pejorative connotations of what would otherwise be called "backdoor" spending, because it avoids the appropriations committees in favor of automatic disbursement of funds through the treasury.

For present purposes, the two forms of treasury budgeting that constitute alternatives to traditional appropriations are tax expenditures and mandatory entitlements. When concessions are granted in the form of tax reductions for home ownership or college tuition or medical expenses these are equivalent to budgetary expenditures except that the money is deflected at the source. In the United States, tax expenditures now amount to more than $100 billion a year. In one sense this is a way of avoiding budgeting before there is a budget. Whether one accepts this view is a matter of philosophy. It is said, for instance, that the United States government has a progressive income tax. Is that the real tax system or is it a would-be progressive tax as modified by innumerable exceptions? The budgetary process is usually described as resource allocation by the president and Congress through its appropriations committees. Is that the real budgetary process or is it that process together with numerous provisions for "backdoor" spending, low interest loans, and other devices? From a behavioral or descriptive point-of-view actual practices constitute the real system. Then the exceptions are part of the rule. Indeed, since less than half of the budget passes through the appropriations committees, the exceptions must be greater than the rule, and some would say the same could be said about taxation. If the exceptions are part of the rule, however, tax expenditures stand in a better light. Then the government is not contributing or losing income but legitimately excluding certain private activities from being considered as income. There is no question of equity—people are just disposing of their own income as they see fit in a free society. Unless whatever is, is right, tax and budget reformers will object to sanctifying regrettable lapses as operating principles. To them the real systems are the ones which we ought to perfect—a progressive tax on income whose revenues are allocated at the same time through the same public mechanism. Tax expenditures interfere with both these ideals.

Mandatory, open-ended entitlements, our second category of treasury budgeting, provide that anyone eligible for certain benefits must be paid regardless of the total. Until the legislation is changed or a "cap" limits total expenditure, entitlements constitute obligations of the state through direct drafts on the treasury. Were I asked to give an operational definition of the end of budgeting, I would say "indexed, open-ended entitlements." Budgeting would no longer involve allocation within limited resources but only addition of one entitlement to another, all guarded against fluctuation in prices.

Obviously, treasury budgeting leaves a great deal to be desired in controlling costs of programs, which depend on such variables as levels of benefits set in prior years, rate of application, and severity of administration. Legal control is possible but difficult because of the large number of individual cases and the innumerable provisions governing eligibility. If the guiding principle is that no one who is eligible should be denied even if some who are ineligible must be included, expenditures will rise. They will decline if the opposite principle—no ineligibles even if some eligibles suffer—prevails.[8]

Whether or not entitlement programs are efficient or effective, the budgetary process will neither add to nor subtract from that result simply because it plays no part. To the extent that efficiency or effectiveness are spurred by the need to convince others to provide funds, such incentives are much weakened or altogether absent. The political difficulties of reducing benefits or eliminating beneficiaries speak eloquently on this subject. No doubt benefits may be eroded by inflation. Protecting against this possibility is the purpose of indexing benefits against inflation (thus doing for the individual what volume budgeting does for the bureaucracy).

Why, then, in view of its anti-budgetary character, is treasury budgeting so popular? Because of its value in coping with conflict, calculation, and economic management. After a number of entitlements and tax expenditures have been decided upon at different times, usually without full awareness of the others, implicit priorities are produced ipso-facto, untouched as it were, by human hands. Conflict is reduced, for the time being at least, because no explicit decisions giving more to this group and less to another are necessary. Ultimately, to be sure, resource limits will have to be considered, but even then only a few rather than all expenditures will be directly involved, since the others go on, as it were, automatically. Similarly, calculation is contracted as treasury budgeting produces figures, allowing a large part of the budget to be taken for granted. Ultimately, of course, days of reckoning come in which there is a loss of flexibility due to the implicit preprogramming of so large a proportion of available funds. For the moment, however, the attitude appears to be "sufficient unto the day is the (financial) evil thereof."

For purposes of economic management, treasury budgeting is a mixed bag. It is useful in providing what are called automatic stabilizers. When it is deemed desirable not to make new decisions every time conditions change, as pertains to unemployment benefits, an entitlement enables funds to flow according to the size of the problem. The difficulty is that not all entitlements are counter-cyclical (child benefits, for example, may rise independently of economic conditions) and the loss in financial flexibility generated by entitlements may hurt when the time comes to do less.

Nevertheless, treasury budgeting has one significant advantage over appropriations budgeting, namely, time. Changes in policy are manifested quickly in changes in spending. In order to bring considerations of economic management to bear on budgeting, these factors must be introduced early in the process of shaping the appropriations budget. Otherwise, last-minute changes of large magnitude will cause chaos by unhinging all sorts of prior understandings. Then the money must be voted and preparations made for spending. In the United States under this process—from the spring previews in the Office of Management and Budget, to the president's budget in January, to congressional action by the following summer and fall, to spending, in the winter and spring—eighteen to twenty-four months have elapsed. This is not control but remote control.

"Fine-tuning expenditures," attempting to make small adjustments to speed up or slow down the economy, do not work well anywhere. Efforts to increase expenditure are as likely to decrease the expenditure in the short run due to the effort required to expand operations. Efforts to reduce spending in the short run are as likely to increase spending due to severance pay, penalties for breaking contracts, and so on. Hence, even as efforts continue to make expenditures more responsive, the attractiveness of more immediate tax and entitlement increases is apparent.

The recalcitrance of all forms of budgeting to economic management is not so surprising; both spending programs and economic management cannot be made more predictable if one is to vary to serve the other. In an age profoundly influenced by Keynesian economic doctrines, with their emphasis on the power of government spending, however, continued efforts to link macro-economics with microspending are to be expected.

The Structural Budget Margin

One such effort is the "Structural Budget Margin" developed in the Netherlands. Due to dissatisfaction with the Keynesian approach to economic stabilization, as well as disillusionment with its short-term fine-tuning, the Dutch sought to develop a longer-term relationship between the growth of public spending and the size of the national economy. Economic management was to rely less on sudden starts and stops of taxation and expenditure, and greater effort was to be devoted to controlling public spending. (The closest the United

States has come is through the doctrine of balancing the budget at the level of full employment which almost always would mean a deficit). The Dutch were particularly interested in a control device because of the difficulty of getting agreement to hold down expenditures in coalition governments. Thus, spending was to be related not to actual growth but to desired growth, with only the designated margin available for new expenditure.[9]

Needless to say there are differences in definition of the appropriate structural growth rate and it has been revised up and down. Since the year used as a base makes a difference, that has also been in dispute. As we would also expect, there are disagreements over calculation of cash or volume of services with rising inflation propelling a move toward cash. Moreover, since people learn to play any game, conservative governments used the structural budget margin to hold down spending and socialists used it to increase it, for then the margin became a mechanism for figuring out the necessary increases in taxation. Every way one turns, it appears, budgetary devices are good for some purposes and not for others.

Why the Traditional Budget Lasts

Every criticism of traditional budgeting is undoubtedly correct. It is incremental rather than comprehensive; it does fragment decisions, usually making them piecemeal; it is heavily historical looking backward more than forward; it is indifferent about objectives. Why, then, has traditional budgeting lasted so long? Because it has the virtue of its defects.

Traditional budgeting makes calculations easy precisely because it is not comprehensive. History provides a strong base on which to rest a case. The present is appropriated to the past which may be known, instead of the future, which cannot be comprehended. Choices that might cause conflict are fragmented so that not all difficulties need be faced at one time. Budgeters may have objectives, but the budget itself is organized around activities or functions. One can change objectives, then, without challenging organizational survival. Traditional budgeting does not demand analysis of policy but neither does it inhibit it. Because it is neutral in regard to policy, traditional budgeting is compatible with a variety of policies, all of which can be converted into line-items. Budgeting for one year at a time has no special virtue (two years, for instance might be as good or better) except in comparison to more extreme alternatives. Budgeting several times a year aids economic adjustment but also creates chaos in departments, disorders calculations, and worsens conflict. Multiyear budgeting enhances planning at the expense of adjustment, accountability, and possible price volatility. Budgeting by volume and entitlement also aid planning and efficiency in government at the cost of control and effectiveness. Budgeting becomes spending. Traditional budgeting lasts, then, because it is simpler, easier, more controllable, more flexible than modern alternatives like PPB, ZBB, and indexed entitlements.

A final criterion has not been mentioned because it is inherent in the multiplicity of others, namely, adaptability. To be useful a budgetary process should perform tolerably well under all conditions. It must perform under the unexpected—deficits and surpluses, inflation and deflation, economic growth and economic stagnation. Because budgets are contracts within governments signifying agreed understandings, and signals outside of government informing others of what government is likely to do so they can adapt to it, budgets must be good (though not necessarily great) for all seasons. It is not so much that traditional budgeting succeeds brilliantly on every criterion, but that it does not entirely fail on any one that is responsible for its longevity.

Needless to say, traditional budgeting also has the defects of its virtues. No instrument of policy is equally good for every purpose. Though budgets look back, they may not look back far enough to understand how (or why) they got where they are. Comparing this year with last year may not mean much if the past was a mistake and the future is likely to be a bigger one. Quick calculation may be worse than none if it is grossly in error. There is an incremental road to disaster as well as faster roads to perdition; simplicity may become simplemindedness. Policy neutrality may degenerate into disinterest in programs. So why has it lasted? So far, no one has come up with another budgetary procedure that has the virtues of traditional budgeting but lacks its defects.

At once one is disposed to ask why it is necessary to settle for second or third best: Why not combine the best features of the various processes, specially selected to work under prevailing conditions? Why not multiyear volume entitlements for this and annual cash zero-base budgeting for that? The question answers itself; there can only be one budgetary process at a time. Therefore, the luxury of picking different ones for different purposes is unobtainable. Again, the necessity of choosing the least worst, or the most widely applicable over the largest number of cases is made evident.

Yet almost a diametrically opposite conclusion also is obvious to students of budgeting. Observation reveals that a number of different processes do, in fact, coexist right now. Some programs are single year but others are multiyear, some have cash limits while others are open-ended or even indexed, some are investigated in increments but others (where repetitive operations are involved) receive, in effect, a zero-base review. Beneath the facade of unity, there is, in fact, diversity.

How, then, are we to choose among truths that are self-evident (there can be only one form of budgeting at a time and there are many)? Both cannot be correct when applied to the same sphere, but I think they are when applied to different spheres. The critical difference is between the financial form in which the budget is voted on in the legislature, and the different ways of thinking about budgeting. It is possible to analyze expenditures in terms of programs, over long periods of time, and in many other ways without requiring that the form of analysis be the same as the form of appropriation. Indeed, as we have seen, there are persuasive reasons for insisting that form and function be different. All this can be summarized: The more neutral the form of presenting appropriations, the easier to translate other changes—in program, direction, organizational structure—into the desired amount without making the categories into additional forms of rigidity, which will become barriers to future changes.

Nonetheless, traditional budgeting must be lacking in some respects or it would not be replaced so often by entitlements or multiyear accounts. Put another way, treasury budgeting must reflect strong social forces. These are not mechanisms to control spending but to increase it. "The Budget" may be annual, but tax expenditures and budget entitlements go on until changed. With a will to spend there is a way.

I write about auditing largely in terms of budgeting and budgeting largely in terms of public policy. The rise of big government has necessarily altered out administrative doctrines of first and last things. When government was small so was public spending. Affairs of state were treated as extensions of personal integrity, or the lack thereof. The question was whether spending was honest. If public spending posed a threat to society it was that private individuals would use government funds to accumulate fortunes as sources of power. State audit was about private avarice. As government grew larger, its manipulation meant more. Was it doing what it said it would do with public money? State audit became state compliance. However, when government became gigantic, the sheer size of the state became overwhelming. The issue was no longer control of the state—getting government to do what it was told—but the ability of the state to control society. Public policy, i.e., public measures to control private behavior, leapt to the fore; and that is how auditing shifted from private corruption to governmental compliance to public policy.

Social forces ultimately get their way, but while there is a struggle for supremacy, the form of budgeting can make a modest difference. It is difficult to say, for instance, whether the concept of a balanced budget declined due to social pressure or whether the concept of a unified budget, including almost all transactions in and out of the economy, such as trust funds, makes it even less likely. In days of old when cash was cash, and perpetual deficits were not yet invented, a deficit meant more cash out than came in. Today, with a much larger total, estimating plays a much more important part, and it's anyone's guess within $50 billion as to the actual state of affairs. The lesson is that for purposes of accountability, and control, the simpler the budget the better.

Taking as large a view as I know how, the suitability of a budgetary process under varied conditions depends on how well diverse concerns can be translated into its forms. For sheer transparency, traditional budgeting is hard to beat.

Notes

1. But, for a beginning, see Allen Schick, "The Road to PPB: The Stages of Budget Reform," *Public Administration Review* (December 1966): 243-258.
2. Hugh Heclo, Aaron Wildavsky, *The Private Government of Public Money: Community and Policy Inside British Political Administration,* (London: Macmillan; Berkeley and Los Angeles: University of California Press).
3. Ibid.
4. Robert A. Hartman, "Multiyear Budget Planning, in *Setting National Priorities: The 1979 Budget,* ed. Joseph A. Pechman (Washington, DC: The Brookings Institution, 1978), p. 312.
5. Naomi Caiden, Aaron Wildavsky, *Planning and Budgeting in Poor Countries* (New York: John Wiley and Sons, 1974).
6. This and the next eight paragraphs are taken from my "Policy Analysis is What Information Systems are Not, *New York Affairs,* Vol. 4, No. 2 (Spring 1977): 10-23.
7. See Jeanne Nienaber and A. Wildavsky, *The Budgeting and Evaluation of Federal Recreation Programs, or Money Doesn't Crow on Trees* (New York: Basic Books, 1973).
8. The importance of these principles is discussed in my book, *Speaking Truth to Power: The Art and Craft of Policy Analysis* (Boston: Little, Brown and Co.).
9. J. Diamond, "The New Orthodoxy in Budgetary Planning: A Critical Review of Dutch Experience, *Public Finance,* Vol. XXXII, No. I (1977): 56-76.

2

The Political Economy of Efficiency: Cost-Benefit Analysis, Systems Analysis, and Program Budgeting

"The encroachment of economics upon politics is not difficult to understand. Being political in perspective is viewed as bad; having the perspective of the economist is acclaimed as good. As a discipline, economics has done more with its theory, however inadequate, than has political science. Under some conditions economists can give you some idea of what efficiency requires. It is a rare political scientist who would even concern himself with political rationality. Economists claim to know and work to defend their interests in efficiency: political scientists do not even define their sphere of competence. Thus the marketplace of ideas is rigged at the start."

There was a day when the meaning of economic efficiency was reasonably clear. An objective met up with a technician. Efficiency consisted in meeting the objective at the lowest cost or in obtaining the maximum amount of the objective for a specified amount of resources. Let us call this "pure efficiency." The desirability of trying to achieve certain objectives may depend on the cost of achieving them. In this case the analyst (he has graduated from being a mere technician) alters the objective to suit available resources. Let us call this "mixed efficiency." Both pure and mixed efficiency are limited in the sense that they take for granted the existing structure of the political system and work within its boundaries. Yet the economizer, he who values efficiency most dearly, may discover that the most efficient means for accomplishing his ends cannot be secured without altering the machinery for making decisions. He not only alters means and ends (resources and objectives) simultaneously but makes them dependent on changes in political relationships. While he claims no special interest in or expertise concerning the decision apparatus outside of the marketplace, the economizer pursues efficiency to the heart of the political system. Let us call this "total efficiency." In this vocabulary, then, concepts of efficiency may be pure or mixed, limited or total.

A major purpose of this paper is to take the newest and recently most popular modes of achieving efficiency—cost-benefit analysis, systems analysis, and program budgeting—and show how much more is involved than mere economizing. Even at the most modest level of cost-benefit analysis, I will try to show that it becomes difficult to maintain pure notions of efficiency. At a higher level, systems analysis is based on a mixed notion of efficiency. And program budgeting at the highest levels leaves pure efficiency far behind its overreaching grasp into the structure of the political system. Program budgeting, it turns out, is a form of systems analysis, that is, political systems analysis.

These modes of analysis are neither good for nothing nor good for everything, and one cannot speak of them as wholly good or bad. It is much more useful to try to specify some conditions under which they would or would not be helpful for various purposes. While such a list could not be exhaustive at this stage, nor permanent at any stage (because of advances in the art), it provides a basis for thinking about what these techniques can and cannot do. Another major purpose of this paper, therefore, is to describe cost-benefit and systems analysis and program budgeting as techniques for decision-making. I shall place particular stress upon what seems to me the most characteristic feature of all three modes of analysis: the aids to calculation designed to get around the vast areas of uncertainty where quantitative analysis leaves off and judgment begins.

Cost-Benefit Analysis

One can view cost-benefit analysis as anything from an infallible means of reaching the new Utopia to a waste of resources in attempting to measure the unmeasurable.[1]

The purpose of cost-benefit analysis is to secure an efficient allocation of resources produced by the governmental system in its interaction with the private economy. The nature of efficiency depends on the objectives set up for government. In the field of water resources, where most of the work on cost-benefit analysis has been done, the governmental objective is usually postulated to be an increase in national income. In a crude sense, this means that the costs to whomever may incur them should be less than the benefits to whomever may receive them. The time streams of consumption gained and foregone by a project are its benefits and costs.

The aim of cost-benefit analysis is to maximize "the present value of all benefits less that of all costs, subject to specified restraints." [2] A long view is taken in that costs are estimated not only for the immediate future but also for the life of the project. A wide view is taken in that indirect consequences for others—variously called externalities, side-effects, spillovers, and repercussion effects—are considered. Ideally, all costs and benefits are evaluated. The usual procedure is to estimate the installation costs of the project and spread them over time, thus making them into something like annual costs. To these costs are added an estimate of annual operating costs. The next step involves estimating the average value of the output by considering the likely number of units produced each year and their probable value in the marketplace of the future. Intangible, "secondary," benefits may then be considered. These time streams of costs and benefits are discounted so as to obtain the present value of costs and benefits. Projects whose benefits are greater than costs may then be approved, or the cost-benefit ratios may, with allowance for relative size, be used to rank projects in order of desirability.

Underlying Economic and Political Assumptions

A straightforward description of cost-benefit analysis cannot do justice to the powerful assumptions that underlie it or to the many conditions limiting its usefulness. The assumptions involve value judgments that are not always recognized and, when recognized, are not easily handled in practice. The limiting conditions arise partly out of the assumptions and partly out of severe computational difficulties in estimating costs, and especially benefits. Here I can only indicate some major problems.

Cost-benefit analysis is based on superiority in the marketplace,[3] under competitive conditions and full employment, as the measure of value in society. Any imperfection in the market works against the validity of the results. Unless the same degree of monopoly were found throughout the economy, for example, a governmental body that enjoys monopolistic control of prices or outputs would not necessarily make the same investment decisions as under free competition. A similar difficulty occurs where the size of a project is large in comparison to the economy, as in some developing nations. The project itself then affects the constellation of relative prices and production against which its efficiency is measured. The assumption based on the classical full employment model is also important because it gives prices special significance. Where manpower is not being utilized, projects may be justified in part as putting this unused resource to work.

The economic model on which cost-benefit analysis depends for its validity is based on a political theory. The idea is that in a free society the economy is to serve the individual's consistent preferences revealed and rationally pursued in the marketplace. Governments are not supposed to dictate preferences nor make decisions.

This individualist theory assumes as valid the current distribution of income. Preferences are valued in the marketplace where votes are based on disposable income. Governmental action to achieve efficiency, therefore, inevitably carries with it consequences for the distribution of income. Projects of different size and location and composition will transfer income in different amounts to different people. While economists might estimate the redistributive consequences of various projects, they cannot, on efficiency grounds, specify one or another as preferable. How is this serious problem to be handled?

Benefit-cost analysis is a way of trying to promote economic welfare. But whose welfare? No one knows how to deal with interpersonal comparisons of utility. It cannot be assumed that the desirability of rent supplements versus a highway or dam can be measured on a single utility scale. There is no scientific way to compare losses and gains among different people or to say that the marginal loss of a dollar to one man is somehow equal to the gain of a dollar by another. The question of whose utility function is to prevail (the analyst versus the people involved, the upstream gainers versus the downstream losers, the direct beneficiaries versus the taxpayers, the entire nation or a particular region, and so on) is of prime importance in making public policy.

The literature on welfare economics is notably unable to specify an objective welfare function.[4] Ideally, actions would benefit everyone and harm no one. As an approximation, the welfare economist views as optimal an action that leaves some people better off and none worse off. If this criterion were applied in political life, it would result in a situation like that of the Polish Diet in which anyone who was damaged could veto legislation. To provide a way out of this impasse, Hicks and Kaldor proposed approval of decisions if the total gain in welfare is such that the winners could compensate the losers. But formal machinery for compensation does not ordinarily exist and most modern economists are highly critical of the major political mechanism for attempting to compensate, namely, log-rolling in Congress on public works projects.[5] It is a very imperfect mechanism for assuring that losers in one instance become winners in another.

Another way of dealing with income distribution is to accept a criterion laid down by a political body and maximize present benefits less costs subject to this constraint. Or the cost-benefit analyst can present a series of alternatives differing according to the individuals who pay and prices charged. The analyst must not only compute the new inputs and outputs, but also the costs and benefits for each group with whom the public authorities are especially concerned. No wonder this is not often done! Prest and Turvey are uncertain whether such a procedure is actually helpful in practice.[6]

Income redistribution in its most extreme form would result in a complete leveling or equality of incomes. Clearly, this is not what is meant. A more practical meaning might be distributing income to the point where specific groups achieve a certain minimum. It is also possible that the operational meaning of income redistribution may simply be the transfer of some income from some haves to some have nots. Even in the last and most minimal sense of the term it is by no means clear that projects that are inefficient by the usual economic criteria serve to redistribute income in the desired direction. It is possible that some inefficient projects may transfer income from poorer to richer people. Before the claim that certain projects are justified by the effect of distributing income in a specified way can be accepted, an analysis to show that this is what actually happens must be at hand.

Since the distribution of income is at stake, it is not surprising that beneficiaries tend to dominate investment decisions in the political arena and steadfastly refuse to pay for what they receive from government tax revenues. They uniformly resist user charges based on benefits received. Fox and Herfindahl estimate that of a total initial investment of $3 billion for the Corps of Engineers in 1962, taxpayers in general would pay close to two-thirds of the costs.[7] Here, greater use of the facilities by a larger number of beneficiaries getting something for nothing inflates the estimated benefits which justify the project in the first place. There may be a political rationale for these decisions, but it has not been developed.

In addition to redistributing income, public works projects have a multitude of objectives and consequences. Projects may generate economic growth, alleviate poverty among some people, provide aesthetic enjoyment and opportunities for recreation, improve public health, reduce the risks of natural disaster, alter travel patterns, affect church attendance, change educational opportunities, and more. No single welfare criterion can encompass these diverse objectives. How many of them should be considered? Which are susceptible of quantification? The further one pursues this analysis, the more impassable the thicket.

Limitations in the Utility of Cost-Benefit Analysis

One possible conclusion is that at present certain types of cost-benefit analysis are not meaningful. In reviewing the literature on the calculus of costs and benefits in research and development, for example, Prest and Turvey comment on "the uncertainty and unreliability of cost estimates . . . and . . . the extraordinarily complex nature of the benefits." [8]

Another conclusion is that one should be cautious in distinguishing the degree to which projects are amenable to cost-benefit analysis:

When there are many diverse types of benefits from a project and/or many different beneficiaries it is difficult to list them all and to avoid double counting. This is one reason why it is so much easier to apply cost-benefit analysis to a limited purpose development, say, than it is to the research and development aspects of some multi-purpose discovery, such as a new type of plastic material....It is no good expecting those fields in which benefits are widely diffused, and in which there are manifest divergences between accounting and economic costs or benefits, to be as culti-vable as others. Nor is it realistic to expect that comparisons between projects in entirely different branches of economic activity are likely to be as meaning-ful or fruitful as those between projects in the same branch. The technique is more useful in the public-utility area than in the social-services area of govern-ment.[9]

If the analysis is to be useful at all, calculations must be simplified.[10] The multiple ramifications of interesting activities can be taken into account only at the cost of introducing fantastic complexities. Prest and Turvey remark of one such attempt, that "This system . . . requires knowledge of all the demand and supply equations in the economy, so is scarcely capable *of* application by road engineers." [11] They suggest omitting consideration where (1) side effects are judged not terribly large or where (2) concern for these effects belongs to another governmental jurisdiction.[12]

If certain costs or benefits are deemed important but cannot be quantified, it is always possible to guess. The increasing use of recreation and aesthetic facilities to justify public works projects in the United States is disapproved by most economists because there can be a vast, but hidden, inflation of these benefits. For example, to attribute the same value to a recreation day on a reservoir located in a desert miles from any substitute source of water as to a day on an artificial lake in the heart of natural lake country is pa-tently wrong. Economists would prefer to see recreation facilities listed in an appendix so that they can be taken into account in some sense, or, alterna-tively, that the project be presented with and without the recreation facilities, so that a judgment can be made as to whether the additional services are worth the cost.[13]

Economists distinguish between risk, where the precise outcome cannot be predicted but a probability distribution can be specified, and uncertainty, where one does not even know the parameters of the outcomes. The cost-benefit ana-lyst must learn to live with uncertainty, for he can never know whether all relevant objectives have been included and what changes may occur in policy and in technology.

It is easy enough to cut the life of the project below its expected economic life. The interest rate can be raised. Assumptions can be made that costs will be higher and benefits lower than expected. All these methods, essentially conser-vative, are also highly arbitrary. They can be made somewhat more systematic, however, by sensitivity analysis in which length of life, for instance, is varied over a series of runs so that its impact on the project can be appraised.

Lessening uncertainty by hiking the interest or discount rate leads to greater difficulties, for the dominance of "higher criteria over economic analysis is apparent in the frustrating problem of choosing the correct interest rate at which to discount the time streams of costs and benefits essential to the enterprise. Only an interest rate can establish the relationship between values at different periods of time. Yet people differ in preferences for the present versus the intermediate or long-run value. Moreover, the interest rate should also measure the opportunity cost of private capital that could be used to produce wealth elsewhere in the economy if it had not been used up in the form of tax income spent on the project under consideration. Is the appropriate rate the very low cost the government charges, the cost of a government corporation like TVA that must pay a somewhat higher rate, the going rate of interest for private firms, or an even higher rate to hedge against an uncertain future? As Otto Eckstein has observed, "the choice of interest rates must remain a value judgment."[14]

If the efficiency of a project is insensitive to interest costs, then these costs can vary widely without mattering much. But Fox and Herfindahl discovered that if Corps of Engineer projects raised their interest (or discount) rate from 2 5/8 to 4, 6, or 8 percent, then 9, 64, and 80 percent of their projects, respectively, would have had a benefit-cost ratio of less than unity. [15] This single value choice among many has such large consequences that it alone may be decisive.

The Mixed Results of Cost Benefit Analysis

Although cost-benefit analysis presumably results in efficiency by adding the most to national income, it is shot through with political and social value choices and surrounded by uncertainties and difficulties of computation. Whether the many noneconomic assumptions and consequences actually result in basically changing the nature of a project remains moot. Clearly, we have come a long way from pure efficiency, to verge upon mixed efficiency.

Economic analysts usually agree that all relevant factors (especially nonmarket factors) cannot be squeezed into a single formula. They therefore suggest that the policy maker, in being given the market costs and benefits of alternatives, is, in effect, presented with the market value he is placing on nonmarket factors. The contribution of the analyst is only one input into the decision, but the analyst may find this limited conception of his role unacceptable to others. Policy makers may not want this kind of input; they may want *the* answer, or at least an answer that they can defend on the basis of the analyst's legitimized expertise.

The dependence of cost-benefit analysis on a prior political framework does not mean that it is a useless or trivial exercise. Decisions must be made. If quantifiable economic costs and benefits are not everything, neither would a decision-maker wish to ignore them entirely. The great advantage of cost-benefit analysis, when pursued with integrity, is that some implicit judgments are made explicit and subject to analysis. Yet, for many, the omission of explicit consideration of political factors is a serious deficiency.

The experience of the Soil Conservation Service in lowering certain political costs may prove illuminating. For many years the Service struggled along with eleven major watershed projects involving big dams, great headaches, and little progress. Because the watersheds were confined to a single region, it was exceedingly difficult to generate support in Congress, particularly at appropriations time. The upstream/downstream controversies generated by these projects resulted in less than universal local approval. The SCS found itself in the direct line of fire for determining priorities in use of insufficient funds.

Compare this situation with the breakthrough which occurred when SCS developed the small watershed program. Since each facility is relatively inexpensive, large numbers can be placed throughout the country, markedly increasing political support. Agreement on the local level is facilitated because much less land is flooded and side payments are easier to arrange. A judicious use of cost-benefit analysis, together with ingenious relationships with state governors, places the choice of priorities with the states and yet maintains a reasonable level of consistency by virtue of adherence to national criteria. Errors are easier to correct because the burden of calculation has been drastically reduced and experience may be more easily accumulated with a larger number of small projects.

Consider the situation in which an agency finds it desirable to achieve a geographical spread of projects in order to establish a wider base of support. Assume (with good reason) that cost-benefit criteria will not permit projects to be established in some states because the value of the land or water is too low. One can say that this is just too bad and observe the agency seeking ways around the restriction by playing up benefits, playing down costs, or attacking the whole benefit cost concept as inapplicable. Another approach would be to recognize that federalism—meaning, realistically, the distribution of indulgences to state units—represents a political value worth promoting to some extent and that gaining nation-wide support is important. From this perspective, a compromise solution would be to except one or two projects in each state or region from meeting the full requirement of the formula, though the projects with the highest benefit-cost ratio would have to be chosen. In return for sacrificing full adherence to the formula in a few instances, one would get enhanced support for it in many others.

Everyone knows, of course, that cost-benefit analysis is not the messiah come to save water resources projects from contamination by the rival forces of ignorance and political corruption. Whenever agencies and their associated interests discover that they cannot do what they want, they may twist prevailing criteria out of shape: Two projects may be joined so that both qualify when one, standing alone, would not. Costs and benefits may be manipulated, or the categories may be so extended that almost any project qualifies. On the other hand, cost-benefit analysis has some "good political uses that might be stressed more than they have been. The technique gives the responsible official a good reason for turning down projects, with a public-interest explanation the Congressman can use with his constituents and the interest-group leader with his members.

This is not to say that cost-benefit analysis has little utility. Assuming that the method will continue to be improved, and that one accepts the market as the measure of economic value, it can certainly tell decision-makers something about what they will be giving up if they follow alternative policies. The use of two analyses, one based on regional and the other on national factors, might result in an appraisal of the economic costs of federalism.

The burden of calculation may be reduced by following cost-benefit analysis for many projects and introducing other values only for a few. To expect, however, that the method itself (which distributes indulgences to some and deprivations to others) would not be subject to manipulation in the political process is to say that we shall be governed by formula and not by men.

Because the cost-benefit formula does not always jibe with political realities—that is, it omits political costs and benefits—we can expect it to be twisted out of shape from time to time. Yet cost-benefit analysis may still be important in getting rid of the worst projects. Avoiding the worst where one can't get the best is no small accomplishment.

Systems Analysis

The good systems analyst is a *chochem*, a Yiddish word meaning "wise man," with overtones of "wise guy." His forte is creativity. Although he sometimes relates means to ends and fits ends to match means, he ordinarily eschews such pat processes, preferring instead to relate elements imaginatively into new systems that create their own means and ends. He plays new objectives continuously against cost elements until a creative synthesis has been achieved. He looks down upon those who say that they take objectives as given, knowing full well that the apparent solidity of the objective will dissipate during analysis and that, in any case, most people do not know what they want because they do not know what they can get.

Since no one knows how to teach creativity, daring, and nerve, it is not surprising that no one can define what systems analysis is or how it should be practiced. E. S. Quade, who compiled the RAND Corporation lectures on systems analysis, says it "is still largely a form of art" in which it is not possible to lay down "fixed rules which need only be followed with exactness." [16] He examined systems studies to determine ideas and principles common to the good ones, but discovered that "no universally accepted set of ideas existed. It was even difficult to decide which studies should be called good." [17]

Systems analysis is derived from operations research, which came into use during World War II when some scientists discovered that they could use simple quantitative analysis to get the most out of existing military equipment. A reasonably clear objective was given, and ways to cut the cost of achieving it could be developed, using essentially statistical models. Operations research today is largely identified with specific techniques: linear programming; Monte Carlo (randomizing) methods; gaming and game theory. While there is no hard and fast division between operations research and systems analysis, a rough separation may perhaps be made. The less that is known about objectives, the more they conflict, the larger the number of elements to be considered, the more uncertain the environment, the more likely it is that the work will be called a systems analysis. In systems analysis there is more judgment and intuition and less reliance on quantitative methods than in operations research.

Systems analysis builds models that abstract from reality but represent the crucial relationships. The systems analyst first decides what questions are relevant to his inquiry, selects certain quantifiable factors, cuts down the list of factors to be dealt with by aggregation and by eliminating the (hopefully) less important ones, and then gives them quantitative relationships with one another within the system he has chosen for analysis. But crucial variables may not be quantifiable. If they can be reduced to numbers, there may be no mathematical function that can express the desired relationship. More important, there may be no single criterion for judging results among conflicting objectives. Most important, the original objectives, if any, may not make sense.

It cannot be emphasized too strongly that a (if not the) distinguishing characteristic of systems analysis is that the objectives are either not known or are subject to change. Systems analysis, Quade tells us, "is associated with that class of problems where the difficulties lie in deciding what ought to be done—not simply how to do it—and honors go to people who . . . find out what the problem is." [18] Charles Hitch, the former Comptroller of the Defense Department, insists that:

> Learning about objectives is one of the chief objects of this kind of analysis. We must learn to look at objectives as critically and as professionally as we look at our models and our other inputs. We may, of course, begin with tentative objectives, but we must expect to modify or replace them as we learn about the systems we are studying—and related systems. The feedback on objectives may in some cases be the most important result of our study. We have never undertaken a major system study at RAND in which we are able to define satisfactory objectives at the beginning of the study. [19]

Systems analysts recognize many good reasons for their difficulties in defining problems or objectives. Quade reaches the core: "Objectives are not, in fact, agreed upon. The choice, while ostensibly between alternatives, is really between objectives or ends and nonanalytic methods must be used for a final reconciliation of views." [20] It may be comforting to believe that objectives come to the analyst from on high and can be taken as given, but this easy assumption is all wrong. "For all sorts of good reasons that are not about to change," says Hitch, "official statements of national objectives (or company objectives) tend to be nonexistent or so vague and literary as to be non-operational." [21] Objectives are not only likely to be "thin and rarified," according to Wohlstetter, but the relevant authorities "are likely to conflict. Among others there will be national differences within an alliance and within the nation, interagency, interservice, and intraservice differences." [22]

Moreover, even shared objectives often conflict with one another. Deterrence of atomic attack might be best served by letting an enemy know that we would respond with an all-out, indiscriminate attack on his population. Defense of our population against death and destruction might not be well served by this strategy, [23] as the Secretary of Defense recognized when he recommended a city-avoidance strategy that might give an enemy some incentive to spare our cities as well. Not only are objectives large in number and in conflict with one another, they are likely to engender serious repercussion effects. Many objectives, like morale and the stability of alliances, are resistant to quantification. What is worth doing depends on whether it can be done at all, how well, and at what cost. Hence, objectives really cannot be taken as given; they must be made up by the analyst. "In fact," Wohlstetter declares, "we are always in the process of choosing and modifying both means and ends." [24]

Future systems analysts are explicitly warned not to let clients determine objectives. A suggestive analogy is drawn with the doctor who would not ignore a patient's "description of his symptoms, but . . . cannot allow the patient's self-diagnosis to override his own professional judgment." [26] Quade argues that since systems analysis has often resulted in changing the original objectives of the policy-maker, it would be "self-defeating to accept without inquiry" his "view of what the problem is."[26]

I have stressed the point that the systems analyst is advised to insist on his own formulation of the problem because it shows so closely that we are dealing with a mixed concept of efficiency.

Adjusting objectives to resources in the present or near future is difficult enough without considering future states of affairs which hold tremendous uncertainty. Constants become variables; little can be taken for granted. The rate of technological progress, an opponent's estimate of your reaction to his latest series of moves based on his reaction to yours, whether or not atomic war will occur, what it will be like, whether we shall have warning, whether the system we are working on will cost anything close to current estimates and whether it will be ready within five years of the due date—on most of these matters, there are no objective probabilities to be calculated.

An effective dealing with uncertainty must be a major goal of systems analysis. Systems analysis is characterized by the aids to calculation it uses, not to conquer, but to circumvent and mitigate some of the pervasive effects of uncertainty. Before a seemingly important factor may be omitted, for example, a sensitivity analysis may be run to determine whether its variation significantly affects the outcome. If there is no good basis for calculating the value of the factor, arbitrary values may be assigned to test for extreme possibilities. Contingency analysis is used to determine how the relative ranking of alternatives holds up under major changes in the environment, say, a new alliance between France and Russia, or alterations in the criteria for judging the alternatives, such as a requirement that a system work well against attacks from space as well as earth. Contingency analysis places a premium on versatility as the analyst seeks a system that will hold up well under various eventualities even though it might be quite as good for any single contingency as an alternative system. Adversary procedures may be used to combat uncertainty. Bending over backwards to provide advantages for low-ranking systems and handicaps for high-ranking systems is called a fortiori analysis. Changing crucial assumptions in order to make the leading alternatives even, so that one can judge whether the assumptions are overly optimistic or pessimistic, is called break-even analysis. [27] Since all these methods add greatly to the burden of calculation, they must be used with some discretion.

A variety of insurance schemes may also be used to deal with uncertainty. In appraising what an opponent can do, for instance, one can assume the worst, the best, and sheer inertia. In regard to the development of weapons, insurance requires not one flexible weapon but a variety of alternatives pursued with vigor. As development goes on, uncertainty is reduced. Consequently, basic strategic choice involves determining how worthwhile paying for the additional information is by developing rival weapons systems to the next stage. The greater the uncertainty of the world, the greater the desirability of having the widest selection of alternative weapons to choose from to meet unexpected threats and opportunities. Alchian and Kessel are so wedded to the principle of diversified investment that they "strongly recommend this theorem as a basic part of systems analysis." [28]

As a form of calculation, systems analysis represents a merger of quantitative methods and rules of thumb. First, the analyst attempts to solve the problem before he knows a great deal about it. Then he continuously alters his initial solution to get closer to what he intuitively feels ought to be wanted. Means and ends are continuously played off against one another. New objectives are defined, new assumptions made, new models constructed, until a creative amalgam appears that hopefully defines a second best solution, one that is better than others even if not optimal in any sense. In the famous study of the location of military bases conducted by Albert Wohlstetter and his associates at the RAND Corporation, widely acknowledged as a classic example of systems analysis, Wohlstetter writes:

> The base study . . . proceeded by a method of successive approximations. It compared forces for their efficiency in carrying a payload between the bases and targets without opposition either by enemy interceptors or enemy bombers. Then, it introduced obstacles successively: first, enemy defenses; then enemy bombardment of our bombers and other elements needed to retaliate. In essence, then, the alternative systems were tested for their first-strike capability and then they were compared for their second-strike capacity. And the programmed system performed in a drastically different way, depending on the order in which the opposing side struck. In the course of analyzing counter-measures and counter-countermeasures, the enemy bombardment turned out to be a dominant problem. This was true even for a very much improved overseas operating base system. The refueling base system was very much less sensitive to strike order. It is only the fact that strike order made such a difference among systems contemplated that gave the first-strike, second-strike distinction an interest. And it was not known in advance of the analysis that few of the programmed bombers would have survived to encounter the problem of penetrating enemy defenses which had previously been taken as the main obstacle. The analysis, then, not only was affected by the objectives considered, it affected them.[29]

The advantage of a good systems study is that by running the analysis through in theory on paper certain disadvantages of learning from experience may be avoided.

If the complexity of the problems encountered proved difficult in cost-benefit analysis, the burdens of calculation are ordinarily much greater in systems analysis. Many aspects of a problem simply must be put aside. Only a few variables can be considered simultaneously. "Otherwise," Roland McKean tells us, "the models would become impossibly cumbersome, and . . . the number of calculations to consider would mount in the thousands." [30] Formulas that include everything may appear more satisfactory but those that cannot be reduced "to a single expression are likely to convey no meaning at all." [31] Summing up their experience. Hitch and McKean assert that

> analyses must be piecemeal, since it is impossible for a single analysis to cover all problems of choice simultaneously in a large organization. Thus comparisons of alternative courses of action always pertain to a part of the government's (or corporation's) problem. Other parts of the overall problem are temporarily put aside, possible decisions about some matters being ignored, specific decisions about others being taken for granted. The resulting analyses are intended to provide assis-

tance in finding optimal, or at least good, solutions to sub-problems: in the jargon of systems and operations research, they are sub-optimizations.

Although admitting that much bad work is carried on and that inordinate love of numbers and machines often get in the way of creative work,[33] practitioners of systems analysis believe in their art. "All of them point out how the use of analysis can provide some of the knowledge needed, how it may sometime serve as a substitute for experience, and, most importantly, how it can work to sharpen intuition." [34] Systems analysis can increase explicitness about the assumptions made and about exclusions from the analysis. The claim is that systems analysis can be perfected; sheer intuition or unaided judgment can never be perfect.

Yet there is also wide agreement that systems analysts "do philosophy,"[35] that they are advocates of particular policy alternatives. What Schelling calls "the pure role of expert advisor" is not available for the analyst who "must usually formulate the questions themselves for his clients." [36] Beyond that, Wohlstetter argues that systems analysts can perform the function of integrating diverse values. New systems can sometimes be found that meet diverse objectives. [37] The politician who gains his objectives by inventing policies that also satisfy others, or the leader of a coalition who searches out areas of maximum agreement, performs a kind of informal systems analysis.

All these men, however, work within the existing political structure. While cost-benefit analysis may contain within it implicit changes in existing governmental policies, it poses no direct challenge to the general decision-making machinery of the political system. Program budgeting is a form of systems analysis that attempts to break out of these confines.

Program Budgeting

It is always important, and perhaps especially so in economics, to avoid being swept off one's feet by the fashions of the moment.[38] So this new system will identify our national goals with precision.[39]

On August 25, 1965, President Johnson announced that he was asking the heads of all federal agencies to introduce "a very new and revolutionary system" of program budgeting. Staffs of experts set up in each agency would define goals using "modern methods of program analysis." Then the "most effective and the least costly" way to accomplish these goals would be found.[40]

Program budgeting has no standard definition. The general idea is that budgetary decisions should be made by focusing on output categories like governmental goals, objectives, end products or programs instead of inputs like personnel, equipment, and maintenance. As in cost-benefit analysis, to which it owes a great deal, program budgeting lays stress on estimating the total financial cost of accomplishing objectives. What is variously called cost-effectiveness or cost-utility analysis is employed in order to select "alternative approaches to the achievement of a benefit already determined to be worth achieving." [41]

Not everyone would go along with the most far-reaching implications of program budgeting, but the RAND Corporation version, presumably exported from the Defense Department, definitely does include "institutional reorganization to bring relevant administrative functions under the jurisdiction of the authority making the final program decisions." In any event, there would be "information reporting systems and shifts in the power structure to the extent necessary to secure compliance with program decisions by the agencies responsible for their execution." [42] Sometimes it appears that comprehensiveness—simultaneous and complete examination of all programs and all alternatives to programs every year—is being advocated.

Actually, comprehensiveness has been dropped (though not without regret) because "it may be too costly in time, effort, uncertainty, and confusion." [43] There exists considerable ambivalence as to whether decisions are implicit in the program categories or merely provide information to improve the judgment of governmental officials.

Programs are not made in heaven. There is nothing out there that is just waiting to be found. Programs are not natural to the world; they must be imposed on it by men. No one can give instructions for making up programs. There are as many ways to conceive of programs as there are of organizing activity, [44] as the comments of the following writers eloquently testify:

> It is by no means obvious . . . whether a good program structure should be based on components of specific end objectives (e.g., the accomplishment of certain land reclamation targets), on the principle of cost separation (identifying as a program any activity the costs of which can be readily segregated), on the separation of means and ends (Is education a means or an end in a situation such as skill retraining courses for workers displaced by automation?), or on some artificially designed pattern that draws from all these and other classification criteria.[45]

> Just what categories constitute the most useful programs and program elements is far from obvious . . . .If one puts all educational activities into a broad package of educational programs, he cannot simultaneously include school lunch programs or physical education activities in a Health Program, or include defense educational activities (such as the military academies) in the Defense Program....In short, precisely how to achieve a rational and useful structure for a program budget is not yet evident.[46]

> In much current discussion it seems to be taken for granted that transportation is a natural program category. But that conclusion is by no means obvious.[47]

> A first question one might ask is whether, given their nature, health activities merit a separate, independent status in a program budget. The question arises because these activities often are constituents of, or inputs into, other activities whose purpose or goal orientation is the dominating one. Outlays by the Department of

Defense for hospital care, for example, though they assist in maintaining the health of one segment of the population, are undertaken on behalf of national defense, and the latter is their justification. [48]

The difficulties with the program concept are illustrated in the space program. A first glance suggests that space projects are ideally suited for program budgeting because they appear as physical systems designed to accomplish different missions. Actually, there is a remarkable degree of interdependence between different missions and objectives—pride, scientific research, space exploration, military uses, etc.—so that it is impossible to apportion costs on a proper basis. Consider the problem of a rocket developed for one mission and useful for others. To apportion costs to each new mission is purely arbitrary. To allocate the cost to the first mission and regard the rocket as a free good for all subsequent missions is ludicrous. The only remotely reasonable alternative—making a separate program out of the rocket itself—does violence to the concept of programs as end products. The difficulty is compounded because the facilities that have multiple uses like boosters and tracking networks tend to be very expensive compared to the items that are specific to a particular mission.[49] Simple concepts of programs evaporate upon inspection.

Political realities lie behind the failure to devise principles for defining programs. As Melvin Anshen puts it, "The central issue is, of course, nothing less than the definition of the ultimate objectives of the federal government as they are realized through operational decisions." The arrangement of the programs inevitably affects the specific actions taken to implement them. "Set in this framework," Anshen continues, "the designation of a schedule of programs may be described as building a bridge between a matter of political philosophy (what is government for?) and . . . assigning scarce resources among alternative governmental objectives."[50]

Because program budgeting is a form of systems analysis (and uses a form of cost-benefit analysis), the conditions that hinder or facilitate its use have largely been covered in the previous sections. The simpler the problem, the fewer the interdependencies, the greater the ability to measure the consequences of alternatives on a common scale, the more costs and benefits that are valued in the marketplace, the better the chances of making effective use of programs. Let us take transportation to illustrate some of the conditions in a specific case.

Investments in transportation are highly interdependent with one another (planes versus cars versus trains versus barges, etc.) and with decisions regarding the regional location of industry and the movements of population. In view of the powerful effects of transportation investment on regional employment, income, and competition with other modes of transport, it becomes necessary to take these factors into account. The partial equilibrium model of efficiency in the narrow sense becomes inappropriate and a general equilibrium model of the economy must be used. The combination of aggregative models at the economy-wide level and inter-region and inter-industry models that this approach requires is staggering. It is precisely the limited and partial character of cost-effectiveness analyses, taking so much for granted and eliminating many variables, that make them easy to work with for empirical purposes. Furthermore, designing a large-scale transportation system involves so close a mixture of political and economic considerations that it is not possible to disentangle them. The Interstate Highway Program, for example, involved complex bargaining among federal, state, and local governments and reconciliation of many conflicting interests. The development of certain "backward regions, facilitating the movement of defense supplies, redistribution of income, creating countervailing power against certain monopolies, not to mention the political needs of public officials, were all involved. While cost-utility exercises might help with small segments of the problem, J. R. Meyer concludes that, "Given the complexity of the political and economic decisions involved, and the emphasis on designing a geographically consistent system, it probably would be difficult to improve on the congressional process as a means of developing such a program in an orderly and systematic way." [51]

On one condition for effective use—reorganization of the federal government to centralize authority for wide-ranging programs—proponents of program budgeting are markedly ambivalent. The problem is that responsibility for programs is now scattered throughout the whole federal establishment and decentralized to state and local authorities as well. In the field of health, for example, expenditures are distributed among at least twelve agencies and six departments outside of Health, Education, and Welfare. A far greater number of organizations are concerned with American activities abroad, with natural resources and with education. The multiple jurisdictions and overlapping responsibilities do violence to the concept of comprehensive and consistent programs. It "causes one to doubt," Marvin Frankel writes, "whether there can exist in the administrative echelons the kind of overall perspective that would seem indispensable if federal health resources are to be rationally allocated." [52] To G. A. Steiner it is evident that "The present 'chest of drawers' type of organization cannot for long be compatible with program budgeting." [53] W. Z. Hirsch declares that "if we are to have effective program budgeting of natural resources activities, we shall have to provide for new institutional arrangements." [54] Yet the inevitable resistance to wholesale reorganization would be so great that, if it were deemed essential, it might well doom the enterprise. Hence, the hope is expressed that translation grids or crossover networks could be used to convert program budget decisions back into the usual budget categories in the usual agencies. That is what is done in Defense, but that Department has the advantage of having most of the activities it is concerned with under the Secretary's jurisdiction. Some program analysts believe that this solution will not do.

Recognizing that a conversion scheme is technically feasible, Anshen is aware that there are "deeply frustrating" issues to be resolved. "The heart of the problem is the fact that the program budget in operation should not be a mere statistical game. Great strategic importance will attach to both the definition of program structure and content and the establishment of specific program objectives (including magnitude, timing, and cost)."[55] The implications of program budgeting, however, go far beyond specific policies.

It will be useful to distinguish between policy politics (which policy will be adopted?), partisan politics (which political party will win office?), and system politics (how will decision structures be set up?). Program budgeting is manifestly concerned with policy politics, and not much with partisan politics, although it could have important consequences for issues that divide the nation's parties. *My contention is that the thrust of program budgeting makes it an integral part of system politics.*

As presently conceived, program budgeting contains an extreme centralizing bias. Power is to be centralized in the Presidency (through the Budget Bureau) at the national level, in superdepartments rather than bureaus within the executive branch, and in the federal government as a whole instead of state or local governments. Note how W. Z. Hirsch assumes the desirability of national dominance when he writes: "These methods of analysis can guide federal officials in the responsibility of bringing local education decisions into closer harmony with national objectives."[56] G. A. Steiner observes that comprehensiveness may be affected by unrestricted federal grants-in-aid to the states because "such a plan would remove a substantial part of federal expenditures from a program budgeting system of the federal government."[57] Should there be reluctance on the part of state and local officials to employ the new tools, Anshen states "that the federal government may employ familiar incentives to accelerate this progress." [58] Summing it up, Hirsch says that "It appears doubtful that a natural resources program budget would have much impact without a good deal of centralization."[59]

Within the great federal organizations designed to encompass the widest ramifications of basic objectives, there would have to be strong executives. Cutting across the subunits of the organization, as is the case in the Department of Defense, the program budget could only be put together by the top executive. A more useful tool for increasing his power to control decisions vis-à-vis his subordinates would be hard to find.[60]

Would large-scale program budgeting benefit the Chief Executive? President Johnson's support of program budgeting could in part stem from his desire to appear frugal and also be directed at increasing his control of the executive branch by centralizing decisions in the Bureau of the Budget. In the case of foreign affairs, it is not at all clear whether it would be preferable to emphasize country teams, with the budget made by the State Department to encompass activities of the other federal agencies abroad, or to let Commerce, Agriculture, Defense, and other agencies include their foreign activities in their own budgets. Program budgeting will unleash great struggles of this kind in Washington. An especially intriguing possibility is that the Bureau of the Budget might prefer to let the various agencies compete, with the bureau coordinating (that is, controlling) these activities through a comprehensive foreign affairs program devised only at the presidential level.

Yet is it not entirely clear that presidents would welcome all the implications of program budgeting. It is well and good to talk about long-range planning; it is another thing to tie a president's hands by committing him in advance for five years of expenditures. Looking ahead is fine but not if it means that a president cannot negate the most extensive planning efforts on grounds that seem sufficient to him.[61] He may wish to trade some program budgeting for some political support.

In any event, that all decisions ought to be made by the most central person in the most centralized body capable of grabbing hold of them is difficult to justify on scientific grounds. We see what has happened. First pure efficiency was converted to mixed efficiency. Then limited efficiency became unlimited. Yet the qualifications of efficiency experts for political systems analysis are not evident. [62]

We would be in a much stronger position to predict the consequences of program budgeting if we knew (a) how far toward a genuine program budget the Defense Department has gone and (b) whether the program budget has fulfilled its promise. To the best of my knowledge, not a single study of this important experiment was undertaken (or at least published) before the decision was made to spread it around the land. On the surface, only two of the nine program categories used in the Defense Department appear to be genuine programs in the sense of pointing to end purposes or objectives. Although strategic retaliation and continental defense appear to be distinct programs, it is difficult to separate them conceptually; my guess is that they are, in fact, considered together. The third category—general purpose forces—is presumably designed to deal with (hopefully) limited war anywhere in the world. According to Arthur Smithies, "The threat is not clearly defined and neither are the requirements for meeting it. Clearly this program is of a very different character from the other two and does not lend itself as readily to analysis in terms either of its components or of its specific contribution to defense objectives." [63]

What about the program called airlift and sealift? These activities support the general purpose forces. Research and development is carried on presumably to serve other defense objectives, and the same is true for the reserve forces.

No doubt the elements that make up the programs comprise the real action focus of the budget, but these may look less elegant when spread into thousands of elements than they do in nine neat rows. When one hears that hundreds of program elements are up for decision at one time,[64] he is entitled to some skepticism about how much genuine analysis can go into all of them. Part of the argument for program budgeting was that by thinking ahead and working all year round it would be possible to consider changes as they came up and avoid the usual last minute funk. Both Hitch[65] and Novick [6] (the RAND Corporation expert on defense budgeting) report, however, that this has not worked out. The services hesitate to submit changes piecemeal, and the Secretary wants to see what he is getting into before he acts. The vaunted five-year plans are still in force but their efficacy in determining yearly decisions remains to be established.

One good operational test would be to know whether the Department's systems analysts actually use the figures from the five-year plans in their work or whether they go to the services for the real stuff. Another test would be whether or not the later years of the five-year projections turn out to have any future significance, or whether the battle is really over the next year that is to be scooped out as part of the budget. From a distance, it appears that the services have to work much harder to justify what they are doing. Since McNamara's office must approve changes in defense programs, and he can insist on documentation, he is in a strong position to improve thinking at the lower levels. The intensity of conflict within the Defense Department may not have changed, but it may be that the disputants are or will in the future be likely to shout at a much more sophisticated level. How much this is due to McNamara himself, to his insistence on quantitative estimates, or to the analytic advantages of a program budget cannot be determined now. It is clear that a program budget, of which he alone is master, has helped impose his will on the Defense Department.

It should also be said that there are many notable differences between decision-making in defense and domestic policy that would render suspect the transmission of procedures from one realm to the other. The greater organizational unity of Defense, the immensely large amounts of money at stake, the extraordinarily greater risks involved, the inability to share more than minimal values with opponents, the vastly different array of interests and perceptions of the proper roles of the participants, are but a few of the factors involved.

The Armed Services and Appropriations Committees in the defense area, for example, are normally most reluctant to substitute their judgment on defense for that of the president and the Secretary of the Department. They do not conceive it to be their role to make day-to-day defense policy, and they are apparently unwilling to take on the burden of decision. They therefore accept a budget presentation based on cavernous program categories even though these are so arranged that it is impossible to make a decision on the basis of them. If they were to ask for and to receive the discussion of alternative actions contained in the much smaller program elements on which McNamara bases his decisions, they would be in a position to take the Department of Defense away from its Secretary.

There is no reason whatsoever to believe that a similar restraint would be shown by committees that deal with domestic policies. It is at least possible that the peculiar planning, programming, and budgeting system adopted in Defense could not be repeated elsewhere in the federal establishment.

Political Rationality

Political rationality is the fundamental kind of reason, because it deals with the preservation and improvement of decision structures, and decision structures are the source of all decisions. Unless a decision structure exists, no reasoning and no decisions are possible....There can be no conflict between political rationality and . . . technical, legal, social, or economic rationality, because the solution of political problems makes possible an attack on any other problem, while a serious political deficiency can prevent or undo all other problem solving....Nonpolitical decisions are reached by considering a problem in its own terms, and by evaluating proposals according to how well they solve the problem. The best available proposal should be accepted regardless of who makes it or who opposes it, and a faulty proposal should be rejected or improved no matter who makes it. Compromise is always irrational; the rational procedure is to determine which proposal is the best, and to accept it. In a political decision, on the other hand, action never is based on the merits of a proposal but always on who makes it and who opposes it. Action should be designed to avoid complete identification with any proposal and any point of view, no matter how good or how popular it might be. The best available proposal should never be accepted just because it is best; it should be deferred, objected to, discussed, until major opposition disappears. Compromise is always a rational procedure, even when the compromise is between a good and a bad proposal. [67]

We are witnessing the beginning of significant advances in the art and science of economizing. Having given up the norm of comprehensiveness, economizers are able to join quantitative analysis with aids to calculation of the kind described by Lindblom in his strategy of disjointed incrementalism.[68]

Various devices are employed to simplify calculations. Important values are omitted entirely; others are left to different authorities to whose care they have been entrusted. Here, sensitivity analysis represents an advance because it provides an empirical basis to justify neglect of some values. Means and ends are hopelessly intertwined.

The real choice is between rival policies that encapsulate somewhat different mixes of means and ends. Analysis proceeds incrementally by successive limited approximations. It is serial and remedial as successive attacks are made on problems. Rather than waiting upon experience in the real world, the analyst tries various moves in his model and runs them through to see if they work. When all else fails, the analyst may try an integrative solution reconciling a variety of values to some degree, though meeting none of them completely. He is always ready to settle for the second or third best, provided only that it is better than the going policy. Constrained by diverse limiting assumptions, weakened by deficiencies in technique, rarely able to provide unambiguous measures, the systems, cost-benefit, and program analysis is nonetheless getting better at calculating in the realm of efficiency. Alas, he is an imperialist at heart.

In the literature discussed above there appears several times the proposition that "the program budget is a neutral tool. It has no politics." [69] In truth, the program budget is suffused with policy politics, makes up a small part of President Johnson's partisan politics, and tends towards system politics. How could men account for so foolish a statement? It must be that they who make it identify program budgeting with something good and beautiful, and politics with another thing bad and ugly. McKean and Anshen speak of politics in terms of "pressure and expedient adjustments," "haphazard acts . . . unresponsive to a planned analysis of the needs of efficient decision design." From the political structure they expect only "resistance and opposition, corresponding to the familiar human disposition to protect established seats of power and procedures made honorable by the mere facts of existence and custom." [70] In other places we hear of "vested interests," "wasteful duplication," "special interest groups," and the "Parkinson syndrome." [71]

Not so long ago less sophisticated advocates of reform ignored the political realm. Now they denigrate it. And, since there must be a structure for decision, it is smuggled in as a mere adjunct of achieving efficiency. Who is to blame if the economic tail wags the political dog? It seems unfair to blame the evangelical economizer for spreading the gospel of efficiency. If economic efficiency turns out to be the one true religion, maybe it is because its prophets could so easily conquer.

It is hard to find men who take up the cause of political rationality, who plead the case for political man, and who are primarily concerned with the laws that enable the political machinery to keep working. One is driven to a philosopher like Paul Diesing to find the case for the political:

> the political problem is always basic and prior to the others....This means that any suggested course of action must be evaluated first by its effects on the political structure. A course of action which corrects economic or social deficiencies but increases political difficulties must be rejected, while an action which contributes to political improvement is desirable even if it is not entirely sound from an economic or social standpoint. [72]

There is hardly a political scientist who would claim half as much. The desire to invent decision structures to facilitate the achievement of economic efficiency does not suggest a full appreciation of their proper role by students of politics.

A major task of the political system is to specify goals or objectives. It is impermissible to treat goals as if they were known in advance. "Goals" may well be the product of interaction among key participants rather than some "deus ex machina" or (to use Bentley's term) some "spook" which posits values in advance of our knowledge of them. Certainly, the operational objectives of the Corps of Engineers in the Water Resources field could hardly be described in terms of developing rivers and harbors.

Once the political process becomes a focus of attention, it is evident that the principal participants may not be clear about their goals. What we call goals or objectives may, in large part, be operationally determined by the policies we can agree upon. The mixtures of values found in complex policies may have to be taken in packages, so that policies may determine goals at least as much as general objectives determine policies. In a political situation, then, the need for support assumes central importance. Not simply the economic, but the *political* costs and benefits turn out to be crucial.

A first attempt to specify what is meant by political costs may bring closer an understanding of the range of requirements for political rationality.[73] Exchange costs are incurred by a political leader when he needs the support of other people to get a policy adopted. He has to pay for this assistance by using up resources in the form of favors (patronage, logrolling) or coercive moves (threats or acts to veto or remove from office). By supporting a policy and influencing others to do the same, a politician antagonizes some people and may suffer their retaliation. If these hostility costs mount, they may turn into reelection costs—actions that decrease his chances (or those of his friends) of being elected or reelected to office. Election costs, in turn, may become policy costs through inability to command the necessary formal powers to accomplish the desired policy objectives.

In the manner of Neustadt, we may also talk about reputation costs, i.e., not only loss of popularity with segments of the electorate, but also loss of esteem and effectiveness with other participants in the political system and loss of ability to secure policies other than the one immediately under consideration. Those who continually urge a president to go all out—that is, use all his resources on a wide range of issues—rarely stop to consider that the price of success in one area of policy may be defeat in another. If he loses popularity with the electorate, as President Truman did, Congress may destroy almost the whole of his domestic program. If he cracks down on the steel industry, as President Kennedy did, he may find himself constrained to lean over backwards in the future to avoid unremitting hostility from the business community.

A major consequence of incurring exchange and hostility costs may be undesirable power-redistribution effects. The process of getting a policy adopted or implemented may increase the power of various individuals, organizations, and social groups, which later will be used against the political leader. The power of some participants may be weakened so that the political leader is unable to enjoy their protection.

The legitimacy of the political system may be threatened by costs that involve the weakening of customary political restraints. Politicians who try to suppress opposition, or who practice election frauds, may find similar tactics being used against them. The choice of a highly controversial policy may raise the costs of civic discord. Although the people involved may not hate the political leader, the fact that they hate each other may lead to consequences contrary to his desires.

The literature of economics usually treats organizations and institutions as if they were costless entities. The standard procedure is to consider rival alternatives (in consideration of price policy or other criteria), calculate the differences in cost and achievement among them, and show that one is more or less efficient than another. This typical way of thinking is sometimes misspecified. If the costs of pursuing a policy are strictly economic and can be calculated directly in the marketplace, then the procedure should work well. But if the costs include getting one or another organization to change its policies or procedures, then these costs must also be taken into account.[74] Perhaps there are legal, psychological, or other impediments that make it either impossible or difficult for the required changes to be made. Or the changes may require great effort and result in incurring a variety of other costs. In considering a range of alternatives, one is measuring not only efficiency but also the cost of change.

Studies based on efficiency criteria are much needed and increasingly useful. My quarrel is not with them as such, at all. I have been concerned that a single value, however important, could triumph over other values without explicit consideration being given these others. I would feel much better if political rationality were being pursued with the same vigor and capability as is economic efficiency. In that case I would have fewer qualms about extending efficiency studies into the decision-making apparatus.

My purpose has not been to accuse economizers of doing what comes naturally. Rather, I have sought to emphasize that economic rationality, however laudable in its own sphere, ought not to swallow up political rationality—but will do so, if political rationality continues to lack trained and adept defenders.

Notes

I am more than ordinarily indebted to the people who have improved this paper through their comments. Win Crowther, John Harsanyi, John Krutilla, Arthur Maas, Arnold Meltsner, Nelson Polsby, William Riker, and Dwight Waldo saved me from errors and contributed insights of their own. The responsibility for what is said is entirely my own.

The paper, written while the author was a Research Political Scientist at the Center for Planning and Development Research, University of California, Berkeley, was originally presented at a conference on public policy sponsored by the Social Science Research Council.

1. A. R. Prest and R. Turvey, "Cost-Benefit Analysis: A Survey," *Economic Journal,* Vol. LXXV (December 1965): 683-75. I am much indebted to this valuable and discerning survey. I have also relied upon Otto Eckstein, "A Survey of the Theory of Public Expenditure Criteria," in *Public Finances: Needs, Sources, and Utilization,* National Bureau of Economic Research (New York: Princeton University Press, 1961), pp. 439-504. Irving K. Fox and Orris C. Herfindahl, "Attainment of Efficiency in Satisfying Demands for Water Resources," *American Economic Review,* May 1964, pp. 198-206. Charles J. Hitch, *On the Choice of Objectives in Systems Studies* (Santa Monica, CA: The RAND Corporation, 1960). John V. Krutilla, "Is Public Intervention in Water Resources Development Conducive to Economic Efficiency," *Natural Resources Journal,* January 1966, pp. 60-75. John V. Krutilla and Otto Eckstein, *Multiple Purpose River Development* (Baltimore, MD: Johns Hopkins University Press, 1958). Roland N. McKean, *Efficiency in Government Through Systems Analysis with Emphasis on Water Resources Development,* (New York: 1958).
2. Prest and Turvey, ibid., p. 686.
3. In many important areas of policy such as national defense it is not possible to value the product directly in the marketplace. Since benefits cannot be valued in the same way as costs, it is necessary to resort to a somewhat different type of analysis. Instead of cost-benefit analysis, therefore, the work is usually called cost-effectiveness or cost-utility analysis.
4. A. Bergson, "A Reformulation of Certain Aspects of Welfare Economics," *Quarterly Journal of Economics*, February 1938; N. Kaldor, "Welfare Propositions and Interpersonal Comparisons of Utility," *Economic Journal,* 1939, pp. 549-52; J. R. Hicks, "The Valuation of Social Income," *Economica,* 1940, pp. 105-24; I. M. D. Little, *A Critique of Welfare Economics,* (Oxford: 1950); W. J. Baumol, *Welfare Economics and the Theory of the State* (Cambridge: 1952); T. Scitovsky, "A Note on Welfare Propositions in Economics," *Review of Economic Studies,* 1942, pp. 98-110; J. E. Meade, *The Theory of International Economic Policy, Vol. II: Trade and Welfare* (New York: 1954).
5. For a different view, see James M. Buchanan and Gordon Tullock, *The Calculus of Consent: Logical Foundations of Constitutional Democracy* (Ann Arbor: University of Michigan Press, 1962).
6. Prest and Turvey, "Cost-Benefit Analysis." p. 702. For a contrary view, see Arthur Maas, "Benefit-Cost Analysis: Its Relevance to Public Investment Decisions," Vol. LXXX, *Quarterly Journal of Economics,* May 1966, pp. 208-226,
7. Irving K. Fox and Orris C. Herfindahl, "Attainment of Efficiency in Satisfying Demands for Water Resources," *American Economic Review,* May 1964, p. 200.
8. Prest and Turvey, "Cost-Benefit Analysis," p. 727.
9. Ibid., pp. 729, 731.
10. David Braybrooke and Charles Lindblom, *A Strategy for Decision* (New York: 1963).
11. Prest and Turvey, "Cost-Benefit Analysis," p. 714.
12. Ibid., p. 705.

13. See Jack L. Knetch, "Economics of Including Recreation as a Purpose of Water Resource Projects," *Journal of Farm Economics,* December 1964, p. 1155. No one living in Berkeley, where "a view" is part of the cost of housing, could believe that aesthetic values are forever going to remain beyond the ingenuity of the quantifier. There are also costs and benefits, such as the saving and losing of human life, that can be quantified but can only be valued in the marketplace in a most peculiar (or ghoulish) sense. See Burton Weisbrod, *The Economics of Public Health; Measuring the Economic Impact of Diseases* (Philadelphia: 1961), for a creative attempt to place a market value on human life. Few of us would want to make decisions about public health by use of this criterion, not at least if we were the old person whose future social value contribution is less than his cost to the authorities.

14. Otto Eckstein, "A Survey of the Theory of Public Expenditure," p. 460.

15. Fox and Herfindahl, "Attainment of Efficiency," p. 202.

16. E. S. Quade, *Analysis for Military Decisions* (Chicago: 1964), p. 153.

17. Ibid., p. 149.

18. Ibid., p. 7.

19. Charles J. Hitch, *On the Choice of Objectives*, p. 19.

20. E. S. Quade, *Analysis for Military Decisions*, p. 176.

21. Charles J. Hitch, *On the Choice of Objectives*, pp. 4-5.

22. Albert Wohlstetter, "Analysis and Design of Conflict Systems," in E. S. Quade, *Analysis for Military Decisions*, p. 121.

23. See Glenn H. Snyder, *Deterrence and Defense* (Princeton: 1961).

24. Wohlstetter in Quade, *Analysis for Military Decisions,* p. 122.

25. E. S. Quade, *Analysis for Military Decisions*, p. 157. Quade attempts to soften the blow by saying that businessmen and military officers know more about their business than anyone else. But the import of the analogy is clear enough.

26. Ibid., pp. 156-57.

27. Herman Kahn and Irwin Mann, *Techniques of Systems Analysis* (Santa Monica, CA: The RAND Corporation, 1957), believe that "More than any single thing, the skilled use of a fortiori and break-even analyses separate the professionals from the amateurs." They think that convincing others that you have a good solution is as important as coming up with one.

28. Armen A. Alchian and Reuben A. Kessel, *A Proper Role of Systems Analysis* (Santa Monica, CA: The RAND Corporation, 1954), p. 9.

29. Albert Wohlstetter in E. S. Quade, *Analysis for Military Decisions*, pp. 125-26

30. R. N. McKean, "Criteria," in E. S. Quade, *Analysis for Military Decisions,* p. 83.

31. E. S. Quade, *Analysis for Military Decisions,* p. 310.

32. Charles J. Hitch and Roland N. McKean, *The Economics of Defense in the Nuclear Age* (Cambridge, MA: Harvard University Press, 1961), p. 161.

33. See Hitch on "Mechanitis—putting . . . machines to work as a substitute for hard thinking." Charles Hitch, "Economics and Operations Research: A Symposium. II," *Review of Economics and Statistics,* August 1958, p. 209.

34. E. S. Quade, *Analysis for Military Decisions*, p. 12.

35. Ibid., p. 5.

36. T. C. Schelling, "Economics and Operations Research: A Symposium. V. Comment," *Review of Economics and Statistics,* August 1958, p. 222.

37. Albert Wohlstetter in E. S. Quade, *Analysis for Military Decisions*, p. 122.

38. Prest and Turvey, "Cost-Benefit Analysis," p. 684.

39. David Novick, ed., *Program Budgeting* (Cambridge, MA: Harvard University Press, 1965), p. vi.

40. Ibid., pp. vi.
41. Alan Dean, quoted in D. Novick, ibid., p. 311.
42. R. N. McKean and N. Anshen in D. Novick, ibid., pp. 286-87. The authors say that this aspect of program budgeting is part of the general view adopted in the book as a whole.
43. Arthur Smithies in ibid., p. 45.
44. A look at the classic work by Luther Gulick and Lyndall Urwick, *Papers on the Science of Administration* (New York: Columbia University Press, 1937), reveals considerable similarity between their suggested bases of organization and ways of conceptualizing programs.
45. N. Anshen in D. Novick, *Program Budgeting*, pp. 19-20.
46. G. A. Steiner in ibid., p. 356.
47. A. Smithies in ibid., p. 41.
48. Marvin Frankel in ibid., pp. 219-220. I have forborne citing the author who promises exciting discussion of the objectives of American education and ends up with fascinating program categories like primary, v, secondary, and tertiary education.
49. See the excellent chapter by M. A. Margolis and S. M. Barro, ibid., pp. 120-145.
50. Ibid., p. 18.
51. J. R. Meyer in ibid., p. 170. This paragraph is based on my interpretation of his work.
52. M. Frankel, ibid., p. 237.
53. Ibid., p. 348.
54. Ibid., p. 280.
55. Ibid., pp. 358-59.
56. Ibid., p. 206.
57. Ibid., p. 347.
58. Ibid., p. 365.
59. Ibid., p. 280.
60. See my comments to this effect in *The Politics of the Budgetary Process* (Boston: 1964), p. 140. For discussion of some political consequences of program budgeting, see pp. 135-142.
61. See William H. Brown and Charles E. Gilbert, *Planning Municipal Investment: X Case Study of Philadelphia* (Philadelphia: University of Pennsylvania Press, 1961), for an excellent discussion of the desire of elected officials to remain free to shift their commitments.
62. It may be said that I have failed to distinguish sufficiently between planning, programming, and budgeting. Planning is an orientation that looks ahead by extending costs and benefits or units of effectiveness a number of years into the future. Programming is a general procedure of systems analysis employing cost-effectiveness studies. In this view program budgeting is a mere mechanical translation of the results of high-level systems studies into convenient storage in the budgetary format. No doubt systems studies could be done without converting the results into the form of a program budget. This approach may have a lot to be said for it and it appears that it is the one that is generally followed in the Department of Defense in its presentations to Congress. But if the systems studies guide decisions as to the allocation of resources, and the studies are maintained according to particular program categories and are further legitimatized by being given status in the budget, it seems most unlikely that programming will be separated from budgeting. One is never sure whether too much or too little is being claimed for program budgeting. If all that program budgeting amounts to is a simple transla-

tion of previous systems studies into some convenient form of accounting, it hardly seems that this phenomenon is worth so much fuss. If the program categories in the budget system are meaningful, then they must be much more than a mere translation of previously arrived at decisions. In this case, I think that it is not my task to enlighten the proponents of program budgeting, but it is their task to make themselves clear to others.

63. A. Smithies in Novick, *Program Budgeting*, p. 37.
64. See U.S. House Appropriations Committee Subcommittee on Department of Defense Appropriations for Fiscal 1965, 88th Congress, 2nd Session, IV, p. 133. McNamara asserted that some 652 "subject issues" had been submitted to him for the fiscal 1965 budget.
65. Charles Hitch, *Decision Making for Defense* (Berkeley: University of California Press, 1965).
66. Novick, *Program Budgeting*, p. 100.
67. Paul Diesing, *Reason in Society* (Urbana: 1962), pp. 198, 203-4, 231-32.
68. Braybrooke and Lindblom, *A Strategy for Decision*. See also Lindblom, *The Intelligence of Democracy* (New York: 1965).
69. M. Anshen in D. Novick, *Program Budgeting*, p. 370.
70. Ibid., p. 289.
71. Ibid., p. 359.
72. Paul Diesing, *Reason in Society*, p. 228.
73. I am indebted to John Harsanyi for suggestions about political rationality.
74. In the field of defense policy, political factors are taken into account to the extent that the studies concentrate on the design of feasible alternatives. In the choice of overseas basing, for example, the question of feasibility in relation to treaties and friendly or unfriendly relationships with other countries is considered. Thus it seems permissible to take into account political considerations originating outside of the country, where differences of opinions and preferences among nations are to some extent accepted as legitimate, but apparently not differences internal to the American policy.

3

Rescuing Policy Analysis

Everyone knows that the nation needs better policy analysis. Each area one investigates shows how little is known compared to what is necessary in order to devise adequate policies. In some organizations there are no ways at all of determining the effectiveness of existing programs; organizational survival must be the sole criterion of merit. It is often not possible to determine whether the simplest objectives have been met. If there is a demand for information the cry goes out that what the organization does cannot be measured. Should anyone attempt to tie the organization down to any measure of productivity, the claim is made that there is no truth in numbers. Oftentimes this is another way of saying, "Mind your own business." Sometimes the line taken is that the work is so subtle that it resists any tests. On other occasions the point is made that only those learned in esoteric arts can properly understand what the organization does, and they can barely communicate to the uninitiated. There are men so convinced of the ultimate righteousness of their cause that they cannot imagine why anyone would wish to know how well they are doing in handling our common difficulties. Their activities are literally priceless; vulgar notions of cost and benefit do not apply to them.

Anyone who has weathered this routine comes to value policy analysis. The very idea that there should be some identifiable objectives and that attention should be paid to whether these are achieved seems a great step forward. Devising alternative ways of handling problems and considering the future costs of each solution appear creative in comparison to more haphazard approaches. Yet policy analysis with its emphasis upon originality, imagination, and foresight, cannot be simply described. It is equivalent to what Robert N. Anthony has called strategic planning: "the process of deciding on objectives of the organization, on changes in these objectives, on the resources used to attain these objectives.... It connotes big plans, important plans, plans with major consequences."[1] While policy analysis is similar to a broadly conceived version of systems analysis,[2] Yehezkel Dror has pointed up the boundaries that separate a narrow study from one with larger policy concerns. In policy analysis,

1. Much attention would be paid to the political aspects of public decision-making and public policymaking (instead of ignoring or condescendingly regarding political aspects)...
2. A broad conception of decision-making and policy-making would be involved (instead of viewing all decision-making as mainly resources allocations).
3. A main emphasis would be on creativity and search for new policy alternatives, with explicit attention to encouragement of innovative thinking...
4. There would be extensive reliance on . . . qualitative methods...
5. There would be much more emphasis on futuristic thinking....
6. The approach would be looser and less rigid, but nevertheless systematic, one which would recognize the complexity of means-ends interdependence, the multiplicity of relevant criteria of decision, and the partial and tentative nature of every analysis...[3]

Policy analysis aims at providing information that contributes to making an agency politically and socially relevant. Policies are goals, objectives, and missions that guide the agency. Analysis evaluates and sifts alternative means and ends in the elusive pursuit of policy recommendations. By getting out of the firehouse environment of day-to-day administration, policy analysis seeks knowledge and opportunities for coping with an uncertain future. Because policy analysis is not concerned with projecting the status quo, but with tracing out the consequences of innovative ideas, it is a variant of planning. Complementing the agency's decision process, policy analysis is a tool of social change.

In view of its concern with creativity, it is not surprising that policy analysis is still largely an art form; there are no precise rules about how to do it. The policy analyst seeks to reduce obscurantism by being explicit about problems and solutions, resources and results. The purpose of policy analysis is not to eliminate advocacy but to raise the level of argument among contending interests. If poor people want greater benefits from the government, the answer to their problems may not lie initially in policy analysis but in political organization. Once they have organized themselves, they may want to undertake policy analysis in order to crystallize their own objectives or merely to compete with the analyses put forth by others. The end result, hopefully, would be a higher quality debate and perhaps eventually public choice among better-known alternatives.

A belief in the desirability of policy analysis—the sustained application of intelligence and knowledge to social problems—is not enough to insure its success, no more than to want to do good is sufficient to accomplish noble purposes. If grandiose claims are made, if heavy burdens are placed on officials without adequate compensation, if the needs of agency heads are given scant consideration, they will not desire policy analysis. It is clear that those who introduced the PPB system into the federal government in one fell swoop did not undertake a policy analysis on how to introduce policy analysis into the federal government.

In a paper called "The Political Economy of Efficiency,"[4] written just as PPBS was begun in national government, I argued that it would run up against serious difficulties. There is still no reason to change a single word of what I said then. Indeed, its difficulties have been so overwhelming that there is grave danger that policy analysis will be rejected along with its particular manifestation in PPBS. In this essay I shall assess the damage that the planning-programming-budgeting system has done to the prospects of encouraging policy analysis in American national government. Then I would like to suggest some ways of enabling policy analysis to thrive and prosper.

Why Defense was a Bad Model

A quick way of seeing what went wrong with PPBS is to examine the preconditions for the use of this approach in the Defense Department, from which it was exported throughout the federal government. The immediate origins of PPBS are to be found in The Rand Corporation,[5] where, after the Second World War, a talented group of analysts devoted years of effort to understanding problems of defense policy. It took five years to come up with the first useful ideas. Thus the first requisite of program budgeting in defense was a small group of talented people who had spent years developing insights into the special problems of defense strategy and logistics. The second requisite was a common terminology, an ad hoc collection of analytical approaches, and the beginnings of theoretical statements to guide policy analysis. When Secretary of Defense Robert McNamara came into office, he did not have to search for men of talent nor did he have to wait for a body of knowledge to be created. These requisites already existed in some degree. What was further necessary was his ability to understand and to use analytical studies. Thus the third requisite of program budgeting is top leadership that understands policy analysis and is determined to get it and make use of it.

The fourth requisite was the existence of planning and planners. Planning was well accepted at the various levels of the Defense Department with the variety of joint service plans, long-range requirement plans, logistical plans, and more. Military and civilians believed in planning, in coping with uncertainty and in specifying some consequences of policy decisions. The problem as the originators of PPBS saw it was to introduce cost considerations into planning; they wanted to stop blue-sky planning and to integrate planning and budgeting. They wanted to use the program budget to bridge the gap between military planners, who cared about requirements but not about resources, and budget people, who were narrowly concerned with financial costs but not necessarily with effective policies.

Policy analysis is expensive in terms of time, talent, and money. It requires a high degree of creativity in order to imagine new policies and to test them out without requiring actual experience. Policy analysis calls for the creation of systems in which elements are linked to one another and to operational indicators so that costs and effectiveness of alternatives may be systematically compared. There is no way of knowing in advance whether the analysis will prove intellectually satisfying and politically feasible. Policy analysis is facilitated when: (a) goals are easily specified, (b) a large margin of error is allowable, and (c) the cost of the contemplated policy makes large expenditures on analysis worthwhile. That part of defense policy dealing with choices among alternative weapons systems was ideally suited for policy analysis. Since the cost of intercontinental missiles or other weapons systems ran into the billions of dollars, it was easy to justify spending millions on analysis.[6] The potential effectiveness of weapons like intercontinental missiles could be contemplated so long as one was willing to accept large margins of error. It is not unusual for analysts to assume extreme cases of damage and vulnerability in a context in which the desire for reducing risk is very great. Hence a goal like assuring sufficient destructive power such that no enemy strike could prevent devastation of one's country may be fuzzy without being unusable. If one accepts a procedure of imagining that possible enemies were to throw three times as much megatonage as intelligence estimates suggest they have, he need not be overly troubled by doubts about the underlying theory. If one is willing to pay the cost of compensating against the worst, lack of knowledge will not matter so much. The point is not that this is an undesirable analytic procedure, quite the contrary, but the extreme cases were allowed to determine the outcomes.

Inertia

The introduction of new procedures that result in new policies is not easy. Inertia is always a problem. Members of the organization and its clientele groups have vested interests in the policies of the past. Efforts at persuasion must be huge and persistent. But there are conditions that facilitate change. One of these is a rising level of appropriations. If change means that things must be taken away from people in the organization without giving them anything in return, greater resistance may be expected. The ability to replace old rewards with larger new ones helps reduce resistance to change. The fact that defense appropriations were increasing at a fast rate made life much easier for Mr. McNamara. The expected objections of clientele groups, for example, were muted by the fact that defense contractors had lots of work, even if it was not exactly what they expected. Rapid organizational growth may also improve the possibilities for change. The sheer increase in organizational size means that many new people can be hired who are not tied to the old ways. And speedy promotion may help convince members that the recommended changes are desirable.

The deeper change goes into the bowels of the organization, the more difficult it is to achieve. The more change can be limited to central management, the greater the possibility for carrying it out. The changes introduced in the Defense Department did not, for the most part, require acceptance at the lower levels. Consider a proposed change in the organization of fighting units that would drastically reduce the traditional heavy support facilities for ground forces. Such a change is not easily manipulated from Washington. But the choice of one weapons system over another is much more amenable to central control. The kinds of problems for which program budgeting was most useful also turned out to be problems that could be dealt with largely at the top of the organization. The program budget group that McNamara established had to fight with generals in Washington but not with master sergeants in supply. Anyone who knows the Army knows what battle they would rather be engaged in fighting.

The ability of an organization to secure rapid change depends, of course, on the degree of its autonomy from the environment. I have argued elsewhere[7] that the President of the United States has much more control over America's foreign policy than over its domestic policy. In almost any area of domestic policy there is a well-entrenched structure of interests. In foreign and defense policy, excluding such essentially internal concerns as the National Guard, the territory within the American political system is not nearly so well defended; there are far fewer political fortifications, mines, and boobytraps.

Personnel

Experienced personnel may be a barrier to change. They know something about the consequences of what they are doing. They may have tried a variety of alternatives and can point to reasons why each one will not work. If I may recall my low-level Army experience (I entered as a private first class and was never once demoted), the usual reply to a question about the efficacy of present practice was, "Have you ever been in combat, son?" But the most dramatic changes introduced in the Pentagon had to do with questions of avoiding or limiting nuclear war, in which no one had a claim to experience and in which the basic purpose of analysis is to make certain that we do not have to learn from experience. If the system fails, the game is over. And since McNamara's men possessed a body of doctrines on defense policy, they had an enormous advantage over regular military who were for a long time unable to defend themselves properly in the new field.[8]

The new policy analysts did not accept the currency of military experience. In their view, naked judgment was not a satisfactory answer to why a policy should be adopted. The Army might know the fire-power of an infantry division, but fire-power was not "effectiveness." Competition among the services for appropriations, however, was favorable to PPBS. There was a defense budget that covered virtually all of the Department's subject matter. There were defense missions in which trade-offs could be made between the services. Resources could actually be diverted if the analysis "proved" a particular service was right. Programs could easily be developed because of the facile identification of program with weapons systems and force units. Once the military learned the jargon, they were willing to play the game for an extra division or carrier. So long as dollar losses in one program were more than made up by gains in another, the pain of policy analysis was considerably eased.

The favorable conditions for the limited use of program budgeting in the Department of Defense do not exist in most domestic agencies. There are no large groups of talented policy analysts expert in agency problems outside of the federal government. These nonexistent men cannot, therefore, be made available to the agencies. (The time has passed when eighth-rate systems engineers in aerospace industries are expected to solve basic social problems overnight.) Most agencies had few planners and even less experience in planning. There is no body of knowledge waiting to be applied to policy areas such as welfare and crime. A basic reason for wanting more policy analysis is to help create knowledge where little now exists. There are only a few agencies in which top managers want systematic policy analysis and are able to understand quantitative studies. Goals are not easily specified for most domestic agencies. Nor do they usually have handy equivalents for programs like expensive weapons systems. What Thomas Schelling has so pungently observed about the Department of State—it does not control a large part of the budget devoted to foreign policy—is true for the domestic departments and their lack of coverage as well.[9]

Except for a few individual programs like the proposals for income supplements or assessing the desirability of a supersonic transport, the cost of most domestic policies does not rise into the billions of dollars. Congress and interested publics are not disposed to allow large margins of error. Instead of increasing, the availability of federal funds began declining soon after the introduction of program budgeting. A higher level of conflict was inevitable, especially since the acceptance of proposed changes required the acquiescence of all sorts of people and institutions in the far-flung reaches of the agencies. Social workers, city officials, police chiefs, welfare mothers, field officers, and numerous others were involved in the policies. Program budgeting on the domestic side takes place in a context in which there is both less autonomy from the environment and a great deal more firsthand experience by subordinates. On these grounds alone no one should have been surprised that program budgeting in the domestic agencies did not proceed as rapidly or with as much ostensible success as in the Defense Department.[10]

No One Can Do PPBS

In past writings I argued that program budgeting would run up against severe political difficulties. While most of these arguments have been conceded, I have been told that in a better world, without the vulgar intrusion of political factors (such as the consent of the governed), PPBS would perform its wonders as advertised. Now it is clear that for the narrow purpose of predicting why program budgeting would not work there was no need to mention political problems at all. It would have been sufficient to say that the wholesale introduction of PPBS presented insuperable difficulties of calculation. All the obstacles previously mentioned, such as lack of talent, theory, and data, may be summed up in a single statement: *no one knows how to do program budgeting.* Another way of putting it would be to say that many know what program budgeting should be like in general, but no one knows what it should be in any particular case. Program budgeting cannot be stated in operational terms. There is no agreement on what the words mean, let alone an ability to show another person what should be done. The reason for the difficulty is that telling an agency to adopt program budgeting means telling it to find better policies and there is no formula for doing that. One can (and should) talk about measuring effectiveness, estimating costs, and comparing alternatives, but that is a far cry from being able to take the creative leap of formulating a better policy.

Pattern of Events

On the basis of numerous discussions with would-be practitioners of program budgeting at the federal level, I think I can describe the usual pattern of events. The instructions come down from the Bureau of the Budget. You must have a program budget. Agency personnel hit the panic button. They just do not know how to do what they have been asked to do. They turn, if they can, to the pitifully small band of refugees from the Pentagon who have come to light the way. But these defense intellectuals do not know much about the policy area in which they are working. That takes time. Yet something must quickly come out of all this. So they produce a vast amount of inchoate information characterized by premature quantification of irrelevant items. Neither the agency head nor the examiners in the Bureau of the Budget can comprehend the material submitted to them. Its very bulk inhibits understanding. It is useless to the

Director of the Budget in making his decisions. In an effort to be helpful, the program analysis unit at the Budget Bureau says something like, "Nice try, fellows; we appreciate all that effort. But you have not quite got the idea of program budgeting yet. Remember, you must clarify goals, define objectives, relate these to quantitative indicators, project costs into the future. Please send a new submission based on this understanding."

Another furious effort takes place. They do it in Defense, so it must be possible. Incredible amounts of overtime are put in. Ultimately, under severe time pressure, even more data is accumulated. No one will be able to say that agency personnel did not try hard. The new presentation makes a little more sense to some people and a little less to others. It just does not hang together as a presentation of agency policies. There are more encouraging words from the Budget Bureau and another sermon about specifying alternative ways of meeting agency objectives, though not, of course, taking the old objectives for granted. By this time agency personnel are desperate. "We would love to do it," they say, "but we cannot figure out the right way. You experts in the Budget Bureau should show us how to do it." Silence. The word from on high is that the Bureau of the Budget does not interfere with agency operations; it is the agency's task to set up its own budget. After a while, cynicism reigns supreme.

PPBS must be tremendously inefficient. It resembles nothing so much as a Rube Goldberg apparatus in which the operations performed bear little relation to the output achieved. The data inputs into PPBS are huge and its policy output is tiny. All over the federal government the story is the same: if you ask what good has PPBS done, those who have something favorable to say invariably cite the same one or two policy analyses. At one time I began to wonder if the oil shale study[11] in the Interior Department and the maternal and child health care program[12] in Health, Education, and Welfare were all that had ever come out of the programming effort.

The orders to expand PPBS did not say, "Let us do more policy analysis than we have in the past." What it said was, "Let us make believe we can do policy analysis on everything." Instead of focusing attention on areas of policy amenable to study, the PPBS apparatus requires information on *all* agency policies.

Program Structure

The fixation on program structure is the most pernicious aspect of PPBS. Once PPBS is adopted, it becomes necessary to have a program structure that provides a complete list of organization objectives and supplies information on the attainment of each one. In the absence of analytic studies for all or even a large part of an agency's operations, the structure turns out to be a sham that piles up meaningless data under vague categories.[13] It hides rather than clarifies. It suggests comparisons among categories for which there is no factual or analytical basis. Examination of a department's program structure convinces everyone acquainted with it that policy analysis is just another bad way of masquerading behind old confusions. A mere recitation of some program categories from the Department of Agriculture—Communities of Tomorrow, Science in the Service of Man, Expanding Dimensions for Living—makes the point better than any comment.

Even if the agency head does understand a data-reduction-summarization of the program budget, he still cannot use the structure to make decisions, because it is too hard to adjust the elaborate apparatus. Although the system dredges up information under numerous headings, it says next to nothing about the impact of one program on another. There is data but no causal analysis. Hence the agency head is at once oversupplied with masses of numbers and undersupplied with propositions about the impact of any action he might undertake. He cannot tell, because no one knows, what the marginal change he is considering would mean for the rest of his operation. Incremental changes at the Bureau of the Budget at the agency level are made in terms of the old budget categories. Since the program structure is meant to be part of the budget, however, it must be taken as a statement of current policy and it necessarily emerges as a product of organizational compromise. The program structure, therefore, does not embody a focus on central policy concerns. More likely, it is a haphazard arrangement that reflects the desire to manipulate external support and to pursue internal power aspirations. Being neither program nor budget, program structure is useless. It is the Potemkin Village of modern administration. The fact that generating bits of random data for the program structure takes valuable time away from more constructive concerns also harms policy analysis. The whole point of policy analysis is to show that what had been done intuitively in the past may be done better through sustained application of intelligence. The adoption of meaningless program structures, and their perversion into slogans for supporting existing policies, does not—to say the least—advance the cause of policy analysis.

Gorham Testimony

I do not mean to suggest that the introduction of PPBS has not led to some accomplishments. Before we consider the significance of these accomplishments, however, it is essential that we understand what PPBS has manifestly not done. One could hardly have a better witness on this subject than William Gorham, formerly Assistant Secretary (Program Coordination), Department of Health, Education, and Welfare, and now head of the Urban Institute, who is widely acknowledged to be an outstanding practitioner of program budgeting.

At the highest level of generality, it is clear that PPBS does not help in making choices between vast national goals such as health and defense, nor is PPBS useful in making tradeoffs between more closely related areas of policy such as health, education, and welfare. In his testimony before the Joint Economic Committee, Gorham put the matter bluntly:

> Let me hasten to point out that we have not attempted any grandiose cost-benefit analysis designed to reveal whether the total benefits from an additional million dollars spent on health programs would be higher or lower than that from an additional million spent on education or welfare. If I was ever naive enough to think this sort of analysis possible, I no longer am. The benefits of health, education, and welfare programs are diverse and often intangible. They affect different age groups and different regions of the population over different periods of time. No amount of analysis is going to tell us whether the Nation benefits more from sending a slum child to pre-school, providing medical care to an old man or enabling a disabled housewife to resume her normal activities. The "grand decisions"—how much health, how much education, how much welfare, and which groups in the population shall benefit—are questions of value judgments and politics. The analyst cannot make much contribution to their resolution.[14]

It turns out that it is extremely difficult to get consensus on goals within a single area of policy. As a result, the policy analyst's attempt to find objectives that are more clearly operational and more widely acceptable. Gorham speaks with the voice of experience when he says

> Let me give you an example. Education. What we want our kids to be as a result of going to school is the level of objective which is the proper and the broadest one. But we want our children to be different sorts of people. We want them to be capable of different sorts of things. We have, in other words, a plurality of opinions about what we want our schools to turn out. So you drop down a level and you talk about objectives in terms of educational attainment—years of school completed and certain objective measures of quality. Here you move in education from sort of fuzzy objectives, but very important, about what it is that you want the schools to be doing, to the more concrete, less controversial, more easily to get agreed upon objectives having to do with such things as educational attainment, percentage of children going to college, etc.
>   I think the same thing is true in health and in social services, that at the very highest level objective, where in theory you would really like to say something, the difficulty of getting and finding a national consensus is so great that you drop down to something which is more easily and readily accepted as objectives.[15]

What can actually be done, according to Gorham, are analytic studies of narrowly defined areas of policy. "The less grand decisions," Gorham testified, "those among alternative programs with the same or similar objectives within health—can be substantially illuminated by good analysis. It is this type of analysis which we have undertaken at the Department of Health, Education, and Welfare."[16] Gorham gives as examples disease control programs and improvements in the health of children. If this type of project analysis is what can be done under PPBS, a serious question is raised: Why go through all the rigamarole in order to accomplish a few discrete studies of important problems?

A five-year budget conceived in the hodgepodge terms of the program structure serves no purpose.[17] Since actual budget decisions are made in terms of the old categories and policy analysis may take place outside of the program structure, there is no need to institutionalize empty labels. If a policy analysis has been completed, there is no reason why it cannot be submitted as part of the justification of estimates to the Bureau of the Budget and to Congress. For the few program memoranda that an agency might submit, changes could be detailed in terms of traditional budget categories. Problems of program structure would be turned over to the agency's policy analysts who would experiment with different ways of lending intellectual coherence to the agency's programs. There would be no need to foist the latest failure on a skeptical world. Nor would there be battles over the costs of altering a program structure that has achieved, if not a common framework, at least the virtue of familiarity. The difference is that stability of categories in the traditional budget has real value for control[18] while the embodiment of contradictions in the program structure violates its essential purpose.

Incentives for Policy Analysis

PPBS discredits policy analysis. To collect vast amounts of random data is hardly a serious analysis of public policy. The conclusion is obvious. The shotgun marriage between policy analysis and budgeting should be annulled. Attempts to describe the total agency program in program memoranda should be abandoned. It is hard enough to do a good job of policy analysis, as most agency people now realize, without having to meet arbitrary and fixed deadlines imposed by the budget processes There is no way of telling whether an analysis will be successful. There is, therefore, no point in insisting that half-baked analyses be submitted every year because of a misguided desire to cover the entire agency program. The Budget Bureau itself has recently recognized the difficulty by requiring agencies to present extensive memoranda only when major policy issues have been identified. It is easier and more honest just to take the program structure out of the budget.

The thrust of the argument thus far, however, forces us to confront a major difficulty. Policy analysis and budgeting were presumably connected in order to see that high quality analysis did not languish in limbo but was translated into action through the critical budget process. Removing policy analysis from the annual budget cycle might increase its intellectual content at the expense of its practical impact. While formal program structures should go—PPBS actually inhibits the prospects for obtaining good analysis that is worth translating into public policy—they should be replaced with a strong incentive to make policy analysis count in yearly budgetary decisions. I am therefore proposing a substitute for PPBS that maintains whatever incentive it provided for introducing the results of policy analysis into the real world without encouraging the debilitating effects.

The submission of program memoranda supported by policy analysis should be made a requirement for major dollar changes in an agency's budget. The Bureau of the Budget should insist that this requirement be met by every agency. Agency heads, therefore, would have to require it of subunits. The sequence could operate as follows:

1. Secretary of agency and top policy analysts review major issues and legislation and set up a study menu for several years. Additions and deletions are made periodically.
2. Policy analysts set up studies which take anywhere from six to twenty-four months.
3. As a study is completed for a major issue area, it is submitted to the Secretary of the agency for review and approval.
4. If approved, the implications of the study's recommendations are translated into budgetary terms for submission as a program memorandum in support of the agency's fiscal year budget.

No one imagines that a mechanical requirement would in and of itself compel serious consideration of policy matters. No procedure should be reified as if it had a life of its own apart from the people who must implement it. This conclusion is as true for my suggestion as for PPBS. We must therefore consider ways and means of increasing the demand for and supply of policy analysis.

Increasing Demand and Supply

The first requirement of effective policy analysis is that top management want it. No matter how trite this criterion sounds, it has often been violated, as Frederick C. Mosher's splendid study of program budgeting in foreign affairs reveals.[20] The inevitable difficulties of shaking loose information and breaking up old habits will prove to be insuperable obstacles without steady support from high agency officials. If they do not want it, the best thing to do is concentrate efforts in another agency. Placing the best people in a few agencies also makes it more likely that a critical mass of talent will be able to achieve a creative response to emerging policy problems.

Policy analysis should be geared to the direct requirements of top management. This means that analysis should be limited to a few major issues. Since there will only be a few studies every year, the secretary should have time to consider and understand each one. The analytical staff should be flexible enough to work on his priority interests. Consequently, one of the arguments by which program budgeting has been oversold has to be abandoned. Policy analysis will not normally identify programs of low priority. Top management is not interested in them. They would receive no benefit from getting supporters of these programs angry at them. Instead, agency heads want to know how to deal with emergent problems. Practitioners of policy analysis understand these considerations quite well. Harry Shooshan, Deputy Undersecretary for Programs, Department of the Interior, presents a perceptive analysis:

> We have tried to more heavily relate our PPB work and our analytical work to the new program thrusts, and major issues, not because it is easier to talk about new programs, but rather, there is a good question of judgment, on how much time one should spend on ongoing programs that are pretty well set. So you restate its mission and you put it in PPB wrapping and what have you really accomplished?
>
> There are going to be new program proposals, new thrusts of doing something in certain areas. Let's relate our analyses to that and get the alternatives documented as well as we can for the decision-makers. So it is a combination of on the one hand it being difficult to identify low priorities in a manner that really means something and on the other hand, it is the fact of what have we really accomplished by simply putting old programs in new wrappings when new programs really should get the emphasis right now in terms of what are the decisions now before, in my case, the Secretary of the Interior, in terms of what should he know before he makes decisions relative to where he is attempting to go. If I can relate PPB to the decision on his desk today and the near future, I can sell him and, in turn, our own Department on the contribution that we can make.[21]

The implications of Shooshan's point go beyond making policy analysis more desirable by having it meet the needs of top management. The subjects for policy analysis ought to be chosen precisely for their critical-fluide-mergent character. These are the places where society is hurting. These are the areas in which there are opportunities for marginal gains. Indeed, a major role for top management is scanning the political horizon for targets of opportunity. Yet the characteristics of these new problems run counter to the criteria for selection that PPBS currently enforces, since they are identified by ambiguity concerning goals, lack of data upon which to project accurate estimates of costs and consequences, and pervasive uncertainty concerning the range of possible changes in program.

There would be a much larger demand for policy analysis if it were supplied in ways that would meet the needs of high level officials. Let us consider the example of the President of the United States. He can certainly use policy analysis to help make better decisions. Substantial policy studies would give him and his staff leverage against the bureaucracy. Knowledge is power. Indeed, command of a particular field would enable presidents to exert greater control over the agenda for public decision and would give them advantages in competition with all sorts of rivals. Presidents could use perhaps a dozen major policy studies per year of their most immediate concerns. If even a few of these turn out well, the president may be motivated to make use of them. Contrast this with the present inundation of the Executive Office by endless streams of program "books," summaries, and memoranda that nobody ever looks at.

What is true of the president is also true for important executives in the agencies. Policy-oriented executives will want to get better analysis. Executives wishing to increase their resource base will be interested in independent sources of information and advice. Those who would exert power need objectives to fight for. It is neither fashionable nor efficient to appear to seek power for its own sake. In polite society the drive is masked and given a noble face when it can be attached to grand policy concerns that bring benefits to others as well as to power seekers. The way to gain the attention of leaders is not to flood them with trivia but to provide examples of the best kind of work that can be done. The last years of the Johnson Administration witnessed a proliferation of secret commissions to recommend new policies. The department secretary often became just another special pleader. If they have any interest in curbing this development, secretaries may find that producing their own policy analyses allow them to say that outside intervention is not the only or the best way to generate new policies.

Congressional Demand

If strategically located congressmen demanded more policy analysis, there is little doubt that we would get it. What can be done to make them want more of it? The answer does not lie in surrounding them with large staffs so that they lose their manifestly political functions and become more like bureaucrats. Nor does the answer lie in telling congressmen to keep away from small administrative questions in favor of larger policy concerns. For many congressmen get into the larger questions only by feeling their way through the smaller details.[22] A threat to deprive congressmen of the traditional line-item appropriations data through which they exert their control of agency affairs also does not appear to be a good way of making congressmen desire policy analysis.

Policy analysis must be made relevant to what congressmen want. Some legislators desire to sponsor new policies and they are one clientele for analysis. For other congressmen, however, policy is a bargainable product that emerges from their interactions with their fellows. These members must be appealed to in a different way. They often have a sense of institutional loyalty and pride. They know that Congress is a rare institution in this world— a legislative body that actually has some control over public policy. They are aware that the development of new knowledge and new techniques may freeze them out of many of the more serious decisions. Policy analysis should be proposed to these men as an enhancement of the power of Congress as an institution. The purpose of analysis would be, in its simplest form, to enable congressmen to ask good questions and to evaluate answers. Oftentimes it is hardest for a layman to recognize the significant questions implicit in an area of policy. Are there other and better questions to be asked, other and better policies to be pursued?

A Congress that takes seriously its policy role should be encouraged to contract for policy analysis that would stress different views of what the critical questions are in a particular area of policy. Each major committee or subcommittee should be encouraged to hire a man trained in policy analysis for a limited period, perhaps two years. His task would be to solicit policy studies, evaluate presentations made by government agencies, and keep congressmen informed about what are considered the important questions. In the past, chairmen have not always paid attention to the quality of committee staffs. Following the lead of the Joint Economic Committee, seminars might be held for a couple of weeks before each session. At these seminars discussions would take place between agency personnel, committee staff, and the academics or other experts who have produced the latest policy analysis. If all went well, congressmen would emerge with a better idea of the range of issues and of somewhat different ways of tackling the problems, and the policy analysts would emerge with a better grasp of the priorities of these legislators.

Suppliers of Policy Analysis

Thus far we have dealt solely with the incentive structure of the consumers who ought to want policy analysis—agency heads, presidents, congressmen. Little has been said about the incentive structure of the suppliers who ought to provide it—analysts, consultants, academics. Our premise has been that the supply of policy analysis would be a function of the demand. Now, the relationships between supply and demand have long been troublesome in economics because it is so difficult to sort out the mutual interactions. Upon being asked whether demand created supply or supply created demand, the great economist Marshall was reported to have said that it was like asking which blade of the scissors cuts the paper. There is no doubt, however, that changes in the conditions and quality of supply would have important effects on the demand for policy analysis.

Disengaging policy analysis from PPBS would help build the supply of policy analysis by

1. Decreasing the rewards for mindless quantification for its own sake. There would be no requests from the Bureau of the Budget for such information and no premium for supplying it.
2. Increasing the rewards for analysts who might try the risky business of tackling a major policy problem that was obviously not going to be considered because everyone was too busy playing with the program structure. Gresham's Law operates here: programmed work drives out unprogrammed activity, make-work drives out analysis.

One way of increasing the supply of policy analysis would be to improve the training of people who work directly in the various areas of policy. Instead of taking people trained in policy analysis and having them learn about a particular policy area, the people in that area would be capable of doing policy analysis. Three-day or three-month courses will not do for that purpose. A year, and possibly two years, would be required. Since it is unlikely that the best people can be made available for so long a period, it is necessary to think in terms of education at an earlier period in their lives. There is a great need for schools of public policy in which technical training is combined with broader views of the social context of public policy. Although no one knows how to teach "creativity," it is possible to expose students to the range of subjects out of which a creative approach to public policy could come.

Another way of increasing the supply of policy analysis would be to locate it in an organizational context in which it has prestige and its practitioners are given time to do good work. Having the policy analysis unit report directly to the secretary or agency head would show that it is meant to be taken seriously.[23] But then it is bound to get involved in day-to-day concerns of the agency head, thus creating a classic dilemma.

Tactics

The effective use of a policy analysis unit cannot be specified in advance for all agencies. There are certain tensions in its functions that may be mitigated on a case-by-case basis but cannot be resolved once and for all. Serious policy analysis requires months, if not years, of effort. A unit that spends its time solely on substantial policy analysis would soon find itself isolated from the operational concerns of the agency. There would be inordinate temptations on the part of its members to go where the action is. Before long, the policy unit might become more immediately relevant at the expense of its long-term impact. The frantic nature of day-to-day emergencies drives out the necessary time and quiet for serious study and reflection. What can be done? One tactic is for the policy unit to consider itself an educational as well as an action group. Its task should be to encourage analysis on the part of other elements of the organization. It should undertake nothing it can get subunits to do. The role of the policy unit would then be one of advising subunits and evaluating their output.

A second tactic would be to contract out for studies that are expected to take the longest period of time. The third tactic is the most difficult, because it calls for a balancing act. Immediate usefulness to top management may be secured by working on problems with short lead times while attempting to retain perhaps half of the available time for genuine policy analysis. To the degree that serious policy analysis enters into the life of the organization and proves its worth, it will be easier to justify its requirements in terms of release from everyday concerns. Yet the demand for services of the analysts is certain to increase. Failures in policy analysis, on the other hand, are likely to give the personnel involved more time for reflection than they would prefer. Like headquarters-field relationships, line and staff responsibilities, and functional versus hierarchical command, the problems of the policy unit are inherent in its situation and can only be temporarily resolved.

These comments on incentives for increasing the supply and demand for policy analysis are plainly inadequate. They are meant merely to suggest that there is a problem and to indicate how one might go about resolving it. We do not really know how to make policy analysis fit in with the career requirements of congressmen, nor can we contribute much beside proverbial wisdom to the structure and operation of policy analysis units. There are, however, opportunities for learning that have not yet been used. One of the benefits flowing from the experience with PPBS is that it has thrown up a small number of policy analyses that practitioners consider to be good. We need to know what makes some live in the world and others remain unused. Aside from an impressive manuscript by Clay Thomas Whitehead,[24] however, in which two recent policy analyses in defense are studied, there has been no effort to determine what this experience has to teach us. Despite the confident talk about policy analysis (here and elsewhere), a great deal of work remains to be done on what is considered "good" and why. The pioneering work by Charles E. Lindblom should not be wrongly interpreted as being anti-analysis, but as a seminal effort to understand what we do when we try to grapple with social problems.

Reexamination

Critical aspects of policy analysis need to be reexamined. The field cries out for a study of "coordination" as profound and subtle as Martin Laudau's essay on "Redundancy."[25] That most elemental problem of political theory— the proper role of the government versus that of the individual—should be subject to a radical critique.[26] The fact that cost-benefit analysis began with water resource projects in which the contribution to national income was the key question has guided thought away from other areas of policy for which this criterion would be inappropriate. There are policies for which the willingness of citizens to support the activity should help determine the outcome. There are other policies in which presently unquantifiable benefits, like pleasure in seeing others better off or reduction of anxiety following a visible decrease in social hostility, should be controlling. Although social invention is incredibly difficult, the way is open for new concepts of the role of government to liberate our thoughts and guide our actions.

In many ways the times are propitious for policy analysis. The New Deal era of legislation has ended and has not yet been replaced by a stable structure of issues. People do not know where they stand today in the same way they knew how they felt about Medicare or private versus public electric power. The old welfare state policies have disenchanted former supporters as well as further enraged their opponents. Men have worked for twenty years to get massive education bills through Congress only to discover that the results have not lived up to their expectations; it takes a lot more to improve education for the deprived than anyone had thought. There is now a receptivity to new ideas that did not exist a decade ago. There is a willingness to consider new policies and try new ways. Whether or not there is sufficient creativity in us to devise better policies remains to be seen. If we are serious about improving public policy, we will go beyond the fashionable pretense of PPBS to show others what the best policy analysis can achieve.

Notes

This paper supplements my recent studies. It is meant to be read in conjunction with these other works. Thus I have felt no need to describe the traditional budgetary practices covered in *The Politics of the Budgetary Process* (Boston: Little, Brown & Co., 1964) or modern modes of "efficiency" analysis beyond the account in "The Political Economy of Efficiency (*Public Administration Review*, Vol. XXVI, No. 4, December 1966, pp. 292-310). Nor have I sought to fully set forth my ideas on desirable budgetary reform as found in "Toward A Radical Incrementalism" (Washington, DC: American Enterprise Institute for Public Policy Research, December 1965), also, in *Congress: The First Branch of Government* (Washington, DC: American Enterprise Institute for Public Policy Research, 1966), pp. 115-165.

I wish to thank Arnold Meltsner, a graduate student in the Department of Political Science, for his critical comments and for giving me the benefit of his experience with Defense budgets. I also wish to thank Robert Biller, Yehezkel Dror, Todd LaPorte, Frederick C. Mosher, and Nelson Polsby for helpful comments. Peter Dahl made useful stylistic suggestions. No one who reads this paper will doubt that I mean to take all the blame.

1. Robert N. Anthony, *Planning and Control Systems: A Framework for Analysis* (Boston: Harvard University Press, 1965), p. 16.
2. Aaron Wildavsky, "The Political Economy of Efficiency," *Public Administration Review*, Vol. XXVI, No. 4 (December 1966): 298-302.
3. Yehezkel Dror, "Policy Analysts: A New Professional Role In Government Service," *Public Administration Review*, Vol. XXVII, No. 3 (September 1967): 200-201. See also Dror's major work, *Public Policy-Making Reexamined* (San Francisco: Chandler, 1968).
4. Aaron Wildavsky, "The Political Economy of Efficiency."
5. See David Novick, "Origin and History of Program Budgeting," The RAND Corporation, October 1966, p. 3427.
6. I once tried to interest a graduate student who had experience with defense problems in doing research in the City of Oakland. He asked the size of Oakland's budget. "Fifty million dollars," I said. "Why, in the Air Force we used to round to that figure," was his reply.
7. Aaron Wildavsky, "The Two Presidencies," *Transaction,* Vol. IV, No. 2 (December 1966): 7-14.
8. For further argument along these lines, see my article, "The Practical Consequences of the Theoretical Study of Defense Policy," *Public Administration Review*, Vol. XXV, No. I (March 1965): 90-103.
9. Thomas C. Schelling, "PPBS and Foreign Affairs," memorandum prepared at the request of the Subcommittee on National Security and International Operations of the Committee on Government Operations, U.S. Senate, 90th Congress, First Session, 1968.
10. Dr. Alain Enthoven, who played a leading role in introducing systems analysis to the Defense Department, has observed that "The major changes in strategy, the step-up in production of Minuteman and Polaris and the build-up in our non-nuclear forces including the increase in the Army, the tactical air forces, and the air lift . . . were being phased in at the same time that PPBS was being phased in....We speeded up the Polaris and Minutemen programs because we believed that it was terribly important to have an invulnerable retaliatory force. We built up the Army Land Forces because we believed it was necessary to have more land forces for limited non-nuclear wars. We speeded up the development of anti-guerrilla forces or special forces because we believed that was necessary for counterinsurgency. Those things would have happened with or without PPBS. PPBS does not make the strategy." Subcommittee on National Security and International Operations of the Committee on Government Operations, U.S. Senate, *Hearings, Planning-Programming Budgeting,* 90th Congress, First Session, Part 2, Sept. 27 and Oct. 18, 1967, p. 141.
11. *Prospects for Oil Shale Development* (Washington, DC: Department of the Interior, May 1968).
12. The study is presented in ibid., pp. 10-45.
13. Similar difficulties under similar conditions evidently occur in the business world. It is worth citing Anthony's comments: "Strategic planning [that is, policy analysis] is essentially *irregular.* Problems, opportunities, and 'bright ideas' do not arise according to some set timetable; they have to be dealt with whenever they happen to be perceived....Failure to appreciate the distinction between regular and irregular processes can result in trouble of the following type. A company with a well-developed budgeting process decides to formalize its strategic planning. It prepares a set of forms and accompanying procedures, and has the operat-

ing units submit their long-range plans on these forms on one certain date each year. The plans are then supposed to be reviewed and approved in a meeting similar to a budget review meeting. Such a procedure does not work....There simply is not time enough in an annual review meeting for a careful consideration of a whole batch of strategic proposals....It is important that next year's operating budget be examined and approved as an entity so as to ensure that the several pieces are consonant with one another....Except for very general checklists of essential considerations, the strategic planning process follows no prescribed format or timetable. Each problem is sufficiently different from other problems so that each must be approached differently." *Planning and Control Systems,* pp. 38-39.

14. Joint Economic Committee, Congress of the United States, *Hearings, The Planning, Programming Budgeting System: Progress and Potentials,* 90th Congress, First Session, September 1967, p. 5.

15. Ibid., pp. 80-81. One might think that a way out of the dilemma could be had by adopting a number of goals for an area of policy. When Committee Chairman William Proxmire suggested that more goals should be specified, Gorham replied, "I would like to be the one to give the first goal. The first one in is always in the best shape. The more goals you have, essentially the less useful any one is, because the conflict among them becomes so sharp" (p. 83).

16. Ibid., p. 6.

17. Anthony again supplies a useful comparison from private firms that makes a similar point:

> An increasing number of businesses make profit
> and balance sheet projections for several years
> ahead, a process which has come to be known
> by the name "long-range planning.". . . A five-
> year plan usually is a projection of the costs
> and revenues that are anticipated under policies
> and programs *already approved,* rather than a
> device for consideration of, and decision on,
> new policies and programs. The five-year plan
> reflects strategic decisions already taken; it is
> not the essence of the process of making new
> decisions....In some companies, the so-called
> five-year plan is nothing more than a mechanical
> extrapolation of current data, with no reflection
> of management decisions and judgment; such
> an exercise is virtually worthless *(Planning and
> Control System,* pp. 57-58).

18. An excellent discussion of different purposes of budgeting and stages of budgetary development is found in Allen Schick, 'The Road to PPB: The Stages of Budget Reform," *Public Administration Review,* Vol. XXVI, No. 4, December 1966, pp. 243-258.

19. In another paper ("Toward A Radical Incrementalism"), I have proposed that policy analysis would be facilitated by abolishing the annual budget cycle. One of the great weaknesses of governmental policy making is that policies are formulated a good two years before funds become available. Given the difficulties of devising policies in the first place, the time lag wreaks havoc with the best analysis. Since no one seems disposed to consider this alternative seriously, I mention it merely in passing as a change that would fit in with what has been suggested.

20. Frederick C. *Mosher,* "Program Budgeting in Foreign Affairs: Some Reflections," memorandum prepared at the request of the Subcommittee on National Security and International Operations of the Committee on Government Operations, U.S. Senate, 90th Congress, Second Session, 1968.
21. Joint Economic Committee, *Hearings,* pp. 77-78.
22. Aaron Wildavsky, "Toward A Radical Incrementalism," pp. 27-29.
23. When Charles Hitch was Controller of the Defense Department, the policy analysis unit reported directly to him, as did the budget unit. One reported result is that the policy unit was able to do its work without being drawn into the daily concerns of the budget men. When policy analysis (called systems analysis) was given separate status, with its own assistant secretary, there was apparently a much greater tendency for its members to insist upon control of immediate budgetary decisions. Hence the distinction between longer-run policy analysis and shorter-run budgeting tended to be obscured. It would be interesting to know whether the participants saw it in this way. Optimal placement of a policy analysis unit is bound to be a source of difficulty and a subject of controversy.
24. Clay Thomas Whitehead, "Uses and Abuses of Systems Analysis," The RAND Corporation, September 1967.
25. See Martin Landau, "Redundancy," *Public Administration Review,* Vol. XXIX, No. 4, July/August 1969.
26. For a fine example of original thought on this question, see Paul Feldman, "Benefits and the Role of Government in a Market Economy," Institute for Defense Analysis, Research Paper, February 1968, p. 477.

4

Toward a Radical Incrementalism: A Proposal to Aid Congress in Reform of the Budgetary Process

My purpose in writing this paper is to aid Congress in reforming the budgetary process from the viewpoint of legislators in a representative assembly.[1] The usual proposals for helping Congress by taking its job away or by shifting its responsibilities to the executive or by recommending that it confine itself to those actions of which it is least capable will not be found here. I shall propose a radical incremental approach designed to improve the calculating capability of all governmental participants in the budgetary process. I shall also propose mechanisms for improving the essential political information on budgeting available to Congress, somewhat at the expense of the Chief Executive, though not without some compensations for him as well. Finally, I shall suggest that Congress sponsor research which, for the first time, would be directly geared to improving its ability to act on appropriations in terms best suited to its limitations and opportunities.

My approach is based on considerations (as old as political theory itself) which do not seek vainly to condemn natural political behavior, but rather to so arrange the interaction of political forces as to secure desirable results. At one point in the *Politics,*[2] Aristotle devised a solution to a vexing political problem. It seems that the poor were so busy trying to make a living that they could not afford to attend the Assembly, while the rich found so much profit in their private activities that it did not appear worthwhile for them to participate. This violated the balance of political forces whereby justice emerges from a clash of interests. Aristotle's solution was characteristically ingenious: the poor were to be paid to attend and the rich fined if they failed to attend. We might also recall how the Greeks saw to it that men of wealth paid their subscriptions to the state. If one man claimed he could not pay, any man willing to do so could substitute his property for the property of the man who alleged he could not pay. Children recognize the considerations involved when they divide a valued object by having one of them cut it in half and the other select the piece for himself. Spinoza's *Tractatus Politicus* [3] is full of suggestions for mechanisms by which the passions of men may, by their strength and predictability, be usefully employed. He suggests, for example, that military leaders be paid from the receipts of import and export duties so that they will be motivated to defend the state but not to engage in continual wars, since this would interrupt commerce and with it their source of income. The Constitution of the United States, with its separation and sharing of powers, its federalism, its staggered elections, and overlapping constituencies, is based on this kind of consideration, as the words of the framers so clearly reveal. I would take my stand with the authors of the *Federalist* (especially in their 51st number) who argue that political practices should be so arranged "that the private interest of every individual may be a sentinel over the public rights."

In order to provide necessary background, the first section of the paper is devoted to an analysis of the nature of reform proposals. Following this is a brief description of the budgetary process in the United States. After an analysis of the major criticisms of the budgetary process, the paper ends with an exposition and defense of radical incrementalism as a desirable approach to budgeting in the United States.

The Political Meaning of Budgetary Reform

A large part of the literature on budgeting in the United States is concerned with reform.[4] The goals of the proposed reforms are couched in similar language—economy, efficiency, improvement, or just better budgeting. The president, the Congress and its committees, administrative agencies, even the interested citizenry are all to gain by some change in the way the budget is formulated, presented, or evaluated. There is little or no realization among the reformers, however, that any effective change in budgetary relationships must necessarily alter the outcomes of the budgetary process. Far from being a neutral matter of "better budgeting," proposed reforms inevitably contain important implications for the political system.

A crucial aspect of budgeting is whose preferences are to prevail in disputes about which activities are to be carried on and to what degree, in the light of limited resources. The problem is not only generally "how shall budgetary benefits be maximized," as if it made no difference who received them, but also specifically "who shall receive budgetary benefits and how much." One of the central problems of social conduct consists of somehow aggregating different preferences so that a decision may emerge. How can we compare the

worth of expenditures for irrigation to certain farmers with the worth to motor-
ists of widening a highway, or the desirability of aiding old people to pay
medical bills with the degree of safety provided by an expanded defense program. All this is further complicated by the necessity of taking into account the
relative intensity of preference with which policies are sought by different
people. The process developed for dealing with interpersonal comparisons in
government is not economic but political. Conflicts are resolved (under agreed
upon rules) by translating different preferences through the political system
into units called votes or into types of authority like a veto power. Therefore, if
the present budgetary process is rightly or wrongly deemed unsatisfactory, one
must alter in some respect the political system of which the budget is an expression. It is impossible to make drastic changes in budgeting without also
altering the political system and the distribution of influence within it.[5]

By far the most significant way of influencing the budget would be to introduce basic political changes (or to wait for secular changes like the growing
industrialization of the South). Imagine that the electoral college were changed
to favor conservatives or that the seniority system were altered to favor more
liberal committee chairmen; give the president an item veto or provide him
with more powers enabling him to control the votes of his party in Congress;
enable a small group of congressmen to command a majority of votes on all
occasions so that they can push their program through. Then you will have
exerted a profound influence on the content of the budget.

Since the budget represents conflicts over whose preferences shall prevail,
one cannot speak of "better budgeting" without considering who benefits and
who loses or demonstrating that no one loses. Just as the supposedly objective
criterion of "efficiency" has been shown to have normative implications,[6] so a
"better budget" may well be a cloak for hidden policy preferences. To propose
that the president be given an item veto, for example, represents an attempt to
increase the influence of the particular interests which gain superior access to
the Chief Executive rather than, say, to the Congress. Only if one could eliminate the element of conflict over expenditures could it be assumed that a reform is "good enough" if it enables an official to do a better job from his point
of view; since conflict over expenditures cannot be eliminated, the policy implications for others must be taken into account.[7]

Perhaps there are reforms which promise benefits for all and deprivations
for none, or benefits for some and deprivations for none. But this cannot be
assumed; it must be demonstrated especially to groups which anticipate deprivations for themselves. I am proposing that we be explicit about our intentions
and demonstrate some awareness of the likely consequences of our proposals.
(This advice is meant for the scholars whose task presumably includes being
open with their colleagues, and not for the political participants for whom it
might not always be wise to reveal what they are about.) It is clear, then, that

before reforms are suggested, we need some idea of how the federal budgetary process operates in its political context. Then we may get a better idea of the consequences of reform proposals in comparison with the consequences of the present budgetary process.

The Budgetary Process

For our purposes, we shall conceive of budgets as attempts to allocate financial resources through political processes. If politics is regarded as conflict over whose preferences are to prevail in the determination of policy, then the budget records the outcomes of this struggle. If one asks "who gets what the (public or private) organization has to give?" then the answers for a moment in time are recorded in the budget. If organizations are viewed as political coalitions,[8] budgets are mechanisms through which subunits bargain over conflicting goals, make side payments, and try to motivate one another to accomplish their objectives. In a study such as this, which stresses the appropriations process in Congress, the political context of budgeting can hardly be overemphasized.

The making of decisions depends upon calculation of which alternatives to consider and to choose. Calculation involves determination of how problems are identified, get broken down into manageable dimensions, are related to one another, and how choices are made as to what is relevant and who shall be taken into account. A major clue toward understanding budgeting is the extraordinary complexity of the calculations involved. In any large organization, there are a huge number of items to be considered, many of which are of considerable technical difficulty. Yet there is little or no theory in most areas of policy which would enable practitioners to predict the consequences of alternative moves and probability of their occurring.[9] Man's ability to calculate is severely limited; time is always in short supply; and the number of matters which can be encompassed in one mind at the same time is quite small.[10] Nor has anyone solved the imposing problem of the interpersonal comparison of utilities. Outside of the political process, there is no agreed upon way of comparing and evaluating the merits of different programs for different people whose preferences vary in kind and in intensity.

Participants in budgeting deal with their overwhelming burdens by adopting heuristic aids to calculation. They simplify in order to get by. They make small moves, let experience accumulate, and use the feedback from their decisions to gauge consequences. They use actions on simpler matters that they understand as indices to complex concerns. They attempt to judge the capacity of the men in charge of programs even if they cannot appraise the policies directly. They may institute across-the-board ("meat-axe") cuts to reduce expenditures, relying on outcries from affected agencies and interest groups to let them know if they have gone too far.[11]

By far the most important aid to calculation is the incremental approach. Budgets are almost never actively reviewed as a whole in the sense of considering at one time the value of all existing programs compared to all possible alternatives. Instead, this year's budget is based on last year's budget, with special attention given to a narrow range of increases or decreases. The greatest part of any budget is a product of previous decisions. Long-range commitments have been made. There are mandatory programs whose expenses must be met. Powerful political support makes the inclusion of other activities inevitable. Consequently, officials concerned with budgeting restrict their attention to items and programs they can do something about—a few new programs and possible cuts in old ones.

Incremental calculations, then, proceed from an existing base. By "base" we refer to commonly held expectations among participants in budgeting that programs will be carried out at close to the going level of expenditures. The base of a budget, therefore, refers to accepted parts of programs that will not normally be subjected to intensive scrutiny. Since many organizational units compete for funds, there is a tendency for the central authority to include all of them in the benefits or deprivations to be distributed. Participants in budgeting often refer to expectations regarding their fair share of increases and decreases. The widespread sharing of deeply held expectations concerning the organization's base and its fair share of funds provide a powerful (although informal) means of coordination and stability in budgetary systems that appear to lack comprehensive calculations proceeding from a hierarchical center.[12]

Roles (the expectations of behavior attached to institutional positions) are parts of the division of labor. They are calculating mechanisms. In American national government, the administrative agencies act as advocates of increased expenditure, the Bureau of the Budget acts as presidential servant with a cutting bias, the House Appropriations Committee functions as a guardian of the Treasury, and the Senate Appropriations Committee as an appeals court to which agencies carry their disagreement with House action.

Possessing great expertise and large numbers, working in close proximity to their policy problems and clientele groups, and desirous of expanding their horizons, administrative agencies generate action through advocacy. But how much shall they ask for? Life would be simple if they could just estimate the costs of their ever-expanding needs and submit the total as their request. But if they ask for amounts much larger than the appropriating bodies believe is reasonable, their credibility will suffer a drastic decline. In such circumstances, the reviewing organs are likely to apply a "measure of unrealism"[13] with the result that the agency gets much less than it might have with a more moderate request. So the first decision rule for agencies is: do not come in too high. Yet the agencies must also not come in too low, for the assumption is that if the agency advocates do not ask for funds they do not need them. Since the budgetary situation is always tight, terribly tight, or impossibly tight, reviewing bodies are likely to just accept a low request with thanks and not inquire too closely into its rationale. Given the distribution of roles, cuts must be expected and taken into account. Thus, the agency decision rule might read: come in a little high (padding), but not too high (loss of confidence). But how high is too high? What agency heads usually do is to evaluate signals from the environment—last year's experience, legislative votes, executive policy statements, actions of clientele groups, reports from the field—and come up with an asking price somewhat higher than they expect to get.[14]

Having decided how much to ask for, agencies engage in strategic planning to secure their budgetary goals. (Strategies are the links between the goals of the agencies and their perceptions of the kinds of actions which their political environment will make efficacious.) Budget officers in American national government uniformly act on the belief that being a good politician—cultivation of an active clientele, development of confidence by other officials (particularly the appropriations subcommittees), and skill in following strategies which exploit opportunities—is more important in obtaining funds than demonstration of efficiency. Top agency officials soon learn that the appropriations committees are very powerful; committee recommendations are accepted by Congress approximately 90 percent of the time.[15] Since budgetary calculations are so complex, the legislators must take a good deal on faith; thus, they require agency budget officers to demonstrate a high degree of integrity. If the appropriations committees believe that an agency officer has misled them, they can do grave damage to his career and to the prospects of the agency he represents. While doing a decent job may be a necessary condition for the agency's success in securing funds, the importance of having clientele and the confidence of legislators is so great that all agencies employ these strategies.[16]

In addition to these ubiquitous strategies, there are contingent strategies which depend upon time, circumstance, and place. In defending the base, for example, cuts may be made in the most popular programs so that a public outcry will result in restoration of the funds. The base may be increased within existing programs by shifting funds between categories. Substantial additions to the base may come about through proposing new programs to meet crises and through campaigns involving large doses of advertising and salesmanship.[17] The dependence of these strategies on the incremental, increase-decrease type of budgetary calculation is evident.

The Bureau of the Budget in the United States has the assigned role of helping the president realize his goals (when it can discover what they are supposed to be). This role is performed with a cutting bias, however, simply because the agencies normally push so hard in making requests for funds. The bureau helps the president by making his preferences more widely known throughout the executive branch so that those who would like to go along have a chance to find out what is required of them. Since Congress usually cuts the president's budget, bureau figures tend to be the most that agencies can get, especially when the items are not of such paramount importance as to justify intensive scrutiny by Congress. Yet the power of the purse remains actively with Congress. If the Budget Bureau continually recommended figures which were blatantly disregarded by Congress, the agencies would soon learn to pay less and less attention to the president's budget. As a result, the bureau follows consistent congressional action.[18] It can be shown empirically that recommendations tend to follow congressional actions over a large number of cases.[19]

In deciding how much money to recommend for specific purposes, the House Appropriations Committee breaks down into largely autonomous subcommittees in which the norm of reciprocity is carefully followed.[20] Specialization is carried further as subcommittee members develop limited areas of competence and jurisdiction. Budgeting is both incremental and fragmented as the committees deal with adjustments to the historical base of each agency. Sequential decision-making is the rule as problems are first attacked in the subcommittee jurisdiction in which they appear and then followed step-by-step as they manifest themselves elsewhere.[21] The subcommittee members treat budgeting as a process of making marginal monetary adjustments to existing programs rather than as a mechanism for reconsidering basic policy choices every year.[22] Fragmentation and specialization are further increased through the appeals functions of the Senate Appropriations Committee which deals with what has become (through House action) a fragment of a fragment. When the actions of subcommittees conflict, the difficulties are met by repeated attacks on the problem or through reference to the House and Senate as a whole.[23]

The members of the United States House Appropriations Committee consider themselves guardians of the Treasury who take pride in the frequency with which they reduce estimates.[24] They reconcile this role with their role as representatives of constituency interests by cutting estimates to satisfy one role and generally increasing amounts over the previous year to satisfy the other. As guardians of the public purse, committee members are expected to cast a skeptical eye on the blandishments of a bureaucracy ever anxious to increase its dominion by raising its appropriations. In order to provide an objective check on the effectiveness of the committee's orientation, Fenno[25] examined the appropriations histories of thirty-seven bureaus concerned with domestic policies from 1947 to 1959 and discovered that the committee reduced the estimates it received 77.2 percent of the time.

Tough as they may be in cutting the budgets of their agencies, appropriations committee members, once having made their decision, generally defend the agencies against further cuts on the floor. This kind of action is in part self-interest. The power of the appropriations subcommittees would be diminished if their recommendations were successfully challenged very often. Members believe that the House would "run wild" if "orderly procedure"—that is, acceptance of committee recommendations—were not followed. The role of defender also has its roots in the respect for expertise and specialization in Congress, and the concomitant belief that members who have not studied the subject should not exercise a deciding voice without the presence of overriding consideration. An appeal to this norm usually is sufficient to block an attempt to reduce appropriations.[26]

A member of the Senate Appropriations Committee is likely to conceive of his proper role as the responsible legislator who sees to it that the irrepressible lower house does not do too much damage either to constituency or to national interests. The senators are rather painfully aware of the House committee's preeminence in the field of appropriations and they know that they cannot hope to match the time and thoroughness that the House body devotes to screening requests. For this reason, the Senate committee puts a high value on having agencies carry appeals to it. The senators value their right to disagree on disputed items as a means of maintaining their influence in crucial areas while putting the least possible strain on their time and energy. The Senate role of responsible appeals court is dependent, of course, upon agency advocacy and House committee guardianship.

The Budgetary Process Reconsidered

In describing the budgetary process, we have identified a number of basic characteristics that have called forth a great deal of criticism from many sources. For example, the aids to calculation have been described as arbitrary and irrational. It has been said that, instead of concentrating on grand policy alternatives, the appropriations committees interfere mischievously with the administrative process through excessive concern with small details. Some critics go so far as to state that this petty intervention takes place without adequate information so that administrators are harassed for all the wrong reasons by men who lack knowledge. The specialized, incremental, fragmented, and sequential budgetary procedures have been faulted as leading to a lack of coordination and a neglect of consequences of the actions that are taken. At the same time, Congress is said to be losing its control of appropriations because its meager efforts cannot keep pace with the superior information resources of the federal bureaucracy. Nor, the critics add, are the appropriations committees willing to make the vast increase in staff which would enable them to make their will felt through intelligent decisions on broad policies. Instead, they combine dependence on the executive for information with "irrational" practices such as across-the-board cuts. The participants in budgeting have been taken to task for serving local interests rather than the national public interest. Their roles are considered to be excessively narrow, and the strategies they follow are condemned as opportunistic if not immoral. Finally, the appropriations process is deemed much too slow and too late: actions are taken on material which is out of date, and administrators are left uncertain how much money they will have until long after the previous fiscal year has ended.

It is immediately evident that many of these criticisms are contradictory. Increasing the staff of the appropriations committees hardly seems like a good way to cut down on detailed oversight of administration. Concern with local interests is one way of dealing with the differential consequences of national policy. Congress can hardly interfere less with administrators by making all the basic policy decisions for the executive agencies. That the critics of Congress are confused is an old story; let us make the best sense we can out of the criticisms and deal with the serious concerns which they raise.

The alternative budgetary process envisioned by the critics is quite different from the one we now have. Instead of aids to calculation such as the incremental method, they prefer comprehensive and simultaneous evaluation of means and ends. In their view, coordination should be made the explicit concern of a central hierarchy that should consider a wide range of alternative expenditures and investigate rather fully the consequences of each and the probability of their occurring. Each participant should seek to protect the general interest rather than the particular interests directly within his jurisdiction. Strategies should be eschewed or, at least, based on the merits of the program rather than on making the best possible case. Congressmen should avoid interferences in the administrative process and concentrate on developing superior knowledge and greatly enlarged staff assistance in order to make the most general determinations of governmental policy. The following pages deal in detail with various critical approaches.

Comprehensiveness

One prescription offered by the critics for "rationally" solving problems of calculation is to engage in comprehensive and simultaneous means-ends analysis. But budget officials soon discover that ends are rarely agreed upon, that they keep changing, that possible consequences of a single policy are too numerous to describe, and that knowledge of the chain of consequences for other policies is but dimly perceived for most conceivable alternatives. The result, as Charles Lindblom has demonstrated, is that although this comprehensive approach can be described, it cannot be practiced because it puts too great a strain by far on man's limited ability to calculate.[27] What budget officials need are not injunctions to be rational but operational guides that will enable them to manage the requisite calculations. Commands like "decide according to the intrinsic merits," "consider everything relevant," "base your decision on complete understanding" are simply not helpful. They do not exclude anything;

unlike the aids to calculation, they do not point to operations that can be performed to arrive at a decision.

All that is accomplished by injunctions to follow a comprehensive approach is the inculcation of guilt among good men who find that they can never come close to fulfilling this unreasonable expectation. Worse still, acceptance of an unreasonable goal inhibits discussion of the methods actually used. Thus, responsible officials may feel compelled to maintain the acceptable fiction that they review (almost) everything; and yet when they describe their actual behavior, it soon becomes apparent that they do not. The vast gulf between the theories espoused by some budget officials and their practice stems, I believe, from their adherence to a norm deeply imbedded in our culture, which holds that the very definition of rational decision is comprehensive and simultaneous examination of ends and means. In this case, however, the rational turns out to be the unreasonable. Sad experience warns me that even those who agree with the analysis thus far are prone to insist that governmental officials must "take a look at the budget as a whole," even though neither they nor anyone else has any idea of what that might mean or how it might be accomplished. Surely, considering "the budget as a whole" does not mean merely putting it between the covers of one volume, or letting one's eyes run over the pages, or merely pondering the relationship between income and expenditures. Yet, if (to take current examples) evaluating the most important relationships between the space program, the war on poverty, and aid to education appears to be extraordinarily difficult, what is the point of talking about reviewing "the budget as a whole" in the real sense of analyzing the interrelationships among all the important programs. The perpetuation of myth is an old story. What is unfortunate is that insistence on an impossible standard takes our attention away from real possibilities for change.

Failure to consider the contributions toward calculation of the existing budgetary process distorts the magnitude of the problem. New programs and substantial increases and decreases in old programs do not receive close attention when interest groups, politicians, or bureaucrats, anxious to make an issue, demand an investigation. What escapes intensive scrutiny is not the whole but only certain parts, which carry on as before. The fact that some activities do not receive intensive scrutiny is hardly sufficient reason to do everything over every year. In my recommendations, I shall deal with the problem that remains.

Coordination

The fact that the budgetary process is not comprehensive has given rise to charges that it is uncoordinated. Indeed, the very terms that we have used to describe budgetary practices—specialized, incremental, fragmented, sequential, non-programmatic—imply that at any one time the budget is not effectively considered as a whole so as to systematically relate its component parts to one another. As long as the lack of coordination is the result of ignorance of other people's activities or the complexity of organization, there is a good chance of overcoming it by dedicated staff work or some formal coordinating mechanism. But, in many cases, lack of coordination is a result of conflicting views about policy that are held by men and agencies that have independent bases of influence in society and in Congress. The only way to secure coordination in these cases is for one side to convince or coerce or bargain with the other. When it is understood that "coordination" is often just another word for "coercion," the full magnitude of the problem becomes apparent. For there is no one, the president and congressional leaders included, who is charged with the task of dealing with the "budget as a whole" and who is capable of enforcing his preferences. Vesting of formal power to coordinate the budget effectively would be tantamount to a radical change in the national political system, requiring the abolition of the separation of powers and a federally controlled party system, among other things.

What may be said about coordination, then, if we take the existing political system as not subject to drastic change? By taking as our standard of coordination the existence of a formal structure charged with the task and capable of executing it, we come up with an obvious answer: there is very little coordination excepting what the president can manage through the Budget Bureau. By accepting the possibility of informal coordination, of participants who take into account what others are doing, we can say there is a great deal of coordination that has escaped the notice of observers.

Let us pose the following question: how does an appropriations subcommittee know when things are not working out in other areas affected by its actions? Are its budgetary decisions coordinated with those decisions made by other subcommittees? Part of the answer is found in a comment by a committee member to the effect that "people can't be too badly off if they don't complain." The subcommittees do not consider themselves to be the only participants in budgeting. They expect, in accordance with sequential decision making, that committees and organizations in the affected areas will take corrective action. When an agency shouts more loudly than usual, when an interest group mounts a campaign, when other congressmen begin to complain, subcommittee members have a pretty good idea that something is wrong. If their perceptions of the array of political forces lead them astray, the appropriations subcommittees can be brought back into line by a rebellion within the full committee or by an adverse vote on the floor. For, as we noted earlier, unless members have an exceedingly intense preference, they will try to come up with appropriations that will not be reversed on the floor; to do otherwise would be to risk losing the great prestige the committee enjoys. The subcommittee may be thought of as exercising discretion over a zone of indifference, within which others are not aware enough or not concerned enough to challenge them, but beyond which others will begin to mobilize against them. In this way, a semblance of coordination is maintained. And as time passes, the participants come to develop a tacit understanding as to the general level of most appropriations, a phenomenon we have previously designated by the notion of fair shares. No one has to check up on everyone; it is sufficient that occasional marked departures from commonly held notions of fair shares would generate opposition.

Widespread acceptance of this concept of fair shares may go a long way toward accounting for the degree of coordination (the extent to which participants take into account what others do) that does exist in calculating expenditures totals. The total budget was rarely drastically out of line with expenditures before it was formalized in 1921, and even without control by a central authority today we do not usually get extraordinary increases or decreases except during national emergencies. There has been much more subtle and informal coordination by tacit agreements and accepted limits than there has previously been thought to be.

To some critics the procedure by which the agencies (as well as the appropriations committees and the Budget Bureau to a lesser extent) try to gauge "what will go" may seem unfortunate. They feel that there must be a better justification for programs than the subjective interpretation of signals from the environment. Yet we live in a democracy in which a good part of the justification for programs is precisely that they are deemed desirable by others. What is overlooked is that these informal procedures are also powerful coordinating mechanisms: when one thinks of all the participants who are continuously engaged in interpreting the wishes of others, who try to feel the pulse of Congress, the president, interest groups, and special publics, it is clear that a great many adjustments are made in anticipation of what other participants are likely to do. This, it seems to me, is just another term for coordination, unless one insists that coordination be redefined to require conscious control by a single individual or group.

The interaction between appropriations committees and administrative agencies includes at least seven modes of coordination:

1. Laws commanding specific actions;
2. Committee reports demanding specific action on (implicit) pain of future penalties;
3. Exchange of indulgences;
4. Taking each other's preferences into account with direct contact;
5. Accommodations to prior actions of the other without consultation;
6. Argument in which one side convinces the other;
7. Granting of side payments by one participant in return for action by the other.

Neglect of Consequences

The budgetary process is sometimes attacked for its apparent neglect of consequences, and there can be no doubt that lack of comprehensiveness in budgeting means that a participant making a specific decision will often neglect important values affected by that decision. However, Lindblom has proposed that consequences neglected by one participant may be considered by another, or by the same participant working on another problem.[28] To the extent, therefore, that all significant interests tend to be represented in a fragmented political system, decision-makers may reduce their information costs, by neglecting many alternatives, in the confidence that they will be picked up by others or by themselves at another time. Thus, the budgetary process as a whole may be considered rational even though the actions of individual participants may not seem to be because they omit from their calculations consequences important for others.

The political process in a democracy has a built-in feature that assures that some presently neglected values will be considered. This mechanism exists because politicians and interest-group leaders are motivated, by their hope of retaining or winning office, to find needs that have not been met and proposing to fulfill them in return for votes.

No doubt the neglect of some values (say those dear to blacks) could be better avoided by increasing the weight of the appropriate interests in the political process. There is no point; it seems to me, in faulting the budgetary process for the lamentable failure of some groups to be properly represented in the political life of the nation. Political mobilization of blacks will obviously do much more to protect their neglected interests than any change in the mechanism for considering budgets.

The most powerful coordinating mechanisms in budgeting undoubtedly are the various roles adopted by major participants in the budgetary process. Because the roles fit in with one another and set up a stable pattern of mutual expectations, they do a great deal to reduce the burden of calculations for the individual participants. The agencies need not consider in great detail how their requests will affect the president's overall program; they know that such criteria will be introduced in the Budget Bureau. The appropriations committees and the Budget Bureau know that the agencies are likely to put forth all the programs for which there is prospect of support and can concentrate on fitting them into the president's program or on paring them down. The Senate committee operates on the assumption that if important items are left out through House action the agency will carry an appeal. If the agencies suddenly reversed roles and sold themselves short, the entire pattern of mutual expectations might be upset, leaving the participants without a firm anchor in a sea of complexity. If the agency were to refuse the role of advocate, it would increase the burden on the congressmen; they would not only have to choose among desirable items placed before them with some fervor, but they would also have to discover what these items might be. This is a task ordinarily far beyond the limited time, energy, information, and competence of most congressmen.

The roles appear to be "natural" to the occupants of these institutional positions. A man who has spent many years working in, say, the natural resources area can be expected to believe that his programs are immensely worthy of support. (He may try to eliminate programs he deems unworthy, but there are always others to take their place.) Indeed, he would hardly be worth having as a governmental employee if he did not feel this way in his position. By serving as advocate in the real world, he sees to it that important values in his area are not neglected if he can help it.

The House Appropriations Committee's role of guarding the Treasury, with its emphasis on reducing requests, makes sense in the context of agency advocacy. If the congressmen can be reasonably certain that the agency has put its best foot forward, then their decisions may be viewed as choices along the margins of the top percentage of expenditures advocated by the agencies. The role of guardianship provides the congressmen with a stance that supplies reasonably clear instructions—cut the estimates—while keeping the area within which they must focus their attention (the largest increases) manageable in terms of their limited time and ability to calculate.

Some critics suggest that appropriations committee members should adopt a different role. In this "mixed" role, the congressman would be oriented toward neither cutting nor increasing but to doing both in about equal proportions. Each case would have to be considered on its own merits. To some extent, of course, this balance occurs under the present system. The difference is one of degree, but not less important for being so. For where they are in doubt or do not care to inquire in detail, the congressmen may now follow their prevailing orientation—usually to cut at the margin—expecting to receive feedback if something drastic happens. Under a "mixed" role, however, an exhaustive inquiry into all or most items would be called for. The resulting increase in amounts of calculation required would be immense. And to the extent that other participants adopted a mixed role, the pattern of role expectations upon which participants are now dependent as a calculating device would no longer prove stable. The calculation of preferences, essential in a democratic system, would become far more burdensome since inquiries would have to be instituted to find out what the various groups wanted in specific cases.

Furthermore, the adoption of a mixed role would be likely to lead to a greater neglect of values affected by decisions. Unless the ability of each participant to calculate the consequences of his actions is much more impressive than the evidence suggests, he is bound to neglect more if he attempts to do more. Yet this is precisely what a mixed role would force him to do. Instead of concentrating on a limited range of values within his jurisdiction, as his present role requires, he would have to consider the widest possible range of values in order to make a mixed role work. In place of the reasonable certainty that each participant does a good job of looking after the relatively narrow range of values entrusted to his care, there would be little certainty that any particular value would be protected because no one had been especially directed to look after it. Let us explore this question further as a fundamental problem in normative political theory.

Interests

Why, it may be asked, should the various participants take a partial view? Why should they not simply decide in accordance with what the public interest requires? Actually, this is the principle that participants think they are following now; they all believe that their version of the public interest is correct. It is their differing institutional positions, professional training, and group values that lead to perspectives producing somewhat different interpretations of the public interest. Let us, then, rephrase the question and ask whether it is better for each participant to put first the achievement of his own goals (including the goals entrusted to him by virtue of his position) when he considers what is meant by "public interest," or whether he should view the goals of others as of prime or at least equal importance to this consideration?

I am prepared to argue that the partial-view-of-the-public-interest approach is preferable to the total-view-of-the-public-interest approach, which is so often urged as being superior. First, it is much simpler for each participant to calculate his own preferences than for each to try to calculate the preferences of all. It is difficult enough for a participant to calculate how the interests he is protecting might best be served without requiring that he perform the same calculation for many others who might also be affected. The "partial" approach has the virtue of enabling others to accept as an input in their calculations the determination of each participant as to his preferences, which is not possible under the total approach. The danger of omitting important values is much greater when participants neglect the values in their immediate care in favor of what seem to them a broader view. How can anyone know what is being neglected if everyone speaks for someone else and no one for himself?

The partial approach is more efficient for resolving conflicts, a process that lies at the heart of democratic politics. Because the approach is partial, it does not require its practitioners to discover all or most possible conflicts and to work out answers to problems that may never materialize. It permits each participant to go his own way until he discovers that the activities of others interfere. Effort can then be devoted to overcoming the conflicts that arise. The formation of alliances in a political system requiring them is facilitated by the expression and pursuit of demands by those in closest touch with the social reality from which they issue. It is not, then, noblesse oblige but self-interest that assures that all demands insist on being heard and find the political resources to compel a hearing. A partial adversary system in which the various interests compete for control of policy (under agreed upon rules) seems more likely to result in reasonable decisions—that is, decisions that take account of the multiplicity of values involved—than one in which the best policy is assumed to be discoverable by a well-intentioned search for the public interest for all by everyone.

Strategies

If it is granted that budgetary practices based on a partial view of the public interest are desirable, then it would appear necessary to accept the use of strategies designed to secure appropriation goals. It is not surprising, however, that critics find something basically underhanded, even undemocratic, in the maneuvering of "special interests" for strategic advantage. Would not a straightforward approach based on the "merits" of each program be preferable?

Requiring that an individual commit suicide for the public good may at times have an acceptable rationale; suggesting that it become a common practice can hardly claim as much. I shall take it as understood, then, that asking participants in budgeting consistently to follow practices extremely disadvantageous to themselves and their associates is not reasonable. The participants must be able to maintain themselves in the environment.

The notion that administrators go around telling each other (or believing in secret) that the purposes for which they request funds are not valid but that they want the money anyway in order to advance themselves and build empires is not worthy of consideration. It would be exceedingly difficult to keep people in an organization if they could not justify its purposes to themselves. Such an attitude would be bound to come to the attention of other participants, who would take appropriate action. It would be bad strategically as well as morally. Attempts to reduce a complex distributive process like budgeting to the terms of a western melodrama—the good men ride white horses and advance on their merits; the bad men wear black masks and rely on strategies— do away with the great problem of deciding upon expenditures advocated by officials who are sincere believers in their proposals, and who know that all demands can be satisfied.

Budgetary strategies may generally be characterized as attempts to make the best case for the agency at the best time and thus to get as large an appropriation as possible. This behavior follows from the role of the agency as advocate. As a practical matter, we would expect any agency head worth his keep to respond to opportunities for increasing appropriations and warding off cuts.

The contrary position—making the worst case at the worst time—is not likely to be greeted with enthusiasm by either congressmen or agency staff.

Seizing on the opportune moment for advancing the agency's budgetary goals has much to commend it. The nation is served by initiative in meeting the needs of the time. An element of flexibility is generated that helps ensure that opportunities for action will be taken. "Crisis" strategies belong in this category. What is the difference, we may ask, between using a crisis to increase appropriations and acting to meet the nation's requirements in an hour of need? The desire to present the agency's requests in the best light can be used in a positive sense to improve the thinking of the operating units. The budget office can play an important mediating role because it must explain and justify agency actions to the outside world. By playing devil's advocate to agency personnel, by pointing out that justifications are not clear or persuasive, by saying that the program heads have to do better to convince the Budget Bureau or the appropriations committees, the budget office may compel or encourage thinking from diverse perspectives. In this way, a wider range of interests and values receive consideration.

Clientele and confidence strategies are desirable as well as inevitable in a democratic society. The feedback that clientele give to the participants is essential political information about who wants what programs, at what level, and with what degree of intensity. The establishment of confidence in an agency and its officers provides the trust necessary for congressmen who must live with complexity; the sanctions upon that agency that follow from lack of congressional confidence represent a great safeguard against duplicity. That morality is to some extent the handmaiden of necessity does not make it any less real or valuable.

A naked recital of strategies is bound to suggest that a certain amount of trickery is involved. Some strategies that appear to be deceitful represent amoral adjustments to an environment that does not give the participants much choice. Consider the kind of duplicity that appears to be involved in the game wherein agency people make believe that they are supporting the president's budget while actually encouraging congressmen to ask questions that will permit them to talk about what they would really like to have. Is this behavior immoral or does the immorality belong to the Executive Office directive that tries to compel agency personnel to say things that they do not believe in order to support the president? Congress has the power of the purse and it is difficult to argue that it should not have the kind of information about what the people in charge of the program think they ought to get that might help it to arrive at decisions. If one wants to get rid of Congress, then the problem solves itself. But if one accepts the separation of powers, then it may well be that it would be destructive to deny Congress information it would like to have, especially when for Congress to have it is manifestly in the interests of administrators. The biblical injunction against excessive temptation is appropriate here.

Merits

Despite all that has been said, the very idea that strategies are employed may still appear disturbing. Why cannot programs be presented on their merits and their merits alone? The most obvious answer is that the question presupposes popular, general agreement on what constitutes merit when the real problem is that people do not agree. That is why we have politics. To lay down and enforce criteria of merit in budgeting would be, in effect, to dispense with politics in favor of deciding what the government shall do in advance.

Much of what is meant by merit turns out to be "meets my preferences" or "serves my interests" or "the interests of those with whom I identify." It would be most peculiar for a nation calling itself a democracy to announce that only the most meritorious policies were carried out despite the fact that they were not preferred by any significant group in the population. The degree to which widespread preferences are met not only *is* but *ought* to be *part* of why policies are deemed meritorious.

We all know that people do not always realize what is good for them. They are occupied with many things and may not recognize the benefits flowing from certain policies. They may find it difficult to support policies that are meritorious but not directly related to their own immediate needs. Here is where strategies come in. Where support is lacking, it may be mobilized; where attention is unfocused, it may be directed by advertising; where merits are not obvious they may be presented in striking form. Ability to devise strategies to advance the recognition of merit is immensely more helpful than cries of indignation that political artistry should be necessary.

Merit consists, in part, of the effectiveness with which programs are formulated and carried out. No one should doubt that this criterion is recognized in the budgetary process; estimates, justifications, and presentations are directed to this end. Though effectiveness is indispensable—confidence would be lacking without it, for one thing; clientele would be dissatisfied, for another—agencies find that it does not take them far enough. An agency may be wonderfully effective in formulating and carrying out its programs and yet see its fortunes suffer because of the need for Congress to cut that year or to shift funds to some other vital area. Defense appropriations are often a function of domestic concerns; stabilization policy may be constrained by military needs; the complexity of a project or the difficulty of demonstrating immediate results may militate against it. Consequently, the agency invariably finds that in some areas its good works and best efforts are not being rewarded. Prizes are simply not distributed for good deeds alone. The agency's mode of adapting to this circumstance is to use demonstration of good works as one among a number of strategies. Forbidding agencies to use strategies designed to give its good requests a better chance, because bad requests can also be dressed up, seems inadvisable as well as unlikely to succeed.

Motivation

Instead of bewailing the use of strategies, it would be immensely more fruitful to arrange incentives within the system so as to insure that good strategies and good programs will go together as often as possible. Budgeting would be conceived of in this sense as constituting a problem in human motivation. When motivation is disregarded, it is no wonder that unsatisfactory results ensue. In order to demonstrate that this problem is by no means peculiar to the national budgetary process let us take a brief look at budgeting in Soviet and American industrial firms.

Rewards to managers in Soviet industrial firms depend on their meeting production quotas assigned in economic plans. But necessary supplies—skilled labor and financial resources—are often lacking. The first consequence of this is that the quota is not set from above but becomes the subject of bargaining as the managers seek to convince the ministries that quotas should be as low as possible. Yet the managers find it prudent not to hugely exceed their quota, for in that case next year's quota will be raised beyond attainment. The second consequence is that production is not rationalized to produce the greatest output at the lowest cost, but is geared instead to meeting specific incentives. Heavy nails are overproduced, for example, because quotas are figured by weight. Maintenance may be slighted in favor of huge effort for a short period in order to meet the quota. Funds are hidden in order to provide slack that can be used to pay "pushers" to expedite the arrival of supplies. The list of essentially deceitful practices to give the appearance of fulfilling the quota is seemingly endless: producing the wrong assortment of products, transferring current costs to capital accounts, shuffling accounts to pay for one item with funds designated for another, declaring unfinished goods finished, lowering the quality of goods, and so on.[29] The point is that the budgetary system arranges incentives in such a way that managers cannot succeed with lawful practices. When similar incentives are applied in American industrial firms, similar practices result, from running machines into the ground, to "bleeding the line," tb meeting a monthly quota by doctoring the accounts.[30]

As in the Soviet Union, American firms often use budgets not to reflect or project reality but to drive managers and workers toward increased production. Budgets are conceived of as forms of pressure on inherently lazy people[31] so that (to paraphrase Mao Tse-tung) the greater the pressure the better the budget. Inevitably, managers and workers begin to perceive budgets as "perpetual needlers" or as "the hammer that's waiting to hit you on the head."[32] In some cases, this leads to discouragement because it is apparent that whatever the effort, the budget quota will be increased. Since accounting is separate for subunits in the firm, it is not surprising that fierce negotiations take place to assign costs among them. As a result, top officials find it necessary to engage in campaigns to sell budgets to the units. Otherwise, sabotage is likely.[33] While some attention has been given to human relations in budgeting,[34] only Stedry[35] has attempted to explore the essential motivational problems of budgeting within an organizational framework. Yet, without an understanding of the impact of different goals and incentive systems on human activity, reliable statements about the likely consequences of different budgetary incentives can hardly be made. I shall attempt to deal with this problem in my recommendations.

Power

The strategy which critics of the budgetary process find most objectionable is Congress' use of the appropriations power to alter policies of executive agencies. To say that congressmen interfere too much in the details of administration, however, is to consign them to impotence. Grand policy decisions come few and far between. Most policy is made through interpretation of statutes by administrators or through a succession of marginal adjustments in the form of legislative amendments. If by "administrative detail" one means "trivial," then it would seem that the administrators who are presumably being defended would have little to worry about. A basic analytic problem, preventing meaningful thought, is that "policy" is identified with "Congress" and "administration" with the executive branch. By definition, Congress should not tell administrators what to do, because administrators administrate and Congress is supposed only to make policy. I agree so completely with the position taken by Richard Fenno that I would like to quote his comments at some length:

> To relegate Congress to the making of broad policy decisions and to oversight in terms of broad program management is to prescribe precisely those tasks which Congress is least capable of performing. To criticize Congress for intervening in a specific and detailed fashion is to attack it for doing the only thing it can do to effectively assert its influence. Specifics and details are the indispensable handles which Congressmen use to work inductively toward broader kinds of oversight judgments. Specifics and details are what concern the constituents on whose behalf Congressmen must intervene with the bureaucracy. Specific and detailed requests from an interested Congressman to a bureau head or division chief do more to "galvanize the internal disciplines of administration" (Arthur Macmahon's phrase) than any broad statement of policy. The profusion of committees and subcommittees make possible a degree of specialization which gives to Congressmen the de-

tailed and specific information they find most useful in influencing executive behavior.

Specific and detailed controls by individuals and small committees give Congressmen their maximum influence because these controls are best adapted to the realities of executive decision-making. If executive decision-making is basically piecemeal, incremental and marginal, then congressional control, if it is to be effective, must be basically piecemeal, incremental and marginal. What is or is not "appropriate" congressional control cannot be prescribed *a priori*...Congressional control is or is not appropriate in the context of the realities of legislative and executive decision-making. The legislator ought not to be criticized for using those controls which are available to him and which his experience tells him bring the greatest influence over executive activity. If we do not recognize this, we will continue to prescribe impossible control tasks...[36]

The power of Congress to control budgetary decisions depends on the power of its appropriations committees. For no large assembly of men can develop the expertise, self-direction, cohesiveness, and dispatch which are necessary to do the large volume of budgetary business. A good index of the power of any legislature is whether it develops and follows committees of experts in specific areas of decisions. Where such committees are absent, as in Great Britain, the power of Parliament becomes a fiction. (A common definition of a cabinet is a committee which permits no rivals.) The appropriations committees measure up exceedingly well when we consider that their recommendations are adopted by the houses of Congress approximately 90 percent of the time. Although one might contemplate with equanimity some reduction in this record of success, a drop below, say, 75 percent would seriously compromise the appropriations committees with the president and the agencies. For a great deal of the ability to have agencies follow congressional will is dependent on the knowledge that the appropriations committees are watching and that their actions will be upheld with a high degree of certainty. Once the power gets transferred to Congress as a whole, its exercise becomes so uncertain and diffuse that no one can count on it. Congressmen simply do not have the time and the knowledge to debate a very large number of appropriations with sense and then follow through. The general body of congressmen do well to keep the appropriations committees in line with an occasional defeat on the floor to remind them whom they are ultimately beholden to.

The great power of the appropriations committees consists in the extent to which agencies and the Bureau of the Budget systematically take account of their preferences. Anyone who has seen budget offices in operation knows that the unseen hand of Congress is never far from the surface. The agency practice of holding mock hearings in which some officials are assigned the role of appropriations committee members is a vivid illustration of how Congress makes its will felt indirectly.

The power of the appropriations committees depends on their ability to command regular support in Congress, support which, in turn, is dependent on the cohesiveness of the committees. Fenno has shown that support for the House Appropriations Committee drops markedly when its subcommittees issue split recommendations.[37] The internal norms and calculating mechanisms whereby the committee achieves a high degree of integration are therefore of extreme importance in the maintenance of congressional power. The incremental, fragmented, non-programmatic, and sequential procedures of the present budgetary process aid in securing agreement. It is much easier to agree on an addition or reduction of a few thousand or a million dollars than to agree on whether a program is good in the abstract. It is much easier to agree on a small addition or decrease than to compare the worth of one program to that of all others. Conflict is reduced by an incremental approach because the area open to dispute is reduced. Agreement comes much more readily when the items in dispute can be treated as differences in dollars instead of as basic differences in policy; calculating budgets in monetary increments facilitates bargaining and logrolling. It becomes possible to swap an increase here for a decrease there or for an increase elsewhere without always having to consider the ultimate desirability of programs blatantly in competition. Procedures that de-emphasize overt conflicts among competing programs also encourage secret deliberations, nonpartisanship, and the recruitment of personnel who feel comfortable in sidestepping policy decisions most of the time. The prospects for agreement within the House Appropriations Committee are enhanced by closed hearings and mark-up sessions, and by a tradition against publicity. Were deliberations to take place in public—"open covenants openly arrived at"—committee members might find themselves accused of "selling out" if they made concessions. Willingness to compromise, to be flexible, is a quality sought in choosing members to serve on the appropriations committees. Party ties might be disruptive of agreement if they focused attention on the policy differences between the two political persuasions. Instead, party differences are submerged during committee deliberations, and the usual process of taking something from a program here, adding to a program there, swapping this for that, can go on.

However the committee's practices are subject to attack precisely because of their de-emphasis of large policy considerations. Manifestly, the House Appropriations Committee does not normally consider its task to lie in rehashing every year the arguments over the fundamental desirability of the legislation already considered by the substantive committees and passed by Congress. Fortunately, Richard Fenno has provided us with a splendid analysis of a committee whose members took fierce partisan and ideological positions on virtually all the issues that came before them.[38] The norm of reciprocity—accepting the recommendations of other subcommittees if they accept yours—was unknown on the House Education and Labor Committee in the years after the Second World War. The members went after each other with abandon. They appeared to glory in differences and to stress the ultimate values which divided them. As a result, the committee was supremely ineffective in getting its recommendations accepted in the House. Internal committee warfare contributed to the long delay in producing any important legislation on education. Were these norms to prevail on the appropriations committees it is doubtful that a congressional budget could be produced at all. In the presence of delay and confusion and in the absence of party majorities to resolve these matters consistently on a strict partisan basis. Congress would be faced with the choice of abandoning its budgetary prerogatives or of indulging in the grossest forms of action leading to wild and unpredictable swings in the levels of appropriations.

Reform Proposals

The literature on reform is replete with suggestions for improving the rationality of the budgetary process, which turn out to have vast implications for the distribution of power. Identifying rationality with a comprehensive overview of the budget by a single person or group, Arthur Smithies despairs of the fragmented approach taken by Congress and proposes a remedy. He suggests that a Joint (congressional) Budget Policy Committee be formed and empowered to consider all proposals for revenue and expenditure in a single package and that its decisions be made binding by a concurrent resolution. He presents this reform suggestion as a moderate proposal to improve the rationality of the budget process.[39] If the proposed Joint Committee were unable to secure the passage of its recommendations, as would surely be the case, it would have gone to enormous trouble without accomplishing anything but a public revelation of futility. The impotence of the Joint Committee on the Economic Report,[40] the breakdown of the single congressional attempt to develop a comprehensive legislative budget,[41] and the failure of congressional attempts to control the Council of Economic Advisers[42] and the Budget Bureau,[43] all stem from the same cause. There is no cohesive group in Congress capable of using these devices to affect decision making by imposing its preferences on a majority of congressmen. Smithies' budgetary reform presupposes a completely different political system from the one which exists in the United States. In the guise of a procedural change in the preparation of the budget by Congress, Smithies is actually proposing a revolutionary move which would mean, if it were successful, the virtual introduction of the British Parliamentary system.

In a sophisticated advocacy of budgetary reform, John Saloma suggests a Joint (congressional) Committee of Fiscal Policy, which he believes can operate within the existing political system. The Joint Fiscal Committee would have a small membership drawn from leading members of the two appropriations and the two finance committees of Congress. The Joint Committee would be well staffed. According to Saloma,

> The Joint Committee should not be required to submit a formal legislative budget for congressional enactment. At most it should develop budgetary guidelines to assist the fiscal committees (guidelines that probably would be kept confidential). Primarily it should provide a forum for continuing Congressional consideration of the budget, changing economic and political assumptions on which the budget is based, and the status of authorization and appropriation measures.[44]

Saloma believes that the Joint Fiscal Committee would improve communications between the houses of Congress, enable Congress "to express its sentiments on broad fiscal policy," provide a continuing picture of the budget which Congress does not have, and provide guidelines to a coordinating committee of appropriations subcommittee chairmen on levels of appropriations.[45] Smithies proposal has been made more realistic at the cost of emasculating it. What is the point of the Joint Fiscal Committee if, unlike the Joint Committee on Atomic Energy, it cannot make recommendations for action on the floor of Congress? Why should any other committee pay attention to its recommendations? Experience with the Joint Economic Committee suggests that advisory committees of this character have hardly any influence at all on governmental policy.[46] If the budgetary guidelines of the Joint Fiscal Committee were adopted, which is doubtful, we would have in effect a steering committee of Congress, which Saloma recognizes is unrealistic. If they were rejected, as is likely, disillusionment would be inevitable, despite Saloma's warning that expectations should not be too high. Whatever information is desired on the outstanding authorizations and appropriations can be had through the existing committees of Congress or through some simple information service. It seems to me that Saloma's proposal, a variation of the McClellan Committee bill, is simply a bow to the gods of comprehensiveness. As usual, no demonstration is made of the feasibility of a comprehensive approach; instead, the gods are appeased by providing an umbrella committee, much as if incantation of the Joint Fiscal Committee's name would reveal the divine presence of a rational view of the budget as a whole.

Summary

In appraising the budgetary process, we must deal with real men who know that, in this real world, the best they can get is to be preferred to the perfection they cannot achieve. Unwilling or unable to alter the basic features of the political system, they seek to make it work for them rather than against them in budgeting. Participants in budgeting not only work within the specified constitutional rules, they also make active use of them. Problems of calculation are mitigated by the division of labor in the separation of powers; morality is enforced by substantial external checks as well as by inner motives; a wider range of preferences is taken into account by making the institutional participants responsible for somewhat different ones. A great deal of informal coordination takes place as participants adjust to their expectation of other's behavior. An incremental approach guards against radical departures most of the time, whereas agency advocacy and strategies designed to take advantage of emergent needs help ensure flexibility. A basic conclusion of this appraisal is that the existing budgetary process works much better than is commonly supposed.

There is, however, no special magic in the status quo. Inertia and ignorance as well as experience and wisdom may be responsible for whatever problems exist in the present state of affairs. Improvements of many kinds are undoubtedly possible and desirable. The heart of the problem of budgetary reform lies in the inevitable tension between the practice of incrementalism and the ideology of comprehensiveness. The assumption of all previous proposals for reform has been that incrementalism must be sacrificed to comprehensiveness. But as this section has suggested formal coordination and comprehensive calculation of budgets are unfeasible, undesirable, or both. If comprehensiveness is rejected, however, there turn out to be other significant directions for reform that have not yet been tried. My view is that the present budgetary process should be taken as far as it will go and then corrected for its worst deficiencies. Proposals for reform should advocate a more thoroughgoing incremental approach, not its opposite—a more comprehensive one. There should be greater use of aids to calculation rather than less. Agencies should not be told to give up advocacy, but should be motivated to make their best case even more persuasive. There should be even less formal unity and more conflict in budgeting than there is today.

Radical Incrementalism

The president, the agencies, and Congress are now compelled to give at least pro forma consideration to all the activities in the whole budget in a limited period of time. This results in a brief period characterized by frantic activity and the rote presentation of masses of information, most of which is not subject to change and of no special interest to anyone at that time. Why? Because of unthinking acceptance of the idea that there must be a budget containing all expenditures presented and considered at one time. As the federal budget grows, and life and budgeting become more complex, the demand for central direction increases. Yet the overload of information is already staggering; aids to calculation are used in a desperate attempt to simplify consideration of small parts of the budget. The time has come to cast aside the myth of comprehensiveness. Theory should be brought in line with experience so that there will be a chance of improving the experience. The budget needs to be further fragmented. Attention needs to be directed to matters of political interest which can be changed. Evaluation of budgetary requests must be spread out so that greater time and attention may be devoted to each of them. The development and refinement of further aids to calculation should assume a high research priority. The delays in the budgetary process should be markedly reduced by permitting the most immediate response to budgetary requests.

My proposal is that we abandon the annual budgetary process, as it is now known, and substitute a continuous consideration of incremental changes to the existing base. Each agency will assume that the funds for its programs will automatically be continued. All appropriations will be continuous, except for a small number designed for a limited time period. When an agency wishes to increase or decrease its funds for a program or to eliminate an old program or begin a new one, it will submit a request to Congress through the Bureau of the Budget. The president may submit requests for change to Congress, and have them considered right away. The appropriations committees may call for testimony at any time on any budgetary matter and change appropriations irrespective of the fiscal year. By altering authorizations to spend, the substantive committees may also bring reconsideration of budgetary matters. I call this proposal radical incrementalism because it is based on pushing the evident incremental tendencies in budgeting to encompass the entire process.

A basic purpose of radical incrementalism is to facilitate speedy and continuous adaptation to emergent problems. While some programs may remain in a steady state, others can be reviewed as often as any participant deems it necessary. Supplemental appropriations would become a thing of the past. Demands could be dealt with as they arise. If the latest incremental move suggests a new step requiring changes in appropriations, a decision could be made right then and there. The tyranny of the annual budget—requiring formal review of programs of little immediate interest and inhibiting action on programs which need attention at the moment—would be ended.

Suppose that a subcommittee wished to look at trends in personnel or building costs. It could simply ask for these figures and act on them as it saw fit. Should a subcommittee want to view any budgetary item in relation to an agency's total appropriations, it could request both sets of figures. In order to facilitate this procedure, the appropriations committee should require agencies to develop quick and inexpensive methods of estimating expenditures. The agencies as well as the appropriations committees need to develop better aids to calculation. It may well be the case that much agency budgetary work is far too expensive and cumbersome for the results achieved. The development of rough and ready cost estimates should make it possible for agencies to provide serviceable breakdowns of their activities from a variety of conceptual viewpoints. Instead of being stuck with a rigid set of program categories, terribly expensive to maintain under proper accounting, the agencies and the subcommittees would have the advantage of being able to look at activities from diverse perspectives.

An objection that might be raised to radical incrementalism is that certain programs could escape scrutiny over a period of years. This potential problem may be solved by appointing people to review periodically those programs or activities that do not change very much from year to year, and would, therefore, tend to escape frequent scrutiny. Since they do not alter radically, a thorough going over every five years or so would be sufficient. Nor need any one organization do it all; the incremental approach can make use of the division of labor that is a part of the national system. Departmental budget offices, the bureaus themselves, the Bureau of the Budget, and the House and Senate appropriations subcommittees and their investigating staffs, might use sampling techniques so that each would review a few programs of this kind every year. The results could then be used to see if congressional scrutiny were warranted the next year. In this way, a large part of the problem may be met while adding only a little to the burden of the participants. Should the appropriations committees decide that they wish to review every activity as often as every five to eight years, they could make it a rule that each appropriation lapses five to eight years after the last congressional act.

Narrowing, fragmenting, and dispersing these budgetary reviews has considerable advantage from the viewpoint of encouraging experimentation and innovation: because no one organization is overburdened, the most thorough analysis is facilitated; more active participation by high level officials is encouraged because the material to be considered at any one time is not overwhelming; as the knowledge and interest of top officials is fed back down the line, the significance of the activity and the importance of those who engage in it is likely to be enhanced. If budgetary reviews can be liberated to some extent from the peak periods of the formal budgetary cycle, imagination and creativity can be given freer play. The absence of immediate deadlines may encourage speculation and experimentation, while the increased probability that hierarchical superiors have time to listen gives greater promise that the efforts may lead to tangible results. The variety of organizations involved should also lead to consideration of a broad range of values and perspectives.

At first glance, it might appear that problems of coordination would be made more difficult than they are today. I think not; unless, of course, one is prepared to define coordination as placing all appropriations within the cover of one huge book at one time. Nor does it make much sense to define coordination as a central review, since this begs the question of whether policies have actually been related to one another in a reasonable way. It is a lot easier to mesmerize oneself with talk about central coordination than it is to practice it. Radical incrementalism, however, can be practiced. Each increment of the budget can be considered as it comes up. Attempts can be made to adapt the new policy, through successive approximation, to major features of the environment as revealed by experience. Thus, a series of rapid adjustments can be made in a budgetary system which encourages (indeed, compels) decision makers to take into account the preferences of others and to mitigate the adverse consequences that policies may have for them. Under radical incrementalism, adaptation can be undertaken with greater intelligence because: (1) the action is close in time to awareness of the problem; (2) changes are smaller, quicker, alterable, and, therefore, more easily made; (3) the decision-makers are enabled to have a better grasp of where they are in relation to where they want to be; (4) each change can be separately evaluated against a general picture of the most relevant programs then in operation instead of, an immensely more complicated task, multitudes of suggested changes being pitted against each other simultaneously; (5) every change is always important in the sense that a major participant in the system wants it.

Nothing in radical incrementalism prevents any participant in the budgetary process from using any and all analytic techniques at his disposal. Everyone is permitted to be as wise as he knows how to be. If the day should come when a simultaneous comparison of all governmental programs appeared desirable, the president or Congress could consider the budget in just that way. If it appears desirable to consider all programs dealing with water or land or any other area of policy, the president or the appropriations committees can call for action. Indeed, a radical incrementalism might foster such an approach by permitting scheduling when other great matters were not up for immediate decision. The endless search for "needless duplication," "sheer waste," and "irrational decisions" could go on with as much, or as little, sense as before.

Consequences of Radical Incrementalism for Major Participants

What would happen to the president's budget? It would represent the president's preferences on any and all budgetary items on which he cared to express an opinion. It could be as complete a document as he (through the Budget Bureau) knows how to make, or it could contain positions only on selected matters. It would go to Congress as a source of information, but it would not be the action document that it is now. Instead, action on presidential requests would take place when he sent specific demands for specific items to the appropriations committees. The president's budget would be much like his State of the Union Message where he presents his legislative priorities and shopping list, but where he does not necessarily comment on policies he does not wish changed. When he wants action, he follows up his address by submitting a series of concrete proposals for action. Then, as his pending requests are acted upon, the president takes these decisions into account in submitting his next wave of requests. The president would gain flexibility he does not have now because he would not have to commit himself in advance on all appropriations requests as is the case under the annual budget approach. Nor would he and his chief advisers have to engage in the chaotic activity of the fall, when tired and overburdened men work furiously to put together all appropriations. Outgoing presidents would not have to go through the charade of developing a budget with which to stick their successor, and incoming presidents would not have to face the immediate task of putting together another full-scale budget to counteract the one that is then operative. The new president could deal with the most vital matters first, and then take up the rest in a more leisurely way.

The president's ability to pursue economic policies would be enhanced rather than diminished by radical incrementalism. There would be no decrease in his ability to plan for a desired relationship between revenue and expenditures. He could set out the relationship he believes desirable in his budget message or in his economic report or in any other way he deems appropriate. And he could propose action to meet his preferences through regular legislation, appropriations, or executive action. But he would not be compelled to do this at any specific time as is now the case. He could wait until he thought a change was necessary, receive the most current predictions of current revenue and expenditure, and act at once. When emergencies require increased expenditure, as in the Vietnam situation, or when long-range estimates proved to be faulty, as frequently happens, he could modify his plans. Since the possibility of substantial change in expenditures is confined to a few areas of policy, these could be re-studied when necessary. While automatic stabilizers, such as unemployment compensation, work well in guarding against depressions voluntary action by the federal government has not proved effective.[47] Perhaps the flexibility provided by radical incrementalism will permit speedier and more appropriate adaptation to contemporary needs.

A possible objection to radical incrementalism might be that Congress would suffer because agencies would not have to come before the appropriations committees every year for all the appropriations that (aside from trust funds and the like) are usually included in the annual budget. However, instead of concentrating their attention on appropriations requests only in the once-a-year period when all requests are made, agencies would be continually thinking of the prospect of making their next request. On vital matters, the agencies might be called for repeated appearances. To the extent that Congress is more often on their mind its influence should grow rather than decrease.

Opinion on radical incrementalism will probably be divided in Congress. Some members who identify with a presidential constituency might object on the grounds that welfare policies would be hurt by enhancing the power of the appropriations committees to cut in crucial places. However, this would not happen, because, while conservatives now gain somewhat by the special positions they hold on committees, this advantage is rapidly disappearing.[48] There is good reason to believe that the seniority system will increasingly benefit proponents of welfare legislation. Both presidents and the formal congressional leadership have ample means at their disposal to place members who represent preferences of the party majority on the appropriations committees, and they have already used this to good effect in the House. Deviance from the party majority is largely a southern, Democratic phenomenon and will diminish in size and importance with the growth of black voting, population shifts out of the deep South, and increased Democratic party representation elsewhere. Moreover, the best analysis we have of the appropriations committees in Congress (see book by Professor Richard F. Fenno, Jr. of the University of Rochester, Rochester, New York) suggests that they do not markedly transgress on the preferences of the mass of other legislators. While it is true that service on the appropriations committees does tend to make members suspicious of executive advocacy, it is also true that the substantive committees are generally packed with legislators whose constituency interests suggest a more expensive view of governmental programs. A creative tension between the somewhat differing orientations of the two levels of committees does not appear to be a bad thing.

Fiscal conservatives might also oppose radical incrementalism for fear that it would result, in general, in higher governmental expenditures. Such critics might argue that, in considering programs one at a time, Congress would lose track of the implications for the total rate of expenditure. However, there would be little difficulty in arranging for a reporting service in Congress that would issue frequent statements on total approved expenditures. The solution to the problem of securing decreases, or holding down increases, in expenditure lies in the elimination of programs and not in budgetary procedures. If fiscal conservatives wish to make a drastic impact on expenditures, they will have to elect many more legislators who support their views than is now the case. Barring this unlikely development, there is no point in making the appropriations process the whipping post for developments that represent secular trends in the political system as a whole. Where appropriations subcommittees appear to stand in the way of expenditures desired by a significant majority of their colleagues, they may be out-voted on the floor, or congressional majorities may resort to backdoor spending or to other devices that take control of appropriations out of the offending subcommittees' hands. When fiscal conservatives, or liberals for that matter, are able to assert themselves in Congress, radical incrementalism should provide somewhat better opportunities for selective intervention than now exist.

In my opinion, the most serious obstacle to the acceptance of radical incrementalism is an ideological one. The proposals may not receive serious consideration because they run counter to the reigning ideologies of comprehensiveness and annual budgeting. But I still think them useful to have at hand if and when Congress gets serious about improving its capabilities as an institution.

Strategic Political Knowledge

By reducing the information requirements of budgetary decisions, radical incrementalism increases the possibility of reasonable action. Whatever knowledge exists can be brought to bear on the problem by some participant in the system. Knowledge may be increased in the sense that the data are more recent and the feedback from one action can be immediately used in the next appraisal. But knowledge about how to deal with problems is only one kind of knowledge There is a prior knowledge which often assumes greater political importance: namely, what problems should be considered? A radical incrementalism provides an important aid to calculation in that it focuses attention on those changes from the status quo which are important to some participant. But there are other ways of being alerted to matters of importance which would be especially useful to congressmen.

The Budgeting and Accounting Act of 1921 provides for presidential submission of agency budgets to Congress through the Bureau of the Budget. The appropriations committees do not formally receive original agency requests but only those requests as amended or deleted by the Chief Executive. We all know, to be sure, that when ties between agencies and appropriations committee chairmen are close the original agency demands may be brought out in private or in committee hearings. But, agency officials are under restrictions in how far they can go in open advocacy. In any event, junior members of the appropriations committees may never discover this information, and the same will most certainly be true of most other members of Congress.

As political men in a representative assembly, legislators are, above all, dealers in preferences. Since they are makers, shapers, molders, brokers, and bargainers of preferences, the most important information for them to have is information about what people want. Related to this as an aid to calculation is information on where preferences of key participants differ and why, for it alerts legislators to a conflict of preferences in which they may wish to intervene. Congress could well use Franklin D. Roosevelt's well-known practice of programming for conflict, which was designed to assure him that he would be called in on important matters, that is, matters on which preferences and policies differed. This kind of strategic political knowledge is of special importance to congressmen because they appear to be more skilled in reconciling conflicting preferences than in evaluating complicated sets of budgetary figures.

Therefore, I propose that, along with radical incrementalism, there should be a legal requirement that the original requests of agencies be made public, together with a statement by the Budget Bureau giving its reasons for making changes. Congressmen would be immediately alerted to a conflict of preferences and would have the rationales of both the agency and the Budget Bureau presenting rival arguments. Both the agencies and the Budget Bureau would be highly motivated to make the best possible case for their demands. If they were also motivated to reach an agreement through bargaining, the very fact of their success would be one indicator that the matter was not of the highest priority for congressional attention. While some agencies might try to raise their demands inordinately for bargaining purposes, a series of attempts would soon reveal that consistently coming in too high would not serve their interests and would be abandoned.

Thus far I have deliberately used the general word "agency" to avoid complicating the argument with distinctions between bureaus and departments. My initial recommendation is that each department retain its present power to make secret recommendations to the president on behalf of the bureaus within its jurisdiction. In this way, general presidential influence on initial bureau requests could be maintained through his power to hire and fire cabinet members and other heads of organizations. Since department heads must maintain themselves in an environment which necessarily differs from that of the president, their recommendations may sometimes be expected to differ from his on crucial matters. (If this were not the case, the president would have much less need for a Budget Bureau and an Executive Office.) The congressional purpose of unearthing significant political matters through the airing of conflicts would be served. Should this proposal prove insufficient, Congress could go further and require department heads to present in writing their reasons for disagreements with the Budget Bureau request.

Under a system of congressional programming for conflict, the president would lose his ability to maintain the fiction that agencies uniformly support his budget. If this means that congressmen would learn more about where to intervene, there might be a corresponding decrease of the presidential influence now gained by keeping Congress in the dark. Undoubtedly, the proposal will be fought for that reason. But, in fact, the president's support would still be terribly important to the agencies. Congress would still rely on the president's figures as a starting point for their consideration and as a benchmark for making cuts or (less frequently) increases. Agencies would almost always be better off with the president's support than without it; since Congress tends to cut the president's budget, an agency would have to mount a special campaign, with no certain prospect of success, in order to have a chance for victory. It would hardly be advisable, therefore, for agencies to flaunt the Chief Executive. The president might gain in another direction through his ability, under radical incrementalism, to intervene continuously in the appropriations process rather than to confine his energy largely to consideration of the annual budget.

I have no intention of proposing a system that would interfere with the confidential relationship between the president and the Bureau of the Budget. All communications from the Budget Bureau to the president would be as privileged as they are today. Nothing would prevent the Budget Bureau from presenting one kind of argument to the president and another to Congress. The only requirement would be that the president (through the Bureau of the Budget) comment on the differences between his recommendations and those of the agency involved.

A painful adjustment on the part of the Bureau of the Budget would undoubtedly be required. It has grown up in an environment which nurtures secrecy. Its confidential relationship with the president has been used to prevent public scrutiny of its action. Rationalizations of its positions on issues, which have become partly implicit in the subculture of the Executive Office, would have to be raised to the surface at some point. The bureau's claim to a more rational mode of decision making in the public interest (as opposed to irrational procedures in agencies surrounded by special interests) would become open to public examination. The Bureau of the Budget could no longer operate entirely as if it were guided by an informal version of the Official Secrets Act, which so effectively shields executive personnel in Great Britain from outside intervention. While bureau personnel would gain by being liberated from the physically and mentally exhausting task of putting together an entire governmental budget in a few frantic weeks, they might not be happy with a radical incremental approach to budgeting.

By raising conflict to a more public and hence more visible level, interest groups may be stimulated to greater activity. In a democracy, where public knowledge is generally deemed good, this hardly appears to provide an objection to radical incrementalism. Recent scholarship has suggested that in many cases the power of interest groups in relation to public officials has been exaggerated. Where interest groups are already very powerful, as in the case of the Rivers and Harbors Congress, the chances are that they are privy to the additional information that would be made public under the new system. Thus, the proposals for increasing the availability of strategic information might work to strengthen groups presently weak while adding little or no additional power to the strong.

Knowledge about Policies

Although it might be agreed that strategic political information is of the highest importance to a political body like Congress, knowledge about the fields of policy themselves is also significant. Since the specialization of subcommittee members, together with long service in particular areas of policy, undoubtedly does more to augment the substantive information of the legislators than anything which might be suggested, it follows that proposals that drastically increase the turnover of legislators or prevent them from specializing should be resisted. One minor suggestion, however, might be useful. The appropriations committees might hire one or two staff members whose purpose would be to recruit ad hoc teams of scholars and practitioners to give a special kind of advice. These men would produce very brief reports telling the subcommittees two things: the questions deemed to be of greatest importance in the relevant field of policy, and the best known ways of looking at the problems involved. Then, if the members of a subcommittee were interested, they could spend a few days at the beginning of the session discussing general policy considerations with their consultants. The best that could be said for this approach would be that it might sensitize congressmen to different kinds of questions and approaches divorced from the immediate need to make a decision. The worst would be that nothing useful would happen. The approach seems worth a try on a low priority basis.

Under a radical incremental approach, with programming for conflict, each organizational unit in the executive branch would be highly motivated to bring forth its best programs and to back them up with the best knowledge at its command. Congress could then use the resources in the executive branch to improve the quality of information that goes into its own decisions. It could still be possible, however, for situations to exist in which all the participants lack useful knowledge. No amount of competition or conflict or reconciliation of divergent preferences would produce reasonable decisions where everyone is poverty-stricken in regard to knowledge. One can say that in the midst of universal lack of knowledge a centrally directed and enforced policy would be by far the worst kind since its impact would be more far-reaching and its reversal would be far more difficult. Such a problem is not peculiar to Congress; universal ignorance is a defect of the society, not merely of a single institution. Yet Congress does have an obligation to increase the sum total of knowledge relevant to carrying out its policy-making functions. The best way for individual congressmen to become aware of gaps in information is to carry on intimate association with program personnel in the agencies and with experts from industry and academic life who might be most sensitive to what we do not know. Beyond this, the task force of experts described above might make suggestions for research in areas where crucial knowledge is lacking. The aid given governmental bodies by organizations such as RAND, also suggests that Congress should look kindly upon the establishment of research corporations in all major areas of policy. Although these corporations would have ties to executive agencies, the increase in information which they would generate would also be useful to Congress. By increasing the number of men trained in various policy areas, research corporations like RAND also increase the possibilities for Congress to gather information from knowledgeable men during and (especially) after their term of employment has ended.

The usual solution suggested for the problem of lack of knowledge in Congress is simply to add to staff resources. In this undifferentiated form, however, the proposal is not terribly helpful. How great an increase in staff, for whom, and for what purpose? The appropriations committees now are entitled to as many staff assistants as they want. In addition, they have virtually unlimited call on the General Accounting Office and other agencies for as much help as they ask for. However, while the staff members are by and large immensely knowledgeable—they may well know more about programs than the highest executive officials—they tend to serve the subcommittee chairmen and ranking minority members rather more than the junior members. But not all junior members would want an additional staff person, responsible only to themselves, who would help out on appropriations. Some members might be tempted to engage in subterfuge by using their appropriations staff for other purposes they deem more valuable. To encourage open behavior it would be advisable to give all legislators a couple of extra staff people at high pay. Then those appropriations committee members who wanted extra assistance could use a staff man for that purpose or not as they saw fit. In this way, a few members might be helped without encouraging a direct conflict with subcommittee chairmen and regular committee staff who might view the earmarking of additional staff for appropriations work as a threat to them. Of course, some conflict over new staff is probably inevitable. A very large increase in personnel or committee staff would seem undesirable on the ground that congressmen are valuable as representatives and not as office managers.

But this discussion still begs the question of what kind of knowledge congressmen need. As a self-respecting body, Congress ought to have research carried on which is expressly designed to help its members in the context in which they work. There is no point in preparing vast volumes of general data to be added to the tomes congressmen already have no time to read. Nor is there much point in preparing comprehensive decision procedures which Congress could not and would not use. It would be most desirable, however, for researchers to study ways and means of developing and introducing scanning mechanisms which would tell congressmen what matters were worth their attention. Forcing conflicts to the surface is one such mechanism. So is increase-decrease analysis. Congressmen need more devices which gear the budgetary process toward producing signals which direct attention to important problems or to strategic opportunities for intervention at low cost in time and high payoff in control. A research group on "aids to calculation" might prove exceedingly useful in this respect.

To the best of my knowledge no one has ever undertaken a study designed to tell congressmen how they might best get compliance with their directives.

The lack of knowledge of budgetary motivation has previously been mentioned. What relationship should there be between agency and Budget Bureau requests and grants of funds to secure the highest degree of sensitivity to congressional preferences? What kind of division of functions between and within agencies would maximize opportunities for congressional knowledge and intervention? What simple budgetary forms could be devised to remind executives of congressional interest? The president has found a new Machiavelli in Richard Neustadt; Congress finds no one to give it advice about its special power stake.

Increase in conflict

A predictable consequence of the adoption of the reforms proposed here would be a moderate increase in conflict within Congress over specific appropriations. By highlighting the matters that do receive consideration by the appropriations committees, a radical incremental approach should moderately increase the awareness of interested congressmen. By increasing staff possibilities for junior members of the committees, their ability to disagree with the more senior members should be enhanced somewhat. Emphasizing differences between the president and the agencies should increase political knowledge for all interested members of Congress. Since committee recommendations now receive such a high level of support in Congress, a modest increase in conflict would enable ordinary congressmen to have a little more influence without disrupting the budgetary process. The ability of the system to withstand conflict would also be enhanced by a radical incremental approach because it decreases the need to reach formal agreement on the entire budget. If conflict within Congress leads to lack of agreement and some delay, the agencies can continue to spend at the same level while waiting for a decision on proposed changes. Moreover, only incremental parts of the budget would be delayed while the rest would continue as before. By relaxing the inhibitions created by the overwhelming need to agree on a whole budget every year, the creative aspects of conflict would be given greater scope in budgetary matters as they are in other legislation.

Conclusion

The change to radical incrementalism would not require as great a change in budgetary practices as it would in perceptions of these practices. Incremental practices are a part of the present budgetary process; but, because participants believe that the ideal budgetary process is comprehensive and coordinated hierarchically, they view incrementalism, with an attitude somewhere between desperation and contempt, as a necessary evil that was adopted only because they did not know any better. At present, incremental practices take place within the framework of annual considerations of the entire budget; this arbitrary time schedule, which is designed to give the appearance of comprehensiveness, actually serves neither the theory of comprehensiveness nor the practice of incrementalism. While comprehensiveness, which cannot be practiced, is touted as a lofty ideal, incrementalism, which could be practiced, is hidden in the scullery like an unloved but necessary Cinderella.

If Congress were willing or able to delegate its powers to an executive committee of compatible legislators, it could, of course, achieve central direction in the same limited sense as the president has: the final word on budgetary decisions would come from a single source whose unity would be visible. But, if Congress is unwilling and unable to do this, as is surely the case, then it should seek to manifest its influence in ways appropriate to a body of legislators capable of unity on an ad hoc basis but not consistently over a wide range of measures. Its ability to continually form and reform ad hoc coalitions addressed to emergent political problems should be enhanced through a radical incrementalism. Congress is in the business of correcting mistakes—consequences of decisions with adverse impact on people—and should improve its ability to do so with dispatch. The weaknesses of Congress as a highly fragmented institution are self-evident. I am suggesting that Congress could gain strength by making use of its essential nature rather than by running away from it.

Notes

1. I wish to make it perfectly clear that I do not subscribe to the view that the executive branch is a scheming ogre gleefully squeezing the life out of our innocent and defenseless Republic. My views are quite different; I would not regard such a characterization as either accurate or helpful in the analysis of public policy. I have been asked to take the viewpoint of Congress in writing about policy. This I have gladly done, for our Congress deserves our best. As a citizen and a political scientist, I would just as gladly perform a similar service for the executive. My intention is not to disparage the great institutions of our democracy but to contribute to understanding and perfecting them.
2. Richard McKeon, ed., *Basic Works of Aristotle* (New York: 1941), pp. 1185-87, 1212-24.
3. A. G. Wernham, *Benedict de Spinoza, The Political Works* (Oxford: The Clarendon Press, 1958), inter alia.
4. Arthur E. Buck, *Public Budgeting* (New York: Harper and Brothers, 1929); Jesse Burkhead, *Government Budgeting* (New York: John Wiley and Sons, Inc., 1956); Hoover Commission on the Organization of the Executive Branch of the Government, *Budget and Accounting* (Washington, DC, 1949); Edward A. Kolodziej, "Congressional Responsibility for the Common Defense: The Money Problem," *The Western Political Quarterly* 16 (1963):149-160; Arthur Smithies, *The Budgetary Process in the United States* (New York: McGraw-Hill, 1955); Robert Ash Wallace, "Congressional Control of the Budget," 99 *Midwest Journal of Political*

Science 3 (1959):151-167; and William Franklin Willoughby, *The National Budget System* (Baltimore, MD: Johns Hopkins University Press, 1927).

5. Aaron Wildavsky, *Politics of the Budgetary Process* (Boston: Little, Brown & Co., 1964), pp. 127-44.
6. Dwight Waldo, *The Administrative State* (New York: The Ronald Press, 1948) inter alia; Herbert A. Simon, *Administrative Behavior,* 2d ed. (New York: Macmillan, 1957), pp. 172-97.
7. Wildavsky, *Politics of the Budgetary Process,* pp. 127-44.
8. Richard Cyert and James March, eds., *A Behavioral Theory of the Firm* (Englewood Cliffs, NJ: Prentice-Hall, 1963).
9. David Braybrooke and Charles Lindblom, *A Strategy of Decision* (New York: Free Press of Glencoe, 1963).
10. Simon, *Administrative Behavior.*
11. Wildavsky, *Politics of the Budgetary Process,* pp. 1-13.
12. Ibid., pp. 16-18.
13. J. S. Hines (Research Officer) and R. W. Edwards (Chairman) *Budgeting in Public Authorities* (New York: A Study Group of the Royal Institute of Public Administration, 1959), p. 245.
14. Wildavsky, *Politics of the Budgetary Process, pp.* 21-32.
15. Richard F. Fenno, Jr., "The House Appropriations Committee as a Political System: The Problem of Integration," *American Political Science Review* LVI (1962): 310-324.
16. Wildavsky, *Politics of the Budgetary Process,* pp. 65-98.
17. Ibid., pp. 101-123.
18. Ibid., pp. 4-42.
19. Otto Davis and Aaron Wildavsky, "An Empirical Theory of Congressional Appropriations," (Mimeograph, 1965).
20. Fenno, "House Appropriations Committee."
21. Wildavsky, *Politics of the Budgetary Process, pp.* 56-64.
22. Fenno, "House Appropriations Committee."
23. Wildavsky, *Politics of the Budgetary Process.*
24. Fenno, "House Appropriations Committee."
25. Ibid., p. 312.
26. Ibid.; Wildavsky, *Politics of the Budgetary Process.*
27. Charles Lindblom, "The Science of Muddling Through, *Public Administration Review,* 19 (1959): 79-88.
28. See his *Decision-Making in Taxation and Expenditures, Public Finances, Needs, Sources and Utilization* (Princeton, NJ: National Bureau of Economic Research, 1961), pp. 295-336.
29. Joseph S. Berliner, *Factory and Manager in the USSR* (Cambridge, MA: Harvard University Press, 1957).
30. Frank Jasinsky, "Use and Misuse of Efficiency Controls, Harvard *Business Review* 34 (1956): 107; Chris Argyris, *The Impact of Budgets on People* (New York: Controllership Foundation, Inc., 1952), pp. 12ff.
31. Argyris, *The Impact of Budgets on People,* pp. 6ff.
32. Ibid., pp. 12-13.
33. Ibid., inter alia; Bernard H. Sord and Glenn A. Welsch, *Business Budgeting: A Survey of Management Planning and Control Practices* (New York: Controllership Foundation, Inc., 1958), pp. 140-150.
34. Arnold A. Bebling, "A Look at Budgets and People," Business *Budgeting* 10 (1961): 16.

35. Andrew C. Stedry, *Budget Control and Cost Behavior* (Englewood Cliffs, NJ: Prentice-Hall, 1960).
36. Richard F. Fenno, Jr., review of Joseph P. Harris, "Congressional Control of Administration," in *American Political Science Review*, XVIII: 3 (1964): 673-675.
37. Fenno, "The House Appropriations Committee."
38. Frank Munger and Richard Fenno, Jr., *National Politics and Federal Aid to Education* (Syracuse, NY: Syracuse University Press, 1962), pp. 106-36.
39. Smithies, *Budgetary Process in the United States*, pp. 192ff.
40. Avery Leiserson, "Coordination of the Federal Budgetary and Appropriations Procedures under the Legislative Reorganization Act of 1946," *National Tax Journal* I (1948): 118-26.
41. Wallace, "Congressional Control of the Budget"; Dalmas H. Nelson, "The Omnibus Appropriations Act of 1950," *Journal of Politics* 15 (1953): 274-88; John Phillips, "The Hadacol of the Budget Makers," National *Tax Journal* 4 (1951): 255-68.
42. Roy Blough, "The Role of the Economist in Federal Policy-Making," *University of Illinois Bulletin* (1953): 51; Lester Seligman, "Presidential Leadership: The Inner Circle and Institutionalization," *Journal of Politics*, 18 (1956): 410-26; Edwin G. Nourse, *Economics in the Public Service: Administrative Aspects of the Employment Act* (New York: Harcourt Brace 1953); Ronald C. Hood, "Reorganizing the Council of Economic Advisers," *Political Science Quarterly*, LXIX (1954): 413-37.
43. Fritz Morstein Marx, "The Bureau of the Budget: Its Evolution and Present Role, II, *American Political Science Review* 39 (1945): 869-98; Richard Neustadt, "Presidency and Legislation: The Growth of Central Clearance," *American Political Science Review XLVIII* (1954): 641-71; Seligman, "Presidential Leadership."
44. John S. Saloma, "The Responsible Use of Power," in Saloma and Murray L. Weidenbaum, *Congress and the Federal Budget* (Washington, D C: The American Enterprise Institute for Public Policy Research, 1965), p. 182.
45. Ibid., pp. 175-93.
46. Ralph K. Huitt, "Congressional Organization and Operations in the Field of Money and Credit," in *Fiscal and Debt Management Policies: A Series of Research Studies prepared for the Commission on Money and Credit*, William Fellner et al. (Englewood Cliffs, NJ: Prentice-Hall, 1963), pp. 399-495.
47. Wilfred Lewis, Jr., *Federal Fiscal Policy in the Postwar Recessions* (Washington, DC: The Brookings Institution, 1962).
48. Raymond E. Wolfinger and Joan Heifetz, "Safe Seats, Seniority and Power in Congress," *American Political Science Review* LIX (1965): 337-49.

5

The Annual Expenditure Increment

Why does a president whose administration is responsible for a deficit of over $30 billion in the last fiscal year suddenly appear as a protector of the purse? Why do congressmen who vote for their share of spending increases express unhappiness with the collective results of their individual actions? How can a president get away with impounding funds when Congress has the power of the purse? The answer to all these questions is the same: because Congress is losing faith in its appropriations process. If congressmen believed in what they were doing, they would support each other enough to get their way. The president prevails because secretly congressmen think he is right. Since they do not believe in themselves, they espouse the heresy that it is the president who knows best.

It is true that the president is forcing the issue by insisting that he need not spend even after Congress passes bills over his vetoes. In this he should be beaten back. And no doubt innumerable ways will be found of tying his hands. But if the congressional response is confined to that level, the same pattern will recur as soon as the issue leaves the headlines: Congressmen will again vote for appropriations one day and rely on the president to impound them the next. Feeling that the financial situation has got out of control, they will give the president far more of their power than he is capable of wresting from them. Yet the belief that the presidency is a better institution to do budgeting than the Congress, that it somehow knows more or acts more rationally, is just what I said it was—a heresy. What is more, it is an illusion, created with mirrors; it is produced by sleight of hand or, to be more precise, by sleight of mind.

The Magic of Totals

Why does the president, who spends perhaps twenty hours a year on the annual budget, seem more rational than the chairman of the House Appropria-

111

tions Committee, who must spend 2,000 hours on it? It is simply because the former announces himself with trumpet blasts from on high, while the latter sounds more like the Tower of Babel than the Heavenly Chorus. The president's budget is made in private, the congressional budget in public. Congressmen see how their budget is made; knowing what went into it they are, like sausage-makers, leery of what will come out of it. Unaware of what has been going on in the Executive Office of the president, they respect its products more because they know the ingredients less. Thus have congressmen come to prefer other people's errors to their own.

The magic is in the totals. If the president seems more rational, if he somehow appears to be in control and to know what he is doing, it is because he announces his desired totals of government spending with an air of conviction. presidents naturally make up in assurance what they lack in knowledge. Although the executive's total is not entirely plucked out of the air, neither is it turned out down to the last decimal by some infallible sausage machine of modern economic science. The total so authoritatively proclaimed by one man is in fact a product of the fair guesses and wild surmises of many within the executive branch.

What is in a total? On the expenditure side, it is a thing of shreds and tatters. Ability to project, or predict, federal expenditures is poor. Estimates can easily be off by $5 or $10 billion. Underspending usually runs a good 2 to 3 percent, creating the possibility of an additional error of $4 to $6 billion. More than half of the total is left over from previous years in the form of unobligated balances, and no one is quite certain how large they are or how soon they will be liquidated. Aficionados of the craft also recognize that exactly what is included in the budget as an expenditure is, at the all-important margin, a matter of convenience rather than of necessity. Give me my way or give them theirs, and either of us will be able to make that budget larger or smaller by anything from $10 to $50 billion with just a flick of the projection or a twist of the definition.

But we are all Keynesians now, the trite phrase runs, from which we seem to conclude that an allowable total expenditure figure emerges from economic theory untouched by human hands. Keynesian doctrine is universally popular because the instructions it conveys—spend when underemployed, save when overemployed—are simpleminded enough for all of us to pretend we understand the economy. But the argument for impounding goes beyond this maxim by making the further suggestion that there is a direct and immediate connection between expenditures not made and the health of the economy. Yet spending changes, unlike variations in tax rates, make awkward tools for short-term economic management. In many cases no one knows what the employment or inflationary impact of an expenditure will be. It is quite possible for a short-term cut in authorization to lead to a middle-term increase in expenditure because closing costs have to be paid and permanent leave has to be given to workers that are laid off. By the time the effects of expenditure cuts are felt, the chances are that the economic circumstances at which they were aimed will have changed. No one can be certain that presidential spending targets are correct for economic spending purposes; or, if they are, that the limits proposed will come near to meeting them; or, if they do, that the contrary effect will not occur. The totals are hunches, on top of guesses, wrapped in conjectures.

Because the president announces his preferred total only once, the impression grows that it is the total he has always had in mind. Nothing could be further from the truth. The most obvious feature of the presidential total is never mentioned, no doubt because it appears self-evident: He announces it at the end—not the beginning—of his consideration of the budget. The total changes up to late December, when the government printer imposes the final deadline. True, there is a planning figure bandied about within the Office of Management and Budget (OMB) during the spring. This preliminary total is not necessarily devoid of meaning, but neither is it binding. Everyone knows it is subject to change, not only in response to events, but as the actual process of having to decide further reveals to the participants their preferences. In the last month, week, or day, the president must weigh his expenditure desires on, say, six to ten major programs against the prospect of raising or lowering taxes within the context of the economic situation. If he changes his total a dozen times, only his budget director will know.

Just because the importance of budgetary totals has been exaggerated does not mean that Congress should not be interested in them. If congressmen will not think well of themselves (or outsiders think well of congressmen) unless they come up with a total, then Congress must equip itself to produce the magic number. If many Americans, including congressmen, believe that the nation is spending too much and want to return more purchasing power to individuals, that is another and better reason for being interested in the totals. Indeed, it is the widespread feeling that Congress is indifferent to the total that explains its vulnerability to presidential impounding.

Imperfect Budgets and Negligent Guardians

The last decade has revealed certain imperfections in the congressional political arena. Members of Congress who vote for spending proposals find themselves unhappy with the resulting totals or the tax rates related to them. It appears undesirable either to turn down spending bids or to raise taxes to accommodate them. The president accuses Congress of wanting the credit for spending but not the blame for taxing. Impoundment is his challenging response: Either take the onus for raising taxes or allow me to make my limits stick by refusing to spend beyond them.

Power and responsibility go together: Irresponsibility equals impotence. Democratic legislatures are often enfeebled by making unreal decisions. When legislatures typically authorize several times the amount of expenditure that is available to the national treasury, as has been the case, for instance, in the Philippines, the actual allocation of money is necessarily transferred to the executive. The price of depriving no one is inability to indulge anyone.

In the past, Congress maintained the power of the purse because it played the role of guardian of the treasury. In most cases it cut requests the president made on behalf of the spending agencies. While Congress did not formally set a total, expenditures as a whole were kept within tacit boundaries acceptable to most legislators. Today guardianship still exists but it has declined. Congress still cuts more than it increases, but not by much nor with the regularity for which it was once (in)famous, and the appropriations subcommittees are more likely to try to hold the line at the president's request than they are to assume it will be cut.

If Congress goes all the way in abandoning guardianship, the show will still go on, but the president's men will act as guardians. The role of advocacy is already built into the system through the spending agencies. Congress cannot do better than the original cast in crying, "More, more!" Left unchecked, the agencies' desires would know few bounds. So there must be guardians. What is now being decided is whether Congress will continue to play the role of guardian effectively or will see another actor take over its role, and so its power.

The decline of guardianship as a congressional role has been accompanied by the erosion of reciprocity as a congressional norm. No large body of men can make as many decisions as an annual budget requires without breaking up into specialized groups and then deferring to the judgments of these groups. Reciprocity has been attacked from two separate directions with a single result—higher appropriations. The recommendations of appropriations subcommittees are being overturned on the floor more frequently than in the past, usually in order to increase the amount appropriated. Legislative committees have begun to rail against their opposite numbers on the appropriations side for exercising more power with less information, usually on the ground that expenditures should be greater than they are, even if that means getting around the annual appropriations process through direct (backdoor spending) or indirect (tax subsidies) access to the treasury. Being the adaptive creatures they are, the members of appropriations subcommittees have tried to reestablish the deference customarily shown to them by raising the price they are prepared to pay. Yet few like the total cost.

What is to be done? When we say that economic markets are imperfect, what we mean is that they do not produce essential information for buyers and sellers, with the result that optimal decisions are unlikely to be made. The solution is to "rig the market by changing the rules governing permissible exchanges. When the budgetary process produces imperfections in the form of discrepancies between preferences on specific programs and the overall expenditure total, comparable steps have to be taken. Now it may be that rules which would make it easier to reconcile desired totals with programmatic preferences are the last thing congressmen want to see, and will go the way of Thomas Edison's old scheme for instantaneous recording of votes. Maybe congressmen do not wish to face the totals arising from individual spending actions. Perhaps they would rather avoid confrontation between desirable expenditures and unavoidable taxes. In that case, impounding would not be the abominable action of a pugnacious president but the routine undertaking of a conscientious chief executive. It would represent a systemic adaptation to the decline in congressional guardianship. Congress would still be allowed to act as if it were budgeting, with the understanding that the president would cut back the total when he deemed that advisable. As a result, congressmen would stand to lose not only the power over totals they conveniently wish to give up, but the power over spending they still wish to retain.

It is possible that the cries of outrage against impounding are merely the death rattles of a Congress inclined to self-destruction—possible, but hardly certain. There is nothing inevitable about what is happening. All the signs point to strong citizen concern over the decline of Congress. Many congressmen are at least ambivalent enough to wish it were otherwise. Most congressmen stand to lose the power that makes their job worth having; they should respond to proposals for maintaining that power. My own view is that it is both desirable and possible to maintain—and even enhance—the congressional power of the purse. As evidence that different procedures are possible and that some actually work, let us consider the budgetary practices of France, Great Britain, and Japan in comparison to those of the United States.

Budgeting in the Modern Democracies

Because most of the budget is a product of previous decisions, the largest determining factor of the size and content of this year's budget is last year's budget. The budget is thus like an iceberg: By far the largest part of it is below the surface, outside the control of anyone. Long-range spending commitments have been made; this year's share is included as part of the annual budget. There are mandatory programs, such as veterans' pensions, whose expenses must be met. Powerful political support makes the inclusion of other activities inevitable. Budgeting, therefore, is incremental, not comprehensive. The beginning of wisdom about an agency budget is that it is almost never actively reviewed as a whole every year, in the sense of reconsidering the value of all existing programs as compared to all possible alternatives. Instead, it is based on last year's budget with special attention given to a narrow range of increases or decreases. *Thus the men who make the budget are concerned with relatively small increments to an existing base.*

The near-universal practice of incrementalism in budgeting has been attacked as mindless and irrational—mindless because most of the budget is not subject to scrutiny, and irrational because the full range of relevant comparisons is deliberately excluded from view. But mindless or not, incrementalism and other such devices to simplify and speed decisions are inevitable responses to the extraordinary complexity of resource allocation in governments of any size, a problem that has gotten worse in recent decades as governmental expenditures have soared. With governments undertaking so many new programs and doing so much more under the rubric of old ones, there has been a greater emphasis upon simplifying calculations. More of the total budget has been taken for granted, and a lesser proportion of the changes has been subjected to the serious scrutiny of budget makers.

Incrementalism is becoming institutionalized in rich countries. Three out of the four countries for which information is available—Great Britain, France, and Japan—not only practice incrementalism but have built it into their formal machineries for making the annual budget. This is not incrementalism *sub rosa,* as in the United States, where it is adopted but not applauded, on the grounds that there must be something better, though no one can, for the moment, quite think of what that would be. Rather it is incrementalism with a clear conscience—indeed, with a vengeance. Tendencies to think and act incrementally are reinforced by procedures designed to compel incremental calculations.

Since 1955, France has used the device of the *sertice sote,* in which all past expenditure is considered a continuing commitment. Parliament votes only on additions or, occasionally, subtractions from past totals. What is more important, the Ministry of Finance treats past commitments as if they were inviolable.

Since 1965, Great Britain has replaced the traditional estimates of authorized expenditure with five-year projections of the cost of existing policies. Called by the name of the official committee supervising it, the Public Expenditure Survey Committee (PESC), the new procedure allocates funds in the form of annual white papers. PESC works. It has given the British Treasury considerably greater control than it had previously exercised over the growth of public expenditure. It is now far more difficult than it used to be to sneak in small items with large future expenditure implications. Containing the vices of its virales, as most human mechanisms do, PESC also makes it correspondingly more difficult for old items to be taken out. To make sure that it has an ample margin of safety, the Treasury has adopted two new devices—the relative price effect and productive potential. Based on the (questionable) assumption that productivity in the public sector does not grow at the same rate as in the private sector, the "relative price effect" causes a proportion of each year's budget to be put away for use in case expenditures should go that much beyond expectations. "Productive potential" declares, by fiat, that productivity will increase at something under (or, now, over) 3 percent, thereby building into the budget a small and constant margin for future increases. Thus PESC works within a margin of a margin with a safety factor added on.

Incrementalism is nowhere better practiced than in Japan. The Japanese can get incremental anyway you come at them, bottom-up, top-down, and seemingly sideways as well. To begin with, the Ministry of Finance imposes a 125 percent ceiling over the previous year. A quarter of the previous year's budget might seem large were it not for the fact that past expenditures are not challenged at all, and it is expected that every ministry will get built-in increases amounting to at least half or more of the margin. Therefore, in making up its draft budget, the Finance Ministry adds both "Natural Increases" (cost-of-living and mandatory items) and "Semi-natural Increases" (those that are not required by law or by price increases but which every sensible man knows will have to be made). Should there be any question of whether one ministry is to be preferred over others in obtaining increases, the norm of balance *(baransu) is* applied so that comparable programs and categories receive essentially the same proportion of what there is to give. By the time Finance holds its own "Important Items" discussion, it is hardly necessary to think at all about its draft budget. Still, after all this, only a beginning has been made in performing the Japanese lamenectomy on the yearly budget. Concerned lest there still remain grievances unadjusted, the Ministry of Finance puts away a small percentage of the total so that all those who feel they have lost out in the original process can participate in what are variously called the "resurrection" (literally, to come back from the dead) or the "revival" negotiations. Within this rapidly diminishing margin, itself an increment of an increment, the Ministry of Finance allocates proportions across the board for salary and policy adjustment expenses, so that when top party officials and the Minister of Finance sit down for the final decisions, they are not overburdened with numerous hard choices.

The Rise of the Spenders

It is apparent that central budget control organs in Britain, France, and Japan have largely given up, or retreated from, detailed scrutiny of budgetary proposals. They no longer appear anxious to use the budget as a means of imposing their priorities on the rest of the government. What has happened? Why have they begun to abandon their ancient powers? What, if anything, have they got in return? The answer may be simply put: Finance ministries have trimmed their old expenditure powers in order to preserve their new authority over economic management.

As spending has risen, so have the spenders. Growing ever stronger from their past victories, feeding on popular desire for national grandeur or social justice, righteous in their wrath against those who would deny citizens the necessities of life, they have put their former controllers on the run. Threatened in Japan, for instance, by the Liberal Democratic Party, and elsewhere by the spending ministers (such as those who allegedly ganged up on the British Chancellor of the Exchequer in the 1950s), central control organs have had to reconsider their function. At the same time they have also been deeply affected by the Keynesian revolution in economic thought. Except in the United States, where the Office of Management and Budget is not a part of the same organization as the Treasury Department and the Council of Economic Advisers, the men who control expenditure are part of a larger apparatus whose tasks include economic management. As politician and civil servant alike have grown assured and comfortable with seemingly simple Keynesian decision rules, budgeters have increasingly identified their fortunes with their ability to manage the overall economic situation. One reason they have simplified their burden of calculation by confining their attention to increments to the budget is that their interest in total expenditures now far exceeds their concern with the specific programs that make up the total. Ministers of finance and their civil service advisers are usually selected not for their skill at cost-benefit analysis—which might be appropriate for choosing among expenditure projects—but for their ability to handle fiscal and monetary questions. The politicians' special interest in holding down or manipulating the tax rate is also served by the same macroeconomic approach. Hence an implicit bargain has been struck. Ministries of finance have begun to give up detailed financial scrutiny in return for control over the totals as an aid in economic management.

Though the United States has neither institutionalized incrementalism nor established the equivalent of a Ministry of Finance, there are signs it is moving in the direction of emphasizing totals in order to make expenditures the servant of economic management. What is revenue sharing, after all, but a means of centralizing totals and decentralizing priorities within these umbrella figures? What does the creation of a "supersecretary" in charge of economic affairs with an office near the president mean, but a desire to improve control over economic management? What, indeed, is the significance of recent changes in the Office of Management and Budget—the split between administration and budgeting and the exact parallelism between budget divisions and the policy spheres of the new domestic supersecretaries—other than a greater concern with totals and a lesser emphasis on what goes into them? For the budget arm of the OMB is being transformed into a group of staff assistants to the supersecretaries; their function will be like that of the old military division, which participated directly in drawing up the defense budget as an aid to the Secretary of Defense, except now there will be less need to pretend that they are backed by an independent controller in the person of the Director of the Budget. Who, then, will exercise budget control if the former controllers will not? Who will look beneath the totals to get at the composition of expenditures?

The change from interest in composition of expenditures to concern about their total amount has alleviated certain anxieties and created others. Now there need be less conflict between spending ministries and their financial controllers over who has the expertise in a particular line of policy. Having shored up their positions in this way, however, the central control organs have begun to worry that they might have gone too far, and that only those with an axe to grind are now paying attention to public policy. Conflict has been reduced, authority has been maintained, but the rationality of expenditures has been thrown into greater doubt than ever.

Of course I exaggerate. Budget controllers still exist, and they do on occasion attempt to interject their own ideas about public policy in internal ministerial allocations. But the rationale for such intervention has been seriously weakened by the growth of public-sector activity. The ministry of finance can always justify imposition of a total on the grounds that it is the expert on managing the economy and knows how much expenditure it does or does not require. Its budget arm, by contrast, can hardly claim the expertise to justify detailed control over the composition of expenditure. Traditional financial controllers have therefore become vulnerable to attack from outsiders who demand a share in budgetary decision-making on the ground that they *do* possess knowledge going to the merits of the issues. The old boys have responded to these efforts to trespass on their preserve by sponsoring (or at least tolerating) their own reform: program budgeting.

The Planners' Challenge

The attack from the outside came from the planners. They claimed a comprehensive rationality that would enable them to determine where the nation should go and how it should get there for years ahead, with respect to both economic policy and the allocation of resources among sectors and within major projects. Finance ministries met the challenge by bolstering their capability in economic management and by mobilizing the political power to depart from the plans whenever they thought necessary, which was quite often. Whether it was because the planners in Japan failed to anticipate so much economic growth, or those in England so little, or the ones in France so much inflation, or because the central finance organs refused to implement the plans through the budget, in no case were planned targets met or even roughly approximated.

What matters here, however, is not the fate of the plan, but the nature of the conflict between finance and planning over expenditures. Planners are spenders. Their raison d'etre *is* economic growth. Typically they underestimate expenditures and overestimate revenues in order to create room for the investments they believe necessary to bring about growth. Thus planners are the natural allies of large spending departments, whose projects they believe desirable to promote economic growth. For this same reason, planners are also the natural enemies of financial controllers, who wish to place limits on expenditure and to preserve their authority to do so by maintaining their right to approve allocations within the total.

In Britain, the Department of Economic Affairs (DEA), and the National Economic Development Councils which preceded it, postulated high rates of economic growth. Although there was no theoretical rationale for doing so, spending departments and their allies found it convenient to assume that they could be allowed to grow with the rate of increase in gross national product. When economic growth fell below the announced figures, the Treasury found expenditures rising far more rapidly than incomes, creating balance-of-payments and inflationary difficulties. What the Treasury wanted, in these circumstances, was not a *lower* publicized rate of growth, but no announced rate of growth. It knew that politicians would not allow themselves to be accused of selling the country short, and that the figure would inevitably be higher than experience justified. So it fought the DEA and eventually secured its abolition.

In Japan, the Bureau of the Budget was not at all happy with the publication of planned expenditures years into the future, for it knew that spending ministries would use them as a floor from which they would try to get additional increments. The Budget Bureau insisted on treating the planned figures as maximums from which they were free to cut according to the conditions of the times as they interpreted them.

Power and happiness, however, are not always equivalent. While it was not too difficult for the central finance organs to beat off attacks from the outside without making much change in their own activities, they did respond internally to their own dissatisfaction over the lack of intelligence that seemed to characterize their method of budgetary review.

The Failure of PPBS

If the budget is meant merely to register the constellation of prevailing political forces, there is no need for any special budget review technique. It is sufficient if each actor plays his assigned role so that neither spenders nor guardians get their way entirely. But if there were a way of determining the merits of proposed expenditures that stood outside of the political process, central controllers would have a new rationale. They could better justify their own activity to themselves.

This was the promise of program budgeting. Instead of dealing with budgetary inputs, such as personnel and maintenance, for purposes of narrow control, the budget would be organized around categories emphasizing outputs, so as to improve choice. By providing quantitative indicators of inputs and outputs, and by ranking programs according to their merit as means of achieving these objectives, resource allocation would be done in a more rational way.

The main difference between the old and the new forms of budgeting was that one could be done and the other could not. The burden of calculation imposed by PPBS was literally beyond comprehension. Failing to create this simultaneous equation of society in the sky, understandably unable to come up with theories connecting inputs to outputs across the widest range of public policies, program budgeting everywhere fell of its own weight. While it is also true that there were significant bureaucratic objections from those who felt they benefited more under the old ways or who could not comprehend the new ones, and political objections from participants like American congressmen, who looked at program budgeting as a sort of mumbo-jumbo designed to exclude them, nowhere was an ideal—or even a better—budget created. It was one thing to talk about focusing on future results, considering a wider range of alternatives, and generally getting better information, and something else actually to perform when no one could even remotely specify the required cognitive operations.

From the outset, the central budget agencies were ambivalent, divided functionally between the more traditional types and the program budgeters, who were themselves unsure of how far they could or should go. In Japan, for instance, program budgeting had to fit in with norms mandating equity among participants. If program budgeting could somehow be shown to be more scientific, so that its results were both more desirable and more acceptable, that would take care of the problem. But its sponsors had the usual trouble figuring out what to do and the usual difficulty in getting anyone who was disadvantaged to agree that what they did was good.

The federal government of the United States, which had first introduced program budgeting, was also the first to abandon it. Being initially the most ambitious, it experienced the most extreme difficulties in negotiating the pathways between knowledge and power. The OMB was able neither to produce information from program categories appropriate to the level of the user nor to impose such preferences as it did have on the recalcitrant and unwilling. The spending agencies played along because they thought PPBS was for the OMB, whose favorable opinion was useful to them. When they discovered that the OMB was as much in the dark about what to do as they were, and that program budgeting was supposed to be for them, they used the program structures as the latest in the long series of devices for self-advertisement in the struggle for funds. It was a good two years after PPBS was disestablished, in the midst of a circular commenting on the reduction of unnecessary paperwork in the federal government, before the OMB finally began to receive inquiries from people who noticed something was missing.

The Lesson of the British Experience

Great Britain has been saved for last because the evolution of its thought and practice is most instructive. When all of the publicity surrounding program budgeting reached Britain, the Public Expenditure Group in the Treasury was well served by its customary caution. Observers sent to America came back enticed but wary of the innumerable pitfalls they faced. They proceeded pragmatically in two directions: They encouraged a few departments with interested personnel to try creating program structures and categories, and they gave part of the time of one of their bright young men to work with local government officials in actually introducing program budgeting at that level. Then they let them struggle. When neither group was able to advance because they could not figure out how to make the system work, the Treasury had no substantial investment to abandon.

Yet the Treasury could not sit still. Its own concern about the adequacy of program review was exceeded by that of the Conservative Party and its associated businessmen, who were anxious to give the Prime Minister and Cabinet more adequate tools for making expenditure decisions. Instead of rushing into program budgeting across the board, however, the Treasury persuaded the businessmen to join with them in creating a mechanism for Program Analysis and Review (PAR) that was aimed at encouraging departments to analyze a few major programs each year with the knowledge that they would be subject to Cabinet review. PAR is still in its infancy. It has hardly had time to make an impact, but it exists. Its viability may depend in part on whether another new apparatus, the Central Policy Review Staff (CPRS), which the Conservative businessmen designed to aid the Prime Minister and Cabinet in reviewing policy and adhering to party programs, will also be able to maintain itself in the heretofore closed world of top-level British political administration. Thus the Treasury now faces competition, not from planners with grandiose general schemes, but from analysts who are interested precisely in having an effect on the choice among major alternatives in the annual allocation of resources.

The very success of the Treasury in creating the PESC procedure for controlling expenditures has enabled others to concentrate on improving programmatic choices. Of the rich nations of the world, the British have in the Public Expenditure Survey Committee the only major innovation in budgeting practice that has proven successful. PESC does join knowledge and power. The Treasury does issue explicit instructions that departments can follow. Using the carrot of securing greater safety for vulnerable activities and the stick of its existing powers over expenditure, the Treasury has energetically sought and received substantial departmental cooperation. Departments and the Treasury sometimes agree to disagree, but they produce a five-year projection of existing expenditures that has become the actual mechanism for allocating resources in British government. *The lesson is not that successful budgetary innovation ends problems, but that it is based on making calculations manageable. The least demanding effort in terms of theory and data has had the greatest practical effect. And when the political question is asked—What is in it for us?—all participants, Treasury and departments alike, can find affirmative answers.*

In making recommendations for Congress, I shall draw on the lessons to be learned from other nations' budgetary practices, but there can be no thought of directly imitating them. Congress is not like the parliaments in these other countries: Congress is still powerful. Legislatures that actually exercise power independently of the executive over a wide range of activities have become a rarity in the contemporary world. Members of the Japanese Diet act on the budget not as members of the legislature, or even as adherents of the party in parliament, but by virtue of their association with the extra-parliamentary Liberal Democratic Party. Members of the House of Commons have little influence over expenditures in any capacity, and most of what little they do have comes from being backbenchers in the majority party. Deputies and Senators in France may trade on their extra-parliamentary positions as civil servants or mayors to importune for favors before the executive budget is made up. What is required to convince the executive to accede on one program or another is so involved that few try and fewer still succeed. It is important, then, that in appraising recommendations for change we take account of Congress' special characteristics.

Congressional Realities

Past proposals to reform congressional procedures for budget review failed because they did not take into sufficient account the realities of decision making under congressional condition. Whatever is recommended must be workable in a large, heterogeneous, and independent body of men who operate within an environment of fragmented and dispersed power. There is no sense in treating Congress as if it were, or even were led by, a small, cohesive group of men easily able to agree or to impose their will on others. To avoid these traps, it may be helpful to state the characteristics of the congressional environment in the form of criteria for evaluating alternative budgetary procedures.

1. *Many committees, not one.* If you have a committee that makes a budget which is not then altered by other committees—a committee without rivals, a steering committee of the legislature—it can be called a cabinet on

the British model. Congress is a pluralistic institution; it has many centers of power, depending on the time and the issue. To be effective, Congress must exploit rather than fight against its dispersed, fragmented, and pluralistic nature. A good way to use pluralism is to embrace specialization.

2. *More specialization, not less.* Without specialization, there is no knowledge, and without knowledge there is no power. When executives wish to emasculate legislatures, they break up existing committees and prevent formation of new ones that are specialized enough to look into specific areas of policy and small enough to act with dispatch. It is no good railing at last year's failures or the previous decade's disasters. Unless the legislature can keep up with the executive, it will become an auditor after the fact rather than the budgeter ahead of time.

3. *Revitalize old committees rather than create new ones.* The budget must be passed every year. There is no time for a new committee to learn; it must perform well the first time or its activity will be held in disrepute. Old committees have the virtue of age; they have long been there and legislators expect them to be around. Because they perform other essential purposes (appropriations and finance), they can survive initial disappointments of failing to set a total or having it exceeded. Since they cannot compel other legislators to follow their lead, they also need the advantages of existing power levers. Putting the matter another way, it is too much to ask a new committee to take on a new function; in this case new wine will age better in old bottles. But will old committees be willing to learn new budgetary tricks? That depends on being able to answer the always relevant political question of incentives.

4. *Something for all, not nothing for most.* If budgeting is a game, all players must have a chance to score. There has to be something in it for all— bureaucrats, executives, central control organs, legislators (where relevant)—or they will refuse to play seriously. Ministries could not enhance their control over totals, for instance, unless they were prepared to concede enhanced discretion over allocations within those amounts to spending departments and their ministers. The five-year PESC projections would not have worked unless the spending departments got enhanced security for vulnerable old programs as the price of lesser security for attractive new ones. So, too, the congressional committees, the House and Senate as separate chambers, the leadership of both houses, the president, and the departments must all have something to gain from playing the expenditure game under new rules.

5. *Representation, not bureaucratization.* Congressmen are chosen to provide representation. They are originators, purveyors, and mediators of preferences. Their preferences need to be open to live knowledge, not buried under layers of bureaucracy. Congressmen should not spend their time managing a legislative bureaucracy that is supposed to help them deal with the presidential bureaucracy, which threatens to immobilize the presidency under the guise of helping presidents cope with the executive bureaucracy.

The natural defensive posture of bureaucracies is to bury outsiders in mountains of paper. If legislators are also managers, and managers are bureaucrats, the advantages of differences in role are being lost. Better a lousy legislator than a beautiful bureaucrat.

6. *Simplification, not mystification.* Rationality is supposed to mean effective action, not pretentious inaction. The rationality of results must prevail over the rationality of form. The rational man is not the one who makes believe he compares everything to everything else; the rational person is the one who manipulates the few variables under his control to good effect. If attention is focused on all or most possible relationships, it will be impossible to single out those most in need of change. However badly the chief executive confuses himself, he can always come out with a last-minute decision with a gloss of justification. If congressmen confuse themselves, they will not be able to act at all. They need mechanisms to reduce the number of decisions up for consideration at any one time; they need ways of structuring a series of votes so that these are both meaningful and manageable. Before a legislature can act wisely, it must first be able to act. If congressmen do not employ aids to calculation, they will be unable either to arrive at their own preferences or to settle their differences with others. Making calculations manageable lies at the heart of effective legislative decision-making.

What Should not be Done

The criteria for congressional choice cut two ways: They help determine what should not be done as well as what might be attempted. To clear the way for my positive recommendations, let me begin by explaining why I have rejected a number of frequently proposed reforms.

1. *The president should not be given power to make cuts from a congressionally established ceiling through proportionate reductions.* This proposal would have the unfortunate effect of encouraging spending departments and appropriations subcommittees to inflate their recommendations so as to emerge with more after across-the-board cuts have been made. Moreover, this device creates the unfortunate impression that Congress is not able to handle its own affairs by disciplining itself. In the concluding section I shall try to show that Congress can convey a far more favorable impression by actually keeping budgetary outlays within boundaries it considers reasonable.

2. *Five-year projections of governmental expenditures should not be mandated for most programs.* A formal requirement to this effect already exists and produces no useful results. There is no need to create make-work in an already overburdened federal government. Such projections make sense only if the participants are willing to make commitments for that long a period. Experience with five-year projections under the British Public Ex-

penditure Survey reveals that the spending departments get an implied commitment for continuation of expenditures on existing policies as the price of their cooperation. I do not believe that either the president or Congress is willing to go this far in reducing its already small degree of budgetary discretion, and I do not believe they should. The extreme incrementalism that results from the British procedure may not be desirable and in any event, requires the existence of a central budget organ like the Treasury, which has the power to make commitments that will, for the most part, be followed by government. The essence of American government is that no one actor has (or is supposed to have) this authority.

3. *We should also reject the variety of proposals calling for huge amounts of vaguely specified data on the theory that more data would somehow improve the budgetary process.* These requests range from pilot trials of each new proposal (thus guaranteeing that Congress would be unable to respond to emerging conditions) to cost-benefit analysis before (and evaluation after) the establishment of programs. Part of the difficulty here stems from the failure to distinguish between data—any bit that can be collected, ranging from laundry lists to telephone directories—and information, which is data collected according to a theory relating inputs to outputs, and means to ends, in a particular area of policy. Congress is already inundated with data; what it lacks and needs is information. Unfortunately, creativity is scarce throughout the country; theories telling us how to make effective decisions in education, welfare, and many other areas are hard to find. Congress might well support social research to provide such theories, but there is no point in requiring information that cannot be forthcoming without this knowledge. It is all too easy to suppose that if there were more data, there would be more understanding. But random data are not an aid but a barrier to informed decision. The most certain way for Congress to stultify itself is to collect more data than either it or anyone else can handle. As a general rule, no data should be produced unless there is a client who can specify the bit relevant to the particular theory related to the specific decision he is prepared to make.

4. *The numerous proposals calling for a joint committee on the budget are unwise.* The effect of the proposals would be to transfer congressional power over the budget from the House Appropriations Committee to the joint committee staff without substantially benefiting senators. Senators are few in number; their time and talents are necessarily spread thin. They readily command a wide audience, but they have trouble keeping up with the many subjects that come before them. So it is natural for them to rely more on staff work than do most representatives, who have the time to specialize in the narrower jurisdictions that are their lot. The power of a member of the House Appropriations Committee is tied to his place on this committee far more than is the power of his opposite number in the Senate, who serves on numerous committees and whose role in securing public attention for issues and causes often absorbs a considerable part of his attention. A joint

committee, then, would mean a further overshadowing of representatives by senators. It means giving senators the benefit of the hard work done by representatives, without corresponding return. It means that the senators will use staff to counter the expertise of the House members. The voice may be the voice of the Senate, but the guiding hand will come from the staff.

The worst feature of the joint committee idea is how easily it slides over into a cabinet model without anyone quite realizing what has happened. The result, as the report of the Joint Study Committee on the Budget shows, is to replace an unsatisfactory executive budget bureaucracy with an even less desirable legislative bureaucracy. Their idea is that a committee in each house will fix a budget total, allocate amounts for major categories, and adjust taxes accordingly. Their critical assumption is that orders will go down and obedience will come up. That doesn't sound much like the Congress of our common despair and mutual affection—the Board of Estimate, maybe, or possibly even the Bundestag, but not Congress. Reforms that require Congress to be something other than it is or, worse, that would transform it into something not worth having, are somewhat less than compelling. The virtue of Congress is that its vices are exposed. Can't we keep our Congress and (some of) our money too? I think we can.

The Annual Expenditure Increment

Despite all the difficulties, there is a way in which congressmen can reconcile their desires on individual expenditures with their feelings about the total, and in which Congress can coordinate expenditures and revenues with the economic situation, even in the absence of a central leadership capable of compelling obedience. The procedure would work roughly like this: The president submits his budget. The small and capable staff of the Joint Committee on Internal Revenue Taxation makes its own estimates of income. A similar small staff is created on the expenditure side to estimate likely outlays and to check on what was actually spent in the past year. To these actual expenditures for each agency the expenditure staff adds an estimate of what is essentially a cost-of-living increase based on salary raises, price changes, and population movements. The starting figure of the appropriations process in the House of Representatives, then, would be made up of the previous year's expenditure plus an estimate of what it would take to keep the same activities going in the coming year.

This base expenditure would be calculated in total and for the agencies under the jurisdiction of the dozen or so appropriations subcommittees. They would hold hearings and report out bills as they do now, with the important proviso, which would have to be embedded in House rules, that the total could not exceed the previously determined base expenditure. Within that initial total, agencies could suggest changes and the subcommittees could reallocate as they wished. When the bill came to the floor, the members of the House would have the same rights and obligations; they could decrease the base expenditure or propose reallocations, but they could not move to increase it. A similar procedure would be followed in the Senate, which would have to reorganize its Finance subcommittees so that they corresponded to those of the House. The Senate could still serve as an appeals court in the sense of considering requests from agencies to have their monies raised to the base expenditure or to have a different allocation made. Once an appropriations bill was on the floor, Senate appropriations subcommittees and the senators themselves would have to adopt rules forbidding increases above the base expenditures; the Conference Committee would be bound by the same rules. Thus both houses of Congress would, at this initial stage, concentrate essentially on how to do better what had been done before, or, no doubt less frequently, on whether what had been done ought to continue to be done at all.

Let us suppose that the annual expenditure increment would approximate 3 percent of the total. Indeed, in the absence of compelling macroeconomic considerations to the contrary, a 3 percent real increase in expenditures per year seems reasonable.[1] Something like 3 percent would produce a yearly increase of approximately $8 to $10 billion as expenditures approach $300 billion. The key to my expenditure proposals lies in how this annual increment would be treated.

Just as the base expenditure budget is, in reality, a series of subcommittee budgets, the annual increment is meant to be a budget of the entire committee. Agencies would make their spending bids for a part of the annual increment. Each subcommittee would hold hearings and then make recommendations to the committee as a whole. No doubt the bids would add up to more than the available amount. The Appropriations Committee's task would be to establish an order of priority among them so that they could be made to fit within the total.

It is possible that the Appropriations Committee would become so convinced of the desirability of the spending proposals that it would wish to raise its working total. This should not necessarily be condemned. There is no reason for congressmen to impose on themselves a task—fixing an inflexible total at the beginning of the budget process and sticking to it come what may—that no president could (or has even tried to) accomplish. Circumstances may change from the time the working total is established; the committee members may learn more about their own preferences in the process of considering each request. What they must then do is negotiate with the House Ways and Means Committee, through its leaders, for a new package of revenues and expenditures. The point is not that Congress should always stick to some arbitrary total, but that it should always act (and equally important, that it should appear to act) responsibly in relation to the nation's finances.

The annual increment would be reported as a single bill to the House of Representatives. The answer to the question of what the total should be would not appear in the form of some seemingly disembodied figure, but in the size and composition of the recommended increment. The total would equal the base plus the increment.

At this point I do not believe there should be a rule prohibiting increases in the increment. The House should be allowed to work its will. There seems little point in tying its hands because, when sufficiently determined, it will find a way to do what it wants. If the problem is that congressmen believe they will act unwisely under pressure, the House itself may wish to adopt the suggestion of William Niskanen that increases above the annual increment automatically trigger tax increases.

The Senate Appropriations Committee would receive the annual increment and proceed to hold hearings on appeals to increase the total or to alter the composition of expenditures within it. Then the Senate as a whole would have the opportunity to alter the annual increment bill and the tax package with which it would be associated. The final total, as before, would be the increment that Congress actually votes added to the previous base.

Suppose legislators with a spending mentality deliberately estimate expenditures low and revenues high? Precisely this occurred under the legislative budget proposal after World War II and is a frequent practice of planning commissions in poor countries wishing to encourage higher levels of investment. Suppose legislators with a saving mentality estimate expenditures high and revenues low? It happens all the time in American cities and is practiced by finance ministries in poor countries around the world. People will learn to play any game. You can bring legislators in touch with procedures that will enable them to mix revenues and expenditures, but you can t force them to produce a brew you will like.

Why Almost Everyone Stands to Benefit

The effect of the annual expenditure increment would be to focus congressional attention on important choices at the margin—a huge margin, it is true, but a margin of the total nonetheless. Having previously decided which existing programs it would like to rearrange and which it would like to do without, Congress would be choosing among new ventures and expansions of old ones. By a process of sequential reduction, through successive iterations, Congress would have refined its preferences on spending and related them to notions of desirable tax and economic policy.

Why should anyone want to do this? What's in it for them? What incentives are there for those participants in the budgetary process whose cooperation is essential if anything is to happen at all? Let us start with the House Committee on Appropriations. By dividing itself into subcommittees that are careful of each other's prerogatives, it not only gets the power that goes with expertise, but avoids the conflicts that come from some people minding other people's business. Yet minding other people's business is exactly what the committee members must do if the base expenditure and annual increment proposal is to have a chance. Why should they want to? Because by doing so they can maintain and even enhance their power as congressmen. If they do not, they will lose their power to the president, who will be doing the real budgeting at the margins, which will force them into ruinous experiments with joint committees in which staff and Senate will nibble away at what little importance they have left. It is the old story again: "Harry, how's your wife?" "Compared to what?" he replies. The outcry over impounding is symptomatic of the general disintegration of the congressional appropriations process. Compared to the alternatives, I think members will support a stronger voice for the entire Appropriations Committee.

The Senate is asked to choose between expanding its influence over an increasingly unimportant appropriations process through a joint committee with large staff, and being able to exercise more strategic control at the margin of the base expenditure and annual increment. Moreover, given the national prominence of economic management issues, and the natural interest of senators in prominent national concerns, senators would be able to use their positions on the Finance and Appropriations Committees and their role in relating revenues and expenditures to enter one of the most important realms of national policy. They would not be giving up any control over appropriations they could actually exercise, and would be gaining access to issues of broader national scope.

Spending agencies would enjoy the gain of increased stability in their existing programs through base expenditures, and suffer the cost of more tightly constrained competition for the annual increment. It seems like a fair exchange. Agency opinion will probably be divided: Some will want to protect what they have, while others will prefer to take the chance of getting more. Yet on balance I believe administrative agencies will find this procedure more helpful than not, especially since it guarantees that at least they will know about their base expenditure far earlier than is now the case.

Despite surface noise to the contrary, I do not believe that presidents will find impounding a satisfactory way of life. It will give them greater power over the budget at the cost of enhanced responsibility for everything that happens. Since no one person can possibly do all the work involved, power would, in effect, be transferred to the White House staff and the OMB. And, indeed, there are signs of increasing presidential interest in economic management and decreasing interest in the details of expenditure. Why, otherwise, would the president increasingly relegate the solution of social problems to state and local governments? But in attempting to manage the economy, he will find that it is difficult to gather all the threads in his hands unless there is some body in each house of Congress that he can deal with on the same subject. The more Congress does to develop a mechanism for relating expenditure and revenue, the greater the input the president can make to it. Once the problem of the totals has been resolved, chief executives are unlikely to wish for detailed control over a $300 billion budget. If Congress agrees to take some of the heat, presidents will find it both proper and necessary to make room in the kitchen and share their recipe for making the annual budget.

Now the Appropriations Committees are not the only committees that create expenditures. They control only 45 percent of the total. True, these are the most flexible funds, but being less than half, they now bear a disproportionate share of the pressure when expenditures are thought to be too high. Clearly, the committees that cover revenue sharing, tax subsidies, price supports, housing loans, and the like—the committees that do their financing by the back door, so to speak—must play their part, and it is true that they will have less reason to support this proposal. The actor that has the least incentive is the Ways and Means Committee, which may find in its new power to agree on totals with Appropriations slender compensation for having to give others a voice in revenue sharing and tax subsidies. Yet even these congressmen may come to see the advantage for them in the annual expenditure increment. They know that Congress lives or dies in its committees. If Congress loses power, this will happen because of its failure to work out appropriate relationships among its many committees. As is true for the rest of us, the harm others can do to Congress is vastly exceeded by the damage it can do to itself.

Regaining Control of the Budget

Imagine a legislature that actually exercises power in this world! Few people, including congressmen, realize how rare a flower our Congress is. Many Americans, like myself, have a special affection for this exotic plant. But it does require special care. And if it is to survive, it must regain control over the budget.

If Congress is willing to accept the responsibility that goes with power, it can relate its preferences on expenditure with those on taxation and economic management. The trick is to break down the budget so that it can be handled by a large number of independent and diverse legislators who must coordinate their activities without central control. What has to be done is to take advantage of precisely those features of the congressional system that are most characteristic: its independence, its diversity, its large size, its capacity for specialization, and its representation and brokerage of preferences. The annual expenditure increment is designed to accomplish this task. Congress first decides whether it wants to reallocate funds for existing programs in around a dozen major areas of policy. Then it relates the last $10 billion or so to its desire for new expenditures, together with its preferences on taxation. Congress thus has a chance to work its will; no more than this can be done.

Note

1. A case can be made for leaving expenditures out of short-term economic management, relying instead on taxes, money supply, and similar factors. But this paper already has too heavy a load to bear, and I will not now pursue the subject further.

6

Budgetary Reform in an
Age of Big Government

It is time to ask whether there should be fundamental changes in federal budgeting. This chapter partially describes but mostly evaluates the budgetary process of the United States government. We will compare the traditional line-item budget with other forms of budgeting and discuss why the line-item budget, if not the best form, is certainly the most durable. We will explore why the idea of a balanced budget has fallen by the wayside and how the traditional institutional guardians of the public's purse have been thwarted.

Along the way we will learn what the budgetary process used to do, what it does now, how it has fallen into disrepute, and how that might be remedied through constitutional limitations on the budget. We begin by describing the budgetary process itself.

The Budgetary Process

Viewed from a sufficiently remote perspective, all budgetary processes look alike. That is because they all attempt to perform similar functions—relate expenditures to revenues, allocate appropriate amounts to agencies, activities, and programs, and *otherwise protect the power of the principals*. Budgets distribute resources, and both choose who spend and choose who receive care greatly and who gets how much. Differences emerge only after close inspection, yet they are in many ways as important as the similarities. For the differences get at critical considerations: Is a budget real? Do its numbers refer to real events that have (or are about to have) happened? Do expenditures determine revenue or is it the other way around? How do the conditions under which budgeting takes place alter the behavior that takes place? Our task is to outline similarities and then differences so as to place the United States budgetary process in proper perspective.

There are constants in budgeting, no matter where it is practiced, that lead to regular patterns of behavior. Everywhere there are spenders and savers. Those in charge of the great purposes of government naturally tend to identify their fortunes with the interests entrusted to their care. So they defend against cuts and seek increases whenever they can.

Relating expenditure to income is likewise an essential state function. Guardians of the treasury will not do well if they are forced into inflationary measures or constantly have to raise taxes because they cannot control spending. So they cut and trim and otherwise seek to keep spending within hailing distance of revenues.

Beyond this elemental division of budgetary roles, all participants in budgeting are overwhelmed by its complexity. No one can relate the myriad factors to one another simultaneously so as to achieve desired allocations. Complexity appears to be a threshold variable; once the number of factors involved has grown beyond the capacity of the human mind, how much more they grow does not seem to matter.

Decision-makers in a city who are overwhelmed by eighty-six variables do not appear to behave that much differently from those in a state who cannot manage 860 or those in a nation who find 8,600 too much. All adopt aids to calculation. All simplify the task of decision-making by proceeding from a historical base, largely accepting what has gone before, in order to concentrate on proposed new departures. Given teams of spenders and savers operating in a world none can quite comprehend, the same practices—padding, across-the-board cuts, increased spending at the end of the fiscal year, and refusal to release a proportion of budgeted funds during the year—are found wherever one cares to look.

Consider the rush to spend toward the end of the fiscal year. This is rational for agencies that stand to lose resources if they are not consumed. Were agencies allowed to keep a portion to use as they see fit, and not penalized for failing to spend by lower appropriations the next year, they would have an incentive to return unused funds to the Treasury.

Administrative agencies, with their great expertise and large numbers, their close relationships to policy problems and clientele groups, and their eagerness to expand their horizons, generate action through advocacy. But how much shall they ask for? Life would be simple if they could just total the costs of their ever-expanding needs and submit them as their request. But if they ask for amounts much larger than the appropriating bodies believe is reasonable, their credibility will suffer. When that happens, the reviewing bodies are likely to apply a "measure of unrealism. As a result, the agency ends up with much less than it might have obtained with a more moderate request.

So the first basic rule for agencies is: Do not come in too high. Yet agencies must not come in too low, either, for the assumption is that if the agency does not ask for funds it does not need them. Since the budgetary situation is always tight—terribly tight, or impossibly tight— reviewing bodies are likely just to accept a low request with thanks and not inquire too closely into its rationale.

Given the distribution of roles, cuts must be expected and taken into account. Thus the agency decision rule might read: Come in a little high (padding), but not too high. But how high is too high? Agency heads usually evaluate signals from the environment—last year's experience, legislative votes, executive policy statements, economic indicators, actions of clientele groups, reports from the field—and come up with an asking price somewhat higher than they expect to get.

The traditional guardians of the Treasury do not function as they used to. The role of the (national) House Appropriations Committee and the Office of Management and Budget used to be to cut back requests. But the House Committee has been thwarted. When the rate of spending, however high, did not rise fast enough to suit many members of Congress, they engaged in successful end runs around the appropriations process. Open-ended entitlements (rights to support if qualified), loan guarantees, and tax expenditures financed activities by direct drafts on the Treasury or by tax rebates rather than by direct appropriations. And the OMB has become conflicted by the doctrine of the Keynesian full-employment surplus, which justified higher spending on grounds of balancing not the budget but the economy. At the same time, the growing complexity of government led to a decline in OMB's effort to exert direct expenditure control. The great task of government became balancing employment and inflation rather than the budget.

The decline of guardianship and the growth of federal governmental agencies reinforced tendencies toward higher levels of expenditure. Budgeting worked by addition but not by subtraction. It was always easier to solve problems between agencies by adding programs together than by fighting. True, some spending programs were emphasized over others, and different priorities did emerge. Less liked items did not disappear, however, so much as slumber. Awakened when wanted, some programs were kept in place, others were increased, but hardly any were terminated. One-way spending selection—bigger but not smaller—would eventually make the economy less adaptive.

Since 1960, fiscal policy has essentially been made by the president on the advice of his "troika"—the director of the budget, the secretary of the treasury, and the chief of the Council of Economic Advisors (CEA). Their instrument is the Spring Preview of the OMB, and their analysis consists of projected revenues from the Treasury, projected expenditures from the OMB staff, data on employment, inflation, and growth from the CEA, and whatever formulae they have for manipulating these facts and figures. The OMB uses its past experience to estimate the likely spending of the thirteen largest agencies (estimating the residual in a single figure) based on presidential preferences, insofar as these are known, new legislation just passed or likely to be passed, and spending plans of agencies as discovered by its examiners. The OMB also estimates a total for defense based on past experience, conversations with the secretary of defense, discussion with the president, and whoever else it thinks important.

The Spring Preview is the time when considerations involve not so much the merit of individual programs, but aggregate totals. The idea is to come up with a total that will withstand the shocks of the ensuing months, give the domestic economy and the defense establishment livable figures, and enable officials to proceed in making suballocations within an agreed-upon framework. The value of this process is that everyone starts with a similar target; the difficulty is that the target keeps moving.

At the end of the Spring Preview, the OMB sends appropriations and expenditure targets to domestic agencies. During the Kennedy and Johnson administrations, apparently, these targets were not sent to Defense but were, in a manner of speaking, kept in Defense Secretary McNamara's head or constituted some tacit understanding between him, the president, and the troika. Since Nixon's time, the military services have been given "fiscal guidance."

That is just what it is—guidance—not the ultimate destination. Bargaining goes on between the secretary of defense and others, fiscal conditions change, domestic programs show lesser or greater volatility, and fiscal guidance is, as they say, updated. Until recently, at least, the Office of the Secretary of Defense (OSD) reviewed the military budget, with the OMB sending observers but not participating directly. A final reconciliation of OSD desires and OMB preferences takes place, as usual, at the last minute.

As John Crecine said, describing the process in 1975:

> The finalization of the "Defense Number" and the "Expenditure Totals" generally occur [s] during the last half of December, after the very latest economic forecasts are available and the year-end "firming up" of the Defense totals. During the Nixon Administration the entire budget has been regularly "re-opened" in response to last-minute changes in fiscal policy. Year-end "budgetary add-ons" and fiscal stimulus (federal spending increases) have occurred several times....It is not the case that the DOD total is fixed once and for all, or for some substantial period of time. Every major shift in the economy or major legislative change that affects the costs of a domestic program (e.g., Social Security benefits) means that the whole pie is up for reslicing, at least at the margin.[1]

Early in the fall, the secretary of defense, the president's national security advisor, the secretary of state, the director of the OMB, perhaps the secretary of the treasury, sit down in an effort to iron out their differences. Not that they necessarily have to bargain; they can take their disagreements to the president. The record shows that Secretary McNamara won on every occasion he took his case to the president, and there is reason to believe that Secretary of State (or National Security Advisor) Kissinger did nearly as well. A secretary of state or defense has to be careful of the sensitivities of OMB, however, not necessarily because of its importance, but because any significant change in the defense totals may mean reallocation among domestic agencies. The president may not wish to suffer through the trauma this implies if he can help it. The OMB is better off making an agreement, instead of being reversed later, and it is not averse to maintaining a cushion of 2 to 4 percent so it will have something to give at the appropriate time. The OMB can usually keep its part of the bargain—whittling down domestic agency requests to agreed target levels—providing others keep their agreements and the world does not change too much in the meantime.

It is often said, with reason, that the final decision on the president's budget is received by the government printer on the midnight before it is scheduled to be delivered to Congress. What can happen? There may be miscalculation on entitlement programs, so they grow much more rapidly than anyone thought, or unemployment may increase faster than the administration had anticipated, or election prospects may look gloomy, or the international situation may deteriorate, or revenues may lag far behind or leap far ahead of predictions. Once any major element in the picture begins to slip—defense or domestic programs, unemployment, inflation, growth, revenue, electoral or foreign policy prospects—they can all begin to go at once, because they are predicated on some rough relationship to one another. How much better for all concerned if they can agree to live within some approximation of the initial totals they set in April and minor adjustments they can agree upon in the fall.

Where there is a will, there is also a way to come to an agreement. Supplemental appropriations are one approach. They put off into the future what cannot be decided now. The budget gets made in late fall, and then the following spring and summer additional amounts enter, especially in defense. Unless the total authorization is exceeded, no new law need be passed. Of course, this practice is limited to hard cases; otherwise everyone would come clamoring for supplements.

Another method of manufacturing agreement is to blur the relationship between outlays, the amount projected to be spent in a given fiscal year, and budget authority, the legal right of agencies to spend over a number of years. Greater budget authority, which has the effect of authorizing expenditures in future years, can be traded for lesser expenditure in the next fiscal year. Total authority to incur expenditure and actual outlays of money vary one with the other without causing major discomfort. Congress cares about immediate expenditures, as do most of those interested in fiscal policy; so they can, in effect, agree to defer decisions or to pass them on to future years and possibly other decision-makers.

The evident volatility of these fiscal and budgetary processes, the visible pulling and pushing that goes on, has suggested to some an irrational political process in which popular priorities become perverted. The people, it is said, want more social programs and instead they get excessive defense spending. Crecine's investigations cast considerable doubt on this interpretation. This is a case in which volatility hides stability.

In the period from 1953 (fiscal 1955), at the end of the Korean War, to 1979, defense expenditure did not increase at all in real terms. Crecine has calculated that defense expenditure increased on the average about 5.4 percent a year which, until recently, has about taken care of inflation. Decisions about defense, therefore, should not be looked upon as being taken on a once-and-for-all basis. Rather, given the inroads of inflation, they are taken over and over again so that popular preferences reflected in the executive and legislative branches do indeed have an opportunity to make themselves felt. Whether as a proportion of the total budget or as a percentage of gross national product, defense has, in fact, declined considerably in relation to domestic social and welfare expenditures. Only recently has proposed defense spending increased.

In the past decade the budgetary process just described has undergone considerable strain. Pressures for vastly increased spending have proved irresistible, but not enduringly attractive. As a result, members of Congress have begun to lose confidence in their appropriations committees and concomitantly in their own budgetary activities. Year by year they have withdrawn spending from the purview of the appropriations committees until only about 44 percent of the total remains. (Where has it gone? To the revenue committees or to entitlements mandating expenditures or to loan guarantees or to special quasigovernmental corporations, or, in other words, all over the place.)

The level of conflict between legislative committees and appropriations committees has risen, as evidenced by the sharp increase in annual authorizations and the frequency of challenges on the floor. The role of guardianship declined as the appropriations committees responded to insistent demands for expenditure.

The most dramatic symptom, which brought matters to a head, was the growing presidential tendency to impound funds after they had been appropriated: for a few months President Nixon virtually assumed the right not to spend even after Congress had passed an appropriations bill over his veto. Though impounding had been done by other presidents, they did not do it so often; nor did they do it after funds had been appropriated again by Congress. No one knows whether Nixon's use of the practice represents a temporary abuse of executive power or functional adaptation to a system in which Congress prefers to take the credit for spending but wishes the president to take the blame for taxing.

The failure of Congress to perform the essential task of relating revenue and expenditures in a way satisfactory to its members led to the Congressional Budget and Impoundment Control Act (Budget Act of 1974). Congress now has new House and Senate budget committees, with staff of their own, reinforced by a new Congressional Budget Office (CBO), whose task is to recommend spending limits and get Congress to make its allocations within them.

The greatest success of the Budget Act reform is its sheer survival. Unlike all other budgetary reforms in recent times it has lasted well beyond the first year. The gains are a marked improvement in the quality of data, due to the presence of CBO, and a modest increase in interest in totals as part of economic management. Congressional confidence in its own procedures, which was crumbling, has also been bolstered.

But the budget reform was not designed to reduce expenditures. If it had been, it would never have passed. The reform is supposed to enabled Congress to relate expenditures and revenues if they are so inclined with-out prejudicing the outcome. It is a procedural change, not a mandatory constraint Hence we would not expect it to alter the outcomes of the budget process To do that, as we shall see, lower limits would have to be imposed on everyone so that subtraction as well as addition, selection out as well as in, become feasible.

The Traditional Budget and Leading Alternatives

Traditional budgeting is annual (repeated yearly) and incremental (departing marginally from the year before). It is conducted on a cash basis (in current dollars). Its content comes in the form of line-items (such as personnel or maintenance). Over the last century, the traditional budget has been condemned as mindless, because its line-items do not match programs; irrational, because they deal with inputs instead of outputs; shortsighted, because they cover one year instead of many; fragmented, because as a rule only changes are reviewed; conservative, because these changes tend to be small and ineffective. Yet despite these faults the traditional budget reigns supreme virtually everywhere, in practice if not in theory. Why?

The usual answer, if it can be dignified as such, is bureaucratic inertia. The forces of conservatism within government resist change; the same explanations are presumed to fit all cases past and present. How, then, do we explain why countries like Britain departed from tradition in recent years only to return to it? It is hard to credit institutional inertia in virtually all countries for a century. Has nothing happened over time to entrench the line-item budgets? In searching for answers, let us first consider what the traditional budget has been expected to accomplish.

Purposes of the Budget

The line-item budget is a product of history, not of logic. It was not so much created as evolved. Its procedures and purposes represent accretions over time rather than propositions postulated at a moment in time. Hence we should not expect to find them either consistent or complementary.

Control over public money and accountability to public authority were among the earliest purposes of budgeting. Predictability and planning—knowing what there will be to spend over time—were not far behind. From the beginning, relating expenditure to revenue was of prime importance. In our day we have added macroeconomic management in order to moderate inflation and unemployment. Spending is varied to suit the economy. *In time the need for money came to be used as a lever to enhance the efficiency or effectiveness of policies.* He who pays the piper hopes to call the tune. Here we have it: Budgeting is supposed to contribute to continuity (for planning), to change (for policy evaluation), to flexibility (for the economy), and to provide rigidity (for limiting spending).

These different and (to some extent) opposed purposes contain a clue to the perennial dissatisfaction with budgeting. No process can simultaneously provide continuity and change, rigidity and flexibility. And no one should be surprised that those who concentrate on one purpose or the other should find budgeting unsatisfactory or that, as purposes change, these criticisms should become constant. The real surprise is that traditional budgeting has not been replaced by any of its outstanding competitors in this century.

We will attempt to explain this phenomenon by systematically comparing the traditional budget, characteristic for characteristic, with the leading alternatives.[2] By doing so we can see better which characteristics of budgetary processes suit different purposes under a variety of conditions. The characteristics, embodied in our earlier description of traditional budgeting, are (1) unit of measurement (cash or volume); (2) time span; and (3) method of calculation (incremental or comprehensive). Last, we will compare two methods of financing: appropriations and Treasury budgeting. As we go along, keep in mind that the ability of a process to score high on one criterion may increase the likelihood of its scoring low on another. Planning requires predictability, and economic management requires reversibility. Thus there may well be no ideal mode of budgeting. If so, this is the question: Do we choose a budgetary process that does splendidly on one criterion but terribly on others, or a process that satisfies all these demands even though it does not score brilliantly on any single one?

Unit of Measurement: Cash or Volume

Budgeting can be done not only in cash but by volume. Instead of promising to pay so much in the next year or years, the commitment can be made in terms of operations performed or services provided. One reason for budgeting by volume (or constant currency) is to aid planning.

If public agencies know they can count not on variable currency but on what the currency can buy, that is, on a volume of activity, they can plan ahead as far as the budget runs. Indeed, if one wishes to make decisions now that could be made at future periods, so as to help assure consistency over time, stability in the unit of effort—so many applications processed or such a level of services provided—is the very consideration to be desired.

So long as purchasing power remains constant, budgeting by volume is the same as budgeting in cash. However, should the value of money fluctuate (and, in our time, this means inflation), the public budget must absorb additional amounts so as to provide the designated volume of activity. Budgeters lose control of money because they have to supply whatever is needed. Evidently, given large and unexpected changes in prices, the size of the budget in cash terms would fluctuate wildly. Evidently, also, no government could permit itself to be so far out of control. Hence, the very stability budgeting by volume is designed to achieve turns out to be its major unarticulated premise. Stability in program levels is achieved at the cost of instability in prices.

Who—which group or positions—pays the price for budgeting by volume? The private sector and the central controller. Budgeting by volume is, first of all, an effort by elements of the public sector to invade the private sector. What budgeting by volume says, in effect, is that the public sector will be protected against inflation by getting its agreed level of services before other national needs are met. The real resources necessary to make up the gap between projected and current prices must come from the private sector in the form of taxation or interest for borrowing. The central controller also pays because he has to either raise taxes or borrow.

Time Span: Months, One Year, Many Years

Multiyear budgeting has long been proposed as a reform to enhance rational choice by viewing resource allocation in a long-term perspective. Considering one year, it has been argued, leads to shortsightedness—only the next year's expenditures are reviewed; overspending—because huge disbursements in future years are hidden; conservatism—incremental changes do not answer needs for major reforms; and parochialism—programs tend to be viewed in isolation rather than in comparison to their future costs in relation to expected revenue. Extending the time span of budgeting to three to five years, it is argued, would enable long-range planning to overtake short-term reaction and substitute financial control for "muddling through." Moreover, the practice of rushing spending to use up resources by the end of the year would decline.

Much depends, to be sure, on how long budgetary commitments last. The seemingly arcane question of whether budgeting should be done on a cash or volume basis will assume importance if a nation adopts multiyear budgeting.

The longer the term of the budget, the more important inflation becomes. If price changes are automatically absorbed into budgets, a certain volume of activity is guaranteed. If agencies have to absorb inflation, their real level of activity declines.

Multiyear budgeting in cash terms during periods of inflation diminishes the relative size of the public sector, leaving the private sector larger. Behind discussion of the span of the budget, the real debate is over the relative shares of the public and private sectors—which one will be asked to absorb inflation and which one will be allowed to expand into the other.

A similar issue of relative shares is created within government by proposals to budget in some sectors for several years, and in others for only one. Which sectors will be subject to the vicissitudes of life in the short term, and which will be protected from them? Like any other device, multiyear budgeting is not neutral but distributes indulgences differently among the affected interests.

Of course, multiyear budgeting has its positive side. If control of expenditure is desired, a multiyear budget makes it necessary to estimate expenditures far into the future. The old tactic of the "camel's nose"—beginning with small expenditures while hiding larger ones later on—is rendered more difficult.

Once an expenditure gets in a multiyear projection it is likely to stay in because it has become part of an interrelated set of proposals that could be expensive to disrupt. Besides, part of the bargain struck when agencies are persuaded to estimate as accurately as they can is that they will gain stability, that is, not be subject to sudden reductions according to the needs of the moment. Thus control in a single year may have to be sacrificed to maintaining limits over the multiyear period; and, should the call come for cuts to meet a particular problem, British experience with multiyear volume budgeting shows that reductions in future years (which may or may not come about) are easily traded for maintenance of spending in the all-important present.[3]

Suppose, however, that the government deemed it desirable to reduce significantly some expenditures in order to increase others. Because of the built-in pressure of continuing commitments, what can be done in a single year is extremely limited. Making arrangements over a three-to-five-year period (with constant prices, 5 percent a year more for five years compounded would bring about a one-third change in the budget) would permit larger changes in amount in a more orderly way. On the other hand, prices—or priorities or politicians—seldom remain equal. While the British were working under a five-year budget projection, prices and production could hardly be predicted for five months at a time.

Calculation: Incremental or Comprehensive

Just as the annual budget on a cash basis is integral to the traditional process, so is the budgetary base—the expectation that most expenditures will be continued. Normally, only increases or decreases to the existing base are considered in any one period. If traditional budgetary practices may be described as incremental, the main alternative to the traditional budget is one that emphasizes comprehensive calculation. So it is not surprising that the main modem alternatives are planning, programming, and budgeting (PPB) and zerobase budgeting (ZBB).

Let us think of PPB as embodying horizontal comprehensiveness— comparing alternative expenditure packages to decide which best contributes to larger programmatic objectives. ZBB, by contrast, might be thought of as manifesting vertical comprehensiveness—every year, alternative levels of expenditure from base zero are considered for all governmental activities or objectives treated as discrete entities. In a word, PPB compares programs and ZBB compares alternative funding levels.

Planning, Programming, and Budgeting

The strength of PPB lies in its emphasis on policy analysis to increase effectiveness. Programs are evaluated, found wanting, and presumably replaced with alternatives designed to produce superior results. Unfortunately, PPB engenders a conflict between error recognition and error correction. There is little point in designing better policies so as to minimize their prospects of implementation. But why should a process devoted to policy evaluation end up stultifying policy execution? Because PPB's *policy rationality* is countered by its *organizational irrationality*.

If error is to be altered, it must be relatively easy to correct,[4] but PPB makes it hard. The "systems" in PPB—the money, material, personnel, and practices designed to achieve given ends—are characterized by their proponents as highly differentiated and tightly linked. The rationale for PPB lies in its connectedness—like programs are grouped together. Program structures are meant to replace the confused concatenations of line-items with clearly differentiated, nonoverlapping boundaries: only one set of programs to a structure.

This means that a change in one program element or structure must result in change reverberating throughout every element in the same system. Instead of alerting only neighboring units or central control units, which would make change feasible, all are, so to speak, wired together, so the choice is effectively all or none.

Imagine one of us deciding whether to buy a tie or a kerchief. A simple task, one might think. Suppose, however, that organizational rules require us to keep our entire wardrobe as a unit. If everything must be rearranged when one item is added, the probability we will do anything is low. The more tightly linked the elements, and the more highly differentiated they are, the greater the probability of error (because the tolerances are so small), and the less likelihood that the error will be corrected (because with change, every element has to be recalibrated with every other one that was previously adjusted). Being caught between revolution (change in everything) and resignation (change in nothing) has little to recommend it.

PPB increases rather than decreases the cost of correcting error. The great complaint about bureaucracies is their rigidity. As things stand, the object of organizational affection is the bureau as serviced by the usual line-item categories from which people, money, and facilities flow.

Viewed from the standpoint of bureau interests, programs, to some extent, are negotiable; some can be increased and others decreased while keeping the agency on an even keel or, if necessary, adjusting it to less happy times without calling into question its very existence. Line-item budgeting, precisely because its categories (personnel, maintenance, supplies) do not relate directly to programs, is easier to change. PPB, because money flows to objectives, makes it difficult to abandon objectives without abandoning the organization that gets its money for them. It is better that nonprogrammatic rubrics be used as formal budget categories, thus permitting a diversity of analytical perspectives, than that a temporary analytic insight be made the permanent perspective through which money is funneled.

Zero-Base Budgeting

The ideal, ahistorical information system is zero-base budgeting. The past, as reflected in the budgetary base (common expectations as to amounts and types of funding), is explicitly rejected. Nothing is to be taken for granted. Everything at every period is subject to searching scrutiny. As a result, calculations become unmanageable. The same is true of PPB, which requires comparisons of all or most programs that might contribute to common objectives.

To say that a budgetary process is ahistorical is to conclude that it increases the sources of error while decreasing the chances of correcting mistakes. If history is abolished, nothing is settled. Old quarrels become new conflicts. Both calculation and conflict increase exponentially, the former worsening selection, and the latter, correction of error. As the number of independent variables grows, because the past is assumed not to limit the future, ability to control the future declines. As mistrust grows with conflict, willingness to admit and, hence, to correct error diminishes. Doing without history is a little like abolishing memory—momentarily convenient, perhaps, but ultimately embarrassing.

ZBB and PPB share an emphasis on the virtue of objectives. PPB is designed to relate larger to smaller objectives among different programs, and zero-base budgeting promises to do the same within a single program. The policy implications of these methods of budgeting, which distinguish them from existing approaches, derive from their overwhelming concern with ranking objectives. Thinking about objectives is one thing, however, and making budget categories out of them is quite another. Of course, if one wants the objectives of today to be the objectives of tomorrow, which is to say if one wants no change in objectives, then building the budget around objectives is a brilliant idea. However, if one wants flexibility in objectives (sometimes known as learning from experience), it must be possible to change them without simultaneously destroying the organization by withdrawing financial support.

Both PPB and ZBB are expressions of the prevailing paradigm of rationality in which reason is rendered equivalent to ranking objectives. Alas, an efficient mode of presenting results in research papers—find objectives, order them, choose the highest valued—has been confused with proper processes of social inquiry. For purposes of resource allocation, which is what budgeting is about, ranking objectives without consideration of resources is irrational. The question cannot be, What do you want? as if there were no limits, but should be, What do you want compared to what you can get? Ignoring resources is as bad as neglecting objectives, as if one were not interested in the question, What do I want to do this for? After all, an agency with a billion dollars would not only do more than it would with a million dollars but might well wish to do different things. Resources affect objectives as well as the other way around, and budgeting should not separate what reason tells us belongs together.

Insofar as financial control is concerned, ZBB and PPB raise the question of control over what? Is it control over the content of programs or the efficiency of a given program or the total costs of government or just the legality of expenditures? In theory, ZBB would be better for efficiency, PPB for effectiveness, and traditional budgeting for legality. Whether control extends to total costs, however, depends on the form of financing, a matter to which we now turn.

Appropriations or Treasury Budgeting

A traditional budget depends on traditional practice—authorization and appropriation followed by expenditure, postaudited by external authorities. In many countries, traditional budgeting is not, in fact, the main form of public spending. Close to half of public spending in the United States, as well as in other countries, does not take the form of appropriations budgeting, but what we can call "treasury budgeting." This nomenclature does not have the pejorative connotations of "backdoor spending," so called because it avoids the appropriations committees in favor of automatic disbursement of funds through the treasury.

For present purposes, the two forms of treasury budgeting that constitute alternatives to traditional appropriations are "tax expenditures" and "mandatory entitlements." When concessions are granted in the form of tax reductions for home ownership or college tuition or medical expenses, these are equivalent to budgetary expenditures except that the money is deflected at the source. In the United States, tax expenditures now amount to more than $100 billion a year.

Mandatory, open-ended entitlements, our second category of treasury budgeting, provide that anyone eligible for certain benefits must be paid regardless of the total. Until the legislation is changed or a "cap" limits total expenditures, entitlements constitute obligations of the state through direct drafts on the treasury. Were one asked to give an operational definition of the end of budgeting as allocation of resources, one would say "indexed, open-ended entitlements." Budgeting would no longer involve allocation within limited resources but only addition of one entitlement to another, all guarded against fluctuation in prices.

Obviously, treasury budgeting leaves a great deal to be desired in controlling costs of programs, which depend on such variables as levels of benefits set in prior years, rate of application, and severity of administration. Legal control is possible but difficult because of the large number of individual cases and the innumerable provisions governing eligibility.

Why, then, in view of its antibudgetary character, is treasury budgeting so popular? Because of its value in coping with conflict, calculation, and economic management. After a number of entitlements and tax expenditures have been decided upon at different times, usually without full awareness of the others, implicit priorities are produced *ipso facto,* untouched, as it were, by human hands. Conflict is reduced, for the time being at least, because no explicit decisions, giving more to one group and less to another, are necessary. Ultimately, to be sure, resource limits will have to be considered, but even then only a few, rather than all, expenditures will be directly involved, since the others go on automatically.

Similarly, calculation is contracted as treasury budgeting produces figures, allowing a large part of the budget to be taken for granted. Here, too, however, days of reckoning will come in which there is a loss of flexibility due to the implicit preprogramming of so large a proportion of available funds. For the moment, however, the attitude appears to be "sufficient unto the day is the (financial) evil thereof."

Nevertheless, treasury budgeting has one significant advantage over appropriations budgeting, namely, time. Changes in policy are manifested quickly in changes in spending. In contrast, the appropriations process requires that considerations of economic management that bear on budgeting must be introduced early in the process of shaping the appropriations budget. Otherwise, last-minute changes of large magnitude will cause chaos by unhinging all sorts of prior understandings. Then the money must be voted and preparations made for spending. In the United States, under this process—from the spring previews in the Office of Management and Budget, to the president's budget in January, to congressional action by the following summer and fall, to spending, in the winter and spring—eighteen to twenty-four months have elapsed. This is not control but remote control.

"Fine-tuning expenditures," attempting to make small adjustments to speed up or slow down the economy, do not work well anywhere. Efforts to increase expenditure are as likely to decrease the expenditure in the short run due to the effort required to expand operations. Efforts to reduce spending in the short run are as likely to increase spending due to severance pay, penalties for breaking contracts, and so on. Hence, even as efforts continue to make expenditures more responsive, the attractiveness of more immediate tax and entitlement increases is apparent.

Why the Traditional Budget Lasts

Every criticism of traditional budgeting is undoubtedly correct. It is incremental rather than comprehensive; it does fragment decisions, usually making them piecemeal; it looks backward more than forward; it is indifferent about objectives. Yet it has lasted because it has the virtue of its defects.

Traditional budgeting makes calculations easy precisely because it is not comprehensive. History provides a strong base on which to rest a case. The present is appropriated to the past, which may be known, instead of the future, which cannot be comprehended.

Choices that might cause conflict are fragmented so that not all difficulties need be faced at one time. Budgeters may have objectives, but the budget itself is organized around activities or functions. One can change objectives, then, without challenging organizational survival.

Traditional budgeting does not demand analysis of policy but neither does it inhibit it. Because it is neutral in regard to policy, traditional budgeting is compatible with a variety of policies, all of which can be converted into line-items.

Budgeting for one year at a time has no special virtue (two years, for instance, might be as good or better) except in comparison to more extreme alternatives. Budgeting several times a year aids economic adjustment but also creates chaos in departments, disorders calculations, and worsens conflict. Multiyear budgeting enhances planning at the expense of adjustment, accountability, and possible price volatility. Budgeting by volume and entitlement also aid planning and efficiency in government at the cost of control and effectiveness. Budgeting becomes spending. Traditional budgeting lasts, then, because it is simpler, easier, more controllable, and more flexible than modem alternatives like PPB, ZBB, and indexed entitlements.

A final criterion has not been mentioned because it is inherent in the multiplicity of others, namely, adaptability. To be useful a budgetary process should perform tolerably well under all conditions. It must perform under the unexpected—deficit and surpluses, inflation and deflation, economic growth and economic stagnation. Because budgets are contracts within governments signifying agreed understandings, and because they are signals outside of government informing others of what government is likely to do so they can adapt to it, budgets must be good (though not necessarily great) for all seasons. It is not so much that traditional budgeting succeeds brilliantly on every criterion, but that it does not entirely fail on any one that is responsible for its longevity.

Nevertheless, the defects of traditional budgeting remain. No instrument of policy is equally good for every purpose. Though budgets look back, they may not look back far enough to understand how (or why) they got where they are. Comparing this year with last year may not mean much if the past was a mistake and the future is likely to be a bigger one. Quick calculation may be worse than none if it is grossly in error. The road to disaster may be incremental as well as comprehensive; simplicity may become simplemindedness. Policy neutrality may degenerate into disinterest in programs. But so far, no one has come up with another budgetary procedure that has the virtues of traditional budgeting but lacks its defects.

Spending Limits

In the beginning of American history, the public sector was so small it was scarcely noticeable. By the turn of this century, the public sector was on tap, as used to be said of experts, but we-the-people in the private sector were on top. Spending at all governmental levels was just under 7 percent of the gross national product, and within that total the states and localities spent just under twice as much as the federal government.

Today federal spending has increased almost ten times (see Table 6.1), from 2.4 to over 22 percent of the GNP. And state and local spending is barely above half of the federal level. If money is power, relationships between citizens and government and between state and central government are not what they used to be.

Public spending has been growing much faster than the economy. Where one worker in twenty-five worked for the government in 1900, now the figure is closer to one in five. Projecting this trend over two decades would bring total expenditure to nearly two-thirds of whatever is produced. The United States would have changed from a predominantly private to a preponderantly public country.

Today's estimated total of loans on which the federal government has committed itself to pay all or part of the interest or principal should the borrower

TABLE 6.1

Year	Billions of spending			Per capita spending			Percentage of GNP		
	Total	Federal	Nonfederal	Total	Federal	Nonfederal	Total	Federal	Nonfederal
1902	3.2	1.1	2.1	41	14	27	6.8	2.4	4.4
1913	5.0	1.5	3.5	52	16	36	8.0	2.4	5.6
1922	9.5	3.7	5.7	87	35	52	12.6	5.1	7.5
1932	15.4	5.5	10.8	140	44	86	21.3	7.3	14.0
1940	24.0	11.8	13.2	190	90	100	20.3	10.0	10.3
1950	46.5	28.7	17.9	307	189	118	24.7	15.7	9.0
1960	79.6	48.9	30.6	439	270	169	30.1	19.4	10.7
1970	135.5	79.8	56.7	667	389	278	34.1	21.3	12.8
1977*								22.4*	

*Economic Report of the President, 1978

Source: Thomas E. Borcherding, ed., *Budgets and Bureaucrats: The Sources of Government Growth* (Durham, NC: Duke University Press, 1977), p. 26. Reprinted by permission of Duke University Press. Copyright 1977 by Duke University Press.

default is a breathtaking $400 billion (see Figure 6.1). If the borrower pays, there is no apparent cost to the country; defaults made good by Uncle Sam are included in the budget as outlays. But this form of accounting is fundamentally flawed. Credit is as good as cash; the difference between market rates and rates with government guarantees is a subsidy established by the credit of the United States federal government.

The outcome most of us would choose for total spending is smaller than the sum of individual items we choose to make it up. Deciding on the items with a total in mind is different from deciding without one. (A National journal poll shows three-quarters of Congress agreeing that spending is way too high while simultaneously failing to support a presidential cut in the first money bill of the new sessions.)

Of course, the Budget Act of 1974 allows Congress to deal with this problem by setting ceilings in advance. But these ceilings are projections or predictions, not firm limits. Nothing stops a legislator from voting for a lower ceiling and higher individual amounts. Had the reform act been a one-way street, admitting lower but not higher spending, it could not have been passed.

Where is the Institutional Breakdown?

We must ask ourselves how and why the invasion of the private by the public sector was allowed to begin and has been able to succeed. Perhaps the answer is simpler than anyone suggests: Working their will through democratic procedures, people are doing and getting what they want. Otherwise, as Brian Barry states so well, it is "important to know if the forces of electoral competition can be expected to operate in some systematic way to give people what they don't want, or more specifically to give them something that would be defeated by some alternative in a straight vote. For this would suggest that there is some kind of internal flaw to democracy... [6] Barry is inclined to believe there is no such flaw, or if there is, not of the kind that would lead to undesirably high expenditures.

FIGURE 6.1

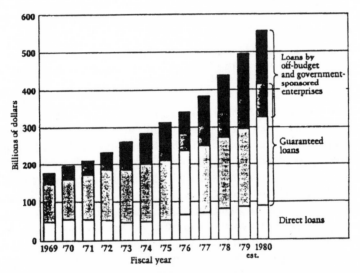

The funds advanced in a given year are simply the difference between the amount of loans outstanding at the beginning and at the end of that year. The accompanying chart shows the growth of federal and federally assisted credit outstanding in the last decade. Since 1969, the total amount of loans outstanding has risen by $263 billion, to $440 billion in 1978, an increase of 147 percent.

While most direct federal outlays are subject to periodic review in both the executive and congressional budget processes, several direct lending programs are excluded from the budget outlay totals as are all loan guarantees, except for payments of claims on defaults, certain repurchases, interest subsidies, or other installment payments. As a result, the budget understates the extent of government involvement in credit markets. In the interest of the development of a more rational credit policy, the administration OMB is proposing a new system for credit review and control.

Source: Office of Management and Budget, Executive Office of the President, *Special Analyses, Budget of the United States Government, Fiscal Year 1980*, Part F.

When I was writing *The Politics of the Budgetary Process* in the early 1960s, the federal budgetary process appeared to be a marvelous example of coordination without a coordinator. Without a central direction, expenditures were close to revenues, evidencing a slow and gentle rise that could be accelerated or reversed in incremental steps without too much trouble. What was remarkable, it seemed, was that the games the participants played fell within well-defined boundaries, their crudities and inefficiencies compensated for by keeping within the rules.

Suddenly the mechanisms of coordination—belief in a balanced budget, national political parties, congressional cohesion, a slow rate of development that allowed programs and their finances to grow together—all disappeared or were weakened. Within a generation, expenditures went only one way—up—and no one knew how to make them come down.

Why can't we recapture the "old time religion" (at least in regard to expenditure)? How can we explain the seemingly inexorable growth of federal spending—an escalation that both personal observation and opinion polls show to be unwanted by the public? A number of explanations have been advanced.

Explaining the Growth in Government Spending

Some theories hold that bureaucratic conspiracy or manipulation explains the growth of public expenditure. But as Brian Barry says, "What could anyone hope for from a system characterized by a collection of rogues competing for the favors of a larger collection of dupes?" [7]

It is necessary, once and for all, to puncture the preposterous Parkinsonian proposition that bureaucrats expand their programs indefinitely by "hoodwinking" the population. Were these programs not deeply desired by strong social elements, they would not prosper. As Frank Levy told this writer, it is not the conspiracy theory, but the "Pogo theory" that is applicable: *We have seen the enemy and they is us.*

The elegant theory of bureaucracy propounded by William Niskanen is far more intuitively appealing and aesthetically pleasing than putting the blame on ourselves. By what criteria, he asks, are bureaucrats judged and rewarded? The difference between the results they achieve and the resources their agencies consume are not among them. Bureaucrats cannot appropriate savings; neither can their agencies carry over funds. Rather, their opportunities for promotion, for salary, and for influence increase with size irrespective of success. So they will want more (much more) for their agencies and programs than citizens would prefer under similar circumstances. [8] So far so good. But why would citizens as voters elect governmental officials who would go along with this? If citizens think taxes are too high or expenditures too large, what stops them from using the ballot box to enforce these views?

One must reject the conspiratorial views of the left, known as "false consciousness," or of the right, called "fiscal illusion," not because they are wholly wrong but because a partial truth is often worse than none at all. Baldly stated, the "doctrine of false consciousness" alleges that the mass of people in a capitalist country are indoctrinated by schools, churches, the communications media, and other institutions to prefer policies contrary to their real interests. No doubt all of us mistake our interests sometimes: no one can pretend to be immune from the presuppositions of his society. On the other hand, none of us can claim to have a "true consciousness"—to know what is better for others than they do when they vote this way or that. In any event, in the current context, false consciousness would signify that expenditures are too low rather than too high, led by corporate propaganda to prefer private to public spending, which is not, as social workers say, the "presenting problem."

Stripped of its surface of complex calculation, the "fiscal illusion" view contends that because no one understands ramifications of innumerable taxes and expenditures, citizens systematically underestimate what they pay and what the government spends.[9] Undoubtedly, in view of the unfathomable billions involved, citizens may underestimate the costs of various programs. That they pay a lot, however, in sales, real estate, state and federal income taxes, and all the rest is obvious to most people. Witness Proposition 13. Moreover, at the federal level the United States uses far fewer indirect taxes, which might escape notice, than do most Western industrial nations. In short, the fiscal illusion theory appears to rest on shaky grounds.

Both false consciousness and fiscal illusion serve the function of explaining to followers why a left- or right-wing movement fails. They are the doctrines of inveterate losers. "It can't be that the people are against us, so it must be they are misguided." This is not the people of whom Alexander Hamilton spoke ("Your people, sir, are a great beast!"), but virtuous and benevolent people who, if they had the right information, would decide with full consciousness and without illusion to make the right (or is it left?) choice.

Arguing that society was affluent but public facilities were starved, John K. Galbraith insisted that individuals were indoctrinated by advertising into having artificial wants—consumption for its own sake. Government, by contrast, is unable to advertise. Citizens would be better served, he asserted, if they gave more income to government for public purposes.[10] Aside from the fact that advertising is not always successful and that people in countries without advertising appear to have remarkably similar preferences, the great question is why what Galbraith wants or what government does is superior to private preferences. Governmental advertising, in the form of public relations, actually is ubiquitous; Galbraith's complaint must really be that it is ineffective. Is he arguing that politics is superior to economics?

Not quite. Is he saying that some wants are superior to others? No doubt. What, then, distinguishes his or my preferences from yours and theirs?

Another view is Gordon Tulloch's theory that "the growth of the bureaucracy to a large extent is self-generating."[11] The trouble with bureaucrats is that they vote: the more of them there are, the more votes they have, the larger the bureaucracy grows. In support of this hypothesis, some evidence may be adduced. Civil servants on average are about twice as likely to vote as other people. Governments at the state and local levels, where most civil servants are employed, are much more labor-intensive than private industry, not only where they perform services, as Baumol's theory of increasing cost of service suggests but across-the-board. And the larger the size of government, the higher its proportion of administrative costs.[13] All this is tantalizing but far from conclusive.

Bureaucrats are by no means a majority. If one is correct in believing that, as citizens, they don't like big government much more than the rest of us, they wouldn't vote for expansion in general. (Indeed, polls report that 48 percent of those who worked for the California state government said that they would support Proposition 13.) It's only their part of the public purse they defend. The grand queries remain: Why don't the rest of us stop them or, even better, why don't their private interests win out over their public ones?

The Pogo theory, as stated before, is that we-the-people (which includes citizens, politicians, and civil servants) are doing this to ourselves. Cooperation is necessary for this game to work. We find that we don't like the end result of our actions, but that does not stop us from doing it. What makes us continue on this path?

Citizens like some governmental programs; not all, of course, but enough to want to see them go up. Unfortunately, the only way to do that is to push everything up, partly because that's the price of support from other citizens (you vote for the increase of my program and I'll vote for the increase of yours); partly because that's the necessary exchange with politicians who support our programs but others as well; partly because there is usually no way to express a position on total spending aside from the items that make it up.

Citizens want their priorities to prevail. But among these priorities is a preference for lower expenditure. Only the existence of the referendum route in California permitted voters to say that real estate taxes were too high without simultaneously having to repudiate their political parties or their representatives in the state legislature whom they may still have preferred on other grounds. Public policy requires not only an aim but an avenue of redress.

The Case for a Constitutional Amendment

A major concern about public policy is that it contains no "principle of selection," that it just grows like Topsy, mixing the best with the worst without distinction. That is one reason why constitutional amendments have been proposed in Congress that would limit spending to a proportion of the gross national product. A constitutional expenditure limitation would establish restraints that prevent piling up all solutions (old and new, good and bad), and constraints within which all have to compete, because not all can survive at the same level.

As things stand, the purveyors of public policy within government have every incentive to raise their spending income while reducing their internal differences. They can accomplish both ends by increasing their total share of national income at the expense of the private sector. As they see it, there is no need to fight among their public selves if private persons will pay. They present a bill to Congress that, in effect, must be paid by higher taxes or bigger debt. They are supported by those who view government as an engine of income redistribution to increase equality. Together, they do battle against those who stress leaving resources in the private sector so as to increase wealth. Thus conflict is transferred from government to society.

Broadly speaking, a constitutional expenditure limitation would increase cooperation in society and conflict in government. Citizens in society would have a common interest whereas the sectors of policy would be plunged into conflict. This change in the pattern of perceiving interests would come about because society would be united on increasing productivity and government would be divided over the relative shares of each sector within a firmly fixed limit. Organizations interested in income redistribution in favor of poorer people would come to understand the fatal fact: the greater the increase in real national production, the more there will be for government to spend on welfare programs and the like. Instead of acting as if it didn't matter where the money came from, they would have to consider how they might contribute to enhanced productivity. Management and labor, majorities and minorities, would be thinking about common objectives, about how to get more out of one another rather than about how to take more from the other.

So far it seems one-sided: the private economy and its supporters have always stood to gain from productivity. But in return they will accept welfare programs within the specified size of the public sector. The overriding objection to social welfare programs is not to improving living conditions of the economically deprived but is due to the fear that the public sector will grow and grow . . . until it swallows up the private sector, irreversibly altering the way of life in this country. This fear is responsible for the reluctance to accept governmental assistance to the needy as a permanent (and desirable) part of American life. Given a constitutional guarantee that government cannot keep growing by absorbing new resources, the private sector can either leave the public to its own devices or join in a common endeavor to improve the efficacy with which it delivers support to universally accepted public services.

Public involvement with private enterprise would take on a decidedly different character. "Produce more to distribute more" might be the slogan. Criticism of corporations would not be based on alleged obstruction of public purposes but on failure to increase private productivity. Industry would be instructed to perform its tasks better rather than lectured as lacking in social conscience or lagging in assuming social services. Governmental regulations that impose financial burdens on business would not be viewed as desirable in and of themselves, as if they were free, but would be balanced against the loss to the economy, on which the size of social services would depend.

Before too long, when expenditure limitation takes hold, for every major addition to federal expenditure there will have to be an equivalent subtraction. The "doctrine of opportunity costs," which states that the value of an act is measured in terms of opportunities foregone, will flourish in government agencies and the supporters of their programs will know that more for one means less for the other.

Two things will be happening at once: each agency will be figuring out how to defend what it has and how to steal a march on the others in getting new programs approved. Agencies will not be able to argue (as they always have) that their proposal in and of itself is desirable (for there are few programs utterly without merit or benefit for someone); instead they will have to show that it deserves a higher priority than others currently being considered. They will need to demonstrate defects in other agency programs. Naturally, these other agencies will defend themselves.

Instead of Congress and interested public officials having to ferret out weaknesses in agency programs, the agencies themselves will do that for us. Competition will improve information. In addition to outsiders demanding that agencies evaluate their own activities, insiders will insist that they do so as well. The opaque agency will become transparent.

Does this idyllic picture have no potential flaws? Might not the bureaucracy's accumulation of evil, like that of Dorian Gray, eventually become apparent for all to see? Might not agencies be embattled and therefore emboldened to mobilize their clientele in something like Thomas Hobbes' "War of All Against All"? Might there not, in a word, be more politics in spending rather than less? Of course. Part of the point of expenditure limitation is to make politics richer and more revealing for citizens in society. Vaunted claims for programs would be countered by opposition that is not only vigorous but informed. Political interaction can produce desirable outcomes; it is not the amount of activity but the quality that counts.

Budgetary reform would also be enhanced by expenditure limitation. Practically every year the "principle of inclusiveness"—all expenditures should be in the budget and compete on the same basis—is subject to repeated violation. Tax expenditures, as we have seen, leave sums that would otherwise be paid to government in the hands of taxpayers. These subsidies could just as well be made direct expenditures, subject to the disciplines of the appropriations process. The same is true of spending by governmentally sponsored corporations and by rapidly growing loan guarantees, the bulk of which never pass through the appropriations process. Since under an expenditure limitation amendment one program's escape from the appropriation process becomes another's deprivation, those who are dependent on appropriations will seek to ensure that those who are not are included in the process.

Kicking the Spending Habit

Each part of public expenditure is wanted by some; only the whole is unwanted. Bringing the two types of decisions together—totals over time and particular parts one at a time—is the essence of expenditure limitation. "It's only worthwhile for me to act in my best interest if I know you are also doing the same." Unless we all work within the same total, at the same time, some of us stand to get more for our favorite programs. Unless we all slow spending simultaneously, therefore, your forbearance will be my reward. So to be free to pursue what we know is best over time, we must bind ourselves against deciding issues one at a time.

This is the rationale for a constitutional amendment: If the advantages are to be obtained, sacrifices must be symmetrical There is no point in your sacrifice if I don't make mine, because the end result depends on both of us. As Vice President Walter Mondale observed, everybody is for cutting the federal budget "as long as it doesn't affect them specifically."[14] Everybody must know (to paraphrase Benjamin Franklin) that they are going to hang separately before they will be willing to hang together.

A constitutional amendment is being considered precisely because it is not an ordinary but an extraordinary rule, a rule, so to speak, that governs other rules. Such a rule is necessary because a social contract dividing the relative shares of the public and private sectors requires a solemn formulation and a secure resting place. Without a firm rule, few will make the sacrifices required to keep spending down.

A constitutional rule is also necessary to accurately reflect public opinion. Were substantial spending desired by strong and lasting majorities, the rules of the political game permit this opinion to be registered in budgetary decisions. But should there be an opposite opinion, reflecting a desire to slow down spending, it would not have an equal opportunity to manifest itself in the budget. Without the amendment there would be no way for slow spenders to get together to enforce equal sacrifice so that this became part and parcel of the calculus involved in individual spending decisions.

To increase spending, no coordination is required; everyone just does what he wants. To decrease spending, however, all big spenders must agree or those who refuse will reap the benefits. Only a constitutional expenditure limitation can create a spending constraint to which all are subject at the same time and in the same way for the foreseeable future.

Budgeting by addition, as we know, only adds up to more. That is why the people in their public capacities need to be allowed to take a standing decision on the relative size of the sectors. Not to do so is not neutral: it is a decision in favor of addition in the public sector and subtraction only in the private.

Getting Around a Spending Limitation

Skeptics have good reason to say that where there's a will to spend, there's a way around limits. At first blush, the "hydraulic analogy"—water blocked one way will flow another—would appear to promise a veritable flood of tax expenditures and guaranteed credit. On second thought, however, it's not so simple.

Expenditure limitation, as we know, will lead to a decline in the need for revenue. The normal way for this decline to manifest itself would be in a reduction in tax rates, more at the lower end, perhaps, but across-the-board as well. Lower rates mean less incentive for tax shelters, tax preferences, tax loopholes of all kinds. The moral case for tax preferences—rates are so high they penalize initiative and thwart industry—will also be weaker because, in a context of general reduction, they are less necessary.

Similarly, it would be easier to get excited over government guaranteed credit if there weren't already $550 billion worth. Imagine a politician turning the argument upside down: lower expenditures, in this view, justify higher taxes so that tax monies can be used for purposes for which direct expenditures are unavailable. One doesn't think this approach will be popular.

There would be no need to turn expenditures into "reverse taxes" if the definition or calculation of the gross national product could be expanded at will. This is unlikely. Though there is no way to guarantee that calculating the GNP differently won't happen, once it is understood that consistency—the same procedures followed two years in a row to arrive at the percentage change—is more important than content, the proper calculation is self-evident.

Alphonse and Gaston on Public Spending, or Who Will Make the First Move?

As things stand today, without a constitutional amendment limiting spending who would take the lead in reducing expenditures? Each sector of policy is concerned with its own internal development, and more money makes it easier to settle internal quarrels. Those who believe more is better for their agency or their clientele come to this position naturally. Those who favor radical restructuring of programs soon discover that such a change is exceedingly difficult without "sweetening the pie." The lessons of experience (as well as the lore of politicians) tell us that social welfare policies can only be changed if their successors are larger (and costlier) than their predecessors. Since no one once included may be left out and no level of benefit once raised may be lowered, every change leads to increased coverage and higher benefits.

What about Congress then? The congressional budget reform—the Budget Act of 1974—is superior to what it replaced, but it is a modest ameliorative move rather than a radical reform. It does for Congress what the Budgeting and Accounting Act of 1921 did for the executive by setting up procedures for relating expenditures to revenue. Its purpose is to increase the sense of self-mastery in Congress by making appropriations within a sense of total expenditures. The way it works is that the Senate and House pass a first concurrent resolution, containing an approximation of this relationship, which is then modified to take account of decisions on individual items and is codified in a second resolution whose total cannot be raised without special procedures. The budget process is now somewhat more orderly with running totals taken of decisions along the way.

The Congressional Budget Office has improved the accuracy of budget committee members by providing a competitive source of expertise, and it has made competent analysis more widely available to those who want it. But (a big but) the Budget Act, as we have seen, is not designed to act as a one-way street to reduce expenditure. Congress is encouraged to consider totals, but it has no greater incentive than before to reduce those totals. Indeed, legislators may vote to increase individual items and simultaneously vote to lower the target totals. Old entitlements are entirely outside its jurisdiction, and it only need be notified of new ones. When Congress is so disposed, the Budget Act enables it to relate desired totals to individual appropriations. This is desirable. But it is not meant to be (and it is not) inevitable.

So-called sunset laws have been suggested as another way of cutting spending. But compared to a constitutional expenditure limitation, these laws are but pale reflections of the real thing. Passed in a number of states and proposed in Congress, they require that agencies expire after a number of years, instead of continuing indefinitely, unless there is an affirmative vote. Because sunset legislation does not get at the causes of continuance but only at their outward appearance, it fails to affect anything except small and defenseless units.

Termination, as Robert Behn has written, requires terminators. It requires political attack and political defense. None of this is forthcoming. The assumption that government grows because no one pays attention is worse than foolish, for it ignores deep-seated difficulties. Actually, attention *is* focused on all agencies that matter by those who are affected by what the agencies do. Since there are so many agencies and more programs, voting for their continuance becomes *pro forma*. Because no advice or incentive is given on how to overcome entrenched interests, the sunset solution is ineffective. Why should legislators who spend all their waking hours establishing new programs and defending old ones suddenly "take the pledge"? Expenditure limitation pits agencies and programs against one another; sunset laws enable them to say they have all given one another the stamp of approval.

Is Item-by-Item Intelligent?

The last approach to be considered here is perhaps the most obvious and direct alternative to a constitutional expenditure limitation—and that is, acting intelligently on major items of expenditure. If we believe that expenditures are too high, this argument goes, we should say specifically which ones should be cut and by how much. From this standpoint, a general injunction to keep within expenditure limits is the height of irresponsibility.

The idea has much to commend it. Efforts to improve efficiency, reduce overlap or duplication, perfect procedures, all of which may be valuable as far as they go, ordinarily do not involve substantial sums that quickly cumulate into large savings. Nibbling at the edges of programs is no substitute for taking the big bites that are needed. True enough, as far as it goes, truer than the pronouncements of the alternatives mentioned previously, true under certain conditions, but not necessarily a timeless and circumstanceless truth. As useful as the approach may be in dealing with less sweeping issues, investigating individual items is misleading as a general guide to expenditure decision-making.

It is all so seductively simple it's almost sad. We decide each case on its merits and we will have a meritorious outcome. Unfortunately, things don't turn out that way. Adding one decision to another—without having to abide by a ceiling—inevitably results in a total expenditure that by common consent is too high. We conclude either that wrong results must be right, because the procedures that produce them appear reasonable, or that there is something not quite correct in what we are doing.

The traditional budgetary process has served the federal government well for most of its history. Reasonable choices have been made, conflict has been contained, legitimacy has been served. Now, in our era of big government, the traditional process appears to give us more programs and expenditures, rather than better ones. It is a good time to consider fundamental change.

Conclusion

Our purpose has been to review and appraise the federal government's budgetary process. Along the way we have considered different forms of budgeting, from PPB to ZBB, and a variety of proposed changes in the process of budgeting. If larger government is desired, the present process is pretty good. While PPB and ZBB will not do much good, they won't do much harm either. If it is deemed desirable to limit spending, not absolutely but relatively to the gross national product, radical changes must be contemplated. Asking why spending keeps rising helps us understand why existing controls are unsatisfactory. Is the present budgetary process biased in favor of spending? Is that good? If not, how might limits be made meaningful? These are the critical questions in the era of big government.

Notes

1. John P. Crecine, "National Security Resource Allocation Process" (draft, 1975), ch. 2, p. 96.
2. Cf. Allen Schick, "The Road to PPB: The Stages of Budget Reform," *Public Administration Review*, December 1966, pp. 243-58.
3. Hugh Heclo and Aaron Wildavsky, *The Private Government of Public Money: Community and Policy Inside British Political Administration* (London: Macmillan; Berkeley: University of California Press, 1974; 2nd ed., London: Macmillan, 1981).
4. This and the next eight paragraphs are taken from Aaron Wildavsky, "Policy Analyses Is What Information Systems Are Not," *New York Affairs* 4, No. 2 (Spring 1977).
5. "Lobbying over the 1980 Budget—Can Congress Say No?" *National Journal* 24 (March 1979): pp. 464 69. "If we cannot now do the job," says the chairman of the House Budget Committee, Robert N. Giaimo, "then the American people, led by the balance-the-budget people, will impose a discipline on us that we refuse to impose on ourselves" (p. 464). All of us know better—this is where we came in. The question addressed by constitutional expenditure limitation is how to get out of this box.
6. Brian Barry, *Does Democracy Cause Inflation?* Brookings Project on the Politics and Sociology of Global Inflation, September 1978, p. 53.
7. Ibid., pp. 34, 35.
8. William A. Niskanen, *Bureaucracy and Representative Government* (Chicago, IL: Aldine-Atherton, 1971).
9. On fiscal illusion, see Richard P Wagner, "Revenue Structure, Fiscal Illusion and Budgetary Choice," *Public Choice* 24 (Spring 1976): 45-61.
10. John K. Galbraith, *The Affluent Society* (Boston: Houghton Mifflin Co., 1958).
11. Gordon Tulloch, "What Is to Be Done?" in *Budgets and Bureaucrats: The Sources of Government Growth*, ed. Thomas E. Borcherding (Durham, NC: Duke University Press, 1977), p. 285.
12. William I. Baumol, "Macroeconomics of Unbalanced Growth: The Anatomy of the Urban Crisis," *American Economic Review* 57 (June 1967): 415-26.

13. Work by Elinor Ostrom and her colleagues on police suggests that size leads to over-specialization, which results in a top-heavy administration without equivalent increases in productivity. Thus small police forces keep as many men on patrol per unit of population as the larger ones. See, for example, Elinor Ostrom and Roger B. Parks, "Suburban Police Department Too Many or Too Small?" in *Urban Affairs Annual Review* 7, eds. Louis H. Masotti and Jeffery K. Hadden (Beverly Hills, CA: Sage Publications, 1970), pp. 367 402.
14. *New York Times,* 2 March 1979, all.
15. Robert Behn, "The False Dawn of the Sunset Laws," *The Public Interest,* No. 49 (Fall 1977): pp. 103-18, and *Policy Sciences* 7, No. 2 (June 1976).

References

Borcherding, Thomas E., ed. *Budgets and Bureaucrats: The Sources of Government Growth.* Durham, NC: Duke University Press, 1977.

Center for the Study of American Business, Washington University. The Congressional Budget Process: Some Views from the Inside. Proceedings of a Conference, Washington University, St. Louis, MO, July 1980.

Doern, G. Bruce, ed. *Spending Tax Dollars: Federal Expenditures,* 1980-1981. Ottawa, Canada: Carleton University, The School of Public Administration, 1980.

Doern, G. Bruce, and Allan M. Maslove, eds. The Public Evaluation of Government Spending. Proceedings of a conference sponsored by the Institute for Research on Public Policy and the School of Public Administration, Carleton University, Ottawa, Canada, October 19-21, 1978. Toronto, Canada: Butterworth, 1979.

Havemann, Joy. *Congress and the Budget.* Bloomington and London: Indiana University Press, 1978.

LeLoup, Lance T. *Budgetary Politics: Dollars, Deficits, Decisions.* Brunswick, OH: King's Court Communications, Inc., 1977.

Levine, Charles H. *Managing Fiscal Stress: The Crisis in the Public Sector.* Chatham, NJ: Chatham House Publishers, 1980.

Lindblom, C. E., "Decision-Making in Taxation and Expenditure." In *Public Finances: Needs, Sources, Utilization: A Conference of the Universities— National Bureau Committee for Economic Research,* National Bureau for Economic Research Special Conference Series, 12. Princeton, NJ: Princeton University Press, 1961.

Merewitz, Leonard, and Stephen H. Sosnick. *The Budget's New Clothes: A Critique of Planning-Programming Budgeting and Benefit-Cost Analysis.* Series in *Public Policy Analysis.* Chicago, IL: Markham, 1971.

Pechman, Joseph A., ed. *Setting National Priorities: The 1980 Budget.* Washington, DC: The Brookings Institution, 1979.

Schick, Allen, ed. *Perspectives on Budgeting.* Washington, DC: The American Society for Public Administration, 1980.

Van Gunsteren, Herman R. *The Quest for Control.* New York: John Wiley and Sons, 1976.

Wildavsky, Aaron. *Budgeting: A Comparative Theory of Budgetary Processes.* Boston and Toronto: Little, Brown & Co., 1975.

_____. *How to Limit Government Spending.* Berkeley: University of California Press, 1980.

_____, and Hugh Heclo. *The Private Government of Public Money: Community and Policy Inside British Political Administration.* 2nd ed. London: Macmillan 1981.

Wilensky, Harold L. *The Welfare State and Equality: Structural and Ideological Roots of Public Expenditures*. Berkeley: University of California Press, 1975.

Wright, Maurice, ed. *Public Spending Decisions: Growth and Restraint in the 1970s*. London: George Allen & Unwin, 1980.

7

Equality, Spending Limits, and the Growth of Government

This essay is not about why governments should choose to limit spending. If governments wish to increase spending, that is obviously their prerogative. Moreover, the evidence indicates that they are very good at it. Governments therefore need no advice on doing what comes naturally. There need be no solution when there is no perceived problem.

The problem of expenditure limitation exists only when there is a public will but not yet a public way to hold down spending. For whatever reason, governments may wish to reduce the rate of spending increases or to hold spending to a fixed level (either absolutely or in proportion to national product or national income) and find themselves frustrated.

A desire to limit spending, of course, does not necessarily mean that citizens or governments dislike all or even any individual items of expenditure. They may well like each one considered separately and yet dislike the totals to which their desires add up. The people's preferences on totals may well be at variance with their preferences on individual programs. Indeed, so far as one can judge from opinion polls, this is precisely the state of the public mind: most expenditures are approved but total spending is disapproved. Reconciling these incompatible demands constitutes the contemporary political problem of public spending.

In this context, control over spending signifies that governments are able to set totals and stick to them. Obviously, this "setting and sticking" does not happen very often. Rather, the record is one of unrelieved failure interrupted only occasionally and for brief periods with temporary successes. Both absolutely and relatively to the size of the economy, public spending keeps climbing.

Why does government grow inexorably? Why do all of the efforts in the OECD countries fail to slow spending for other than short periods? Obviously, there must be a lack of correspondence between the causes of growth and the methods heretofore employed to contain them. What measures, we must ask in conclusion, would be efficacious? We must ask this question because, if there are no solutions, there are, in effect, no problems. "Imperfection" can still be "perfect" in the prudential sense that there are no known ways of perfecting performance. But before we reach that dismal conclusion, which I believe is unwarranted, we want to review and reappraise existing theories on the rise of public spending.

Economic Determinism is a Two-Way Street

The most frequently used and accepted explanation for the growth of government is that it is caused by increasing wealth and industrialization. Whether known as Wagner's Law of Increasing State Activity (government grows faster than the economy)[1] or merely the observation that wealth and growth are related, the implication is teleological, i.e., there is an inherent logic of industrialization that propels such societies toward a greater growth of government.[2] Not so, I say. There is nothing inherent or predetermined about it. Of course, the wealthier a society, the more it has to protect; and the easier it is to spend, the larger the absolute increase in public spending. But why should industrialization, with its concomitant increase in wealth, lead to ever-increasing instead of ever-decreasing proportions of gross national product spent by government? Why, indeed, should a wealthier society be unable to provide both absolutely more and relatively less government spending? Why, to ask an even more pointed question, should people who have prospered from capitalism use that very prosperity to turn against it by diminishing the size of their economy and increasing the size and scope of their bureaucracy? The usual answer, not without its share of truth, is that capitalism not only solves certain problems but also creates others with which government is better suited to deal. But if capitalism creates more problems than it solves and does not produce enough to pay for them, resulting in perennial and growing deficits, that fails to explain why all capitalist countries are better off than their predecessors. More important for this discussion, the finding that capitalism is not worth its cost would eventually (say, within half a century) lead to its demise as the state absorbed the economy.

Viewed from a different perspective, there is nothing inevitable about the government growing faster than the economy. It is said, for instance, that in poor countries only government can raise capital for large projects. Why, then, does government grow in rich ones? It is said that capitalism causes urban growth, which leads to high-density living and the need for government to intervene so as to prevent some people from harming others. One could as easily argue that capitalism leads to urban sprawl or that big cities spawn cultural life or even that the per capita costs of public health and police services are lower in industrial centers. Although education is supposed to be essential to industrialization, to take a final example, Western nations spend from 8 to 40 percent of their budgets on that function—an observation suggesting that there is a lot of discretion left in this supposedly deterministic universe. What is missing is an explanation of why societies would want to expand the size of government.

A glance at the relative growth of public programs offers a clue. Since the end of World War II, in every Western nation, with only the partial exception of the United States since 1980, defense has continuously declined as a proportion of the budget and of GNP. Income transfer to individuals in the form of pensions and unemployment compensation and indirect transfer through medical benefits and, to a lesser extent, education account for most of the increase.[3] Observing what has gone up and down leads to the unremarkable conclusion that growth of government is fueled by a belief in greater equality of condition. When we also observe that movements to decrease social distinctions— between men and women, black and white, endangered species and underprivileged minorities, experts and laymen, authority and citizens—aim to achieve equality of condition, the growth of public spending is clearly part and parcel of the movement toward equality of condition. As long as this value increases in importance, and as long as government is viewed as an agent of redistribution of resources, government spending will continue to grow.

Where is the Institutional Breakdown?

Perhaps the explanation of institutional breakdown is simpler than anyone has suggested: working their will through democratic procedures, people are doing and getting what they want. Otherwise, as Brian Barry has stated, it is "important to know if the forces of electoral competition can be expected to operate in some systematic way to give people what they don't want, or more specifically to give them something that would be defeated by some alternative in a straight vote. For this would suggest that there is some kind of internal flaw to democracy..." [4] Barry is inclined to believe there is no such flaw, or if there is, not of the kind that would lead to undesired high expenditures. Those who hold opposing views are also troubled by the thought that the political process is right and they are wrong. Their perplexity is worth pursuing. According to James Buchanan and Richard Wagner:

> The question we must ask, and answer, is: Why do citizens support politicians whose decisions yield the results we have described? If citizens are fully informed about the ultimate consequences of alternative policy choices, and if they are rational, they should reject political office seekers or officeholders who are fiscally irre-

sponsible. They should not lend indirect approval to inflation-inducing monetary and fiscal policy; they should not sanction cumulatively increasing budget deficits. . . .Yet we seem to observe precisely such outcomes. [5]

There is a paradox of sorts here. A regime of continuous and mounting deficits, with subsequent inflation, along with a bloated public sector, can scarcely be judged beneficial to anyone. Yet why does the working or ordinary democratic process seemingly produce such a regime? Where is the institutional breakdown? [6]

Where indeed?

I emphatically do not subscribe to theories of bureaucratic conspiracy or manipulation by politicians to explain the growth of public expenditure. "What," Barry asked, "could anyone hope for from a system characterized by a collection of rogues competing for the favors of a larger collection of dupes?"[7] I wish to puncture the preposterous Parkinsonian proposition that bureaucrats expand their programs indefinitely by hoodwinking the population. Were these programs not deeply desired by strong social elements, they would not prosper. It is not the conspiracy theory but the Pogo theory (named after the comic strip character) that is applicable: *We has met the enemy, and it is us.*[8]

"They" are Doing It to Us

The elegant theory of bureaucracy propounded by William Niskanen is far more intuitively appealing and aesthetically pleasing. By what criteria, he asks, are bureaucrats judged and rewarded? The differences between the results they achieve and the resources their agencies consume are not among them. Bureaucrats cannot appropriate savings; neither can their agencies carry over funds. Rather, their opportunities for promotion, for salary, and for influence increase with size irrespective of success. Thus they will want more (much more) for their agencies and programs than citizens would prefer under similar circumstances.[9] So far, so good. But why would voters elect government officials who would go along with this? If citizens think taxes are too high or expenditures too large, what stops them from using the ballot box to enforce these views?

I reject the conspiratorial views of the left known as "false consciousness" and those of the right called "fiscal illusion," not because they are wholly wrong but because a partial truth is often worse than none at all. Bluntly stated, the doctrine of false consciousness alleges that the masses in a capitalist country are indoctrinated to prefer policies that are contrary to their real interests by a biased transmission of culture, from schools to churches to the media. No doubt all of us mistake our interests: no one can jump out of his skin and pretend that he was born anew, untouched by human hands or immune from the presuppositions of his society. None of this, however, signifies that others have a "true consciousness"—enabling them to claim authoritatively that they know what is better for us than we do. In any event, in the current context, false consciousness would signify that expenditures are too low rather than too high, led by corporate propaganda to prefer private to public spending, which is not, as social workers say, the presenting problem.

Stripped of its surface of complex calculation, fiscal illusion can be understood by everyone, because no one understands all the ramifications of innumerable taxes and expenditures.[10] And citizens may systematically underestimate what they pay and what the government spends. That they pay a lot directly and indirectly, however, is obvious to most people. Witness Proposition 13 in California. Undoubtedly, in view of the unfathomable billions of dollars involved, citizens also underestimate the costs of various programs. Since it would take only a few minutes for them to find out, however, I am not persuaded this matters much. Illusions exist, no doubt, but I doubt that they result in the euphoric feeling of escape from taxation.

Both false consciousness and fiscal illusion serve the function of explaining to followers why a left- or right-wing movement fails. They are the doctrines of inveterate losers. It cannot be that the people are against us; it must be they are misguided. If they had the right information, would the people decide with full consciousness and without illusion to make the right (or is it the left) choice?

Another view, with which I also disagree, though only in part, is Gordon Tulloch's theory that "the growth of the bureaucracy to a large extent is self generating."[11] The trouble with bureaucrats is that they vote: the more of them there are, the more votes they have and the larger they grow. In support of this hypothesis, (un)certain evidence may be adduced. Civil servants are more likely to vote than other people. Governments are much more labor intensive than private industry, not only where they perform services, as Baumol's theory of increasing cost of service suggests,[12] but also across-the-board. And the larger the size of government, the higher its proportion of administrative costs. All this is tantalizing but far from conclusive. Bureaucrats are by no means a majority. If I am correct in believing that in their role as citizens they do not like big government much more than the rest of us, they would not vote for expansion in general. It is only their part of the public purse they defend. Indeed, according to poll data, 47 percent of state employees in California said they voted for Proposition 13. The grand queries remain: Why don't the rest of us stop them or, even better, why don't their private selves stop their public selves?

Doing It to Ourselves

The Pogo theory, by contrast, is that we the people (including citizens, politicians, and civil servants) are doing it to ourselves. This is a cooperative game. We do not like it—no one said that people necessarily like what they do to themselves—but we do do it. How? Why?

It is not only the bureaucrats and their political protectors but all of us who are at the root of our own problems. Citizens like some of those programs—not all, of course, but enough to want to see them go up. Unfortunately, the only way to do that is to push everything up, partly because that is the price of support from other citizens, partly because that is the necessary exchange with politicians who support our programs but others as well and partly because there is usually no way to express a position on total spending aside from the items that make it up. Citizens want some spending more than others; they want their priorities to prevail; and among these priorities is a preference for lower total expenditure.

Bureaucrats are no better than other people. Because they actively want more, or passively cannot resist, does not mean they want the government to grow, at least not so fast. It is just that everybody is doing the same thing or they cannot get theirs without going along with other programs. Like the citizenry (indeed, they are the citizenry—at least a good part of it) bureaucrats bid up the cost of government without knowing they are doing it. As the hero used to say in those old-fashioned seduction scenes, when he was inexperienced and she was eager, "It's bigger than the both of us."[13]

Legislatures and cabinets also enjoy spending more than saving. Of all those writing on these subjects, William Riker's explanation of legislative expansion of the public sector comes closest, in my view, to the correct spirit. He said,

I think it is probably the case that, if everyone (or if all rulers in a society) agreed to do so, they could obtain the benefits of reducing the size of the public sector. But no such agreement occurs and our question is to explain why it does not. The explanation I offer is that rulers are trapped in a system of exchange of benefits that leads to disadvantageous . . . results.

The system works in this way:

Step 1: Some legislators (or the leaders of some identifiable group with access to legislators) see an opportunity for gain for some of the legislators constituents by the transfer of some activity from the private sector to the public sector. Usually such gain involves the transfer of a private cost to the public treasury....Typically, of course, the beneficiaries of the transfer are relatively small groups of citizens and only a minority of legislators have constituents in the benefiting groups. Typically also there exist other groups and other minorities of legislators who see opportunities for private gain in other transfers from private to public sectors. The combination of several minorities of legislators acting to benefit constituents are enough to make a legislative majority and so together they can produce significant expansions of the public sector.

Step 2: Such a coalition would be ... socially harmless (though perhaps unfair)....But, of course, this successful coalition is only one of many. Entirely different coalitions, some overlapping, some not, obtain other kinds of transfers to the public sector: coalitions around public works, around military bases and contracting, around regulatory bodies and the favors they pass out to various small economic interests, etc. Beyond economic interests there are ideological interests around which legislators can ally themselves to win support by satisfying deeply felt values of some constituents: racial, ethnic, linguistic, religious, moral, patriotic, etc.—all of which can be promoted by expansions of public sector activities.

The consequence is that nearly every conceivable interest, economic and political, has some legislators promoting its own fortunes in future elections by promoting governmental service to that interest.

Step 3: Since each citizen with one or several interests served by these (usually minority) coalitions of legislators benefits as the coalitions succeed and since each legislator benefits in some degree from the gratitude thus generated in marginally important voters, nearly everyone benefits from successful actions to expand the public sector. Consequently, every legislator has a driving motive to form more or less ad hoc majority alliances of these minority coalitions in order to obtain some public benefits for every interest represented in the alliance. Were a legislator to refrain either from promoting some minority interests or from joining in larger alliances to obtain benefits, he (and his constituents) would merely suffer the costs of paying for the benefits for others while obtaining no benefits for themselves.

Yet in the end the society has a greatly expanded public sector with very high costs and considerable inefficiencies. It seems very likely to me that these disadvantages are so great that nearly everybody is worse off than if the public sector expansion had never taken place. It might be supposed, therefore, that everybody would have a motive to agree to forego public sector benefits—and indeed they do. But an agreement for a grand coalition for abstinence seems well nigh unenforceable. Everyone has a motive to desert the grand coalition in the hope of getting some public sector benefit before others do so.[14]

The only difference between us is one of emphasis: Riker sees the governors exploiting the governed, and I see all of us in it together. Why did this not happen in the past and why is it happening now?

Decline of Madisonian Theory

In what he called the theory of a "compound republic," James Madison expressed his belief that the large geographic size of the country, as well as the variety of its peoples, would retard the formation of factions (which we would call pressure groups) acting adversely to the interests of others. It would, he thought, be too difficult for them to organize, confer, and act unless they were numerous and until they had secured widespread agreement. Organized interests would be few in number but large in size, reflecting in the very process of formation a general interest likely to be in accord with a shared view of justice. In his own words:

The smaller the society, the fewer probably will be the distinct parties and interests composing it; the fewer the distinct parties and interests, the more frequently will a majority be found of the same party; and the smaller the number of individuals composing a majority, and the smaller the compass within which they are placed, the more easily will they concert and execute their plans of oppression. Extend the sphere, and you take in a greater variety of parties and interests; you make it less probable that a majority of the whole will have a common motive to invade the rights of other citizens; or if such a common motive exists, it will be more difficult for all who feel it to discover their own strength, and to act in unison with each other. Besides other impediments, it may be remarked that, where there is a consciousness of unjust or dishonorable purposes, communication is always checked by distrust in proportion to the number whose concurrence is necessary.[15]

Modern technology has undermined these Madisonian premises. It is far easier and cheaper for people to get together than he could have imagined.

If modern means of communication were unanticipated, the reversal of political causality, comparable perhaps to redirecting magnetism, was not even dreamed about. Factions exerted force on government, not the other way round. Government might resist but it could never create factions. These might, as in Madison's famous phrases, be sown in the nature of man but not at the behest of government. Yet this is exactly what happens with big government. The more government does for industry and individuals, the more they have to do for it. Instead of imagining industry instigating action by government, for instance, we now know that government often acts and industry reacts, its organization being a response to an interest government has, by its behavior, newly created. Other levels of government also organize after they observe incentives created by the central government.[16] Indeed, government now pays citizens to organize, lawyers to sue, and politicians to run for office.

The larger government grows, the more policies become their own causes. The more government does, the more it needs to fix what it does. The larger government becomes, the less it responds to events in society and the more it reacts to the consequences of its past policies. Thus big government exacerbates the spending pressure it has difficulty overcoming. [17]

How is coordination carried out? Since they cannot predict the consequences of their activities, the sectors of policy adopt a cybernetic solution. They tacitly agree to cope with the consequences caused by other agencies, just as the others agree to cope with theirs. The cost of coordination is reduced to a minimum. The center becomes another sector, specialized to macroeconomic management. In return for deference on adjusting the economy, it agrees (again, tacitly) not to interfere in agency operations, which, in any case, are too many and misunderstood to be dealt with in detail. Thus, as government grows more centralized, in the sense that there are super-departments, the center disappears.

This line of sectors, each with a hand on the shoulder of the one nearest to it, could be described as engaging in a game of reverse musical chairs—when the music stops there are extra chairs to fill. Their golden rule is that each may do unto the other as the other does unto it so long as there is more for both. The litany is well known: doing well deserves more and doing badly deserves mountains of money because these unfortunate conditions must be alleviated. What must never happen to shatter the chain is for one sector to take resources from another. The rule of "fair-shares," dividing increases over the prior year and decreases from requests equally among agencies is characteristic. Funds for extraordinary programs, with special appeal, may go up so long as those for other programs do not go down. There is, in the language of evolution, selection "up" but not "out." Thus defense will not decrease but may be kept constant while welfare grows, or vice versa. How are these happy accommodations possible? Because the public sector has been able to solve its internal problems both by absorbing the growth and by decreasing the share of the private sector.

The system of incentives in central government spending makes addition easier than subtraction. Whenever there is a crunch, administrative agencies will add on the costs of their programmatic proposals; they will not, unless compelled, subtract one from the other. Subtraction suggests competition in which there have to be losers; addition is about cooperation in which (within government) there are only winners. When the economy produces sufficient surplus, spending grows painlessly; when there are shortages, spending grows noiselessly as inflation increases effective taxation or tax expenditures and loan guarantees substitute for amounts that would otherwise appear in the red. The budget grows. A downward dip now and again does not slow its inexorable progress. Budgets used to be balanced. What has happened to throw them out of kilter?

Balancing the Budget versus Balancing the Economy

Following the rule of a balanced budget was an effective mechanism for keeping expenditures down. The dislike of raising taxes exerted restraint on expenditure. Deficits were tolerated during emergencies—wartime and recession. But politicians expected retribution if they disobeyed the rule.

To say that public officials once believed in the doctrine of the desirability of a balanced budget may seem like answering one question with another. What we want to know is why this doctrine was abandoned. All these questions may be answered by focusing on the doctrine that replaced it, the neo-Keynesian idea of balance called the full-employment surplus, a doctrine under which there would almost always be a deficit. The balanced budget was everything the full employment surplus was not.

The attraction of Keynesianism itself is easy to understand. It involves just two variables—spend more when the economy is too slow and spend less when it is going too fast—that politicians on the run believe they can understand and, what is more important, can manipulate. The full employment surplus is even more attractive. Don't just balance the budget, balance the economy! Why worry about a purely technical balance when resources and people are underutilized? Spend to save. Old-fashioned ideas about the government being like the family, which must not spend more than it takes in, or inflation being connected to using debt financing and money creation to cover deficits, went by the boards. Eventually, higher levels of economic activity would generate greater revenues to bring the budget into balance. The important thing is that once balancing the economy becomes the norm, expenditure can undergo enormous expansion with the blessing of economic doctrine. The full-employment surplus norm, in a word, was a license (almost a commandment) to spend.

The old-fashioned balanced budget norm meant more than we understand today. On one side, it signified a common understanding among elites on the extent of tolerable taxation. Tax rates might go up or down but not much. Given the belief in a balanced budget in peacetime, revenues limited expenditure. The norm of the balanced budget imposed, in effect, a global limit on expenditures. Hence the maxim of opportunity costs—much more for one large program meant much less for others—actually applied.[18] Working together with the other two classical budgetary norms—annualarity and comprehensiveness—the requirement of balance meant that all major spending interests in and out of government have a common interest in restraining budget-busting behavior. No more.

Is Item-by-Item Sensible?

I have not specifically stated the most obvious and direct mode of expenditure limitation—acting intelligently on major items of expenditure. If you and I believe that expenditures are too high, the argument goes, we should say specifically which ones should be cut and by how much. If you want to cut expenditures, you must cut programs. Simply stated, these words have much to commend them. I have used them myself. I do not regret having gone along with this argument on micro matters, but analyzing individual items is misleading as a general guide to limiting expenditures.

That is what we have always done; there must be something wrong with "item-by-item" or it would have worked by now. Moreover, the lack of a limit, especially since the decline of the balanced-budget ideology, means that items need not compete with one another. Comparison of increments at the margins might indeed be sensible if it ever happened. But what really happens is that each item is not compared with but added to the others; and what we want is to substitute some subtraction for all the addition. How?

Who would take the lead in reducing expenditures? Each sector of policy is concerned with its own internal development. More money makes it easier to settle internal quarrels. Those who believe more is better for their agency or their clientele come to this position naturally. Those who favor radical restructuring of programs soon discover that this is exceedingly difficult to do without sweetening the pie. The price of policy change is program expansion. All internal incentives work to raise expenditures.

Suppose you and I agree to cut our preferred programs in the common interest. What good would that do unless everyone else does the same? And why should we if "our" loss is "their" gain?

The political process is biased against limiting spending item-by-item. Were substantial spending desired by strong and lasting majorities, the rules of the political game permit this preference to be registered in budgetary decisions. Spending is simple. Even in the face of indifference, letting things go on as they are automatically leads to increases. But should there be an opposite opinion, reflecting a desire to slow down spending, it does not have an equal opportunity to manifest itself in the budget. There is now no way for slow spenders to get together to enforce equal sacrifice so that the general rule becomes part and parcel of the calculus involved in individual spending decisions. To increase spending, no coordination is necessary; to decrease it, an enormous amount is required.

It appears that we have reached a dead end. If there were an effective ceiling, every participant would have to accept the prospect of getting less. The very thing that is desired—expenditure limitation itself—appears to be its own requisite. To explain the futility of expenditure limitation, a feeling common among would-be controllers, let us conduct a mental experiment.

Imagine an expenditure limit to which all governmental activities were subject for at least a decade and from which none could escape. Would budgetary behavior be different? What would happen inside the government and in society? Placed in wide perspective, the purpose of expenditure limitation is to increase cooperation in society and conflict in government. As things stand, the purveyors of public policy within government have every incentive to raise their spending income while reducing their internal differences. How? By increasing their total share of national income at the expense of the private sector. Why fight among their public selves if private persons will pay? They present a bill that, in effect, must be paid by higher taxes or bigger debt. Once there was a limit, however, the direction of incentives would be radically reversed.

Organizations interested in income redistribution will come to understand that the greater the increase in real national product, the more there will be for government to spend on these purposes. Instead of acting as if it did not matter where the money came from, they would have to consider how they might contribute to enhanced productivity. Management and labor would be thinking about common objectives, about how to expand their joint product rather than about how to take more from the other. Government regulations that impose financial burdens would not be viewed as desirable in and of themselves, as if they were free, but would be balanced against the loss to the economy on which the size of social services depend.

The incentive to improve internal efficiency will be immense. Knowing that they are unlikely to get more and may well get less (depending on the state of the economy and disposition of the polity), agencies will try to get the most out of what they have. Efficiency will no longer be a secondary consideration, to be satisfied if nothing else is pressing, or no consideration at all if evidence that they can do with less would reduce their future income: efficiency will be the primary path of the steady state in which they find themselves.

Two things will be happening at once: each agency will be figuring out how to defend what it has and how to steal a march on the others in getting new programs approved. An agency will no longer be able to argue that its proposal in and of itself is desirable (for there are few programs utterly without merit or benefit for someone) and that it deserves a higher priority than others being considered. Agencies will need to demonstrate defects in other agency programs. Naturally, these other agencies will defend themselves. Instead of interested public officials having to ferret out weaknesses in agency programs, they themselves will do that for us.

It would be in the interest of each participant to keep the others in line. Subtraction from someone else would become the necessary handmaiden of addition for oneself. The fiction that central controllers can do it all themselves would be replaced by the reality of spenders saving from one another. Who guards the guardians? They guard one another.

Practicing the Theory

The theory is a pleasing thought (some would say "pipe dream"), but the question of how to get from here to there, from resource entitlements (where we are now) to resource limits (where we would like to be), remains unanswered. Some countries have coalition governments that make it difficult to resist demands by one of the partners. Other countries have minority governments too weak to resist majorities. All countries have parties and politicians and pressure groups that like to preempt the process by making their expenditure preferences mandatory. In all, the politics of indexing proceeds apace: conservatives want to index taxes; progressives want to index spending; the likely result is that everything (and therefore nothing) will be indexed and we are back to square one.

Yet, without appearing to have learned much, we have learned a good deal. Negative knowledge—knowledge of what does not work—is not to be despised. Impossibility theorems make up much of what is valuable in science. So, reasoning backwards, we may begin the long march to limitation by looking at what will not work at all and what might.

There is no method that will tell governments how much to spend on this or that or whether to spend at all.[19] The methods leave much to be desired and are themselves based on value premises that require defense. How much you want, moreover, depends in part on how much you can get. Totals are not merely made out of items; items of expenditure, under any rational scheme, depend on totals. Just as one would do not only more but different things with a billion instead of a million dollars, just as where you go has to depend on what you have to get there with, a decision on totals is part of a rational choice on the parts.

Instead of searching for a magic method that would only evaporate in the mist, budgeters should seek procedures and processes that give spenders an interest in saving. Establishing global expenditure limits is one such incentive.

Are global limits desirable? That depends on what way of life one prefers—competitive individualism (capitalism), hierarchical collectivism (socialism), or equality of condition (egalitarianism). The greater the preference for equality, the larger the growth of government. If the desire for equal results declines, however, global limits to ensure that spending does not exceed economic growth would work. Two things are necessary to curb spending: a decline in egalitarianism and institutional incentives to make good that change in values.

Notes

1. See Patrick D. Larkey, Chandler Stolp, and Mark Winer, "Theorizing About the Growth of Government: A Research Assessment," *Journal of Public Policy,* vol. 1, pt. 2 (May 1981): 157-220.
2. See Harold L. Wilensky, *The Welfare State and Equality* (Berkeley/Los Angeles/ London: University of California Press, 1975); and Frederick Pryor, *Public Expenditures in Communist and Capitalist Nations* (Homewood, IL: Irwin, 1968).
3. Richard Rose, "The Programme Approach to the Growth of Government" (Paper prepared for the American Political Science Association Annual Meeting, Chicago, 1-4 September 1983).
4. Brian Barry, *Does Democracy Cause Inflation?* Brookings Project on the Politics and Sociology of Global Inflation, September 1978, p. 53.
5. James M. Buchanan and Richard E. Wagner, *Democracy in Deficit: The Political Legacy of Lord Keynes* (New York: Academic Press, 1977), p. 125.
6. Ibid., p. 44.
7. Barry, pp. 34-35.
8. See Aaron Wildavsky, *How to Limit Government Spending* (Berkeley: University of California Press, 1980).

9. William A. Niskanen, *Bureaucracy and Representative Government* (Chicago, IL: Aldine-Atherton, 1971).
10. On fiscal illusion, see Richard E. Wagner, "Revenue Structure, Fiscal Illusion and Budgetary Choice," *Public Choice* 24 (Spring 1976): 45-61.
11. Gordon Tulloch, "What Is to Be Done?" in *Budgets and Bureaucrats: The Sources of Government Growth*, ed. Thomas E. Borcherding (Durham, NC: Duke University Press, 1977), p. 285.
12. William J. Baumol, "Macroeconomics of Unbalanced Growth: The Anatomy of the Urban Crisis," *American Economic Review* 57 (June 1967): 415-26.
13. Two sophisticated studies of the causes of governmental growth are Daniel Tarschys, "The Growth of Public Expenditures: Nine Modes of Explanation," *Scandinavian Political Studies* 10 (1975): 29; and Richard Rose and Guy Peters, *Can Government Go Bankrupt?* (New York: Basic Books, 1978).
14. William H. Ricker, *The Cause of Public Growth* (Rochester, NY: University of Rochester, 1978), pp. 24-28.
15. Alexander Hamilton, John Jay, and James Madison, *The Federalist* (New York: Random House, Modern Library, 1937), pp. 60-61.
16. Samuel H. Beer, "In Search of a New Public Philosophy," in *The New American Political System,* ed. Anthony King (Washington, DC: American Enterprise Institute, 1978).
17. See "Policy as Its Own Cause," in Aaron Wildavsky, *Speaking Truth to Power* (Boston: Little, Brown & Co., 1979), chap. 4.
18. See "The Transformation of Budgetary Norms" in Aaron Wildavsky, *The Politics of the Budgetary Process,* 4th ed. (Boston: Little, Brown & Co., 1983), pp. xv-xxxi.
19. A persuasive essay is by W. Irwin Gillespie, "Fools' Gold: The Quest for a Method of Evaluating Government Spending," in *The Public Evaluation of Government Spending,* eds. G. Bruce Doern and Allan M. Maslove (Toronto: Institute for Research on Public Policy, 1979), pp. 39-60.

Part 2

The Culture of Budgeting

8

Toward a Comparative Theory
of Budgetary Processes

This book is about budgetary processes. It covers budgeting in rich countries, numerous poor ones, and American cities and states. Its focus is on budgetary processes as political instruments. Its purpose is explicitly comparative. Before the operation of the many budgetary processes we shall consider can be understood in their full "particularity," we must understand the forces at work in their utmost "generality." In this chapter, I shall define budgeting, develop a simplified model of budgetary relationships, and present a scheme for comparative analysis of budgetary processes. Why is budgeting, whatever it is, the way it is? The reason as far as I know, is because the variables I am about to discuss interact to make it so.

Definition: Budgets Serve Diverse Purposes

Budgeting is translating financial resources into human purposes. Behind currencies stand human limitations; unless nations possess an alchemist's stone for turning base metals into gold, resources are limited. But human desires are not. Hence, some way must be found to apportion available funds among competing people and purposes. Behind every government budget— which necessarily takes revenues from some citizens and distributes them to others—lies conflict. Given the infinite variety of human desires, the budget of a government can never be just one thing—it must be many.

A budget is a record of the past. Victories, defeats, bargains, and compromises over past allocations are reflected in the items included and, by inference, those left out. A budget also is a statement about the future; it attempts to link proposed expenditures with desirable future events. Budgets, therefore, must be plans; they try to determine future states of affairs through a series of current actions. Hence, budgets also are predictions; they specify connections between words and numbers on the budget documents and future human behavior. Whether or not the behavior intended by the makers of a budget actually takes place, however, is a matter of empirical observation rather than of definitional postulation.

We know there must be plans—present actions—with future consequences. Therefore, the real questions are (1) who will plan: a central ruler, decentralized (or delegated) rulers, or noncentralized (independent and competitive) rulers, and (2) how will they plan: by regulation through a central body issuing regulations or by noncentralized units acting through a price system?

Since funds are more scarce than desires, a budget becomes a mechanism for allocating resources. If the aim is to obtain desired objectives at the lowest cost, a budget may become an instrument for pursuing efficiency. When efforts are made to make money increase by considering spending a form of investment, budgets become the means for securing economic growth. Expenditures, in this market context, are economically rational insofar as they add to, rather than detract from, a nation's wealth. To the extent that governments take money from some people in the form of taxes and give it to others who benefit from the expenditures, budgets become the means of income distribution. Expenditures in an egalitarian context become culturally rational to the degree that differences in resources available to individuals and groups in society are reduced. And insofar as spending is used to maintain differences in status and power, budgets support a hierarchical culture.

The size and distribution of budgets have a good deal to say about the ways of life of a people, or, at least, the ruling elites. Like other human artifacts, budgets are cultural constructs expressing the desired relationships among people—maintaining, increasing, or decreasing the differences among them.

If organizations are seen as political coalitions, budgets are mechanisms through which subunits bargain over conflicting goals, make side-payments, and try to motivate one another to accomplish their objectives. A budget may represent an organization's expectations; it may contain the amounts the organization expects to spend. A budget may also reflect organizational aspirations; it may contain figures the organization hopes to receive under favorable conditions; since amounts requested for one purpose rather than for another often affect amounts received, budget proposals often are strategies. The total amount of money and its distribution among various activities may be designed to support an organization's goals. When a budget is used to keep spending within set bounds and to fixed purposes, it becomes a device through which some actors try to control the behavior of others. Budgets are forms of power.

Budgets are signals. As participants act on the budget, they receive information on the preferences of others and communicate their own desires through the choices they make. Here a budget is a network of communications, where information is being continuously generated and fed back to participants. Once enacted, a budget becomes a precedent; the fact that something has been done before vastly increases the chances that it will be done again. Should the document lack predictive value, however, should actual expenditures not flow from inclusion within it, a budget cannot act as a compass. No one can take bearings from it. Then one must look elsewhere for the real mechanisms of resource allocation.

Budgets with predictive value may be seen as expressing the part played by government as the most operational expression of national priorities in the public sector. Compared to party platforms and legislative laws (other than entitlements), inclusion in the budget carries a higher probability of concrete action. Little can be done without money, and what will be tried is embedded in the budget. If one asks, "Who gets what the government has to give?" then the answers for a specific moment in time are recorded in the budget. If politics is regarded as conflict over whose preferences are to prevail in the determination of policy, then the budget records the outcomes of this struggle. Let us, then, conceive of budgets as *attempts to allocate financial resources through political processes in order to serve different ways of life*. The emphasis on "different ways of life" is especially important in this second edition, deserving special emphasis. Therefore, I will attempt to show how budgeting is shaped by people supporting or attempting to change different cultures.

Model: A Simplified Set of Budgetary Relationships

To define is not necessarily to describe. Should we treat budgets as hypotheses—if the funds requested be granted, then they will be spent as promised? It remains to be seen whether and to what degree testing will validate them. It will prove useful to start by outlining a simplified model of budgeting apart from any particular environment or specific conditions other than scarcity, societal complexity, and (at least partially) conflicting preferences for expenditures. The total amount of public spending is in dispute; people partially disagree on how to spend it, and they cannot fully understand the consequences of their actions. But they do have some discretion; their actions are not totally determined by others. In this way I shall set out the terms for future discussion.

Making decisions depends on calculating which alternatives to consider and to choose. Calculation involves determining how problems are identified, broken down into manageable dimensions, and related to one another; calculations include choices as to what is relevant and who shall be taken into account. There is, therefore, a cultural component of calculation. Problems are not just out there; human determination is required to define them as worth solving. Inequalities of income may be regarded as desirable in some settings and undesirable in others, considered a problem here and a solution elsewhere.

A major clue to understanding budgeting is the extraordinary complexity of the calculations involved. In any large organization, a huge number of items must be considered, many of which are of considerable technical difficulty. Yet in most areas of policy, there is little or no theory that would let practitioners predict the consequences of alternative moves and the probability of their occurring. Man operates according to the principle of "bounded rationality." He sees "through a glass darkly." His ability to calculate is severely limited. Time is always in short supply, and the number of matters that can be encompassed in one mind at the same time is quite small. Nor has anyone solved the imposing problem of the interpersonal comparison of utilities: outside of the political process, there is no widely accepted method of comparing and evaluating the merits of different programs for different people whose preferences vary in kind and intensity.

Those who budget deal with their overwhelming burdens by adopting heuristic aids to calculation. They simplify in order to get by. They make small moves, let experience accumulate, and use the feedback from their decisions to gauge consequences. They use actions on simpler matters (which they do understand) as indices to complex concerns. They try to judge the capacity of the people in charge of programs even if they cannot appraise the policies directly. They may institute across-the-board cuts to reduce spending, relying on outcries from affected agencies and interest groups to let them know if they have gone too far.

By far the most important aid to calculation is the incremental approach. Budgets are almost never actively reviewed as a whole, in the sense of considering at one time the value of all existing programs compared to all possible alternatives. Instead, this year's budget is based on last year's budget, with special attention given to a narrow range of increases and decreases. The greatest part of any budget is a product of previous decisions. Long-range commitments have been made. There are mandatory programs whose expenses must be met. Powerful political support makes the inclusion of other activities inevitable. Consequently, officials concerned with budgeting restrict their attention to items and programs they can do something about—a few new programs and possible cuts in old ones.

Incremental calculations, then, proceed from an existing base. By "base" I refer to commonly held expectations among participants in budgeting that programs will be carried out at close to the going level of expenditures. The base of a budget, therefore, refers to accepted parts of programs that will not normally be subjected to intense scrutiny. By encapsulating the past in the present through the base, budgeters limit future disputes. Since many organizational units compete for funds, there is a tendency for the central authority to include all of them in benefits or deprivations to be distributed. Budgeters often refer to expectations regarding their *fair share* of increases and decreases. The widespread sharing of deeply held expectations concerning the organization's base and its fair share of funds provides a powerful (although informal) means of coordination and stability in budgetary systems.

The lack of an accepted base wreaks havoc with common calculations. Spending agencies do not know how much they will need. Reviewing bodies do not know how much they should allocate. Requests for spending and actual appropriations fluctuate wildly. Both supplemental appropriations, when the initial amounts are too low, and underspending, when the agency cannot spend what it has, become commonplace. New agencies and new programs frequently encounter these difficulties because they lack a necessary historical pattern of requests, allocations, and actual expenditures from which everyone can take their bearings, or, when, for any number of reasons—from lack of trust among the main participants to changes in demand for agency services to alterations of the party in power—past allocations are no longer good guides to future ones. Relationships between budgetary actors have shifted; there is a break with prior patterns, and budgeting becomes nonincremental. Over a period of years, however, a new budgetary base is negotiated as the spending agencies and reviewing organs seek stability—the one in expenditure flows, the other in disbursements. The sources of this strain toward predictability lie in the differing but complementary roles assumed by the participants in the process of budgeting.

Roles (the expectations of behavior attached to institutional positions) are part of the division of labor. Administrative agencies act as advocates of increased expenditure, and central control organs function as guardians of the treasury. Each expects the other to do its job; agencies can advocate, knowing the center will impose limits, and the center can exert control, knowing that agencies will push expenditures as hard as they can. Thus, roles serve as calculating mechanisms. The interaction between spending and cutting roles makes up the component elements of budgetary systems. Why do the main actors—advocates and guardians—behave as they do?

Wherever one unit depends on another for its income, the same kind of situation will arise; each considers its own expenditure increases to be too small to affect the total; each feels free, then, to aggrandize itself without considering the effect of that action on the nation's financial position; it does not see revenues as fixed. Agencies have seen totals altered so often they come to regard them as a kind of sleight of hand—now you see it, now you don't. Let somebody else worry about what it all adds up to.

Every agency wants more money; the urge to survive and expand is built in. Clientele groups, on whom an agency depends for support, judge the agency by how much it does for them. The more clients receive, the larger they grow, and the more they can help the agency. In order to grow larger, moreover, agencies and their clientele often seek to expand their coalitions by including more beneficiaries and increasing the funds they receive.

Resource allocation within an agency is much easier with a rising level of appropriations. The prestige of the chief within an agency depends on being able to meet employee demands for higher salaries, amenities, and programs, all of which mean additional funds. Rather than cutting some to increase others, agency heads can mitigate internal criticism by doing better for all or at least not doing worse for anyone. So long as additional funds for one agency and its programs and clientele need not mean less for others—the added amounts being taken up by increasing the overall size of government—the relationships among agencies and their associated interest groups may be cooperative rather than conflictive.

There is also the problem of relative prestige among agencies. Chiefs who can get more than their previous share of the total for new or expanded programs believe themselves (and are believed by others) to be more powerful. Since their reputations become identified with the budgetary success of their agencies, chiefs come to believe that financial growth is the road to fortune; self-interest, joined with the demands of organizational life, reinforces the tendency to overemphasize the importance of one's own unit. Thus, agencies are advocates of their own expenditures, not guardians of the nation's purse. They all want more.

And the job of a finance ministry (as central control organs will now be called) is to see that they don't get it. It is not merely cynicism or even a widespread belief that the center alone sees the whole picture. It is more that incentives for the finance ministry lie in expenditure limitation. People do not complain about a surplus, but if there is a large deficit leading to increased taxes or inflation, the ministry of finance will take the blame. Finance usually is entrusted with administering the tax process so that there is money on hand to meet pressing obligations. Its power motive can rarely be satisfied by advocating more expenditure—spending agencies take care of that. Setting priorities is done more easily by cutting at the margins than by taking over the entire work of the agencies. To exercise leadership demands a balance of sanctions and rewards, not elimination of those who are to be led.

Guardians and advocates play in a mixed motive game. Though they conflict, they must also cooperate. Both require trust. Each role implies its opposite; guardianship expects advocacy to provide a choice among items to cut, and advocacy needs guardianship to supply at least tacit limits within which to maneuver. Resources, after all, cannot be allocated without either proposals for spending or boundaries within which to fit them. The classic strategies participants use to improve their position—asking for more than they expect to get and making percentage cuts across the board—depend on keeping within accepted limits so that budgets have meaning.

Meaningful budgets, then, depend on trust and their ability to be calculated, which in turn are related to each other. A finance ministry that cannot figure out how much money it has on hand cannot determine what is available for spending agencies. Either it will give them too much in the budget, so that the money has to be reclaimed later despite the earlier commitment, or it will provide too little, so that agencies run out of funds before the end of the fiscal year. Agencies that do not know how much they can spend will ask either for too much (leaving money idle), or too little (resulting in emergency requests at unpredictable intervals). Any of these patterns of behavior necessarily reduce trust as the participants learn they cannot rely on one another or the budget. Without trust, guardians must improve the strictest controls; these controls lead to evasive action by the overly constrained advocates. Without trust, advocates are tempted to engage in gross deception or to go outside the central budget altogether; guardians then impose further restraints, until no one can count on anyone and all learn to disregard the formal budget. And disregard it they will if the connection between the amounts provided in the formal budget and the funds actually made available lose their close links.

Without general agreement on the total allowable spending, however, there is less reason for the participants in budgeting to pay attention to each other. If there is a lack of understanding of how high taxes and revenues can go, either from an inability to calculate or from disagreement over proposed levels, cooperation breaks down. There are neither sanctions for substantially exceeding past spending bids, because the sense of fair shares depends on an implicit sense of total limits, nor rewards for staying within the formal allotments, because finance cannot guarantee these funds will be forthcoming.

Variables: Size, Wealth, and Predictability

The lament of the working woman—"It's the same the whole world over"— sounds a responsive cord in regard to budgeting. Familiar behavior appears wherever one goes. Yet dramatic differences do appear among cities, states, and the federal government in the United States; between England, France, Japan, and America; and rich and poor countries. My task is to account for both similarities and differences.

First the similarities. There are constants in budgeting, no matter where practiced, that lead to regular patterns of behavior. Everywhere, though in different proportions, there are spenders and savers. Those in charge of the great purposes of government naturally tend to identify their fortunes with the interests entrusted to their care. So they defend against cuts and seek increases whenever they can. Relating expenditure to income is likewise an essential state function. Guardians of the treasury will not do well if they are forced into inflationary measures or constantly have to raise taxes because they cannot control spending. So they cut and trim and otherwise try to keep spending within hailing distance of revenues. When they fail more than they succeed, as has happened in most of the Western world since the early 1970s, or when they succeed more than they fail, as was true in the preceding quarter century, we shall want to know why. Was it their wealth, the uncertainties in their environment, or the uses their political regimes made of their opportunities?

Beyond this elemental division of budgetary roles, all participants in budgeting are overwhelmed by its complexity. None can relate the myriad factors to one another simultaneously so as simply to achieve desired allocations. Complexity appears to be a threshold variable; once the number of factors involved has grown considerably beyond the capacity of the human mind, it does not seem to matter how much more it grows. Decision-makers at the city level who are overwhelmed by eighty-six variables do not behave that much differently than those at the state level who cannot manage 860, or those at the national level who find 8,600 too much. All adopt aids to calculation. All simplify the task of decision-making by proceeding from a historical base, largely accepting what has gone before, in order to concentrate on proposed new increments. When these increments go upward and onward, life is easy for spending agencies, but hard for central controllers; when there is an allocation of increments downward, life is difficult for spenders, but easier for the treasury. All must operate in a world they can't quite comprehend. The same practices of padding, across-the-board cuts, increased spending at the end of the fiscal year, and refusal to release a proportion of budgeted funds during the year are found wherever one cares to look. At a sufficiently remote level of observation, to be sure, all objects begin to look alike. Therefore, closer inspection is in order.

Wealth matters a great deal. It can produce a surplus of resources that leads to predictability. It can but, as we are discovering, it need not. Just as wealth is created, so may it be dissipated. Needs may stay below or at the level of existing resources; however, they may also exceed them. When that happens, as we will see, uncertainty will result as surely in rich as it does in poor nations. The difference between the rich and the poor nations is that wealth provides a cushion, which takes time to dissipate. But if spending rises faster than revenue, the result is inevitable—uncertainty becomes endemic.

Now for the differences. The most important differences stem from wealth, predictability, political culture, and size. It is convenient to begin with the last. Size alone can alter relationships in the budgetary process. Although city, state, and federal budgetary practices in the United States may be described as incremental, the base from which increments proceed differs enormously. The national budget is larger by several orders of magnitude than any city or state budget. The salary for a janitor or the rental of a Xerox machine, for example, is about the same for governments of all sizes, but the expenditure represents a vastly different percentage of the total for each. Although absolute costs increase arithmetically when moving from city to state to federal levels, relative costs decrease in more of a geometric direction. For example, with a total budget of some $60 million a year, a decision to innovate with one-tenth of one percent of a city's income would involve $600,000—enough, perhaps, to set up a small office. A state spending $6 billion a year would end up with $60 million—enough, perhaps, to support a small program. A similar decision at the federal level, where spending approximates $900 billion a year, would involve $900 million—enough to fund a substantial program. A federal decision on how to spend that money might actually involve several decisions with composite alternatives. The state decision would be just that, a single decision. The city decision might look more like a reflex action than a considered choice. Scale profoundly changes the practical importance of making decisions by increments. To no one's surprise, how much there is to spend makes a great difference not merely in how much is spent but in the mechanisms for making the expenditure.

The poor and the rich nations budget in dramatically different ways. Their distinctive features can be traced to two variables: wealth and predictability. Wealth refers to gross disparities in per capita gross national product (above $2,000, below $1,000) that can be mobilized, and predictability to degrees of certainty or uncertainty regarding available resources versus likely demands for spending. Budgetary poverty, accordingly, means inability to mobilize sufficient resources (because they are lacking or because spending increases even faster) or to control expenditures or both. Budgetary uncertainty means inability to control the flow of expenditures, revenues, or both in the immediate past and to project them into the near future. Budgetary certainty stipulates precisely the opposite conditions.

The combination of certainty and largesse produces budgeting by increments. Past decisions determine most future expenditures; as commitments are kept, so present choice focuses on a small percentage (the increment) over the existing base. It is not the increment, however, but the base that is crucial, for it signifies acceptance of the past. Old quarrels will not be argued again.

In American cities that are in a poor resource position because balanced budgets are required and revenues are inelastic, we find an almost entirely control-oriented, less strategic maneuver than among the rich, and generally little opportunity for decision. Budgeting becomes a form of revenue behavior; income determines outgo. City officials know where they are, but they cannot go very far. Thus, their increments, whether up or down, are very small indeed.

The degree of incremental change varies with the type of budgetary process. Central governments in rich and certain nations exhibit the positive incrementalism that goes with growth. Their mode is onward and upward. They may use growth in resources to expand most programs proportionately, or they may create priorities by increasing some programs more than others. This is how defense spending, which was double that of welfare spending in the United States in 1960, moved to half by 1976 without declining in real terms. The incrementalism of revenue budgeting, by contrast, is smaller and, being tightly constrained, leaves less room for changing priorities.[1] The budgeting of poor nations is nonincremental because they lack the stability to maintain the base.

In poor countries, we find repetitive budgeting under which budgets are made and remade throughout the year amid endless strategic by-play. Poverty leads them to delay lest they run out of money; uncertainty leads them to reprogram funds repeatedly to adjust to the rapidly changing scene. Poor countries do not know where they are now, and the budget does not help them learn where they will be next year. Most in need of stable budgets, the poor nations are least able to secure them. They lack redundancy—the duplication that provides a margin of safety to cope with emergencies and the overlap to compensate for imperfect arrangements that is essential for reliable performance. The combination of poverty and uncertainty is devastating; these countries have little to spend because they are poor, and they find it hard to spend wisely because they are uncertain.

I cannot do better, in summary, than to reproduce Jan Erik-Lane's restatement of the budgetary theory of the first edition:

What distinguishes budget behavior in rich and poor countries is the difference in stability....If the budget behavior typical of instability is to be called "repetitive," and if the behavior typical of stability is to be called "incremental"—as Wildavsky implies—then revenue behavior is a subtype within the category incrementalism. There may be occasion to distinguish between two types of incremental budgeting: zero growth or revenue behavior, and growth incrementalism. Of course, a further distinction may be made between two types of growth incremental behavior: general growth or proportionality, and special growth within priorities. The typology must then be rendered as:

				Proportionality
		Growth		
	Incremental			Priorities
Budgeting			Revenue	
	Repetitive[2]			

Poverty homogenizes behavior. When nations are extremely poor and woefully uncertain, the consequences are so pervasive and profound as to determine almost all budgetary behavior. But this is a limiting condition. Nations may by luck or by effort get richer. They may exert self-control so as to reduce resource requirements. Were this not true, poverty would be permanent, and there would be no change. But we know this is not the case.

Rich and certain nations produce budgets with predictive value—most things that are supposed to happen during the year will happen. The redundancy created by wealth absorbs uncertainty to create the minimum stability necessary for annual budgets to be meaningful instruments of resource allocation. The formal budget and the informal understanding among the participants flash readable signals. By and large the numbers and words in the budget document refer to real events that will probably occur; that is, the specified amounts of money will be spent for something similar to the designated purposes. The ability to make a meaningful budget is a prerequisite for concern over the distributive consequences (the "who gets what") of that budget.

In the first edition, I stated:

> Budgetary processes falling in the rich and uncertain box will not be discussed in detail here because I have not been able to find accounts of contemporary governments with these characteristics. The Third and Fourth French Republics, however, did combine considerable wealth with even greater political instability. One result was the famous practice of voting "twelfths" (one month's appropriations) to pay for government services while the politicians were unable to agree on the budget. Thus, the French experienced alternating incremental and repetitive budgeting depending on the political situation.

Now, with the use of cultural theory, it is possible to explain how wealth and uncertainty may go together. The French experience should have furnished a clue: The advantage of wealth may be nullified if the differences among elites are too great (and the institutional arrangements magnify rather than mitigate these differences) to secure agreement. Similarly, if the combination of political cultures in a given country lead to a growing gap between revenue and expenditure, uncertainty may rear its ugly head. Wealth provides the wherewithal to do the work; wealth cannot, apart from human volition, determine what people do to and with it. Before we modify the old theory, however, we should seek to understand it.

Using wealth and predictability to create a fourfold table, I have classified the budgetary processes under consideration so far (see Figure 8.1): Rich and certain environments lead to incremental budgeting; poverty and predictability generate revenue budgeting; unpredictability combined with poverty generates repetitive budgeting; and riches plus uncertainty produce alternating incremental and repetitive budgeting. And this is exactly what has happened. The remaining problem, which I will address, is how to account for budgetary uncertainty in the midst of considerable wealth.

When budgetary processes operate in environments that may be characterized as poor but certain, we expect to find revenue budgeting. When environments are poor and uncertain, the characteristic conditions of repetitive budgeting appear. Rich and certain governments budget incrementally. When wealth

Figure 8.1

Five Budgetary Processes

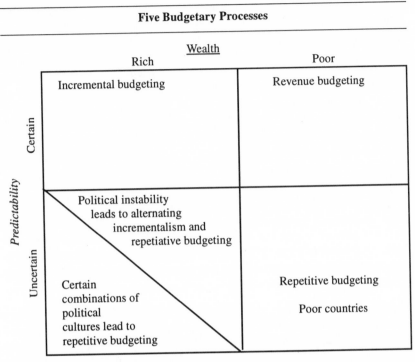

exists side-by-side with uncertainty, repetitive budgeting alternates with incrementalism. The reason for the alternation is that the cause of uncertainty is not inherent in a nation's material condition. When governments get their act together, they reestablish incrementalism; when they continue to create uncertainty, repetitive budgeting manifests itself. Just as certainty can be obtained, despite poverty, by limiting spending to conservative estimates of revenue, uncertainty occurs when wealth is present through overspending or undertaxing or both.

How can we identify and account for differences among wealthy nations? They have more in common with one another than those nations in other boxes; however, there are differences among them. Some spend and tax much more than others. They tax and spend in somewhat different ways and on somewhat different programs. Their various histories have left them with different institutions: Only Japan has an electoral party, the Liberal Democratic party, that plays a regular part in budgeting; only France has a combined presidential-parliamentary regime; only the United States possesses a legislature, independent of the executive, with significant influence over the budget; and only Britain has a cabinet that actually makes important decisions. Ways must be found, evidently, to compare the contributions of these singular institutions. Because these nations are all relatively rich, however, distinctions of degree among them must be introduced to permit contrast; unless degrees of wealth are accounted for, it will not be possible to assess the varying contributions of different political arrangements. Dissimilarities in budgeting between Britain and Japan, for example, may relate more to the large gap in growth rates than to political differences.

Absolute wealth matters in politics, but so does rate of growth. It is much easier politically to support spending out of growth, without increasing tax rates, than to take a larger share of income from those accustomed to holding on to what they have. The four rich countries that we shall examine differ substantially in their absolute wealth and relative rates of growth and, hence, in the severity of the problems posed for them in resource allocation.

To compare budgeting among rich countries it is necessary to connect wealth, taxes, and politics. The idea is to gauge the political difficulties posed for the respective governments by the increases in taxes necessary to support spending as compared with the ability of their budgetary processes to handle the conflict generated. Thus, I shall rank these nations on the degrees to which their tax rates and composition provide more or less support for spending. How well each nation handles the resulting conflicts over resource allocation depends on its political structure (relationship among institutions) and political culture (shared values justifying social practices). Evidently, institutions and culture are related. Let us take them up in turn.

Political Structure

Political structures for processing the budget differ both in the absolute number of institutions significantly involved and in their relative power. Budgetary relationships are regulated by the number of levels required to interact and by the formal authority of each.

The elites manning these political institutions are part of an orderly social scene. Interpersonal relationships are mediated by prevailing norms of conduct. The external norms affecting budgeting are as follows: the degree of personal trust among the higher civil service and politicians; preferences for face-to-face versus formal, legal, courtroom-like modes of resolving disputes; and the extent to which decisions are made on proportional grounds—that is, on the basis of treating the competing units in a uniform manner—rather than by deciding each case on its merits.

Norms of conduct—which I shall call proportionality, arbitration, and trust—are intertwined with forms of institutions. The norms of governing elites may shape institutional forms; the less they trust one another, the more levels of decisions may be needed to contain their conflicts. The institutions through which they must work shape their norms; loyalty to the chief executive cannot be the same for an independent legislature that exercises power over the purse as it is for a civil service that is tightly knit.

By combining the number of institutional levels with prevalent elite values, we can identify distinct political styles of handling conflict that percolate up through the budgetary process. The *diversionary style* practiced in the United States combines a large number of levels with extensive use of all three norms. Conflict is not so much resolved as confused, diverted, and sidetracked. The *containment* (or fortress or even "Maginot line") *style* practiced in France is an attempt to keep conflict within bounds by arbitrating disputes at many levels up the hierarchy. The Japanese, whose smaller number of levels is accompanied by an emphasis on proportionality, have an *avoidance style.* No one has to be told he is wrong; all share equally in the benefits or the miseries because proportional rewards (usually comparable increases) are granted at each level. The British follow an *absorption style.* Working with a high degree of trust and a few levels of decision, the British accommodate conflict through anticipatory adjustment: No one is expected to deny differences, but these are carried on within the overall expectation that each actor will work out his position so as to take account of the vital interests of others. That they should be able to settle is usually more important than the substance of the agreement. That is what it means to carry on Her Majesty's Government.

In this small sample of nations, the range of institutional variation is woefully restricted. Unfortunately, the wealthy do not always arrange their political lives to help students of comparative politics. These four rich countries do not vary on all the relevant institutional features, nor differ when it would suit our purposes. For example, how can we discern the general effects of partisanship when all four rich governments rank high on that dimension? How can we establish conditions for legislative effectiveness with only the United States federal government to rely upon?

An increase in the number of budgetary processes that include the desired institutional characteristics would certainly be helpful, even if that means taking account of subnational units of government. Consider partisanship. American cities are useful because they are similar in wealth (which they lack) and predictability (which they have), while differing in partisanship. Thus, it becomes possible so see that partisanship increases both the scope of the alternatives considered in budgeting and the disposition of municipal legislatures to act contrary to the wishes of the executive. The existence of parties creates the need for some sort of program, and the organization of the legislature on a partisan basis increases its cohesion. The weakness of most municipal legislatures may be traced to nonpartisan organization, part-time service, low salaries, and lack of staff support, all of which inhibit the growth of specialization, expertise, and cohesion necessary to counter the executive.

To look at American state governments is even more instructive because they differ on dimensions of special interest to us. Some combine the relative poverty and certainty of cities, while others resemble rich governments in their largesses and certitude. Yet their budgetary institutions vary greatly in authority. Thus, it becomes possible to observe how the role of the legislature and governor changes from guardian to advocate when specific institutional provisions—an item veto for the governor, a balanced budget requirement for the legislature—alter the incentives, calling forth different roles under various financial conditions. A legislature that knows that a governor has an item veto and the state a surplus, for example, is tempted to veto more funds and leave the executive with the onus of reducing them. If a legislative majority and the executive come from different parties, the legislative urge toward advocacy is enhanced.

What was once "normal" can become "deviant." And this is happening to budgeting. The norms internal to budgeting that matter most are the classical ones inherited from the nineteenth century; once so common, they are now left out of contemporary texts. I refer to the norms of balance, comprehensiveness, and annualarity. Balance provides an informal but powerful coordinating mechanism, for it establishes global limits within which spending bids must be adjusted. Spending is not supposed to exceed available revenue. Comprehensiveness requires that all (or most) revenues be placed in the general treasury and that all (or most) spending be done by departmental agencies. Annualarity imparts a regular sequence to the stages of the budgetary process. Taken together, adherence to these norms creates predictability and a sense of shared destiny; the participants are affected by one another's actions. Their transformation into quite different norms—unbalanced, disaggregated, and continuous budgeting—explains the collapse of expenditure control and, with it, the periodic appearance of repetitive budgeting even in wealthy nations. For now each agency and actor is in business for itself. Control collapses because it is overwhelmed by the desire to spend more. I shall try to show that preferences for spending (and taxing) more or less are part and parcel of different political cultures.

Political Culture

This comparison of political cultures is based on the proposition that what matters most to people is other people. Two questions are basic: Who am I—a member of a strong group that takes collective action or an individual able to transact freely with whomever I wish? What should I do? Should I do as I am told, being bound by numerous prescriptions, or should I do as I please, the only norm being the absence of physical coercion? The strength of commitment to the group or institution and the extent to which norms of everyday behavior are prescribed (see Figure 8.2) are the basic dimensions of political cultures from which other combinations are constructed.

Political culture provides motivation for the uses of resources. As soon as physical survival is assured, there is room to mobilize and allocate resources so as to do what matters most—support one's way of life. By invoking political culture, we bring back into budgeting the values and preferences that contain the differing motives for the particular use of resources in a given society.

Strong groups with numerous prescriptions combine to form a hierarchical regime. Strong group boundaries with few prescriptions form a sectarian regime—a life of voluntary consent without inequality. By uniting few prescriptions with weak group boundaries and thereby encouraging endless new combinations, the bidding and bargaining of market regimes creates a self-regulating substitute for hierarchical authority. When boundaries are weak and prescriptions strong, so that decisions are made by people outside the group, such a controlled regime is fatalistic.

Figure 8.2

The Primary Political Cultures

Group Strength

		Weak	Strong
Number		Subordination	Collectivism
of	Many	(Fatalist)	(Hierarchy)
Prescrip			
tions		Individualism	Egalitarianism
	Few	(Markets)	(Sects)

Just as an act is socially rational if it supports one's way of life, governmental budgeting is politically rational if it maintains the political regimes existing in that place and time. In regimes organized on a market basis, for instance, budgets reflect opportunity for gain by bidding and bargaining. Under hierarchical regimes in which the binding rules of social organization differentiate people and their activities by rank and status, budgets reflect that detailed division of labor. And when a sectarian regime emphasizes equality of condition, budgets are devoted to (re)distributing equal shares.

My cultural hypothesis is that hierarchical regimes that strive to exert authority spend and tax high in order to maintain their rank and status. Market regimes, preferring to reduce the need for authority, spend and tax as little as possible. Egalitarian regimes spend as much as possible to redistribute resources, but their desire to reject authority leaves them unable to collect sufficient revenues.

When rich nations mimic the poor ones by coming close to repetitive budgeting, or when poor ones achieve the certitude that used to be obtained only by the rich, governments have transcended their material conditions. When outside the grip of compulsion, governments make more or less of the circumstances in which they find themselves, the way is open for cultural explanations based not only on potential resources but also on what they prefer to do with them.

Why the Rich May be Uncertain

The spur to cultural analysis, it is time to recall, was my inability in the first edition to account for the coexistence of wealth with uncertainty. Why would nations with high per capita GNPs, large amounts of resources and fat, more than enough to get by, and the ability to withstand adversity for long periods of time, end up budgeting like banana republics? Why would these governments fail to fund all or most of their agencies by the end of the fiscal year? Why would their spending budget have to be redone several times a year? Why could agencies no longer count on receiving all the money specified in the budget? This is another way of asking why central control agencies felt it necessary to "claw back" funds previously allocated?

Wealth does provide protection against adversity. Redundancy of resources enables governments to fill in whatever is needed. Wealth is an advantage in gaining greater wealth, as it provides the wherewithal for a diversity of investments, some of which are bound to pay off. But wealth by itself is no certain barrier to its eventual dissipation. Wealth itself does not guarantee it will grow faster than it is used. There is a strong element of preference here that I shall try to tap through political culture.

If market cultures were dominant, they would spend low, tax less, and invest all over the place. If hierarchies were dominant, they would tax high and spend higher, investing enough so that each generation could pay off its promise to the future; that is, to abide by the structured inequalities of the hierarchical way of life so each generation will be better off than the last. Should the typical alliance we call the establishment be formed between hierarchy and markets, the balance between them should assure moderate taxing and spending. Sectarians, however, combine three tendencies leading to financial instability: (1) high spending in the service of equality of condition, (2) inability to collect revenues due to lack of authority, and (3) rejection of the authority exercised by others. When egalitarianism combines with hierarchy, the balance between them may be stable, the high taxing ability of the one supporting the redistributive proclivities of the other. But as the passion for equality grows, the phenomenon Scandinavians call "the scissors crisis" manifests itself: The rate of expenditure increase exceeds the rate of economic growth even in the best years. It is not the absolute decrease of revenues however, but the rapid increase in spending, coupled with the resistance to reduction, that is responsible for the growing difficulty of responding to hard economic times. For it is the purpose of existing programs, especially entitlements, to keep individuals stable while government has to scramble to maintain itself. The budgetary instability of Western nations, far from being something imposed by external forces or a product of unfortunate circumstances, is built into the warp-and-woof of their public policies. Of course, they do not want the collective consequences of the programs they have so willingly adopted. They do not want, but they may nevertheless get, the formula—the security of the citizen equals the insecurity of the government.

The United States has a little different problem, though the results are similar. It still spends and taxes considerably less than European social democracies. Therefore, it has more room to raise taxes or reduce spending. But the United States lacks one thing the social democracies possess—agreement on spending to support the welfare state. The inability to decide whether to raise taxes or to create a new tax, like the value-added tax, to reduce entitlements, to cut taxes to compel lower spending, or to increase spending and thereby insist on more taxes, leads to a continual stalemate. It is political conflict not economic decline that leads to the appearance of repetitive budgeting in the United States federal government.

The tendencies of political regimes to tax and spend in different ways are summarized in the table below. Political culture is not alchemy; it cannot make base metal into gold. But we shall see that it can do nearly the opposite—make rich countries poor in relation to their needs and, hence, make the rich as uncertain as the poor. We take our social selves with us wherever we go.

Table 8.1

Political Regime and Budgetary Process

Political Regime	Markets	Sects	Hierarchies
Power	noncentralized	shared	centralized
Authority	avoided	rejected	accepted
Objective	to increase differences	to reduce differences	to maintain differences
Budgetary Process			
Criterion of Choice	results	redistribution	process
Agreement on Base	high on totals, low on items	low on totals and items	high on totals and items
Taxes	low	medium	high
Spending	high on individual, low on public	low personal, high public	high public, low personal

Notes

1 . I owe this insight to Jan-Erik Lane's splendid review of the first edition, "Yes, Budgetary Analyses May be Conducted in Accordance with Scientific Method," *Statsvetenskaplig Tidskrift* 4 (1979): 294-298.
2 . Ibid., p. 296.

9

Prologue to Planning and Budgeting in Poor Countries

with Naomi Caiden

Imagine a wholly unlikely event: a frank speech on planning and budgeting by the head of a low-income country. While waiting for the next coup to remove him from office, our reckless leader decides to tell it like it is for the first time. He knows he is breaking faith with all other leaders in similar countries, but he is so certain of his own immediate ouster that he doesn't give a damn. And so his last public speech begins:

"My fellow countrymen, we are poor. Our per capita national income is low. In fact, ten years from now we are still likely to be very poor. Basically, it's because we were poor to begin with, and no one knows how to get rich overnight unless it turns out that the whole country sits on top of an everlasting lake of oil. One way to get rich quicker than usual is to get huge infusions of foreign capital, which is unlikely because the richer nations have gotten tired of giving it. Also there are nationalist groups that do not want us to accept the restrictive conditions or the ideological impositions that go with this aid. So, alas, we are left with the prospect of improving our living standards by our own efforts. My fellow citizens; these prospects are bleak. The only way to raise living standards tomorrow is to invest today. These investment funds won't come from heaven and we have seen they are unlikely to come from abroad. They must, therefore, come from the sweat of our own brows. Now, investment is an excess of production over consumption. In the first few years of independence we exhausted any quick and easy methods of improving agricultural production. What surplus capital remains goes toward maintaining projects we began in our first few years. There is nothing left—unless, of course,

199

I can ask you to eat less and work harder. In all the fancy economic talk you have heard from me in the past, I have managed to cloud the issue; the only way to increase funds for investments is to cut down current consumption. You don't like that, and I don't blame you. It is hard to give up the few minor luxuries one has obtained since independence. It is hard for me to turn down salary increases for teachers and civil servants. Are they not worthy? Doesn't the future of our nation depend on them? I find it even harder to say no to the desire of the armed forces for higher pay and better equipment, though I'm never quite sure in which direction their rifles are turned.

"All right, you want miracles. I can't produce them but I certainly can produce a plan. In that beautiful eighteen-volume document is a rosy future; day by day it curls at the edges, but the charts and the graphs stay resplendent. My beloved predecessor, just before he went into exile, whispered that the plan must serve as a substitute for life. As they say in Rome, the five-year plan is 'the book of dreams.'

"There was a time when I first assumed office that I loved the plan. It seemed the very stuff of reason. If our nation were ever to break the bonds of the past which kept it poor and subservient, it could do so only by conscious efforts to build a richer society. And planners were the men who offered to make the blueprints. Month by month I watched sadly as the plan dissolved under my eyes. If reason couldn't prevail, I thought, maybe power could; but I had little enough of that.

"I wish now to reply to those fashionable doctors who accuse me of sabotaging the plan because I loved the budget more. My predecessor, of course, adored the plan. When money to support it ran out, he resorted to the printing press. But inflation didn't make the plan work for long. My finance minister kept telling me there was no money to pay for what the nation wanted. Once I tried to raise taxes and nearly threw away my career. When the price of our national export fell in the world markets I had to deny more people more things. The essentials of life began to crowd out the projects in the plan. With less to spend, it became all the harder to choose among projects for the remaining money. Then I discovered something interesting: learned economists disagreed among themselves about what ought to be done; each one apparently has his own science. In the end I decided it was cheaper to pay the army and leave the planners making plans than to pay the price of the plan and be overwhelmed by the army.

"We would have been better off if we had controlled the nation's wealth, but many groups in our society have their own source of income. I tried to take it away from one after the other but often I was defeated. They were tenacious in holding on to their own. I learned that I could not coerce everyone. My experts kept talking about a national lack of coordination and an unhappy absence of integration, when what they really meant was that I could not help them defeat their opponents.

"The worst thing about the budget was that it kept disappearing on me. Now I had it and then I didn't. It looked ample enough at first. Then I found out that 10 percent went to pay off foreign loans from the past, and 80 percent went for ordinary expenses that recurred every year. Most of it went for salaries, and it was all I could do to keep them from getting higher, much less lower them. At best there was 10 percent over which I had some sort of discretion. But when our exports began to decline or our big hydroelectric projects ran behind schedule or my civil servants insisted they were starving, it turned out that there was almost nothing left. Moreover, the 10 percent of the nation's budget that I might actually allocate was not 10 percent of the nation's revenue. Far from it. Some 35 percent of our total revenue is controlled by organizations that are called autonomous because I can't get hold of their money. Thus the 10 percent of the budget I might distribute was really a much smaller proportion of the nation's total resources. It was not so much that I minded the budget disappearing, but it began to look like I would go with it.

"The parliamentary budget was beautiful. Everyone had a place in it. Why shouldn't they? The M.P.'s just took everything anybody wanted and threw it together. I didn't discourage them; why be half mad? The real budget, of course, I kept in my pocket. It was a list of who really gets what little we have. Even so, I had to revise it every two or three months because it was hard to find out how much was available. Our financial past was almost as great a mystery to me as my uncertain future.

"In the light of these painful confessions you have a right to ask why I continued with the plan. There are many reasons. We have plans because it is fashionable. How would I look if I came to you without a five-year plan? Everyone else has them. You can't get foreign aid without them. And the men we sent abroad for education need jobs someplace. In the beginning I had an idea that planners might be a useful foil against the special interests; maybe I would get some independent advice for a change. But there's no point getting advice you can't use. Mostly they told me to do good, in language I could barely understand. I wanted to be what they wanted me to be—rational, intelligent, far-sighted, etc.—but relating today's charts to tomorrow's sectoral plans was beyond me. Eventually I got the point: if things were only different than they are, we could do better. Yet when a little money was available and I asked for a good project that was well thought out and would add to national income, there never seemed to be any on hand. Or else there were too many projects, each with its own advocates. Or a project would break down repeatedly during implementation. Toward the end I realized that planners too had their own pet projects. Their idea was to invest more. Not one, it seemed, was thinking about me and how I was going to survive next month. Maybe that's why I am not.

"Still, there is one thing I haven't tried to do. There must be ways to create economic growth with a little justice even though we are poor, even though we lack basic information, even though none of us, including me, knows enough, even though we can never tell what will happen tomorrow. I promise to make at least one budget that corresponds to reality and does not rest only on our ability to print worthless money. Where there is a will, there is sure to be a way out of office."

Introduction: A Fearful Symmetry

How is national planning for economic growth carried on in the poorer countries of the world? Does it achieve its objectives? Why do recommendations so seldom end up in the governmental budgets essential for carrying them out? How does the budgetary process work in poor countries? Why do annual budgets often prove so inaccurate a guide to the actual allocation of resources? How might the characteristic conditions of these countries—economic poverty, political instability, financial uncertainty—be used to yield recommendations for reform of planning and budgeting. We shall try to answer these questions in this book. But first we must state our position on economic growth.

Poor nations undoubtedly wish to grow richer. But they also have other goals, such as more equal distribution of income, self-sufficiency, and maintenance of cultural norms, that may be incompatible with the highest rate of economic growth. We do not insist that economic growth be the highest objective, or indeed, be pursued at all. We are not so confident of the benefits of affluence that we would wish (supposing we knew how) to inflict it on everyone. Neither do we wish to suggest that it is good to be poor. There is no reason to suppose that poverty and nobility go together. So we have written this book for those who find economic growth an important (though not the only) objective and who wonder how planning and budgeting might contribute toward its accomplishment.

The quotation from Beckett, which serves as the headpiece of this book, states the elemental condition of poor countries. There is a constant quantity of tears, and of laughter too. Breaking out of these limits is the task set by their leaders.

The prologue, an imaginary speech by a leader in a poor country, evokes the central dilemma. Though he cannot make a realistic annual budget, he is expected to guide the nation through a long-term plan. He believes in planning as the epitome of rationality, but he cannot square its requirements with the conditions under which he must work. The plan provides an "automatic pilot" when he really needs strategies for coping with turbulence. Can he be helped so as to help his people? Or, as is so often implied, does he lack the will to achieve economic growth?

It seems harsh to accuse political leaders who operate under the most difficult circumstances of lacking the will to develop. They have plenty of political drive or they would not get to the top. But their actions do not manifest an unswerving devotion to economic growth. Instead, they try to reward supporters, allay regional animosities, keep prices artificially low to ward off discontent, and otherwise play down what might be called strict economic considerations.

Not everyone benefits from national economic growth; some people (often the most poor) may miss out altogether, and others may be affected adversely. The interests of the elite and the masses, the landholders and the small businessmen, and urban and rural dwellers may coincide in some distant future. But groups concerned with maintaining and increasing their current level of consumption are unlikely to relish sacrifices for the sake of other segments of the population, now or in the future. If leaders act to attain self-sufficiency by producing commodities at home at several times the cost of imports from abroad, they evidently do not place gains to national income above other values. Economic development, for them, may be a byproduct of more important political goals rather than something to be achieved for its own sake.

It would be wise, under these circumstances, to consider economic development a sometime thing. Political leaders rarely are disinterested in or singleminded about it. Those who want reform must recognize that commitment to growth is likely to be incomplete and sporadic, especially since experts disagree on how to achieve it. No doubt political leaders would be motivated to press harder for growth if they were more confident of reward for their sacrifices.

What should be done? The first chapter, "Questions and Answers: The Literature of Solutions," surveys the main lines of recommendations made by students and practitioners of economic growth, political development, and administrative reform since World War II. In most of these we observe similar trends. Faddism: over the past quarter century almost every conceivable recommendation has been made, as has its opposite. Escapism: that if only things were different, they wouldn't need to be the way they are. Confusion: as simple prescriptions fail, they are altered to take account of the innumerable actors originally left out, by which time complexity dooms them to fall of their own weight. The confusion of the reformers becomes the mirror image of the society they were supposed to help. Physician heal thyself!

Rather than assume that something must be wrong with poor countries because they will not take their medicine, we turn it around and say that the remedies have been maladapted to the organism on which they are supposed to operate; the cures will work only if the patient is already healthy. We describe that organism in the second chapter—"Poverty and Uncertainty." Here it becomes necessary to differentiate poor from rich countries. By definition, being poor signifies lack of money. But the reason poor countries have trouble getting rich is that they lack more than money; they lack capable manpower, useful data, and governmental capacity to mobilize existing resources. Less able to cope with the unexpected, poor countries suffer more uncertainty of an extreme kind, like political instability, than do rich ones. In all these respects rich countries possess what the poor countries miss: the redundancy of men, money, and institutions which let organizations function smoothly and reliably in performing complex tasks.

The reader of F. Scott Fitzgerald's novels, especially *The Great Gatsby,* knows that the rich are different from other people. Wealth provides a buffer against the world and its adversities which the poor must face up to personally. The rich man doesn't worry about losing his wallet; there is always more where that came from. Every bad turn in fortune upsets the poor man because he has so little in reserve. He trembles at risks because he has nothing to fall back on when he fails; if he doesn't succeed, he returns to squalor. The rich man can afford to fail. When he does gamble, he can afford to see it through; he need not leave the game at the first bad turn of the cards. The poor man must be better than the rich—more disciplined, more determined, more self-sacrificing—to do half as well.

While the vocabulary in chapter 2 is a little unusual, there is really nothing new in it. All we have done, actually, is to make it hard to ignore the universally recognized, abundantly documented characteristics of poor countries—poverty, uncertainty, instability. These characteristics—not, as frequently portrayed, obstacles to development—are the very stuff of life itself, and they constitute the essential conditions under which planning and budgeting must operate.

The third chapter, "The Disappearing Budget," describes the widespread practice of remaking the budget frequently during the year and explains it as a consequence of combined uncertainty and poverty. Never knowing what will come next, fearful of depleting their meager reserves, and concerned that the merely urgent will take precedence over the absolutely critical, finance ministries continually revise their expenditure priorities. Spending departments (and their clientele) seek to escape these upsets by finding their own sources of funds, further depleting the central treasury and leading to more restrictive practices, new efforts at evasion, and so on.

Because no one is sure of how much he has or will get at any time, all participants engage in the furious and incessant lobbying described in chapters 4 and 5. The cumulative costs of past decisions force out new expenditures, and a chronic shortage of funds for investment exists side-by-side with inability to spend what is available. Too much, it seems, is spent too late for the wrong things.

Enter planning to make up for the defects of budgeting. It will favor the long term over the short, expedite instead of delay, make good decisions that increase national income instead of bad ones that deplete the nation's resources. What happens is that planners end up like budgeters—only without their power.

The sixth and seventh chapters describe the life cycle of formal planning, from the effort to transform society to eventual incorporation within it. When formal planners keep a safe distance from the environmental conditions which characterize their country, they make elegant paper plans that are not implemented. When they engage actively in the decisional processes of their society, so as to increase the chances of implementing their recommendations, planners gradually become indistinguishable from the environment they were supposed to transform. Instead of their changing it, it changes them.

Planners lack power. They cannot determine what their governments will do against opposition. Little resource allocation is done in accord with the plan. Planned expenditure often does not appear in the budget document. Allocative decisions are made by political leaders and personnel in spending departments and ministries of finance in a series of ad hoc encounters throughout the year. Planners also lack knowledge. When they do make decisions, they are unable to determine the consequences. Whether they lose out to finance in the competition for power, as chapter 8 shows, or whether they just cannot control future events, planners are unable to achieve the targets set out in their plans.

How can this be? The reasonable man plans ahead. He seeks to avoid future evils by anticipating them. He tries to obtain a more desirable future by working toward it in the present. Nothing seems more reasonable than planning. And that is where the problem begins; for if planning is reason, then reasonable people must be for it. Reasonable authors, addressing reasonable readers, cannot be opposed to reason. Must we, therefore, condemn people who will not or cannot conform to national planning as irrational?

One good question deserves another: Can it be rational to fail? Now anyone can do the best he can and still not succeed. Suppose, however, that the failures of planning are not peripheral or accidental but integral to its very nature. Suppose planning as presently constituted cannot work in the environment in which it is supposed to function. Is it irrational to entertain this hypothesis? Is it irrational to pursue any hypothesis that does not confirm the rational nature of planning? The struggle for an answer in chapter 9 leads us to wrestle with the meaning of planning, for the traumas and confusions of planning are encapsulated in the multiple and contradictory meanings of that seductive term. This is not an arcane semantic exercise but an essential activity, because the ways in which men think about the word affect how they act in the world. If planning is assumed to be an inherently good way of doing things, then it is definitionally impossible either to make mistakes or to learn from them. Formal planning becomes axiom rather than hypothesis; hence, it turns itself into a mode of problem-avoidance, not problem-solving.

Not that we think badly of planners. Condemnation would only be fair if we thought they had a chance of success and were too mean or incompetent to take it. Harping on their disabilities would be more appropriate if academics and other wise men avoided (instead of plunging into) the pits into which planners have fallen.

No, the fault is not individual but systemic. Thinkers as well as doers make similar mistakes. Modes of thought as much as action are to blame, which is not to say that we know how things should be put right, but that discovering the sources of error is the first step towards overcoming them. Budgeting and planning should be means of correcting errors, not producing them.

Between thought about and action in poor countries there is a fearful symmetry. Experience reveals a convergent evolution. Confronting a similar environment, theorists and practitioners react along similar lines. Starting out to master the complex conditions of poor countries, theorists end up submitting to them. They surrender to the problems by becoming another embodiment of them. Finance ministries and spending departments play a constant sum game in which stability for one can only be bought at the expense of security for the other. They end up playing a minus-sum game in which, whatever their momentary advantage, the government is left worse off than it was at the start. Private virtues, to reverse Mandeville, become public vices. Planners recapitulate the syndrome, beginning by trying to transform their environment and ending by being absorbed into it. They become part of the problem instead of part of the solution.

Like those who have gone before us we know what is wrong with everyone else, but we are not so good at making suggestions which answer our own criticisms. If our viewpoint is accepted, formal planning should be eliminated and useful work for planners should be found elsewhere. That is difficult. Budgeting is harder. After flirting with unlikely possibilities for reducing the uncertainties that lead to repetitive budgeting we recommend making a virtue out of necessity. Rather than make believe the annual budget is meaningful when it isn't, we suggest that poor countries put their experience to good use by institutionalizing procedures for reconsideration during the year. Since the budget must be renegotiated constantly, adoption of continuous budgeting should work better than the present method. Whatever the utility of our suggestions, we do make a vigorous effort to connect them directly with the conditions in poor countries to which they should be responsive. The practices we recommend may be mistaken but they do follow from our theory.

Our proposals do not pretend to be either authoritative or comprehensive. Whatever the merits of the adage, "look after the pennies and the pounds will look after themselves," it has not often provided the answer to the question of how to get rich in a hurry. Budgeting and planning are by no means all it takes. General proposals for improving the lot of poor countries should include recommendations for redistribution of income, population control, and reorganization of international trade—that is, substantive policies as well as different ways of doing things. Some of these recommendations would be unpalatable; others would be impossible to implement; still others would be beyond the scope of the poor country in the grip of forces beyond its control. By stressing budgeting and planning, we do not mean to imply that we are preoccupied solely with capital investment. We know well that noneconomic factors—improvement in health, welfare, and education of the population—play a key part in increased prosperity, and that they are investments no less than are dams, factories, and roads. Changes in attitudes, too, are as crucial as purely technical development.

We want to add to the discussion of public policy concerned with planning and budgeting for economic growth in poor countries. To achieve this objective we must understand the circumstances under which officials in poor countries operate—in their terms as well as our own. By looking at the world the way they do, we are better able to account for their behavior and to consider ways of modifying it. Proposals for reform must be grounded in the conditions to which they are supposed to apply. By quoting extensively from participants, by paying careful attention to the features of their environment as they describe it, and by examining the explanations they give for their own behavior, we hope to create a recognizable context within which recommended change must take place. Hopefully participants in planning and budgeting will recognize in our book the world in which they work and want to use it both to explain to others what they do and to examine their own behavior.

The explanations offered here are straightforward applications of rational choice. Behavior is explained by the ways in which people go about trying to get what they want in the light of the obstacles and opportunities confronting them in their environment. First, we try to set out major constraints (poverty, uncertainty, instability) that the actors must take into account. Then we consider the goals of major institutional participants—planners, members of finance ministries, chief executives, departmental budgeters—as they interact. These actors assume roles attached to positions they occupy in their institutions—guarding the treasury versus advocating expenditures, expanding the economy versus securing financial stability. The patterns of actions observed (targets set out in national economic plans are rarely achieved; expenditures recommended by the plans seldom find their way into the country's budget; the budget documents do not predict well what will be spent) are explained by the interplay of these participants as they seek to achieve their objectives within the existing constraints.

In appraising our efforts, attention must be paid to our methods and their limitations. This study covers over eighty nations and three-quarters of the world's peoples. Membership in our sample requires only that a nation have a gross national product (GNP) per capita of less than $800 per year, a figure adopted for convenience because the $800 figure allowed for variation among the poor but still set them apart from the rich.

Both the extensive literature on planning and the scanty material on budgeting in these countries varied in coverage and quality. There was nothing solid about budgeting at all, and there were no substantial accounts of how expenditures were determined in any country. We had to depend on fragmentary glimpses found in literature devoted to different purposes. Planning was better covered, but the material was uneven in quality (ranging from major classics and insightful country studies to superficial public relations handouts) and disappointing in that there were huge gaps in almost all dimensions. Many plans existed, but there was little information about how they were put together or how planners worked with them. Often it was not possible to compare original aims with later achievements because neither was known. But then a basic characteristic of poor countries is a pervasive lack of essential information. Budgetary data are rarely trustworthy. How, for instance, can one analyze expenditure patterns in Nepal when audits for the years 1950-65 have been abandoned and only about a quarter of the accounts since that time have been scrutinized? Statistics are largely unreliable when they are available, which is seldom. We were forced, therefore, to use information which varied in quantity and quality, and in a large number of countries we could not make consistent comparisons among categories.

In order to supplement written sources and to gather new data, we chose a dozen nations for intensive interviewing, lasting approximately one month each. Our major criteria were geographic location (so as to cover the major continents), relative poverty (so as to include nations with income from under $100 to $800), and availability (to ensure that our time would be spent interviewing people who would talk freely to us). Timely events influenced our prospects. We did not interview in the Middle East because the summer of 1970 was not a propitious time for Americans to be in Arab countries. A special rationale resulted in excluding East European countries; we did not want to become involved in the usual discussions of price systems versus central decision making.

We ended up with Ghana and Uganda in Africa; Argentina, Chile, and Peru in South America; Indonesia, the Philippines, Malaysia, and Thailand in Southeast Asia; and Ceylon and Nepal in South Asia. Their per capita income is appropriately spread out. Beyond that, much fault can be found with our selection.

French-speaking African countries were omitted because our budget did not permit us to send another interviewer; our best trained person spoke only English. Moreover, it was more difficult to interview in Africa than elsewhere, so we dropped one country from our total. We certainly could have picked poorer countries in Latin America than we did, but here was our chance to see if a bit more money made a difference. Why was India omitted from South Asia, in view of her importance? We had read several detailed books and many articles about it, and we thought it too vast for the time available. Wildavsky did spend a few days there chiefly picking up available material from men who had had a chance to study India for long periods. Why did we omit any reader's favorite country? Lack of wisdom, absence of foresight. As a whole we think the group is as defensible as any other, providing one understands it is not possible to study everything, nor desirable to devote a lifetime to a book that, as part of its purpose, hopes to teach us something about contemporary problems.

Our four interviewers were graduate students in the Political Science Department in Berkeley. They conducted the following number of interviews in the countries indicated: Pat Anglim (28 in Ghana and Uganda); Peter Cleaves (76 in Argentina, Chile, Peru, and 3 other Latin American countries); Ted Smith (25 in Indonesia and the Philippines); Vicharat Vichit-Vadakan, a Thai national (26 in Malaysia and Thailand). In addition, Aaron Wildavsky carried out 17 interviews in Ceylon and 29 in Nepal. Thus a total of 204 interviews were used in writing this book. The student interviews were done in the summer of 1970 and Wildavsky's in the spring of 1971.

Interviews lasted from thirty minutes to several hours. They were based on separate questionnaires for planners and budgeters. ("How do you get money for something not in the plan?" "How do you know if the estimates are reliable?") The questions were open-ended to enable each respondent to reveal as much of his experience as he was willing. Interviewers asked the questions, probed each answer as deeply as they could, took notes, and wrote up the responses immediately thereafter in as much detail as they could manage. Not every respondent was willing or able to answer each question. After initial drafts of the chapters describing planning and budgeting were completed, we ferreted out anyone we could find with practical experience to check on disputed points. We consulted well over a hundred people for brief queries, extended conversations, and ultimately for more formal criticism of the manuscript.

We did not subject the protocols of our interviews to a precise frequency count. To say that a certain phrase or theme recurred 61.8 percent of the time would lend our work a spurious specificity, wholly out of keeping with the conditions under which it was collected or the uses to which it is put. Our interviews were affected by such factors as the time an official had available, his disposition to tell what he knew, the sensitivity of certain subjects, political conditions in the country at the time, the health of interviewers in unusual climates, and so on. The best we can hope for is that the interviews do not falsify main tendencies. A better check on their validity than number counts is the test of closure. A basic reason Wildavsky went to Ceylon and Nepal was to determine whether behavior reported in prior interviews reappeared. He was able to determine, to his satisfaction at least, that the data essentially reinforced past impressions. The less new information supplied by later interviews, the more confident a researcher can be that he has exhausted information available from that source.

Note carefully that the purpose of the interviews is not to provide a record of contemporary events but to describe how a process works. Information on parts of the process unobtainable for some countries can be fitted in from places where our access is better. We want a composite picture (with appropriate indication of differences) of poor countries in general rather than any one country in particular.

In this book, we try to describe the process through which plans and budgets are made and to some degree, implemented. At every step we try to point out the central tendency and to illustrate it with many examples. We use phrases like "universal" for a customary practice, and a word like "typical" for one occurring most of the time in countries for which evidence is available. Should practices appear to vary significantly from one country to another, we tell the reader what is happening as best we can. We deal initially with major tendencies and then with variations on the theme. The sense of process thus should be preserved along with a feeling for the inevitable differences around the world. The amazing things, we believe, are not the differences, but rather the remarkable number of similarities, despite variations in wealth, culture, and political systems.

How do we know whether our descriptions of behavior in planning and budgeting are accurate, and our explanations adequate? How could our theory be falsified? New studies could be made that would show markedly different patterns of behavior in planning and budgeting. Contrary to our findings, plans could be shown to be instruments for controlling futures, and budgets, means of implementing them. Certain propositions, such as the tendency of finance ministries to estimate revenues low and expenditures high, could be given better tests by locating appropriate financial data and establishing their validity. We would have liked to have done this, but we could not find data in which we could place sufficient credence.

How do we justify the use of data—scholarly reports, documents compiled by practitioners, and interviews with participants—taken from different countries at various times and incomplete for most countries at any period of the time? We have described the composite method by which we took steps in the processes of planning and budgeting and applied to each whatever data were at hand even though it came from the same country in different periods or from different nations altogether. If our work is seen as an attempt to create theory, then the proper test is not how it was derived but how well it stands up to the tests of experience. Employing a similar method in regard to federal budgeting in the United States, Wildavsky and his associates were able to provide critical empirical tests, not because the descriptive material was collected more systematically, but because good data could be collected to test the most critical hypotheses.[1] There is no reason in principle why the same could not be done for poor countries, although the task of collection and validation would be much more onerous.

A study of the United States, though it may include numerous federal agencies, presumably takes place within a homogeneous cultural context. How can we justify generalizations that do not take culture into account when our study covers nations in different continents of the world whose cultures must vary enormously?

Why haven't we used the concept of culture? Like everyone else, we realize that poor nations around the world display a remarkable variety of cultures that must affect their planning and budgeting. But how? Cultures differ, but behavior in regard to planning and budgeting is remarkably similar; it would undoubtedly be hard to explain the things these nations have in common by the features that separate them. We also confess to being in some doubt about how to use the concept of culture for predictive purposes. There are no standard cultural categories into which these eighty-odd nations can readily be put, nor are there propositions linking a category of culture to a pattern of action. What we do find in the literature, which further explains our reluctance to use the concept of culture, is its casual use as a residual category. When all other explanations fail, the analyst can always try to save the situation by saying that some amorphous glob called culture is responsible for the phenomenon he cannot explain. To explain uniformity in behavior we must seek uniformity in conditions. Poor nations lack a common culture; they share poverty and uncertainty.

As political scientists it may seem strange that we do not provide extensive discussions of political structure. Beyond brief recognition of differences between parliamentary and presidential forms, which may give a different cast to legislatures and finance ministries, we say little about such subjects as single versus multi-party structures or military versus civilian regimes, though we do cover the military's part in resource allocation. Instead, we talk about strong and weak, more or less stable governments. The reason is that we are interested in the ability of governments to mobilize resources, and we get no help in classification from the literature on political development.

At any one time, there is no accepted classification of political variables across nations and little understanding of their consequences. None of the familiar categories are attached to differential capacity to raise revenue or allocate public money. Insofar as we ask the question, "What difference do they make to planning and budgeting?", the answer must be, "Very little that anyone knows about." Politics matters, we conclude, but not in ways that would be illuminated by any extant discussion of political variables more sophisticated than the elementary ones we use.

Forms of planning and budgeting in poor countries are essentially alike, partly because they are copied from Soviet, European, and (in a few instances) American models and partly because they have evolved in response to similar environmental forces. Government is part of the environment of uncertainty and poverty. It also acts on that environment. But governments have not achieved mastery yet; that is part of what it means to be poor. To no one's surprise, poor societies have poor governments. Rulers may be firmly entrenched but they lack ability either to mobilize sufficient resources or to allocate them productively, or both. If anyone understands how to change politics to improve governments so as to enhance welfare, he has made himself scarcer than these other rare goods. Anyway, we think a little work ought to be left for other students of the subject

Our composite approach raises the question also of the degree to which the patterns we describe and the theories we propose to account for them can be applied to any specific country. We think they mostly can, providing their limitations are recognized. If differences between poor countries are overemphasized, each one will have to be treated as entirely unique. Many theories would be required instead of a few. Yet theories would be difficult to construct if comparability with other countries were denied. Of equal practical importance would be the inability of practitioners in different countries to teach one another. The learning experience could go on only within countries (though even national units might contain too much diversity for the lessons of one region to be applied to another). Clearly the plea of uniqueness had to be rejected on practical grounds, as well as on evidence we present on similarities among these countries.

Yet no one doubts that each country is different in many respects and that these differences must be considered. One tack which we have taken from time to time is to attempt to explain noteworthy departures from usual trends. But the main defense against over-generalization is caution in application. The country in which one is interested is likely to differ in some respects from most others. It may be richer, newer, older, more stable, less skilled, and so on. Hence one's description of it and his efforts to understand it may have to be adjusted accordingly.

Suppose the general explanation does not fit the particular situation; then it is a bad one. General explanations are supposed to cover most cases in most ways though they need not apply equally as well to all cases in all ways. Ultimately we must rest on the claim, substantiated as best we can in the rest of the book, that our description of behavior in planning and budgeting and our explanations of these patterns are essentially correct. We believe we have the facts right and have accounted for the way in which they cluster. Since this is essentially the first effort to consider planning and budgeting together, and also the only attempt to study budgeting at all, we await correction by more accurate descriptions and better explanations.

Note

1 . O. Davis, M. Dempster, and A. Wildavsky, "A Theory of the Budgetary Process," *American Political Science Review* 60 (September 1966): 529-547; "On the Process of Budgeting II: An Empirical Study of Congressional Appropriations," R. Byrne et al., *Studies in Budgeting* (Amsterdam and London: North Holland Publishing, 1971), pp. 292-320.

10

The Movement toward Spending Limits in American and Canadian Budgeting

The most important thing about a budget is that it actually be made. The classical sign of political dissensus is inability to agree on the budget. How we Americans used to snicker at the French (Third and Fourth Republics) practice of voting twelfths (one month's budget at a time, continuing at the prior year's rate) until, that is, we found ourselves making wholesale use of continuing resolutions. How we Americans used to deride the "banana republics" of the world for their "repetitive budgeting" under which the budget was reallocated many times during the year, until it became hardly recognizable, truly a thing of shreds and patches.[1] Yet resolutions that continue last year's funding for agencies, for want of ability to agree on this year's, are becoming a way of life in the United States, and furious spending reduction drives, punctuated by half-year budgets, are nearly the norm in Canada. How, then, do we comfort governmental agencies in the United States and Canada who can hardly discover what their budget was for last year, let alone this year, and who are constantly confronted with in-course corrections?

An annual budget is a great accomplishment. Sending out signals on taxing and spending that remain predictable so that others can take them into account for a full twelve months is no mean achievement. If only we could count on that today! In real life, a phenomenon that used to be confined to poor countries - repetitive budgeting, remaking the budget several times a year - has become standard practice in relatively rich nations as well. Whether the budget is formally reconfigured or not, its underlying premises, its financial assumptions and actual allocations, are subject to rapid change measured in months and weeks rather than years. The volatility of the external environment, when it leads to declines in the rates of spending increases, imposes such disagreeable choices upon governments that economic uncertainty is rapidly converted

215

into political disarray: decisions that are difficult to make have to be made not once but several times a year.

This change from micro-control to macro-limits has been foreshadowed by the replacement of the Public Expenditure Survey (PES) in Britain with "cash limits." The original idea behind PES was to improve planning by basing budgeting on the volume of activity in the coming year and the four that followed. In tune with the temper of the times—the attempt to stabilize government in the midst of economic turbulence—PES turned out to be a means by which the public sector diminished the private. Whatever the rate of inflation, the private sector had to come up with the cash to support the public sector. The consternation and contention this caused within the governmental apparatus may be imagined.[2] Eventually, cash limits were placed on departments and their programs so that if things turned out worse than expected, as usual, the departments and their clientele rather than the Treasury would have to make up the difference. Nowadays, the Treasury has pushed this principle into the future so that published projections of future spending are also based on cash limits. This is a halfway house to spending limits. Which way, half-forward or half-back, will the future take us?

Experience in the Western world is mixed: halting efforts to impose some sort of ceiling with little success in doing so. "Governments in many countries" (Austria, Switzerland, Netherlands, Spain and others too numerous to mention), Tarschys tells us, "now seem to be groping for some artificial norm to replace the dethroned ideal of equilibrium between revenue and expenditure." Sometimes this global norm is related to the size of the deficit or borrowing requirement, other times and places to the proportion of public spending to national product.[3]

My purpose in this paper is to appraise American and Canadian movement in the same direction—toward spending limits. Though Canadians apparently prefer higher spending as a proportion of their national product than Americans do, both nations now wish to stay at the same (rather than higher) levels. Both are experiencing hard times. Both are in a depression resulting in a severe shortfall of revenue. For the first time since government grew so big, with so many programs so difficult to control, the economy is out of whack while the budget is out of balance. While the American economy is less subject to external impact, being so much larger, it is by no means self-contained. The same high interest rates that cause trouble for Canada, for instance, also serve to make America s exports more expensive. With Canada and the United States in the throes of budgetary upheavals, budgeting more often and liking it less—this is a good time to see what they have to learn from one another.

There is chaos, all right, which could portend disaster, but there is also opportunity. Adopting the principle of least effort, let us begin with those actions that do not require radical changes in budgeting. Taken together in the

United States, taxing and spending in the past fifteen years have been driven by two conditions: the absence of indexing on taxes, so that government income under a progressive income rises faster than the price level; and the presence of expenditure indexing (cost-of-living increases) on major entitlement programs; especially social security, so that this spending keeps up with the price level.[4] In an inflationary period, the absence of tax and the presence of spending indexation has driven both taxing and spending up, thus increasing the size of the public in relation to the private sector. One way to overcome this spending and taxing bias was for Congress to vote to index tax brackets by 1985 so that people are not automatically pushed into higher levels of payment when their nominal but not their real income increases. This indexing provision, enacted but not yet implemented, is a hostage that might be used to spur other changes. One would be to de-index all or part of existing entitlements, while leaving tax indexing in place. Instead of a pro-spending and taxing bias, consequently, the budget system would be biased in the opposite direction, toward a smaller size of government. Another possibility would be to de-index both taxing and spending, thus restoring the pre-Great Society neutrality of the budget system.

Starting from another direction—personal exemption levels and tax brackets were indexed as were the major social welfare entitlement programs—Canada has also altered indexing, but with a difference. Personal tax indexing has been limited to 6 and 5 percent, as have the major spending entitlements. (By trying to limit wage increases and administered prices, such as phone rates, Canada may soon be called the Six Percent Society.)[5] Note that tax indexing, which reduces revenues, and spending indexing, which increases expenditures, are both to be diminished in Canada. In the United States, by contrast, taxes are to be indexed, decreasing revenues, while social security remains indexed, increasing expenditure. Evidently in Canada government is being better protected against deficits than in the United States.

Turning to statutory efforts (or even internal rule making) to change the budgetary process, concern over deficits and over President Reagan's success in steamrollering cuts through Congress has led some congressmen into an agonizing reappraisal. The president's great success has been in totally dominating congressional discourse. By aggregating cuts and forcing a vote on them in total (the reconciliation procedure), the president simultaneously made large reductions attractive (because they amounted to something) and politically feasible (because mere billion dollar cuts were harder to spot and because there were so many, congressmen could, so to speak, "hide" amongst them). "Packaging," as this phenomenon is called in Europe, whether called a "mini-budget," the "emergency brake," or the "cut-back plan," whether it goes by the numbers or by the calendar (the "September arrangement," the "November agreement," or the "December settlement"), is an effort to make reductions politically feasible.[6] As politicians in both countries discover that they will be faced with deficits for years, they may, in order to get away with lower spending, prefer to combine their cuts in a reconciliation resolution, or a spending package.

Those unfamiliar with budgetary nomenclature may see little of interest in the incipient debate in Washington over whether the second or the first budget resolution should be binding. Between the two, however, may lie a revolution in congressional procedure and in budgetary outcomes. Under the Budget Reform Act of 1974, Congress should pass a first resolution relating revenue to expenditure by setting a tentative total for spending. After Congress has acted on the various programs that make up the total, the second resolution adds them up so they conform to a new total. This is budgeting by addition; each program total is added on to the others and the "resultant" of these independent actions is called the new total. Were Congress to reverse this procedure by making the first resolution binding, it would have to force program items within preexisting totals. More for one would mean less for another. Since the sums will have to come out of their own programs, interest groups and departments will have to be concerned that no one gets too much. Complaints can be handled by saying that everyone is in the same boat (or budget resolution), and by making it difficult to single out individual legislators as the culprits. The growing feeling in Congress that it has lost and should, therefore, regain control of the budget, would receive an institutional manifestation.[7]

A similar radical change in budgeting could come from constitutional amendments, some requiring a balanced budget, others limiting the permissible tax take or the amount that can be spent, usually a proportion of national product. The leading contender, Senate Joint Resolution 58, which has so far failed to gain the necessary two-thirds majority in the House of Representatives, as it did in the Senate, limits spending to the prior year's amount, plus or minus the proportionate increase or decrease in GNP. There is a basic difference between an amendment to balance the budget and limitation amendments. Balance may be achieved through higher levels of taxation; it is compatible with larger government, providing the legislature is willing and able to raise the revenue. The limitation amendments put all the onus on spending; if national product does not rise sufficiently to meet desired spending, it must be cut. The balanced budget/expenditure limitation amendment, as the current hybrid is called, makes balance permissible but spending limits mandatory. Though, as with many other Canadian innovations, it is a well-kept secret to Americans, the Canadian federal government has pioneered the use of total spending limits tied to the trend in the growth of national product. The fact that this has taken place without formal constitutional change and under a cabinet system makes it all the more valuable for comparative purposes.

Among these alternative procedures, which ones are preferable? And which ones are feasible? Answers to these questions, whatever one's point of view, depend on understanding why government spending has continued to rise. Those who wish to see them go still higher may wish to reinforce old patterns; those who wish to see spending reduced will wish to understand where and how they might most effectively intervene. And those who are simply students of politics and budgeting will want to place their bets on how things are likely to turn out. Will opportunity emerge out of chaos, my question is, or will, as often happens, chaos lead to more of the same?

Is There a Pro-Spending Bias in the Budgetary Process?

Is the congressional budgetary process as it now exists neutral in regard to claims for higher or lower spending? Let me put it this way: If the American people sent equal numbers of high and low spenders to Congress and to the White House, would the budgetary process pass through these opposing desires with equal force? Or would the nation end up with increasing or decreasing expenditures because existing institutions are biased one way or the other? The same question can be asked in regard to Canadian federal budgeting before 1975: Was its budgetary process, without spending limits, neutral in regard to spending?

The Budget Act of 1974 expressed Congress's desire to enhance its own power of the purse by giving it the ability to visibly relate revenue and expenditure. Since the broad coalition supporting the act was made up both of high and low spenders, however, the new process was not designed to favor either side. On the one hand, the mere existence of budget committees raised up another possible impediment to higher spending; on the other hand, the need for these committees to maintain collegial relations with the tax and spending committees as well as remain subject to the will of Congress, meant that they had to subordinate themselves to the rampant desires for higher spending. The evidence from Allen Schick's *Congress and Money* is conclusive:

> In almost a hundred interviews with Members of Congress and staffers, no one expressed the view that the allocations in budget resolution had been knowingly set below legislative expectations. "We got all that we needed," one committee staff director exulted. The chief clerk of an Appropriations subcommittee complained, however, that the target figure in the resolution was too high: "We were faced with pressure to spend up to the full budget allocation. It's almost as if the Budget Committee bent over backwards to give Appropriations all that it wanted and then some."[8]

In considering the related question of mandatory spending, required by law and not subject to the annual appropriations process, Schick makes a powerful plea to consider this a conscious choice, not "an inadvertence of the legislative process but a willful decision by Congress to favor non-budgetary values over budgetary control."[9] Since budgeting, like history, is selectivity, Congress makes its most important choices by choosing what not to consider. Uncontrollability is a biased form of control. If much domestic spending is mandated and indexed and most defense spending is not, is that a bias in budgeting or just democracy at work?

Now it is also possible for defense to receive preferred treatment. Were Canada to take seriously its NATO commitment to increase spending in real terms by 3 percent a year, for instance, defense might become a kind of entitlement. I say "might" because the 3 percent rule does not necessarily take account of human ingenuity. Is this 3 percent over and above the costs calculated in the Gross National Expenditure Deflator or is it calculated above the inflation in the defense market basket of goods, which is rising much faster? Since NATO has not resolved the matter, neither have the Canadians.

Reducing the total size of the budget not only requires eternal vigilance but *information* on where to cut, *coordination* among programs so that increases in some do not balance out decreases in others, and *incentives* to make it worthwhile for each department to contribute toward total reduction. Increasing spending is easy, requires little information (any area will do), even less coordination and, normally, no increase in one area requires a reduction in another. Is that natural, like Mother Nature intended, or unnatural, a bias that explains why government grows? It is exactly this syndrome that has impelled Canadian central governments (after 1975) to adopt overall spending ceilings.

Public spending could be described as engaging in a game of reverse musical chairs—when the singing stops there are extra chairs to fill. The golden rule of agencies and program advocates is that each may do unto the other as the other does unto it so long as there is more for both. What must never happen to shatter the chain is for one sector to take resources from another. "Beggar thy neighbor" is verboten. Extraordinary programs, with special appeal, may go up so long as others do not go down. There is, in the language of evolution, selection "up" but not "out."

How are these happy accommodations possible? Because the public sector has been able to solve its internal problems both by absorbing the growth and decreasing the share of the private sector. Once that easy avenue has been blocked by limits on total spending, as it has in Canada for the past seven years, the necessity for resource allocation has been brought home. Observe the Minister of Finance's solemn statement, as if it were a revelation, that "the government. . . has to reallocate resources. What, we may ask, was budgeting about before?

Summing up the system of incentives in American government spending, addition is easier than subtraction. Whenever there is a crunch, administrative agencies will add on the costs of their programmatic proposals; they will not, unless compelled, subtract one from the other. Subtraction suggests competition in which there have to be losers; addition is about cooperation in which (within government) there are only winners. Until Reagan and reconciliation and until 1975 in Canada (both cases involving ceilings), subtraction was not seriously considered.

Up till now I have not specifically stated the most obvious and direct mode of expenditure limitation—acting intelligently on major items of expenditure. If you and I believe that expenditures are too high, the argument goes, we should say specifically which ones should be cut and by how much. If you want to cut expenditures, you must cut programs. Simply stated, these words have much to commend them. Talk about improving efficiency, reducing overlap or duplication, perfecting procedures, and so on, is valuable as far as it goes, but it does not go very far. Analyzing individual items is misleading as a general guide to limiting expenditures. As R. Van Loon, assistant deputy minister, Income Transfer Programs, Ministry of State for Social Development, says,

> The. . .Treasury Board. . .system was based on microeconomics, its watchword was evaluation and its high priest was Douglas Hartle. Its precepts could be stated fairly simply; to make planning more rational it was necessary to evaluate in detail the efficiency and the effectiveness of programs and then to feed the results back to policy-makers who would, when apprised of this rational input, make the "right" policy choices on the basis of this information....Hartle himself...quickly grew disenchanted with the potential for introducing the particular definition of rationality he had espoused into political decision-making unless the rules of the game and the incentives and behaviour patterns of politicians and bureaucrats could be drastically altered.[10]

Who, for instance, would take the lead in reducing expenditures? Each sector of policy is concerned with its own internal development. More money makes it easier to settle internal quarrels. Those who believe more is better for their department or their clientele come to this position naturally. Those who favor radical restructuring of programs soon discover that this is exceedingly difficult to do without sweetening the pie. The price of policy change is program expansion. All internal incentives work to raise expenditures.

Suppose you and I agree to cut out preferred programs in the common interest. What good would that do unless everyone else does the same? If "our" loss is "their" gain, why should we play this game? The budgetary process is biased against limiting spending item-by-item.

If there should be an opposite opinion, reflecting a desire to slow down spending, it does not have an equal opportunity to manifest itself in the budget. In the past, there has been no way for slow spenders to get together to enforce equal sacrifice so that the general rule becomes part and parcel of the calculus involved in individual spending decisions. To increase spending, no coordination is necessary; to decrease it, an enormous amount. Without spending ceilings that require choice among programs, budgeting by addition rather than subtraction will remain common practice. Indeed, just this—the belief that resource allocation cannot make economic sense until it makes political sense by first imposing a limit on total spending must have been the Canadian understanding, for its budgetary process is now based on this premise.

The "substantial disaffection with the budgetary system used by the federal government," that Sandford Borins informs us had arisen by the mid-1970s, was undoubtedly based on the consideration that "Without financial constraint, cabinet committees were thus characterized by unrepentant log-rolling." Policy initiatives were brought before a cabinet committee that recommended approval or disapproval "without much consideration of what its cost would be, or whether the money could better be spent on another project."[11]

In a white paper headed "Attack on Inflation," on October 14, 1975, it was stated that "The federal government shares the view that the trend of total spending by all governments should not rise more quickly than the trend of the gross national product." According to the civil servants in charge,

> This policy of restraint was applied to *total outlays* from the Consolidated Revenue Fund, including both budgetary and non-budgetary (loans, investments and advances) expenditures. The government made itself accountable for this new policy by announcing the target ceiling for total outlays in advance of the fiscal year. This created a very real political commitment and provided incentive for the government to take action to hold spending within the ceiling.[12]

Where in the three prior years outlays had grown an average of 22.1 percent, in the three following years growth had been held to 8.6 percent.[13]

According to a report on "The Policy and Expenditure Management System" by the Privy Council Office in March 1981,

> In its essence, the new system involves two significant features:
> 1. The preparation of a long-term fiscal plan encompassing government revenue and expenditures over a five-year period, i.e., setting out the overall financial constraints within which policy choices must be considered.
> 2. The establishment of specific expenditure limits (resource envelopes) for policy sectors, related to the government's priorities, and the assignment of the responsibility for managing a particular policy sector's resources to the appropriate Policy Committee of Cabinet.

In order to connect policy-making to resource-allocation, decision-making within sectors of policy has been decentralized to formally established cabinet committees, while decisions as to totals has been centralized.

Cabinet government is government by departments. It is their heads who sit in the cabinet. It is essential, therefore, that the sectors of policy designated as "envelopes have some concordance with departmental responsibilities, or else ministers would lose interest (as well as control).

The policy sectors are a compromise between facilitating trade-offs within envelopes and keeping departmental interests coherent. According to the Privy Council Office, the policy envelopes are assigned to cabinet committees in the following way:

1. *Cabinet Committee on Priorities and Planning*
   Fiscal Arrangements
   Public Debt
2. *Cabinet Committee on Social Development*
   Justice and Legal Affairs— . . . government programs aimed at maintaining and enhancing justice and protection of the individual
   Social Affairs - ...all social programs including major statutory programs that involve direct payments to individuals from the federal government (income maintenance), or payments to support essential social services through arrangements with the provinces (Established Programs Financing), as well as cultural programs.
3. *Cabinet Committee on Economic Development*
   Economic Development— ...programs that are directly related to the key economic sectors, including resources, manufacturing and tourism, as well as horizontal policy activities such as competition policy, regional development and transportation.
   Energy—includes energy and energy-related programs.
4. *Cabinet Committee on Government Operations*
   Services to Government—. . .programs whose primary purpose is to provide support and services to...departments or which are primarily service-oriented (e.g., Post Office). It also includes Executive Functions (mainly central agencies) and agencies which report to Parliament but for which the government retains a financial and management responsibility.
   Parliament—a separate envelope has been defined for those elements outside the direct control of the government.
5. *Cabinet Committee on Foreign and Defense Policy*
   External Affairs and Aid. . .
   Defense—both capital and operating expenses for the Department of National Defense.[14]

Think of the Priorities and Planning Committee as an "inner" cabinet, chaired by the prime minister; its leading members are the Minister of Finance, the president of the Treasury Board, the chairmen of the four policy committees (each of which has two policy sectors; Priorities and Planning keeps two that are within the purview of finance, debt and transfers to provinces), as well as three or four influential ministers, making a total of ten or eleven, as compared to something like double that number who may be regarded as sitting on the "outer" cabinet. As Van Loon describes it,

> Over the past fifteen years the cabinet has evolved from a single decision-making body to a series of committees possessing considerable autonomy within their own spheres of activity.
>
> With so many agencies having a role in the coordination and integration of policy, who coordinates the coordinators? In major part this is achieved through the Priorities and Planning Committee of Cabinet where all of the ministerial heads of the integrating agencies sit and where the financial envelopes are established.
>
> In this area the role of the Priorities and Planning Secretariat of the PCO is particularly important. It briefs the Prime Minister on all major issues coming before "his" cabinet committee and since it is there that intractable coordination problems are dealt with, the role of advising the Prime Minister in this respect is obviously crucial to the coordination of the whole system.[15]

The cabinet, acting through its Priorities and Planning Committee, sets out tentative allocations with dollar limits for ten sectors (the envelopes) for the coming year and the following four. On the bases of recommendations by the Minister of Finance in regard to total spending limits and levels for each policy sector, together with recommendations by the chairmen of the committees for each sector on priorities within its own envelope, Priorities and Planning reaches an understanding as to how much is allocated to each of the ten envelopes. The task of Priorities and Planning is to bring the money and the priorities together. This five-year spending limit is revised annually and, recently, more often. In the past two years, in addition, the estimates brought to Parliament contain the spending plan so that members can see the direct relationship between what they vote and the allocations in the plan.[16] Ceilings on total spending for the next year and estimates of what they will be in the following four are then converted into ceilings for the ten policy sectors. Allocations to departments within the sectors are the responsibility of the various cabinet committees, which are encouraged to be creative within their limits. Thus they can exchange tax expenditures (money presumably foregone by the Treasury) for direct spending and this has actually occurred in regard to a reduction of subsidies, although it affected western provinces in which the governing Liberal party has few representatives.[17]

An innovative system of restraint of public spending tied to national product and divided into ten issue areas has its full share of difficulties. To the politicians who are ministers, flexibility is important, partly so they can say they kept within the prescribed limits and partly so they can respond to clientele in view of changing circumstances. From the standpoint of administrative convenience, it would be easier on the civil servants involved if they could use the trend rate of gross national product rather than, as quickly became the custom, the year-by-year rate. The difference is that the trend rate provides more leeway when faced with year-by-year fluctuations in economic growth. The penalty paid for this leeway is that the limit is subject to greater uncertainty and hence more manipulation than the year-by-year calculations. Whether one prefers grueling yearly exercises in expenditure reduction to come within the limit imposed by the growth rate of GNP, as the public has come to expect, or the elbow room of the trend rate that leaves open the possibility of higher spending, is a nice point. Were the year-by-year rate fully accepted, I suspect that the officials in charge would learn how to make the necessary modifications downward so as not to be caught up in continuous crunches. The preference for the trend rate among ministers and civil servants is due not only to their need for flexibility but also, I think, to some residual unwillingness to imagine that the whole thing is really serious.

Whatever game one plays, it has its share of illusions. When GNP increases at a good clip, or more rapidly than expected, it is quite possible to have higher rates of absolute spending and lower rates compared to the growth of national product. This is a healthy illusion because it flows directly from following the rules of the game. A major purpose of spending limits is exactly to give government a stake in economic growth. (Parenthetically, the very definition of perverse policy is one that protects civil servant and ministerial salaries and pensions against inflation, so they do not suffer in the same way as other people.) Since spending departments can suffer when GNP declines, they must be able to benefit when it increases. The same is true within the envelope system in regard to reallocating resources saved in one program by spending them on others. Just as the programs and departments within an envelope must expect to suffer by making reductions to stay within their limits, they must also be able to hope to do new and better things by reallocating resources.

There is, as I see it, over-concern about the logical neatness of the envelopes or policy sectors into which the total is divided. The right attitude is expressed by W. Erwin Gillespie in his splendid article on "Fools Gold: The Quest for a Method of Evaluating Government Spending."[18] Just as there can be no analytical method for the interpersonal comparison of utilities - that is, for authoritatively relating different people's preferences when they disagree - so there is no division among the vast complexity of governmental programs that is absolutely neat and defensible on some set of simple criteria. Nor, I add, is there need for one. The key criteria are administrative convenience and political judgment. Once cabinets have made standing decisions to limit expenditure to the increase in national product, there must still be room for differences about priorities. The prime minister, and perhaps his inner cabinet, the Priorities and Planning Committee, must be able to reorder and respecify the jurisdictions of these committees in order to achieve the outcomes they believe desirable. Following the general rationale of spending limits, which is to vary the parameters of policy rather than to attempt to control details, governmental leaders must be able to exercise their influence by biasing the committee structure in the directions they favor.

Dividing the expenditure budget into policy envelopes requires consideration of the internal politics of a cabinet government. To retain departmental responsibility, it may be necessary to join activities (part of the sums set aside for the Northern Territory, for instance, could go into the social and another part into the economic envelope) within a single envelope that might on substantive grounds be put together. Because ministers head departments, moreover, they have to be able to see things in terms of organizational and not only programmatic interests. It is one thing to shift funds from this to that program within a given policy sector, and another to show a certain department that sacrifices in one of its elements will be compensated for elsewhere. Rooting incentives within departments is a major problem for the Canadian Policy and Expenditure Management system. My guess, based on experience with another form of program budgeting, is that control of spending is enhanced by separating the existence of departments from changes in allocation.

It may also be expected, apart from immediate political pressures, that experience will reveal incompatibilities and cross purposes that it is the task of civil servants to alleviate. It is through interaction within the envelope system that a tolerable modus vivendi should emerge. Its rationality may be retrospective rather than prospective, but that is a quality that both politics and markets share. Since total spending as a proportion of national product at any one time and its division among the major purposes of government is not an intellectual but a historical development, it is only right that it should be modified in the same way it was constructed; "no planning and expenditure management process," as Van Loon tells us, "is forever."[19]

A far more important difficulty is the tendency to trade spending increases in the first and second years for rarely realized reductions in later years. This happened to the Public Expenditure Survey in Britain. In a different way, it happens in the United States as outlays in one year are traded down in order to trade up obligations to spend in future years. Were this to become common practice, it would destroy expenditure control. Far better, then, to give up four-year projections and budget by yearly expenditure limits. If multiyear budgeting becomes another mechanism for increasing expenditure, then we can say it is entirely redundant, because the traditional system, without limits, does that very well.

There is a danger, hinted at above, that fascination with the intricacies of the envelope system[20] will take attention away from the supreme importance of overall spending limits. It is not that allocation of priorities within the limits does not matter; it matters a great deal. It is rather that without overall limits, incentives to stay within programmatic limits are dissipated. If more for one does not lead to less for another, and if cuts do not cumulate, no has the necessary incentive to keep spending within the prescribed bounds.

The truth is that people learn to play any game. Aficionados of the subject know about the numerous end runs that are possible in any budgetary process. These include imposing costs on the private sector through regulations, loans and loan guarantees (where only defaults are charged as expenditures), tax preferences, netting out the difference between the revenue produced by a service and the expenditure so that only the difference rather than the whole amount of spending counts toward the total, and much more.[21] A major criticism of spending limits is that, by damming-up spending at one end, it would encourage greater recourse to end runs all over the place. I doubt this. The reason is not that there will be an absence of efforts to make end runs; we can count on plenty of attempts. The reason is that budgetary processes without spending limits (that is, almost all processes so far as I know) are already full of end runs.

A false analogy is suggested between a pristine process uncontaminated by end runs and their sudden appearance after the imposition of spending limits. What we have now, without spending limits, is a proliferation of spending spigots of all kinds. It can hardly get much larger. With the United States at a level of some $700 billion in loan guarantees, for instance, it would take a lot to convince me that these would rise dramatically under a different process, if only because of the substantial negative effect on borrowers in the loan markets. Nor is it easy to use regulations and other devices to accomplish the kinds of social purposes that usually motivate spending. And should it be discovered that certain end runs, such as accounting changes, have a deep and deleterious effect, it is always possible to go after them.

When one wishes to make spending limits work, one takes the details of implementation as a challenge to win out in a trial of wits. When, whichever side of the border one resides, one wishes to show that the whole idea of imposing limits is ridiculous, one makes implementation seem impossible or idiotic. In the United States, for instance, opponents of a spending limit amendment will argue that since it would be virtually impossible to balance the budget immediately, the whole idea is cockeyed. Proponents talk, as do Canadian implementers, about contingency funds. There are small contingency reserves for cost-overruns in operations and in entitlements. Each policy sector is also encouraged to set aside funds either by being given a certain amount or by cutting costs within the envelope. Given the expenditure management system as it now exists, only the Priorities and Planning Committee can make reallocations across sectors. The question of contingency funds comes down to this:

Shall the sectors be encouraged to milk their own envelopes or shall Priorities and Planning provide the wherewithal? Not either, I think the answer should be, but both. If one were actually to believe there were a limit on resources, and that one could not afford to run over, everyone would invent devices for keeping track of spending (as is done with debt) and for absorbing unexpected increases. That this seems silly to some people is a measure of the rootedness of budgeting by addition in our time.

Though the effort to impose limits in Denmark has been vitiated by the exclusion of some 60 percent of the totals comprising entitlements, Christensen informs us, ceilings have also not worked for the rest of the budget. Governments have not abided by the limits they presumably imposed on themselves. Why not? Christensen explains,

> that for the public sector there is no such thing as resource scarcity. Even if resources may be scarce in the sense that demand for public expenditure always exceeds the resources available, a normal political response to this kind of resource scarcity has been to expand the total amount of resources available for public sector purposes. In other words, if resources are scarce in the public sector, they have to be made so politically....Such processes should...make it politically possible to repudiate claims for supplementary appropriations which exceed the official limits for public sector growth.... Nothing like that happens.[22]

Once it becomes commonly understood that limits are leaky, no one has sufficient incentive to abide by them.

Though the imposition of spending limits may appear arbitrary and therefore anti-analytical, limits provide the essential basis for making analysis meaningful, namely, that the value of what is done is judged greater than what was given up to get it. No limits, no allocation, no need to use analysis. "It is in this sense," Rod Dobell writes in his insightful paper, "that the 'invisible hand' of the envelope mechanism may lead individual ministers and program managers, through pursuit of their own interests, also to pursue the social goal of a more efficient allocation of resources, at least within the policy envelope."[23] Effective decentralization to cabinet committees depends on effective centralization of spending totals within cabinet.

Reconciling Individual and Collective Rationality: A Canadian Cabinet in Congress?

Canadian experience with spending limits enables us to pose several important questions about the institutional requirements of expenditure control. It has been assumed that spending ceilings were inappropriate in a parliamentary system because no one cabinet could bind another. Perhaps. Nevertheless, Canada shows that it is possible for several governments, coming from different parties, to act to continue the same process. Priorities may and do differ within broad programmatic areas (the envelopes) but the size and structure of the spending ceilings are much the same.

The trail-blazing Canadian effort may be used to argue on the opposite side of the street: spending limits can only be imposed and enforced in a parliamentary system run under a super-committee that tolerates no rivals—namely, a cabinet. Obviously, a parliamentary system cannot be a sufficient condition for establishing and enforcing spending limits. After all, Canada alone has done this. And it could hardly be argued, after immense experience to the contrary, that parliamentary regimes are somehow suited for controlling spending. It is America, not the parliamentary democracies, that spends less. Still, a parliamentary system might be a necessary condition.

A capacity for control, without the desire, is no guarantee of achievement. But is desire, without capacity, sufficient? That depends on whether the imposition of a ceiling through a constitutional amendment will prove efficacious or whether party discipline in the legislature must be used to back it up. Which alternative would prove to be most efficacious, then, converting Congress into a cabinet or using a constitutional deus ex machina to supply the limit without altering traditional congressional government?

With or without indexing taxes, Congress could radically revise its budgetary process by imposing an annual limit on spending within which all items have to fit. In current parlance, this means making the first budget resolution binding. Were the total too high, so it accommodated almost all desires, it would be worthless. To matter, it has to cut into current preferences. But how high is too high? As congressmen cast about for a formula, I suspect they will come up with something remarkably similar to tying spending to the last year plus the increase in gross national product. Last year's spending is some indicator of political agreement on the level of spending and the growth (hopefully!) in the economy is some indicator of what is affordable. In order to set a budget ceiling and to manage its internal division among claimants, while retaining their willingness to participate, however, it would be necessary for Congress to accept considerably more central direction, albeit from within the legislature. Would Congress have to become a cabinet, run by a committee which would tolerate no rivals? Not quite, but neither could it remain the same. The governing coalition could change from year to year, but it would have to set total expenditure and stick to it. And that sounds remarkably like a cabinet government in a parliamentary system.

However this committee would be composed—speaker and whips, caucus chairmen, heads of budget, finance, ways and means, rules, or other committees, partisan or non-partisan—the odds against cohesion are considerable. But are they insuperable? That depends on whether Congress has to become a cabinet or whether it can generate a spending limit without one.

The political rationale for a constitutional amendment should now be apparent: if a political bias toward big government is built into the spending and taxing processes, and if, as *The Federalist* calls it, this "discovered fault" cannot be remedied by the normal workings of the political process, then the rules of the game may have to be changed so as to reconcile collective consequences with individual choice.

Though it is often said that the advantage of economic markets is that they make calculations manageable, such a statement, by itself, misses the mark. Central planners probably have the sheer quantitative capacity to mimic markets. Properly stated, what markets provide is calculating capacity tied to incentives for the participants to make efficient choices. This combination of economic calculation and political incentive is also the heart of the argument for spending limits. Once in place, given the expectation limits on totals will stay in place, each organizational participant in the spending process has the incentive to keep others from growing too fast, lest his programs pay the price. Since all participants depend on economic growth for increases, they have common cause to aid productivity; and, should it be necessary to make sacrifices, all contribute to a common pool of cuts. Spending limits are self-enforcing.

Thus the differences among amendments become important. A pure budget balance requirement would encourage revenue-raising to meet higher levels of spending. Since the interest of each citizen in the cost of programs is small, because the tax take is diffused over millions, but the interest of beneficiaries is large, the interest with the greater incentive will prevail. Log-rolling can go on as before, providing that spending interests are successful in their search for new revenues (say, value-added as well as income taxes). Tax or spending limit amendments, by contrast, would drive down both revenues and expenditures.

What is the political feasibility of these amendments? That depends on whether any of the less stringent alternatives preempt the field or whether failure to adopt them leaves expenditure limitation or budget balance or some combination thereof as the only proposed solution to the budget problem. The political context, therefore, assumes extraordinary importance.

The Rise of Reconciliation

All the while this has been going on, appropriations have been delayed, dissensus opened up to public view, and the deficit—the sign that government is out of control—climbing. A sorry spectacle. Indeed, a spectacle so sorry that many congressmen, the majority that adheres to conceptions of responsible finance and responsible government,[24] as do most voters, may wish to rise to the defense of their institution. Whereas the Budget Reform Act of 1974 was a reaction to a president made unpopular by Vietnam and Watergate, the new changes will respond more directly to budget concerns because that is where the problem presents itself.

It is the way of evolution that it need not be consciously intended. The various participants react to emerging conditions and, willy-nilly, find themselves moving in a direction no one intended. The current chaotic economy, I think, will lead congressmen and presidents, big and little government adherents, to support reconciliation. By the time the present budget crisis is over (to be replaced, no doubt, by others), reconciliation may have become a way of life. Experience under it may reveal untapped potential; congressional coherence, by increasing ability to resist external forces, may make members influential. Relations within the legislature would grow in importance compared to those outside. *Congressional Government,* the title with which Woodrow Wilson rebuked Congress, may become more of a reality. For from years of reconciliation could come a binding first budget resolution, which in turn could spawn a leadership capable of making it work. From budgetary acorns (consider the history of parliaments), the oak of more coherent congressional government may grow. Maybe.

When the bloom has gone off the rose of compromise, the reconciliation procedure, that noxious weed in the budget garden, so hateful and discomforting when it was imposed on the recalcitrant last year, will find its poisonous qualities admired anew. Now the tables may be turned. With the president wanting lower domestic and higher defense spending and many congressmen inclined to do otherwise, he may be faced with a new reconciliation resolution so that he also has to take it all in a single package.

Once reconciliation (a nice name for a harsh regimen) acquires a progressive aura, it will grow on spenders. Unless they acquire commanding majorities in both branches of Congress during the midterm elections, they will be unable to undo tax indexing or, if they can gather the courage, to increase taxes over presidential vetoes. Thus they will become responsible for making large into huge deficits. Far better for them to take refuge in reconciliation under whose umbrella they can write-in their own priorities making selective cuts in defense and domestic spending, gaining budget control in both senses—total spending and the division among programs within totals.

How will future presidents respond? They will embrace reconciliation, claiming credit for whatever it produces on the convincing ground that had their administrations not been around, spending and taxing would have been much higher. They will struggle for their total and their program division, of course, but they will bless the outcome, much in the manner of those who wanted the United States to claim victory and leave Vietnam.

Comparing statutory and constitutional approaches, the ironical element is that the more severe constitutional alternative is easier on Congress. There is no requirement for central leadership; that is provided. What Congress has to do is what it is used to doing—divide up shares. It is self-imposed limits and their enforcement that would strain a fragmented political structure in which the fortunes of members do not rise or fall together. Since Congress need not agree on a limit, it could implement an amendment without basic changes in its structure.

Terms like "guarantees," "entitlements," and "open-ended," are not part of the traditional language of budgeting. They are about resource addition, not resource allocation. They introduce elements of uncertainty that lead to repetitive budgeting, not elements of predictability that hold out hope of an annual budget that (Praise be!) lasts a whole year. Properly put, they increase the certainty of beneficiaries at the expense of decreasing the uncertainties of government.

Scanning the budgetary reforms of the past quarter-century from the vantage point of these fast-fading norms, we can now see that they are part of the problem rather than the solution. Performance budgeting accepts the task to be done, asking only how to perform it more efficiently. Program budgeting seeks out an optimal path among policies to achieve general objectives more effectively. Zero-base budgeting asks how these objectives might be achieved if the constraints of the past were removed. None of these reforms are concerned with totals, as in budgetary balance, or with limits on programs ("caps") so as to restore department control of spending.

I have argued that to the extent governments are serious about limiting spending (after all, many people believe government does not spend enough), they will become concerned about overall spending limits. Though different levels of spending will appear more or less appropriate in various countries, those that desire to keep spending from growing to a greater proportion of national product than it already is will move toward some mechanism for imposing limits. Where the budgetary reforms to which we are accustomed are concerned with the quality of spending, the new wave will emphasize quantity. Whereas old-line reforms sought to directly impose detailed methods for improving decisions, the new, streamlined models will work indirectly to increase incentives to value programs according to their best alternative use. Where PPB and ZBB and the rest were avowedly a-political, drawing on economic or management science for legitimacy, spending limits will be openly political, resting on explicit choices about total spending and its major subdivisions. In the language of political economy, budgeting will be concerned less with intellectual cogitation and more with setting the conditions within which social interaction will take place.[25]

As for control of expenditure itself, experience will resolve itself down to this proposition: Limits on total spending do not guarantee control, but without limits on total spending there can be no control.

Notes

1 . Naomi Caiden and Aaron Wildavsky, *Planning and Budgeting in Poor Countries* (New York: John Wiley and Sons, 1974).

2 . See introduction to the second edition of High Heclo and Aaron Wildavsky, *The Private Government of Public Money* (London: Macmillan, 1981).

3 . Daniel Tarschys, "Curbing Public Expenditures: A Survey of Current Trends," a paper prepared for the Joint Activity on Public Management Improvement, OECD, April 1982, pp. 11-12. This paper covers eighteen countries.

4 . For a survey of efforts to cope with indexation in Western nations, see ibid., pp. 20-27.

5 . For details, see Allan J. MacEachen, Minister of Finance, *The Budget*, Department of Finance, Canada, June 28, 1982, who ends his budget speech with a peroration challenging Canadians to move "from the 12 percent world of recession to the 6 percent world of recovery," p. 11.

6 . These terms have been collected by Tarschys, in "Curbing Public Expenditures," pp. 37-38.

7 . ". . . the recommendation for a binding first resolution is included in virtually every bill. . . to amend the budget process..." "Analysts explain that this change would essentially codify in law what is becoming Congress' recent pattern...," *Inside O.M.B.,* An Inside Washington Publication, Vol. 1, No. 19, September 10, 1982, p. 7.

8 . Allen Schick, *Congress and Money* (Washington, DC: The Urban Institute, 1981), p. 313.

9 . Ibid., p. 571.

10 . R. van Loon, "Stop the Music: The Current Policy and Expenditure Management System in Ottawa," *Canadian Public Administration* 24, no. 2 (Summer 1981): 175-99. This essay is essential reading for anyone who wishes to understand the evolution and structure of expenditure management in Ottawa.

11 . Sandford F. Borins, "Ottawa's Expenditure Envelopes: Workable Rationality at Last?" in *How Ottawa Spends Your Tax Dollars: National Policy and Economic Development,* ed. G. Bruce Doern (Toronto: James Lorimer & Co., 1982), p. 64.

12 . "Controlling Public Expenditure—The Canadian Experience," a paper prepared by civil servants for the Organisation for Economic Co-Operation and Development seminar on controlling public expenditure, Paris, 28-30 May 1980, p. 2.

13 . Ibid.

14 . "The Policy and Expenditure Management System," a paper prepared by the Privy Council Office, March 1981, pp. 10-11.

15 . Van Loon, "Stop the Music," pp. 179, 191.

16 . Privy Council Office, "The Policy and Expenditure Management System," March 1981; and Rod Dobell, "Pressing the Envelope: The Significance of the New, Top-Down System of Expenditure Management in Ottawa," *Policy Options* (Nov./Dec. 1981): 13-18.

17 . G. Bruce Doern, "Liberal Priorities 1982: The Limits of Scheming Virtuously," in Doern, ed., *How Ottawa Spends Your Tax Dollars*, p. 23.

18 . In G. Bruce Doern and Allan M. Maslove eds., *The Public Evaluation of Government Spending,* Institute for Research on Public Policy (Scarborough, Ont.: Butterworth & Co., 1979), pp. 39-60.

19 . Van Loon, "Stop the Music," p. 193.

20 . Was this term taken from the practice in some families of allocating the paycheck in cash among a number of envelopes designated for food, clothing, etc.?

21 . Dobell, "Pressing the Envelope" (p. 17), deals with netting out; see also my *How to Limit Government Spending* (Los Angeles/Berkeley: University of California Press, 1980), chapter 6, on "End Runs," pp. 84-105.

22 . Jorgen Gronnegard Christensen, "Growth by Exception: or The Vain Attempt to Impose Resource Scarcity on the Danish Public Sector," *Journal of Public Policy* 2, part 2 (May 1982): 140.

23 . Dobell, "Pressing the Envelope," p. 16.

24 . See my "The Three-Party System—1980 and After," *The Public Interest* 64 (Summer 1981): 47-57.

25 . See Charles E. Lindblom, *Politics and Markets* (New York: Basic Books, 1977); and Aaron Wildavsky, *Speaking Truth to Power* (Boston: Little, Brown and Co., 1979).

11

The Transformation of Budgetary Norms

Budgeting in Turbulent Times

By the late 1970s and early 1980s budgeting got to be so much fun it was done several times a year, for no budget lasted more than a few months. Those whose programs were indexed against everything sat back and watched the budget being busted automatically. They were on an escalator and it only went in one direction—up. Resource allocation became resource addition.

But the central budget unit had to find funds to finance price changes, higher interest rates, wage settlements and all the rest. So the budget office clamped down on the programs that were not protected. These bore the brunt of turbulence. They were kept on a short string (by pre-auditing, monthly apportionments, and hiring and travel freezes, for example), not necessarily because these maneuvers were desirable but because they saved money in the short term.

Naturally, the beneficiaries of these disadvantaged programs protested. They wanted to move into the protected category, or to move out of the budget altogether by latching on to earmarked taxes. Consequently, as its room for maneuver decreased and its proportion of the national product increased, the central budget unit, compelled by circumstances, frequently ratcheted the budget up or down.

But repetitive budgeting was only the beginning. Because the budget was never really fixed for the year, spending departments acted accordingly. They kept the pressure on all year, instead of only at the beginning, because they feared their funds would be taken away. By seeking more in and out of season, the budget became a starting point instead of a commitment. Not only were there more claimants for government funds, they made claims more often and with more tenacity than before. With the distinction between the "off" and "on" budget season erased, the life of the central budget unit was turbulent.

235

Nor were spending departments overjoyed. The demands from clients for additional benefits increased with every past commitment. If they were unable to meet new demands, the departments were deemed to have failed to defend the constituents entrusted to their care. Unkind remarks would be voiced about their lack of manhood. But they could be responsive by transferring their problems to the central budget office through entitlements, loans and guarantees, off-budget corporations, the panoply of modern devices. The resulting financial turbulence tears government apart.

Everywhere, as they try to accommodate to new conditions, government officials are compelled to take actions whose results they cannot control. Higher taxes not only lead to political unpopularity but to higher prices reflected in the cost of living, and through indexing, to increased spending as well. Nevertheless, inflation becomes a major instrument of policy as government tries to do indirectly—lower the cost of the debt, reduce the real value of wage increases, redistribute income—what it is by then too weak to do directly, all the while relying on what it knows to be temporary expedients. Meanwhile, the value of the currency fluctuates, thereby setting off other difficulties such as higher prices, competitive devaluations and rival trade restrictions.

In earlier decades, various conditions helped cushion the financial impact of big government. Increased spending was supported both by accumulated productivity of earlier years, and by increases in economic growth. In addition, during the 1960s and most of the 1970s, there were significant transfers in real spending from defense to social welfare. Social security funds were in surplus, so large increases in benefits could come with small increases in taxes. Moreover, as inflation took hold, people were pushed into higher tax brackets, providing government with larger revenues without raising taxes. Since revenues under progressive taxation increased by approximately 1.5 percent for every percentage increase in income, inflation was good business for government. Where all else failed, governments could borrow to finance deficits that, at first, were small in relation to their national product.

All that has changed. Whatever might be said about small sporadic deficits, large continuing deficits are widely regarded as contributing to rather than fighting inflation. Financing government from growth is possible only when there is some. Defense has been used up as a transfer for domestic spending; indeed, defense spending is expected to rise. Social security funds are being depleted. The specter is raised of fewer and fewer people working to support more and more beneficiaries.

Big government breeds bigger pressures. Each new program creates interests who organize around it. More people make demands on politicians. Decisions need to be made to satisfy them and to cope with the consequences of prior policies. Thus, politicians find themselves busier than before but with less room to maneuver.

External turbulence and internal incoherence radically revise time horizons: time becomes foreshortened, and an enemy instead of a friend. In the good old days, politicians could play the spending tune today and pay the piper tomorrow, or, better still, in the distant future, when someone else would have to cough up the cash. Nowadays the consequences of policies follow so swiftly on their appearance there is no putting off the day of reckoning. The long-term is gone, the mid-term appears beyond grasp; the short-term, measured in months, measured within political terms of office, is all there is. The undeniable truth dawns: politicians are no longer able to pass on the consequences of their policies to their successors.

Our Budgetary Crisis is Different

Though it is often tempting to speak of one's own times as unusually different from others, there are respects in which the financial crisis of the Western world in the 1980s is different from anything that has gone on before. The level of public spending is much, much higher than it ever has been. In addition to requiring far larger revenues and more extensive spending controls, the sheer size of the task creates not only quantitative but qualitative differences. Relationships are more difficult to change simply because there are so many of them and they are so highly interconnected. It is not just that taxes are high and therefore pressure to lower them (or to keep them from growing higher) is intense; it is also that taxes tend to interfere with one another in a densely packed environment, so that an increase here leads to a reduced yield there. It is well and good to increase some form of sales tax but that may lead to decreased economic activity, which in turn will increase unemployment, and in turn reduce both income and payroll taxes. When wage negotiations are tied in with the level of welfare benefits, the difficulty of changing either one is not doubled but at least squared. There have, of course, been worldwide depressions before, but there has never been one when government spending and taxing were so high or there were so many entrenched interests inhibiting change.

Nor is it just special interests. True, these have always been and are now with us. True, there are many more of them because the state has become a target of opportunity, a cause of generating activity to put pressure on it as well as an effect. [1] Now, with as much credit as one can give to interest group activity, it is the changing and expanding role of government that is the major force involved. Instead of limiting itself to national defense, justice, and a few other narrowly defined and widely agreed activities, government has branched out in order to help manage the economy, redistribute income, provide social welfare, and otherwise influence citizen behavior.

The Emergence of Spending Limits

Spending reforms after the Second World War were concerned with improving the process of calculation, not limiting total spending. A broadbrush review of taxation shows that the major emphasis was on developing methods to manage the economy better, or, like the value added tax, to raise revenue without stirring political protest. No limits there. But that was then. Financial turbulence has brought about the first stirrings of a different budget strategy, a strategy of beginning with limits on total spending. From 1979 onwards, Canadian Cabinets, Liberal and Conservative, have sought to keep spending within the prior year's amount plus the increase in national product. More than this small percentage increase for one department or program, therefore, would mean less for another.[2] This same strategy has been followed in proposed amendments to the Constitution in the United States.[3] Were these amendments adopted or were Congress itself to adopt a mandatory spending ceiling, the growth of expenditures would be held to the rate of economic growth—last year's spending times the percentage increase in national product. The imposition of "cash limits" in Britain also works in the same direction. Not only do departments have to keep within these limits, despite unfavorable price changes, but the public expenditure survey for two years ahead is based on the same terms. So far these tendencies have been confined to the English speaking democracies where market forces are stronger than elsewhere. So far, these limits have not been tested either under years of budgetary stringency or under the reappearance of better times with higher revenues. Whether the 1980s usher in an era of resource limits or not, however, their concern with imposing ceilings on the growth of government is bound to recur if the public sector keeps growing faster than the private.

No one can say whether or to what extent these measures will succeed. Past history is against them. And it may be that a renewed bout of economic vigor will rescue the situation, at least for those nations, which make up the vast majority, that would prefer to keep spending at high proportions of national product. But we also know that spending cannot keep rising far faster than revenue indefinitely. Therefore, there will be changes because there must be. What must these changes accomplish?

When we speak of future budgeting we must turn to what we expect in regard to the transformation of budgetary norms.

Budgetary Norms

"In the good old days public expenditure meant merely the sum of departmental programmes . . ."[4]

Were it entirely possible to trace their origins, the basic budgetary norms which the nineteenth century bequeathed to the twentieth go back at least five hundred years; more, perhaps if we allow for numerology and auditing. Over all this time innovations were adopted piecemeal to improve financial control. Often proposals did not work as intended and sometimes they did not work at all. Given so many false starts, the rate of innovation was not constant but in time it did speed up. With improved administrative methods and growing economies, the budgetary process became manageable by the mid-nineteenth century. When improvement in budgetary practices did begin to slow down, that was only because the norms established by then—norms of annualarity, comprehensiveness, and balance—epitomized the best possible arrangements under the circumstances.

Nowadays one hears much less than before about budgetary norms. Having been ingrained in common understanding, the norms now seem timeless; they have retreated to the background. Yet, one by one, these norms have been undermined, while the practices which rest on them continue as if nothing had happened.

Budget balance has been discarded almost everywhere since the Second World War. Retreat from the balance norm occurred so gradually that a trend was not readily apparent; when people did begin to notice, occasional moments of concern were blotted out both by the prevailing consensus that spending for purposes mandated by the public was better than saving and by the revenues derived from economic growth. Loss of comprehensiveness in budgeting has provoked even less attention. While encompassing more aspects of social life than before, increased spending has been obscured by handling growing proportions of total spending in off-budget accounts. New mechanisms for spending now used extensively have made modern budgets into things of shreds and patches. Indeed, we doubt whether in any western nation, the "normal" budgetary process—estimation, authorization, appropriation, execution—is followed for as much as half the total funds involved. However weak one might think the controls exercised in the normal process are, these controls evidently have been considered far too strong; concerted and successful efforts have been made to get around them.

Instead of having the government spend its revenues directly for particular purposes, money may be left in the hands of taxpayers, providing such funds are used for government approved purposes. These "tax expenditures" (so named because they are a substitute for ordinary spending) may be estimated, but are not a formal part of the budget, nor are they counted towards total spending or the size of the deficit. Thus these revenues foregone do not appear in the budget.

Neither do loan guarantees. Government may loan money directly or may pledge its credit, thereby guaranteeing payment of loans. Huge volumes of loan guarantees have been issued in the past two decades. If there is a default, so the government has to pay, loan guarantees may appear in the budget, but not otherwise. The difference between the market rate of interest and the lower guaranteed rate times the sums outstanding may amount to many billions. As potential borrowers change places, some crowding out others, capital markets are affected also. Yet the interested person would be fortunate to find as much as an appendix to the budget document indicating the scope of direct and guaranteed credit.

The third avenue of escape from comprehensiveness is variously called "entitlement," "back-door financing," or "mandatory items." Without requiring a specific appropriation, legislation authorizes payment to people who qualify for unemployment compensation, say, or for child benefits. The monies spent appear in the budget as estimated outlays, but they are not part of the appropriations process unless the enabling legislation is revised.

With loans, loan guarantees and tax expenditures outside the budget, and entitlements, often involving income transfers, in the budget but not subject to annual control under budgetary procedures, what, then remains of the norm of comprehensiveness? In recent years, moreover, a large number of "off budget" corporations have been chartered. Generally engaged in activities (such as housing) which elsewhere are in private hands, the work accomplished by such corporations may be mentioned in the budget, but their expenditures are not listed, and are not included in budgetary totals. When all these developments are taken together, the movement from comprehensiveness becomes a stampede.

The norm of comprehensiveness was established bit-by-bit between the sixteenth and nineteenth centuries. Instead of the multiplicity of public and private revenues then existing, reformers aimed to channel all money spent by government through a single budget instrument. By the late nineteenth century, when the norms had become well established, a comprehensive budget included *all* agency spending. But while budgetary comprehensiveness is still taken for granted in some circles, in reality, a budget which is truly comprehensive is seldom found these days. Most government money is spent by means of income transfers from some citizens to others, by national grants to local governments, and by off-budget entities. Where the doctrine of comprehensiveness assumed a self-contained public sector, the reality of the post-1960 era is that most payments are made to individuals and groups outside government. If we look to the government budget for a monetary measure of the public use of public financial resources, it no longer serves that purpose.

In the old days, the main escape routes from comprehensiveness were earmarked revenues, or, as the British called them, hypothecated funds; bond sales; separate capital funds for development projects; and minor devices that took funds from the general treasury and placed them in accounts devoted to special purposes. Often the difference in purpose between capital budgets, investment budgets, extraordinary spending and other special spending, and the spending in the regular budget proved to be illusory. Nevertheless, by adding these other budgets to the regular budget, the expert reader could get a pretty good idea of how much was being spent, by whom and for what purpose. No longer. Moving between transfers, credit arrangements, regulations imposing costs on private parties, varieties of government industries—fully owned, partially owned, or only regulated—any assessment of the cost of government is bound to be suspect and incomplete. The result is a nameless revolution in budgeting.

While comprehensiveness and balance have overtly declined in significance, the norm of annualarity still seems to be with us. With each passing year, however, appearances become more deceiving. The larger the size of the budget, and the more heterogeneous the items in it, the more necessary and the more difficult it becomes to have uniform rules of application. On items with long-lead times, such as dams and defense procurement, spending must be phased over a decade or more. Recognition of the common tactic of beginning a new program by entering a small wedge, without revealing the immensely larger costs estimated to occur in future years, had led to repeated calls for multiyear budgets. Yet nowhere have multi-year budgets operated to the satisfaction of those in charge, possibly because maintaining the annual budget has itself become problematic. Pervasive uncertainties regarding expenditures and revenues have led to repetitive budgeting—the budget is continuously reformulated. Thus it appears that the annual budget norm is also being attenuated. Just as electronic data processing, introduced during the 1950s, provided the tools for budgetary control, and as near-universal satisfaction was expressed over its achievement, government began to have difficulty estimating the size of the annual budget, let alone choosing its contents.[5]

There is no blinking at the facts: the budgetary norms established during the nineteenth century have been through a metamorphosis. The welfare state, wars of mass mobilization, changes in financial technology, and "socialism for the rich" [6] have transformed traditional budgeting into a new form that is, as yet, unrecognizable. The words heard most often—from "uncontrollable" to "ungovernable"—reflect more than a judgment that government spending is too high. They reflect a feeling, still inchoate but growing, that the budget has become unrecognizable, a monstrous form—one which is grossly incompatible with traditional categories.

A different way of looking at the budget is as a distributive document. "Who pays" and "who receives" become critical questions. The distributional consequences of, say, loan guarantees versus tax credits, versus reliance on general revenues may be quite different, as will the amounts debited against the government budget. Whether adoption of these devices may be explained by a desire to shift the cost, or simply to spend more by taking funds from whatever pocket is open at the moment, control (or even comprehension) is made much more difficult. For the new Newton of governmental cost accounting must figure out how to calculate not merely what appears in the budget or is included in its appendices, but what imposes costs on private parties through other private parties at the instigation of government.

Inadvertence also determines outcomes. At the outset, this or that group may seek distributive advantage. Over time, however, the various spending provisions overlap and intersect with others, producing unintended consequences. A reduction in tax rates, for instance, would greatly reduce the value of tax expenditures. A provision designed to aid kindergartens by subsidizing an extra period may, by other provisions not contemplated at the time, reduce the number of hours for high school classes.[7] In short, a massive mixture of microadvantages may turn out to be a macro-disadvantage in that no one is in control.

Beyond immediate advantages comes the question of government growth; for if prevailing sentiment were against growth, these various forms of finance would have to compete for priority within a fixed total. Among other things, government accountability would be enhanced because all sorts of spending would have to be made fungible. As Sherlock Holmes remarked about the clue of the dog that did not bark, why has there been no effort to keep all spending within a single set of accounts?

Comprehensive accounting once meant accounting by departments; governmental expenditure, except for a special fund here and there, meant departmental expenditure. Control departments, the understanding was, and you controlled expenditure. With spending by departments on goods and services accounting only for some 15 to 31 percent of government spending in industrial democracies, the inescapable conclusion is that the vast bulk of expenditure is not covered by traditional norms. Most money is spent to affect citizen behavior rather than on things government does directly. Since most spending is done by individuals who receive payments or loans and by sub-national governments, the irrelevance of department control is clear.[8]

Control of spending has declined along with the norm of comprehensiveness because one cannot maximize simultaneously in opposing directions. Varying the level of spending to help modulate swings in the economy or to redistribute income or to strengthen family finances is not wholly compatible with a focus on controlling departmental behavior. The more government has become interested in the world outside its confines, it appears, the less able it is to keep its own house in order. Nor can it be said, following the norm of comprehensiveness, that there is a house of budgeting whose conceptual rooms are comparable. Accounting is in a shambles. Money borrowed one way ends up entirely in the budget, another way partially, and a third way not at all. Reallocating resources from loans to tax preferences to entitlements to departmental spending to government corporations is not possible (not, at least, in the sense of being intended), because there is no common currency. Annualarity signifies predictability. Applicability of this norm signifies that it is not only desirable but feasible—the budget will last a year. That being the common expectation, agencies have an incentive to make accommodation with central controllers. Though it is not spelled out, this is the mutual understanding: because the treasury promises to pay the amount passed in the budget, agencies will both exercise restraint in requests and try to stay within the allotted amounts. Once that implied contract is broken, a number of consequences ensue. Because the treasury cannot guarantee payment of the allotted amount, agency political activity increases, not merely to get what it asks for but to keep it. If the budget sends a signal to "get it if you can," early accommodation is unwise, resulting in later decisions and enhanced uncertainty. Should agencies find this uncertainty intolerable, they will try to escape from prior restraints by making demands for even more, so there will be more left when cuts come. Thus initial bids become even less reliable as a gauge of agency expectations. Rather than remain within the appropriations process, thereby absorbing considerable uncertainty, agencies seek to escape from it through direct drafts on the treasury (called "backdoor spending" or entitlements), through loans or loan guarantees, through shifting functions to "off-budget" entities, through special funds called "earmarked taxes," and through imposing regulations on private parties, so that they have to bear the cost, which does not then appear in the agency budget. Inevitably, as funds available to the central treasury become scarce, representing a lesser proportion of the total, and as it grows less able to calculate how much is being spent, since it lacks direct control over loan guarantees, entitlements and the rest, it seeks to impose a harsher regime on what is left, tempting agencies and program advocates to attempt further escape measures.

We see where we are: the decline of the predictability that used to be based on the norm of annualarity worsens the treasury's ability to maintain comprehensiveness. Revenues are diverted through increasing use of tax preferences (called tax expenditures by those who dislike them) and special funds. Expenditures are rendered incomparable by the numerous devices just mentioned for getting around the appropriations process. No one can say how much an appropriation is worth compared to a direct loan, a guarantee, or any of a number of other spending devices.

The decline of comprehensiveness weakens control. Not knowing how much is being spent, central budget offices are in a weaker position to say that any amount (in which account, please?) is too much. Looking good, as opposed to doing well, becomes tempting. Since treasurers tend to be judged by the degree of budget imbalance, they can improve their position by shifting spending to accounts such as loan guarantees that, except for a small amount for defaults, do not show up in the budget. Or they can (a practice intensified in President Lyndon Johnson's time) trade lower spending outlays in one year for larger authorizations in future years. Without rules that equate all major forms of spending, accounting sleight-of-hand substitutes for spending control. Naturally, this is a game that program advocates are more than willing to play.

It might be different if there were acknowledged limits on expenditure and/ or taxation. For then advocates bidding for spending would be restrained by knowing that much more for them would mean much less for others. And central controllers, besides holding on to an acceptable level of spending, could make the classic argument that understandings about levels of taxation would be violated, thus incurring penalties at the polls. But, as things stand, without widespread agreement on either taxing or spending, the inner restraint that kept the budget battle within tolerable limits is eroded. With the interdependence that resulted from a belief that balance is eroded, because the effects of spending here do not necessarily implicate others elsewhere, budget control gives way to a free-for-all.

There is a supportive relationship between the classical budgetary norms, so that a decline in one causes a contraction in the applicability of the others. Once predictability diminishes, advocates are encouraged to sidestep the appropriations process. The new forms of financing they develop wreak havoc with any notion of a single set of accounts. And as comprehensiveness withers away, predictability in expenditure increases or decreases accordingly. From this exercise we learn that it was the achievement of comprehensiveness that facilitated predictability and the delivery of a budget that could be counted on that encouraged the fungibility of funds across revenue and expenditure categories.

Instead of an energy enhancing, there is an energy depleting relationship between budgetary norms. Less of one leads to less of the other. Nowhere is this more apparent than in the deleterious effect the decay of budget balance has had upon annualarity and comprehensiveness. Budget balance comprises two kinds of equivalencies: accepted limits on revenue and expenditure, and the desire that their totals should come close together. The limits fostered a sense of mutual dependence as all were subject to similar constraints. The balance engendered a sense of self-sacrifice as each of the parts had to sacrifice to achieve a goal outside themselves. Mutual toleration and respect was furthered by the understanding that the actions of the participants impinged on each other. A dual dependence on society was furthered by empathy toward acceptable levels, tested only at the margins, and by knowing that the public looked toward balance as their assurance that the governmental apparatus was in good working order. In a word, limits enhanced predictability; correspondingly, assurance that the budget contract would be kept rewarded the participants for adhering to its provisions. This anticipatory coordination of demands for higher spending and taxing was facilitated by pouring streams of revenue into a single reservoir out of which all (well, almost all) spending flowed. When comprehensiveness became attenuated, the incentive to play the budgetary game by the rules declined with it.

Central control makes most sense against a historical background of past agreement, so that only small proportions of the budget are in dispute. The erosion of limits, predictability and collective concern, however, following from the loss of the traditional budgetary norms, has opened up disputes about the budgetary base: less can be taken for granted because the budget is likely to be redone at almost any time, because unwillingness or inability to share sacrifices means that some agencies become especially vulnerable, and because, given the sheer size and diversity of the budget, it is much more difficult to say whether any particular spending aspiration can or cannot be fulfilled. When increments get very large, or drastic changes are commonly considered, or no one is quite sure how large is large, incremental change is in trouble.

The truth is out: budgeting today does not look like budgeting yesterday because the norms undergirding the process—annualarity, balance, and comprehensiveness—have been undermined. If budgeting seems shaky, that is because the pillars on which it used to rest—predictability, limits, and mutuality—are shaking.

There are, to be sure, other explanations for the demise of the traditional budgetary process. The main explanation in the period from the end of the Second World War to the present is economic growth, its presence until the mid-1970s and its lessening or absence thereafter. It is easy to reach agreements, the growth theory holds, when everyone is getting more, though some get more than others. Incrementalism, Schick says, is based on the expectation of continued plenty. Now that prosperity has declined, incrementalism has gone with it, to be replaced by the harsher feelings of what Tarschys calls a "decremental decade."[9]

There is no doubt that the decline of expected revenues, consequent upon the fall-off in economic growth, makes things harder all the way around. The question we wish to raise is whether the change in budgetary behavior is a cause or a consequence of the transformation of norms. Is it economic growth (or its absence) that regulates budgetary behavior or is it the prevailing norms that determine what happens when growth goes up or down?

Consider the consequences of economic growth. Since it is possible to raise revenue without reducing personal income below what it was, budget balance could be easier, not more difficult, to maintain. Tax rates could remain stable, or even decline, while spending rose, thus raising budget balance to a higher level. Comprehensive accounts could be facilitated, precisely because there was more to go around. There could be less objection to maintaining the regular appropriations process. Why go the route of backdoor spending when the front door is wide open?

Yet that—the proliferation of spending sources during a time of plenty, from the mid-sixties to the mid-seventies, is exactly what happened. To us it seems more reasonable to suppose that a widespread desire to increase spending was behind the weakening of budgetary norms. Once one believes that government spending is laudatory, so that the more the better, it follows that balance and comprehensiveness are obstacles, because they restrict opportunity, and annualarity is an impediment because the money must be voted every year rather than coming in a continuous stream from the treasury. By contrast, open-ended, "no-year" entitlements, loans, regulations, off-budget entities, tax expenditures, and the rest enable government to do good by spending more.

If budgetary norms are being transformed, an observation beyond doubt, it is by no means clear what will replace them. Take annualarity. There are two ways to go: either learn to live with frequent changes or extend the time period to several years. The method of relaxing and enjoying it is now called the continuing resolution (in the United States) or, elsewhere, mid-year corrections.

Lip service to budget balance obscures deep differences. The Reagan Administration, for instance, committed to smaller government, would certainly like to achieve balance, but not if that means higher taxes or (through printing too much money) inflation. When push comes to shove, it would choose a smaller government with a larger deficit (say a $600 billion total, with a $200 billion deficit) to a larger government with a smaller deficit (say a $950 billion total, with a $50 billion deficit). Except when incurred by conservative governments, progressives favor deficits that help achieve employment or that redistribute income. If deficits must be brought down, progressives favor higher taxes, to be paid by people with higher incomes. In the end, it is the size of government, not the balance between revenue and expenditure, that matters most to progressive and conservative political activists.

Comprehensiveness is a cause without a constituency. Or, to put it differently, comprehensiveness has become a means to other ends. For partisans of smaller government, credit budgets and regulatory budgets and getting off-budget entities into the budget are all means of limiting spending. For proponents of expanded government, imposing limits on tax expenditures is a way of increasing revenue taken from upper-income taxpayers to promote higher spending.

The battle over budgetary reform has been joined by the worldwide efforts to impose limits on total spending. In order to work within spending limits, much more careful records of the rate of spending must be maintained. The definition of spending, called outlays, must be sharpened. Reserves against a rainy day will have to be kept. Inevitably, the constraints surrounding spending will be found oppressive. Those who wish to loosen them will find comprehensive accounting useful in enlarging the range of spending sources among which resources may be found. Those who wish to protect limits will want to get everything they can within their purview. Just as the deterioration of any of the classical norms of budgeting adversely affected the others, so too the strengthening of limits will give added impetus to balance and comprehensiveness.

The purpose of having budgetary norms in the first place was to restrain spending and taxing. No one thought it necessary to invent norms for doing what came naturally, that is, the opposite. It was universally thought that reform of budgeting would enable government to do whatever it was doing more efficiently and honestly. No one dreamed of taxes and spending at today's levels. Terms like "entitlement" or "uncontrollable" might have entered into other aspects of government, but they were never conceived as applicable to the budget. The traditional norms are designed to support resource allocation (assuming limits), not resource addition (assuming unlimited resources).

The new reforms—reconciliation packages, spending limits—are proposals to do formally what was previously done informally through acceptance of the norms of annualarity, balance, and comprehensiveness. The irony of contemporary budgetary reform is that radical changes are being advocated in order to bring back the traditional norms of budgeting.

Notes

1. See Aaron Wildavsky, "Policy as its Own Cause," in *Speaking Truth to Power* (Boston: Little, Brown and Co., 1979).
2. See Aaron Wildavsky, "From Chaos Comes Opportunity: The Movement Toward Spending Limits in American and Canadian Budgeting," paper prepared for conference on "The Leading Public Policy Issues of the 1980s," School of Public Administration, Carleton University, Ottawa, Canada, 4-6 October 1982.
3. See Aaron Wildavsky, *How to Limit Government Spending* (Berkeley: University of California Press, 1980), and Wildavsky, "Does Federal Spending Constitute a 'Discovered Fault' in the Constitution? The Balanced Budget Amendment," paper prepared for conference on the Congressional Budget Process, The Carl Albert Center, University of Oklahoma, 12-13 February 1982.
4. Burke Trend, "Policy and the Public," *Times Literary Supplement,* 16 July 1982, p. 755.
5. See Rudolph G. Penner, "Forecasting Budget Totals: Why Can't We Get It Right?" in *The Federal Budget: Economics and Politics*, eds. Michael J. Boskin and Aaron Wildavsky (New Brunswick, NJ: Transaction Publishers, 1982), pp. 89-110.
6. Robert D. Reischauer, "The Federal Budget: Subsidies for the Rich," in Boskin and Wildavsky, *The Federal Budget,* pp. 235-262.
7. See Frank Levy, Arnold Meltsner, and Aaron Wildavsky, *Urban Outcomes* (Berkeley: University of California Press, 1973).

8. Allen Schick, "Off-Budget Expenditure: An Economic and Political Framework," paper prepared for Organisation for Economic Co-Operation and Development, Paris, August 1981. For an insightful effort to get at governmental attempts at self-control, see James Q. Wilson and Patricia Rachal, "Can Government Regulate Itself?" *The Public Interest* 46 (Winter 1977): pp. 3-14.
9. Daniel Tarschys, "Curbing Public Expenditures: A Survey of Current Trends," paper prepared for the Joint Activity on Public Management Improvement of the OECD (Technical Cooperation Service), April 1982.

12

A Cultural Theory of Expenditure Growth and (Un)Balanced Budgets

Why does public spending grow? Because, the literature tells us, nations are rich, because they are poor, because their economies are open, because their economies are closed, because there is consensus, because there is conflict. If all roads lead to Rome, I suggest, that may be because it is the destination not the detours that matter. So I ask a different question: Which political cultures—shared values legitimating social practices—would reject ever-greater governmental growth and which ones would perpetuate it? My hypothesis is that the size of government in any given society is a function (consequence, if you prefer) of its combination of political cultures. The theory also explains the tendencies of political regimes to balance or unbalance their budgets.

Introduction

The question of why government budgets grow may usefully be decomposed into several smaller queries:

1. Why does government spending in Western democracies grow in small steps or large leaps but hardly ever declines as a proportion of Gross National Product?
2. Why do government budgets in some nations grow faster than others? Why does the United States lag behind yet also gradually increase the size of government? Why do the other Anglo-Saxon democracies, such as Canada and Australia, fit the general trend of growth but still spend less than the Western European nations? Why do the Swiss spend so much less proportionately than the Swedes? If there is a logic of industrialization, why does it not operate equally on all industrial nations?

3. Why is most of the growth of government budgets attributable to programs pensions, health, education—that contain a significant redistributive component?

The rising proportion of national product spent through governments in the twentieth century, I contend, cannot primarily be explained by growing wealth or industrialization. Nor can it be attributed, as recent authors do, to the political changes that follow from modernization. On the contrary, the very wealth and technological capacity of these countries would make it possible, were they so inclined, to diminish the proportion of state activity in national economies (Wildavsky, 1985).

Which political cultures (shared values legitimating social practices), I ask, would reject ever-greater governmental growth and which ones would perpetuate it? My hypothesis is that the size of government in any given society is a function (consequence, if you prefer) of its combination of political cultures. This cultural theory also explains the tendencies of political regimes to balance or unbalance their budgets.

People Choose Their Preferences by Constructing Their Institutions

Where do the preferences for different ways of life come from? What sort of social glue holds them together? What are the budgetary consequences of trying to live according to one way of life (or culture) rather than another?

In his now-classic book on *Administrative Behavior* (1976), Herbert Simon spoke of decisions stemming from people's premises about what should count as facts and what they desired, their values. He acknowledged that although these factual and valuational premises could be analyzed separately, in life they were usually found exerting a reciprocal influence on one another. Where, then, did the preferences come from? Simon thought the preferences might exist in the individual, but how they got there remained to be discovered.

If there are an infinite and unrelated number of cultures, no intelligible answer to the question of preference formation can be given except—it depends. History is uniqueness. But, if the types of viable cultures are limited in number and interconnected, formed and reformed along the same dimensions, a comprehensible answer can be given: People's preferences emerge from social interaction in defending or opposing different ways of life.

People choose their preferences as part of the process of constructing building, modifying, rejecting—their institutions. In this way the values people prefer and their beliefs about the world are woven together.

People discover preferences by deciding whether to reaffirm, alter, or abandon their way of life. They continuously construct and reconstruct their culture through decision-making. Just as (but on a more cosmic scale) party identification enables individuals to cut their information costs in choosing among political parties, the continuing reinforcement and rejection of existing authority relationships helps them learn what to prefer as external circumstances change.

The social ideal of market cultures is self-regulation. They favor bidding and bargaining in order to reduce the need for authority. They support equality of opportunity to compete in order to make arrangements between consenting adults with a minimum of external interference. They seek opportunity to be different, not equality of condition to be the same, for diminishing social differences would require a central, redistributing authority.

Hierarchy is institutionalized authority. It justifies inequality on grounds that specialization and division of labor enable people to live together with greater harmony and effectiveness than do alternative arrangements. Belief that hierarchy creates a caring collective is essential to its legitimacy. Hence, hierarchies are justified by a sacrificial ethic: the parts are supposed to sacrifice for the whole. This behavior explains the mildly redistributive policies of governments in societies with strong hierarchies. Why, then, have such societies recently gone further?

Committed to a life of purely voluntary association, sectarian cultures reject authority. They can live a life without authority only by complete equality of condition. The best indicator of sectarian practices, therefore, is their attempt to reduce differences between races, or income levels, or men and women, parents and children, teachers and students, authorities and citizens. Translated into budgetary terms, reducing differences means transferring income from richer to poorer people. Generalized into a desire to do good for the less fortunate, the principle of narrowing differences leads to ever-larger spending programs.

The important decisions individuals make are simultaneously choices of culture. Let us suppose that, as often happens in life, things go wrong. Who is to blame? Sectarians blame the system, the established authority that introduces unnatural inequality into society. Hierarchies blame deviants who harm the collective by failing to follow its rules. Market regimes fault the individual (for failing to be productive) or the government for restricting transactions (not allowing the best bargains to be made). Suppose a new development occurs. Without knowing much about it, those who identify with each particular way of life can guess whether its effect is to increase or decrease social distinctions, impose, avoid, or reject authority—guesses made more definitive by observing what like-minded individuals do. It does not take much for members of a market or a sectarian regime to figure out whether they oppose or approve of a progressive income tax, or for a member of a hierarchical regime to surmise that strengthening the state through a central treasury is better than fragmentation of finance. Of course, people may be, and often are, mistaken. To seek is not necessarily to find a culturally rational course of action. Gramsci's would-be capitalists may try to establish hegemony over others, but they are often mistaken about which ideas and actions will in fact support their way of life. They may, for instance, use governmental regulation to institute a pattern of cumulative inequalities that convert market arrangements into state capitalism, leading to their ultimate subordination. To be culturally rational is the intention, not necessarily the accomplishment.

The dimensions of cultural analysis, taken from the work of Douglas (1982),[1] are the strength of group boundaries, i.e., the degree to which decisions are taken for and binding on a group as a whole, and the extent to which prescriptions of desired behavior are (a) numerous, (b) varied, and (c) compelling to individual members. By observing the actions and verbal behaviors of political parties, government officials, businessmen, environmentalists, and other participants in political life, the cultures to which they adhere may be ascertained. If the budgetary behavior predicted for the regimes identified fails to occur entirely or to the degree specified, the theory falls. Since the definition of regimes is sociological—comprised of group boundedness and internal group prescription—it is possible to separate behavioral consequences, here in budgeting, from their hypothesized cultural causes.

In this paper I will do two things: (1) supply evidence that cultural theory is compatible with other things we know; and (2) argue that it can usefully be extended beyond the growth of spending per se to account for inability to deal effectively with perennial deficits.

Budgeting as a Function of Regime

Just as an act is socially rational if it supports one's way of life, governmental budgeting is rational if it expresses the values and practices of the political regimes existing in that place and time. In regimes organized on a market basis, budgets reflect opportunity for gain by bidding and bargaining. Under regimes in which the binding rules of social organization differentiate people and their activities by rank and status, budgets reflect that detailed division of labor more for some, less for others. And, when a sectarian regime emphasizes purely voluntary organization, budgets are devoted to distributing equal shares. According to this cultural theory, hierarchical regimes, striving to exert authority, spend and tax high in order to maintain each rank and status. Market regimes, preferring to reduce dependence on authority, spend and tax as little as possible. Egalitarian regimes spend as much as possible to redistribute resources but their desire to reject authority leaves them unable to collect sufficient revenues.

But no one of these regimes is viable on its own. No regime is sufficient unto itself. Markets need something—the laws of contract—to be above negotiating; hierarchies need something—a controlled lowerarchy—to set on top of; sects need something—an inegalitarian market and an inequitable hierarchy—to criticize. It takes two poles to make a magnet and it takes (at least) two half-regimes to make a whole regime.

It is time to begin applying the theory. America has historically marched to its own drummers, a combination of weak hierarchy, strong markets, and sects that, before the Civil War, were opposed to strong central government as introducing unnecessary inequality into society, leading to less welfare spending. That was then; today hierarchy is still weak but sectarian forces, which now view government as a force for equality against inegalitarian markets, has impelled the United States part way toward large government. European nations, which share strong hierarchies and moderate to strong sectarianism, all have stepped up spending; and some (i.e., Sweden and the Netherlands) being more egalitarian, spend more than others (i.e., Switzerland). Canada is in between because, while hierarchy remains strong, so do market relationships (Kudrle and Marmor, 1981; Lipset, 1968).

An empirical test of this cultural theory I have been propounding would have to include the reverse causal sequences to that postulated by the numerous camp followers of Wagner's law: increased equality would have to *precede* growth in proportion of public expenditure to national product. The rise of sectarian political cultures would lead to an increased desire for redistribution through government. Soon (say, in a generation) government spending on welfare and in total would rise significantly. Fortunately, Peltzman (1980) has provided exactly the kind of test we require. Peltzman's Law, as I will call it, states that reduced inequality of income stimulates growth of government (p. 263). The greater the inequality between taxpayers in a prior period, Peltzman contends, the less inclined they are to support redistributive spending in a later period (pp. 285-286). Peltzman's Law may be broadened to say that cultural change precedes and dominates budgetary change: the size of the state today is a function of its political culture yesterday.

If cultural theory is superior to alternatives, expenditure should not merely have increased as a proportion of national product; its most egalitarian components should have gone up far faster and the least egalitarian (say, military spending) much slower. This, too, has taken place.

Looking at the programs that dominate budgets in Western nations from 1954 to 1980, Rose (1983) finds that although the overall increase in the share of national product taken by government was 22 percent, the growth rates of major programs differed substantially from one another, and only economic infrastructure (i.e., roads and housing) increased at the average rate. Everywhere spending on defense fell as a proportion of national product, whereas income maintenance, education, health, and interest on the debt greatly increased. In the United States, for instance, spending on health rose 213 percent, whereas defense declined by 59 percent. Our debt interest (which is a product of increasing deficits), programs concerned with income transfers, health (another form of equalizing income), and education (which tends, though not so strongly, in the same direction) have risen sharply.

Because it is, to use the title of Mary Douglas's seminal essay, a theory of cultural bias, the approach I am following is well suited to explaining tendencies to tax and spend a lot or a little, and therefore to predicting the gap (surpluses or deficits) between revenue and expenditure.

Budgetary Balance as a Function of Regime

The Micawber principle—it is not the level of income and outgo but their relationship that matters—is essential to budgeting. It is important, therefore, to ask how expenditure and revenue are related to one another in each political regime. Which regimes run deficits? Which run surpluses? Which spend more than they take in, or take in more than they spend? Which regimes are likely to have what kind of problems—too low revenues, too high expenditure, or inability to vary either one?[2]

The number of ways in which governments can manage spending in relation to their management of resources is quite limited. The following possibilities exist:

1. Governments can manage neither their expenditures nor their revenues.
2. Governments can manage their expenditures but not their revenues.
3. Governments can manage their revenues but not their expenditures.
4. Governments can manage both their expenditures and their revenues.

These logical possibilities, of course, are not all-or-nothing conditions: government may be able to manage a little or a lot. The significance of these all-or-nothing conditions is that they map out the various possible extremes. Governments may have two options: (a) they can act in one way if they have sufficient leeway to manage spending; or (b) they can make different kinds of choices if they have scope to manage their resources. If governments can manage both, they can also manage the overlap. Depending upon how they simultaneously mix increases or decreases in revenue and expenditures, governments can vary the size of the balance or imbalance.

There are five strategies for relating revenues and expenditures so that these are kept within hailing distance (Figure 12.1):

Strategy 1:   Do nothing.
Strategy 2:   Decrease spending.
Strategy 3:   Increase revenues.
Strategy 4:   Increase revenue and increase spending.
Strategy 5:   Decrease revenue and decrease spending.

Figure 12.1

Budgetary Strategies under Political Regimes

Regime: Fatalism	Regime: Hierarchy
Fatalists cannot manage expenditure or revenue	Can manage revenues but not expenditures
Strategy: 1. Do nothing Balance: Spending equals revenue by imposition from above	Strategy: 3. Maximize revenue Balance: Spending marginally exceeds revenue with both at high levels
Regime: Market Can manage both expenditure and revenue at low levels	Regime: Sect Can manage expenditure but not revenue
Strategy: 5. Minimize expenditure and revenue	Strategy: 2. Redistribute resources at high levels of expenditure and low levels of revenue
Balance: Expenditure exceeds revenues at low levels	Balance: High expenditure greatly exceeds low revenue

In order to present a broader and hence more symmetrical array of preferences, I am adding a regime of fatalism,[3] groups with weak boundaries upon whom strong prescriptions are imposed from the outside. Budgets are made for them not by them. (Since they do not budget, I have not discussed them earlier.)

To understand budgeting by competitive individualists in market regimes, we must compare private and public budgeting. In the private sphere, each member competes with the others for goods, for credit, and for followers. Competition for resources increases spending. If investments bear fruit, individualists are able to pay off; if not, competitors take their place. At the governmental level, however, there is little motivation to legislate spending that does not directly benefit particular entrepreneurs. The state is kept poor; only wealthy persons in the private sector have resources for ostentatious display. While market regimes spend as little as possible for public purposes, they are even more averse to taxing. Hence, there are deficits at low levels.

The egalitarian collectives I call sects try to hold down personal consumption. Wealth is regarded as both a sign of inequality, and a temptation to give up an ascetic life. By abjuring wealth, egalitarians implicitly criticize the individualists they oppose, and whose wealth egalitarians cannot, in any event, match, for they find accumulation difficult. Lacking internal authority, they cannot make large revenue demands on members. Because capital accumulation is a source of inequality, it is rejected. Whatever wealth exists in society is soon redistributed. This regime eschews the private conspicuous consumption of market regimes or the public display that goes with hierarchical authority. Budgets are imbalanced by the combination of low revenues and high expenditures.

A hierarchical regime is able to expand its revenues. Collective investment through forced saving enables past commitments to be made good in the future. Taxes, like other rules, are imposed from the top and punctiliously collected. But spending is less easily controlled. Each role within the hierarchy has its prescribed duties, including the kinds of display that are required. New rules limiting display are hard to formulate or accept because they upset prevailing distinctions. Hierarchies can raise revenue far more successfully than reduce spending. Hence, their budgets are unbalanced with high revenues being exceeded by even higher expenditures.

The careful reader will observe that one of the available budgetary strategies—4. Increase both revenue and expenditure—has not been attributed to any of the four regimes. Perhaps this strategy represents a logical possibility, though not an empirical actuality. But I think not. The reason for the omission is that heretofore I have considered only basic types (primary colors, if you will) and not the hybrid regimes that may be formed among them. In a social democracy composed of hierarchies and sects, for instance, the impulses toward equality of result is strengthened, thus leading to greater redistribution of income by the state. Social democracies, therefore, both tax and spend at maximal levels, thus fitting the fourth budgetary strategy.[4]

All Western nations are pluralist democracies. In my terms, that means they have elements of the primary political cultures; they differ in the proportions of each, and it is the differing shapes of these hybrid regimes that create the kinds of imbalances experienced in recent decades. As hierarchy becomes even weaker in the United States than it was, the ever strong market elements combine with a renascent egalitarianism to produce deficits fueled from rising social entitlements (the sectarian contribution) and lower tax rates (a product of the market mentality). With stronger hierarchical and egalitarian political cultures—think of Sweden and the Netherlands and weaker market forces, we find a combination of very high taxation and still higher expenditure. Where market forces are stronger and sectarian elements weaker, but hierarchy is still dominant (as in Germany, U.K., France, and Japan), spending, though still high, diminishes, and deficits are not quite so large.

Notes

1. See also Douglas and Wildavsky (1982) and Webber and Wildavsky (1986). For a systemic presentation of indicators for classifying regimes, see Gross and Rayner (1985).
2. This section is adopted from my joint work with Michael Thompson.
3. For an analysis of fatalism, there called a political regime of slavery, see Wildavsky (1984).
4. How can hierarchies make sure that the public spends its money for collective purposes? How can sects make sure that goods are not used to create invidious distinctions? The solution to this dilemma (there is no telling what people will do with money) is to take it from the populace in cash and give it back in services. In this way the state can determine that income is used for what it considers good causes (the hierarchical preference), and it can also regulate the degree of display (the sectarian preference). In the seemingly simple act of shopping, for instance, the individual is likely to pay less for certain foods, because they are subsidized, pay more for others, because they are heavily taxed, and to pay a sales tax to boot, so that even experts find it difficult to calculate real prices. It is this sucking in and spitting out of resources that leads to the churning between taxation and expenditure that is so pronounced a feature of the modern welfare state. It might well be cheaper to calculate the gross effects of all these subsidies and sanctions (hence the complaints), but this is to miss the point or, rather, the objective, which is to increase state direction of private spending.

References

Douglas, Mary. 1982. "Cultural Bias." In *In the Active Voice*. London: Routledge & Kegan Paul.

Douglas, Mary, and Aaron Wildavsky. 1982. *Risk and Culture*. Berkeley: University of California Press.

Gross, Jonathan, and Steve Rayner. 1985. *Measuring Culture: A Paradigm for the Analysis of Social Organization*. New York: Columbia University Press.

Kudrle, Robert T., and Theodore R. Marmor. 1981. "The Development of Welfare States in North America." In *The Development of Welfare States in Europe and America*, edited by Peter Flora and Arnold J. Heidenheimer. New Brunswick, NJ: Transaction Publishers.

Lipset, Seymour M. 1968. *Agrarian Socialism: The Cooperative Commonwealth Federation in Saskatchewan*. Garden City, NY: Anchor Books.

Peltzman, Sam. 1980. "The Growth of Government." *Journal of Law and Economics* 23 (October).

Rose, Richard. 1983. The Programme Approach to the Growth of Government. Paper presented at American Political Science Association Annual Meeting, Chicago.

Simon Herbert. 1976. *Administrative Behavior*, 3rd ed. New York: Free Press.

Webber, Carolyn, and Aaron Wildavsky. 1986. *A History of Taxation and Expenditure in the Western World*. New York: Simon and Schuster.

Wildavsky, Aaron. 1984. *The Nursing Father: Moses as a Political Leader* University, AL: University of Alabama Press.

Wildavsky, Aaron. 1985. "The Logic of Public Sector Growth." In *The Politics of the Public and the Private*, edited by Jan-Erik Lane. London/Beverly Hills: Sage Publications.

13

The Budget as New Social Contract

Budgets reflect social orders; what is true of one is soon enough true of the other. Living one way and budgeting another is too contradictory to last. When we experience basic changes in budgeting, or hear that radical changes in budgetary relationships are afoot, we know that society is not what it was or will be. Political cultures are in contention.

To assess the potential for and desirability of budgetary changes in the 1980s, therefore, it is worth considering how this nation used to budget, why these budgetary relationships were transformed, and why Americans are now contemplating reforming their prior reforms. Knowing where we have been will help us understand today's choices about where we might go. This historical review is especially necessary because earlier patterns of budgetary thought and action have been lost to our contemporary consciousness.

The Original Compact

The winning side of the American Revolution was composed of three social orders: a weak social hierarchy that wanted to replace the English king with a native variety better suited to colonial conditions, emerging market men who wanted to control their own commerce, and the heirs of a continental republican tradition that stressed small, egalitarian voluntary associations.[1]

The balanced budget at low levels, except in wartime, was the crucial compromise that allowed these three social orders to coexist. Of course, unlike the signing of the Declaration of Independence, the compromise was not made in a single day, nor was there a formal declaration. The informal understanding, however, lasting for a century and a half, was undone in the 1960s, and whether our generation can forge a new consensus that will do as well in our time and last as long as the old is being decided now.

What was this understanding? How was it verified and enforced? And what was in it for everyone concerned?

It is well to remember that the Revolution was fought against the power of the English king. Even the Federalists, who joined social hierarchy and market forces to form the first independent American establishment, had their qualms about how strong the executives, like the president and the departmental secretaries, should be. They wanted political unity and economic order, but on a minimal, not a maximal, basis. Republicans—first the social order, then the political party, originally known as Anti-Federalists—knew best what they were against: established churches, standing armies, and powerful executives. They were *for* life on a smaller scale and limitations on status and economic differences so as to permit people to manage their own affairs.[2]

Left to their own devices, our social hierarchs would have wanted relatively high revenues and expenditures to support a stronger and more splendid central government. Since the market men would have to pay, they preferred a smaller central apparatus, except where spending and taxing provided direct aid. Together this establishment supported what, in American political life, were called "internal improvements"—subsidies for canals, harbors, railroads, and the like.

But the establishment had to contend with the republican believers in small, egalitarian collectives who threatened to withdraw consent to union unless the size and scope of the central government were severely limited. For these egalitarians did not believe that government spending was good for the common man, the small farmer and artisan of their day. Government took from the people (or so they believed) for the establishment. Limiting, not expanding, central government was the byword of republicanism.

Governments that ran deficits might have been acceptable to the hierarchical social order as a necessary accompaniment of domestic grandeur. The "public interest" was their phrase. But continuous deficits were unacceptable to market forces, who feared financial instability, debasement of currency, and inflation. So market men would pay more to balance the budget. It was the egalitarian republicans who insisted on lower levels of taxing and spending. Alone, they might have allowed imbalance—lower revenue than expenditure—since taxes discriminated against the ordinary citizen.

In the compromise that emerged, market men—adherents of competitive individualism—won the opportunity to seek economic growth with government subsidy (i.e., internal improvements) and gained the stability that comes from knowing that spending will be limited by willingness to increase revenues. Egalitarian republicans were able to place limits on the establishment. And the supporters of social hierarchy obtained a larger role for collective concerns, provided they were able to gather sufficient revenue. No order of society got purely what it wanted, but all got assurances that they would not be subject to severe disadvantages.

Thus the doctrine of the balanced budget, a doctrine that became so powerful over time that terrible things were supposed to happen should it be violated with impunity, was far more than an economic theory. The "balance" referred to was not only between revenue and expenditure but between social orders.

Debt: The Great Equation

Thenceforth, the history of American attitudes toward public debt may be translated into formulas for relating revenues to expenditures that were no less powerful for being simple. The first of these budgetary great equations [3] was simplicity itself: revenues minus interest on the public debt equaled allowable national government spending. The new Constitution provided ample authority for all sorts of taxes, including direct levies on individuals and internal excise taxes. In the debate over ratification, however, the proponents of the Constitution frequently insisted that the bulk of taxes be raised by custom duties and sale of public lands, with income and excise taxes reserved for emergencies. Despite Alexander Hamilton's major effort both to exert executive authority and simultaneously to give the government a sounder financial basis by invoking internal taxes,[4] Jefferson and his republican followers soon reverted to their preferred version in which tariffs predominated. Given the widespread agreement on balanced budgets and parsimony in government, as well as the desire to pay off the public debt, the first great equation had appeal.

Life soon provided the circumstances that lawyers say alter cases. In times of war, the second great equation prevailed: revenues, this time including internal taxes, equaled ordinary civilian expenditures minus wartime debt. When surpluses appeared or the attractiveness of internal improvements proved irresistible, or both, a third equation operated: revenues in surplus minus interest on debt, minus ordinary spending, minus internal improvements, equaled central government spending. It was only with the revolution in fiscal thought following the Great Depression of the 1930s that the fourth equation, sometimes called a full-employment surplus, took center stage. The idea was to balance not the budget but the economy at full employment. The fourth great equation stipulated that revenues plus a deficit sufficient to secure full employment equaled spending. The formulation of a fifth equation is under discussion today.

The Faith in Balance

In the nineteenth century, American presidents did not believe government spending would further redistribution from the rich to the poor; to the contrary, "melancholy is the condition of that people," President Polk (1845–1849) wrote, "whose government can be sustained only by a system which periodically transfers large amounts from the labors of the many to the coffers of the few."[5] For these men, as for the citizens they governed, debt was equated with privilege.

Faith in the balanced budget ideal was strengthened by an economic theory that tied wages negatively to debt. As Secretary of the Treasury Robert J. Walker claimed in 1838, "Wages can only be increased in any nation, in the aggregate, by augmenting capital, the fund out of which wages are paid....The destruction or diminution of capital, by destroying or reducing the fund from which labor is paid must reduce wages." This wage–fund argument had the added value of suggesting that the wage earner would be hurt by any effort to go into debt to improve his lot.[6] During the recession of 1837 and 1838, when efforts were made to increase federal spending in order to alleviate suffering, President Van Buren invoked the sagacity of the founding fathers who "wisely judged that the less government interferes with private pursuits the better for the general prosperity."[7] The economy would improve by reducing the deficit, not by building railroads or canals. President Buchanan blamed the financial panic and recession of 1857 and 1858 on "the habit of extravagant expenditures."[8]

Thus, for the federal government, the era before the Civil War remained a time of tiny government. Between 1800 and 1860, as Table 13.1 shows, federal expenditures rose from almost 11 to 63 million dollars in total. More than half were military expenditures. The general category of "civil and miscellaneous" included a substantial amount for the postal deficit, thus covering everything except defense, pensions, Indians, and interest on the debt. Kimmel is correct in his conclusion that "federal expenditures made little or no contribution to the level of living. Only a minor portion of Civil and miscellaneous expenditures were for developmental purposes ..."[9]

The Civil War changed all that. The government grew from tiny to small. It promoted the interests of businessmen and farmers, sometimes aiding railroads and other times intervening to regulate them in the interests of farmers. Beginning with the Morrill Act of 1862, which gave huge land grants to states for the purpose of establishing agricultural and mechanical universities, a variety of measures were adopted to aid education. Post–Civil War presidents generally, like Thomas Jefferson before them, regarded education as an exception to whatever strictures they laid upon unnecessary expenditures. And as the nation was settled and the frontier neared its end, the beginnings of a movement to set aside land for conservation purposes appeared. Still, it is not in these modest departures from the strict doctrine of the minimum state that one can find the sources of budgetary conflict or the seeds of future spending.

Deficit and Surplus

The Civil War also marked the first break in the consensus on debt reduction. Balanced budgets, to be sure, remained the norm, but the growth of presi-

Table 13.1

Federal Expenditures
Fiscal Years 1800, 1825, 1850, and 1860
(in millions of dollars)

	1800	1825	1850	1860
Civil and miscellaneous	1.3	2.7	14.9	28.0[a]
War Department	2.6	3.7	9.4	16.4
Navy Department	3.4	3.1	7.9	11.5
Indians	—	0.7	1.6	2.9
Pensions	0.1	1.3	1.9	1.1
Interest	3.4	4.4	3.8	3.2
Totals	$10.8	$15.9	$39.5	$63.1[a]

a Includes postal deficit of $9.9 million

Source: Lewis H. Kimmel, *Federal Budget and Fiscal Policy, 1789–1958* (Washington, DC: The Brookings Institution, 1959), p. 57. Data from *Annual Report of the Secretary of the Treasury on the State of the Finances for the Fiscal Year Ended June 30, 1934.*

dential discretion and the rise of industrial expansion left the role of debt open to argument. Abraham Lincoln (1860–1865) thought that citizens "cannot be much oppressed by a debt which they owe to themselves." His idea, followed by President Rutherford B. Hayes a decade later (1877–1881), was to secure a wider distribution of the debt among citizens. Considering that the debt might be paid over time, President Ulysses S. Grant (1869–1877), usually not considered a father of supply-side economics, asserted that the capacity to pay grew with the wealth of the nation. Rather than raising taxes to pay the debt in a shorter time, he would cut taxes to increase wealth and hence provide greater subsequent revenues.[10] During a time of expansion, the desire for internal improvements seemed compatible with fiscal prudence.

Money may or may not be the root of all evil. But the availability of substantial surpluses in the post-Civil War period proved a greater temptation than most private interests and public officials were able to withstand. No one can say whether it was the change in national opinion accompanying revenues generated by the growing protective tariff or the attendant changes in the process of budgeting that mattered most. Suffice it to say that soon enough even the $3 billion Civil War debt became readily manageable and that higher tariffs still produced substantial surpluses. Repeating the litanies of the presidents of old, Grover Cleveland (1885–1889) voiced the fear that growing surpluses would "tempt extravagance" and, what was worse, that public extravagance "begets extravagance among the people."

Yet between 1870 and 1902 there was no growth in per-capita expenditures in the federal government of the United States. Spending in absolute terms increased approximately 3.3 percent per year, but gross national product, adjusted for inflation, increased by more than 5 percent per year. Thus the federal sector of government was continuously growing smaller in regard to the size of the economy.[11]

Viewing debt as something a people owes itself (to be judged not as an inherent evil, but relative to a country's ability to pay) is not far from the idea that the size of the deficit matters less than the government's (and through it the people's) return on monies expended. Although the presidents from 1898 to 1920 (McKinley, Roosevelt, Taft, and Wilson) all said they were opposed to unbalanced budgets, the number of deficits began to increase at a rapid rate. For this new breed of presidents, efficient organization and "value for money," as the English say today, mattered more than parsimony.[12] The American people, Woodrow Wilson said, "are not jealous of the amount their Government costs if they are sure that they get what they need and desire for the outlay, that the money is being spent for objects of which they approve, and that it is being applied with good business sense and management."[13] Whether the idea was to do what was being done at less expense, or to do more, was left unclear.

Fiscal prudence, both against the growing debt and for a balanced budget, reasserted itself in the 1920s. World War I had largely been fought on borrowed money. From 1914 to 1918, the government's role in directing economic activity expanded enormously. In response, there was sudden public concern that the profligate habits of wartime would carry over into peacetime civilian life. The Victory Liberty Loan Act of 1919 established a sinking fund to reduce the debt, which was cut by a third (from $24 to $16 billion) by the end of the decade. Wilson's secretary of the treasury, Carter Glass, pointed out the "grave danger that the extraordinary success of the Treasury in financing the stupendous war expenditures may lead to a riot of public expenditures after the war, the consequences of which could only be disastrous." His successor under President Harding (1921-1923), David F. Huston, similarly observed that "we have demobilized many groups, but we have not demobilized those whose gaze is concentrated on the Treasury."[14]

Reform and Expansion

The Budget Act of 1921 was thought by its sponsors to be the reform to end all reforms. The executive budget, introduced by the president with the aid of his new Bureau of the Budget, through which all agency requests had to go, would simultaneously introduce order, expertise, and economy. And for a time there was more of all of these good things. But not for long. Just as there was more volatility in the money supply after the creation of the Federal Reserve

Bank than before,[15] spending expanded much more rapidly after than before 1921. Those of us (present company included) enamored of structural solutions may say that the Budget Act of 1921 did not change basic political incentives, which is true enough, but the other truth is that life overwhelmed the expectations of the reforms. There was greater coherence, which was expected, but also far greater spending, which was not.

Using 1902 as a benchmark, federal spending constituted 2.4 percent of GNP, and this had more than doubled by 1922 to 5.1 percent. Nonfederal spending had also grown but not as quickly, from 4.4 to 7.5 percent of GNP. By 1932 the budget reform of 1921 had been in operation for a decade. During that time, nonfederal spending almost doubled to 14 percent of GNP; federal spending increased by around 40 percent to 7.3 percent. These comparisons may be taken to mean that the rate of increase in federal spending was about the same from 1913 to 1922 (2.4 to 5.1 percent) as from 1922 to 1932 (5.1 to 7.3 percent), and that the reform of 1921 was essentially extraneous to the forces promoting increased spending. Or the figures could be taken to mean that spending would have been still higher in the absence of reform or that, in ways unmeasured by these brute numbers, the quality of spending improved. Between 1902 and 1932, the larger trend was that spending at all levels of government more than tripled from 6.8 to 21.3 percent of GNP.[16] An alternative theory is that the constitutional amendment ratifying the income tax justified the old concern that whatever revenue was raised would be spent.[17] Whatever the explanation, the inauguration of the executive budget ushered out the era of small government in the United States.

When things go well, one tends to credit the doctrines and practices that one has followed; when things go badly, one may still hope to recover by doing more of the same. Though his administration urged a variety of methods to enhance business activity, Herbert Hoover insisted that "we cannot squander ourselves into prosperity." To President Hoover (1928-1932) a balanced budget was the "very keystone of recovery" without which the depression would continue indefinitely. He stressed lowering federal expenditures and, if that failed, raising taxes.[18]

The Democratic opposition firmly shared his opinion that achieving a balanced budget was essential to ending the depression.[19] The new president, Franklin D. Roosevelt (1933-1945), promised both in his campaign and in his inaugural address to make a balanced budget top priority.

Gradually the federal government's goal of achieving a balanced budget during a depression came under attack. Waddill Catchings and William Trufant Foster wrote against the idea of a negative state that relied on the private sector to generate income and employment; instead, they advocated maintaining employment through long-range public works. Though new debt would be created, the additional economic activity and increased revenue would make repayment of the debt easier than an ongoing depression. "We must conquer the depression by collective action," Foster insisted in 1932. "This necessarily means the leadership of the federal government—the only agency which represents all of us....We must abandon our policy of defeatism, our worship of the budget, our false economy program . . . Instead, we must collectively put into use enough currency and credit to restore the commodity price level of 1928."[20]

As conditions worsened, economists and publicists began to talk about "spending" the nation out of the depression. The publishing magnate William Randolph Hearst promoted a "prosperity" bonds issue in the then–unheard–of amount of $5.5 billion. The philosopher John Dewey, president of the People's Lobby, asked for $3.5 billion for public works and relief. However, instead of debt financing that might be inflationary, he proposed that debts be written down and interest rates reduced.[21] Yet there were still those to counter with the traditional belief that continuously unbalanced budgets lead to inflation, and that that could only weaken an already depressed economy.[22] Petitions of all kinds, signed by economists of all persuasions, both for and against increased government spending, proliferated.[23]

"Virtuous" Deficits

By the early 1930s, a number of Americans in the Democratic Party had begun to seek a rationale for encouraging the government to expand public works and thus increase employment. They found this rationale in the work of John Maynard Keynes and introduced his thought to key figures, including President Roosevelt.[24] Building on ideas advanced in 1931 by his collaborator R. F. Kahn, Keynes argued that it was appropriate, in a deflationary period when vast economic resources went unused, for the government to create deficits as a means of expanding demand. When economic activity was slow, government should step in to speed it up; when the economy overheated, and inflation resulted, government could decrease spending. In short, raising and lowering the deficit became a prime means of economic control. The important point, however, was not the practice of Keynesian doctrine—any student of politics knows that it would be much easier to raise than to lower spending—but that it provided a strong intellectual rationale for doing what many people wanted. At long last politicians could combine spending with virtue.

The triumph of Keynesian doctrine marked both an end to the primacy of the balanced budget and a beginning of variable expenditure as an instrument of economic stabilization. The great budgetary equation had been fundamentally reoriented; the emphasis shifted from matching spending and revenue at the lowest possible level, to manipulation of the difference between them. The Employment Act of 1946 signaled a new equation focusing federal policy on the goal of full employment, with deficits and surpluses apparently left to vary in its wake. Spending and owing, instead of being the great enemies of the economy, had become its greatest friends.

By the mid–to–late 1960s, a new budgetary compromise had been made. Its essence was the unbalanced budget (or, if one prefers, balance at the spending level to achieve full employment, which mostly meant the same thing). Its principle was the change in belief among egalitarians (by then allied with the Democratic Party) to the view that government spending was a good thing, especially if done in a redistributive direction. They could help their friends, whom they hoped to recruit, and hurt their enemies at one and the same time by taking from the rich and giving to the poor. So far, so obvious. The less obvious question is what was in it for the establishment? Belief in hierarchy, which is based on the sacrifice of the parts in favor of the whole, goes along with a sacrificial ethic. So long as status distinctions are maintained (say, officers coming from the upper class), they should be willing to do their all (say, leading the troops, thus suffering higher casualties). So long, therefore, as labor unions, racial minorities, and poor regions, the relevant disadvantaged interests, accepted the existing social structure, hierarchs were willing to buy them off. The other side of the establishment, corporate and commercial interests, obtained their own quid pro quo: while everyone else was getting theirs, thus necessitating higher tax rates, they received direct subsidies, such as those for tobacco and ship building, and indirect subsidies, such as loan guarantees and tax preferences. "Socialism for the rich" went hand–in–hand with redistribution to the poor. In case anyone was left out, the "middle masses" received medical and housing subsidies. And, most important, the elderly of whatever class, because they were numerous and organized, achieved a rapid growth in pension and medical payments. The point is that once the mutual restraint of the budget balance had been replaced by the free–for–all of the welfare state, the necessary social accommodations lacked the necessary income (spending increased as a proportion of national product while taxes went up faster than personal income, as Figure 13.1 and Table 13.2 show), which explains why it lasted only a decade.

All this spending depended upon doing what was done without (a) decreasing the standard of living for most Americans, and/or (b) significantly disadvantaging the major participants in the political process. Within ten to fifteen years, however one counts, roughly from 1965 to 1980, both conditions were violated. The social order favoring equality found welfare insufficient and began a direct attack on corporate capitalism. To the social insurance state and the subsidy state (the old welfare state) was added the regulatory state. Eventually, corporations concluded that subsidy was not worth the cost of regulation. The amalgam of social orders that constituted American culture was coming apart. And this unloosening of the ties that bind was nowhere more evident than in budgeting.

Figure 13.1

**Federal Budget Outlays as Percentage of Gross National Product
Fiscal Years 1955-1981**

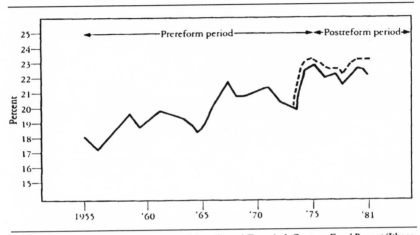

Source: Dennis S. Ippolito, *Congressional Spending: A Twentieth Century Fund Report* (Ithaca, N.Y., and London: Cornell University Press, 1981), p. 205. Data from *Budget of the United States Governement, Fiscal Year 1978 and Budget of the United States Government, Fiscal Year 1981.*

Table 13.2

Amount of and Increase in Per-Capita Personal Income and Individual Income Tax, 1970-1979

	Personal income		Individual income tax	
Year	Amount	Increase (percent)	Amount	Increase (percent)
1970	$3,911	—	$441	—
1971	4,149	6.1	416	− 5.7
1972	4,513	8.8	453	8.9
1973	5,002	10.8	490	8.2
1974	5,449	8.9	561	14.5
1975	5,879	7.9	573	2.1
1976	6,420	9.2	611	6.6
1977	7,061	10.0	727	19.0
1978	7,856	11.2	828	13.9
1979	8,723	11.0	988	19.3

Source: Dennis S. Ippolito, *Congressional Spending: A Twentieth Century Fund Report* (Ithaca, N.Y., and London: Cornell University Press, 1981), p. 210. Data from *Economic Report of the President, 1980.*

Figure 13.2

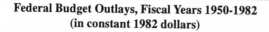

Federal Budget Outlays, Fiscal Years 1950-1982
(in constant 1982 dollars)

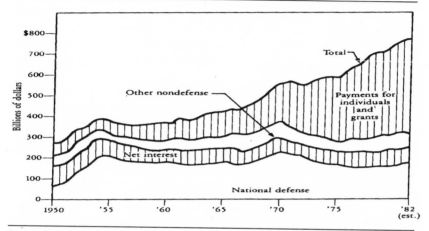

Source: Dennis S. Ippolito, *Congressional Spending: A Twentieth Century Fund Report* (Ithaca, N.Y., and London: Cornell University Press, 1981), p. 27. Data from *Budget of the United States Budget in Brief, Fiscal Year 1982.*

As long as the rate of economic growth exceeded the rate of spending, government could be supported without increasing taxes. The actual decline in growth and the increase in spending, whatever the reasons, meant that this easy exit was closed. The next step (see Figure 13.2) was to decrease defense as a proportion of total spending, from some 49 percent in 1960 to about 23 percent in 1978.[25] This reversal of priorities would work providing that the adherents of hierarchy did not become overly worried about the puncturing of their precious social system by foreign forces. This changed, for any number of reasons from the Soviet arms buildup to the invasion of Afghanistan to pure paranoia, but it changed. At the same time, whether the responsibility lies with oil price increases, declining labor productivity, lack of sufficient savings, overpopulation, deficit spending, or all or none of the above, inflation rose and take–home pay declined.

Quarrel within the Establishment

The budgetary crunch occurred because everyone wanted out. The hierarchical social order wanted to slow down domestic spending, speed up defense expenditure, and, if necessary, raise taxes, though this would be done sub rosa— in the manner of hierarchies—by "bracket creep" as people were pushed into higher brackets, by social security increases, and by the excise taxes on oil. Egalitarians wished to expand domestic spending, keep defense down, and either raise taxes or run deficits as preferable to unemployment or income disparity. Competitive individualists wanted to give market mechanisms freer play by cutting both taxes and spending. When one arrays these preferences—raising versus reducing taxes and spending—their incompatibility becomes evident. So does the difficulty the major political parties have in coming to an internal accommodation. The Republican party of today is something like two–thirds market to one–third hierarchy (some would say 55–45). Its internal conflict is between the hierarchs whose overriding consideration is social stability and the market forces that want to expand the private and contract the public sectors. The quarrel of these semirival and semicooperative social orders, the quarrel within the establishment about budget balance, is not at all surprising, for one side cares about size and the other about the composition or balance' among expenditures.[26] Because he takes a hierarchical, collectivist view of defense and a free–market, individualist view of domestic policy, President Ronald Reagan encapsulates these conflicts within his own administration.

The Democratic Party is divided in a different direction between its hierarchical and egalitarian wings. Once the restraint of budget balance was removed, they came together in support of the welfare state. With the hierarchical elements returning to support of higher defense and lower domestic spending in an effort to reestablish a social and financial equilibrium, the Democratic coalition is in danger of splitting.

The thesis of this analysis is that narrowly focused conflict over budgeting is best understood as part and parcel of a broad–gauged concern over the role of government in society. The rule that budget balance was desirable in peacetime (and that wartime debt was to be paid off in the next generation) enabled market, hierarchical, and egalitarian social orders to live with one another within the same political framework. The alternative rule, the unbalanced budget of the welfare state, created cohesion while it lasted but by 1980 had run its course. The question Americans must answer is whether any new rule will help create (or express) a social compact that the adherents of the various American social orders will find desirable or at least satisfactory. From this social perspective, the odd vocabulary (budget reconciliation means budget conflict, and loan guarantees for some mean lack of loans for others) and the arcane technical terms, which leave people wondering why there is so much fuss over the relative importance of the first versus the second congressional budget resolutions, should make much more sense.

One sign of the times is the proliferation of constitutional amendments designed, in the view of their sponsors, to remedy what James Madison referred to as the "discovered faults" in our basic political arrangements Regardless of the remedy proposed, the terms of discourse—*defects* in the existing political process, *biases* in political arrangements, structural *impediments* to spending limits—suggest a renegotiation of long–standing arrangements. Let us begin looking at the implications of current choices by inquiring into possible pro– or antispending tendencies in the existing federal budgetary process. Then we can examine constitutional versus statutory approaches to improving budgeting either by making it more neutral or by giving it a different bias.

A Biased Budgetary Process?

Is the congressional budgetary process as it now exists neutral in regard to claims for higher or lower spending? The Budget Act of 1974 expressed Congress's desire to enhance its own power of the purse by giving it the ability to visibly relate revenue and expenditure. Since the broad coalition supporting the act was made up both of high and low spenders, however, the new process was not designed to favor either side.[27] On the one hand, the mere existence of budget committees raised another possible impediment to higher spending; on the other hand, the need for these committees to maintain collegial relations with the tax and spending committees, as well as to remain subject to the will of Congress, meant that they had to subordinate themselves to the rampant desires for higher spending. The evidence from Allen Schick's *Congress and Money is* conclusive:

> In almost a hundred interviews with Members of Congress and staffers, no one expressed the view that the allocations in budget resolution had been knowingly set below legislative expectations. "We got all that we needed," one committee staff director exulted. The chief clerk of an Appropriations subcommittee complained, however, that the target figure in the resolution was too high: "We were faced with pressure to spend up to the full budget allocation. It's almost as if the Budget Committee bent over backwards to give Appropriations all that it wanted and them some."[28]

In considering the related question of mandatory spending, required by law and not subject to the annual appropriations process, Schick makes a powerful plea to consider this a conscious choice:

> "Uncontrollability" is not an accident or an inadvertence of the legislative process but a willful decision by Congress to favor nonbudgetary values over budgetary control.[29]

Since budgeting, like history, is a matter of selectivity, Congress makes its most important choices by choosing what not to consider. Uncontrollability is a form of control. If much domestic spending is mandated and indexed and most defense spending is not, is that a bias in budgeting or just democracy at work?

Just as consumers find it more difficult to organize than producers, so spending interests are advantaged because their concern is concentrated while taxpayers' are diffused. A billion–dollar program has a greater effect on recipients than on taxpayers who contribute only a few hundred cents apiece. Are those advantages and disadvantages built into political life, a natural process like photosynthesis, or are they helped along by voting on items rather than on totals? Is budgeting by addition of items rather than subtraction under ceilings the only natural way?

Reducing the total size of the budget requires not only eternal *vigilance* but *Information* on where to cut and *coordination* among programs so that increases in some do not balance out decreases in others. Increasing spending is easy, requires little information (any area will do), and even less coordination. Without a spending limit, no spending agency has an incentive to cut its budget because the contribution to the total is small and uncertain.[30] Is that natural, as Mother Nature intended, or unnatural, a bias that explains why government grows?

The difference between an out–and–out balanced budget and an expenditure limitation constitutional amendment is this: balance can take place at any level of spending, provided it is matched by revenues, whereas limits are designed to secure a specific (always lower) size of government. The balance people may wish to raise taxes; the limits people always want to lower spending. Thus the two pro–amendment sides would differ in the way in which they would answer a critical question: would they prefer a $600 billion budget with a $100 billion deficit, or a $900 billion budget with no deficit? Is it the size of government or the balance between taxing and spending that matters?

Size v. Balance

The crucial character of the difference between size and balance also emerges from Congress's consideration of reforming the budget process it reformed in 1974. Political life is speeding up. The seemingly obscure debates over the relative importance of the first and second budget resolutions are in fact over whether, by statute or rule, Congress will impose on itself spending ceilings.

Nowadays budgeteers speak in strange tongues—e.g., "first resolution" and "second resolution" (the first setting a ceiling for total outlays, the second fixing allocations for specific categories). What would happen if the last became the first? That depends. The Budget Reform Act of 1974 did not decree lower spending, nor did it alter political incentives one whit. What the act did do was change calculations so that Congress could work its will, whatever that was, more effectively. The purpose of the second resolution, as was clear from discussion at the time, was to legitimize budgeting by addition by formalizing the usual congressional tendency to lump together its item–by–item decisions and call this a budget, much as presidents do when the document has to be sent to the printer. Making the first resolution binding might signify a desire to introduce budgeting by subtraction (or "resource allocation," as the old–fashioned phrase had it), through which agencies and programs compete under a fixed total. It might but it might not.

Those who wish to make the first resolution binding argue that the Budget Reform Act of 1974, setting up House and Senate Budget Committees and establishing the Congressional Budget Office, does not work well enough. There remains a lack of control over entitlements (see Figure 13.3); the size of the budget has increased more afterwards than before; and delays in passing the budget have, if anything, proved worse.[31] The hope is that by setting a ceiling and requiring competition among programs, Congress would become financially responsible. But would it?

An easy way out would be for Congress to set the ceiling so high that no increase in one place implied a decrease in another. The result of trying to make the first resolution all–important would be to make it trivial.

If the ceiling set by the first resolution is to be meaningful, it must be at or below the level where the budget is today. If the resolution is to be helpful, it must be consistent over a period of years, for otherwise the size of programs would vary in fits and starts, leaving everyone worse off.

Figure 13.3

Entitlement and Other Uncontrollable Spending as Percentage of Federal Budget, Fiscal Years 1967-1980

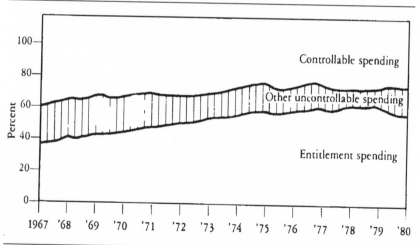

[a] Spending required by contracts made in past years, borrowing authority, guaranteed loans, and other obligations.

Source: Dennis S. Ippolito, *Congressional Spending: A Twentieth Century Fund Report* (Ithaca, N.Y., and London: Cornell University Press, 1981), p. 214. Data from *Congressional Quarterly Weekly Report,* January 19, 1980.

Willy–nilly, therefore, supporters of an effective first resolution must be interested in a semipermanent rule for setting ceilings. Tying spending to national product, the rule that the size of government should not increase faster than the growth of the economy may not be the best rule, but it is hard to see how there could be a significant departure from it that would still leave a significant ceiling.

A major difficulty with a spending limit, whether constitutional or statutory (or by cabinet agreement, as in Canada), is that it does not include a commitment to a balanced budget, which, as it turns out, has most of the popular political support. In order to overcome this drawback, a substantial number of senators reached agreement on Senate Joint

Resolution 58. Though it is called a balanced budget amendment, its title actually inverts its priorities. S. J. Res. 58 requires, insists upon, enforces expenditure limitation related to economic growth. Indexing for tax brackets is also mandated. But budget balance, though expected, is only suggested. According to the calculations of those who support a spending limit, it would lead to balanced budgets most of the time without demanding balance when the economy was in recession or increasing the size of government by raising taxes. Nevertheless, the advocates of market methods—and hence smaller government—prefer spending limits, and the adherents of hierarchy—and hence social stability—prefer budget balance.

Two main budgetary alternatives face us. (1) Budgetary balance on a higher level. America will imitate European social democracies. (2) Spending limits with budget balance at a lower level. The conclusion and the questions, both about budgets and social relations, are the same: the conclusion is that there will be balance; the questions are—At what level? How will we get there? Who will pay? And what will that tell us about the American way of life?

Notes

1. J. G. Pocock, *The Political Works of James Harrington* (Cambridge, MA: Cambridge University Press, 1977).
2. Herbert J. Storing, *The Complete Anti-Federalist, Volume 1: What the Anti-Federalists Were For* (Chicago: The University of Chicago Press, 1981); and William A. Schambra, "A Beginning from Old Principles," typescript, American Enterprise Institute, 1981.
3. See Samuel P. Huntington, *Common Defense: Strategic Programs in National Politics* (New York: Columbia University Press, 1961); and Patrick Crecine, "Defense Budgeting: Constraints and Organizational Adaptation," Discussion Paper 86 (Ann Arbor: University of Michigan Press, 1961), for contemporary versions during the administrations of Harry S. Truman and Dwight D. Eisenhower.
4. Dall W. Forsythe, *Taxation and Political Change in the Young Nation 1781–1833* (New York: Columbia University Press, 1977), p. 38.

5. Lewis H. Kimmel, *Federal Budget and Fiscal Policy 1789–1958* (Washington, DC: The Brookings Institution, 1989), p. 23.
6. Ibid., pp. 24–25.
7. Ibid., pp. 25–26.
8. Ibid., p. 26.
9. Ibid., p. 57.
10. Ibid., pp. 65–69.
11. Thomas Borcherding, "A Hundred Years of Public Spending, 1870–1970," in *Budgets and Bureaucrats: The Sources of Government Growth,* ed. Thomas Borcherding (Durham, NC: Duke University Press, 1977), p. 21.
12. Lewis H. Kimmel, *Federal Budget*, pp. 84–85.
13. Ibid., pp. 87–88.
14. Ibid., p. 88.
15. Milton Friedman and Anna Jacobson Schwartz, *A Monetary History of the United States 1867–1960* (Princeton, NJ: Princeton University Press, 1963), pp. 9–10.
16. Thomas Borcherding, "A Hundred Years of Public Spending, 1870-1970," p. 26.
17. William J. Shultz and M. R. Caine, *Financial Development of the United States* (New York: Prentice–Hall, 1937), pp 518–19.
18. Lewis H. Kimmel, *Federal Budget*, p. 160; and Joseph Dorfman *The Economic Mind in American Civilization 1918–1933* (New York: Viking Press, 1959), pp. 610–16.
19. Lewis H. Kimmel, *Federal Budget*, p. 148.
20. Ibid., p. 155.
21. Joseph Dorfman, *The Economic Mind*, pp. 617, 637.
22. Lewis H. Kimmel, *Federal Budget*, pp. 157, 222–23.
23. Joseph Dorfman, *The Economic Mind*, pp. 659–75.
24. For Felix Frankfurter's efforts in this direction, see H. N. Hirsch, *The Enigma of Felix Frankfurter* (New York: Basic Books, 1981), p. 113.
25. Dennis S. Ippolito, *Congressional Spending: A Twentieth Century Fund Report* (Ithaca, NY, and London: Cornell University Press, 1981), p. 179.
26. See Aaron Wildavsky, "The Party of Government, the Party of Opposition, and the Party of Balance: An American View of the Consequences of the 1980 Election," in *The American Elections of 1980,* ed. Austin Ranney (Washington, DC: The American Enterprise Institute, 1981), pp. 329–50. A shorter version, "The Three–Party System—1980 and After," can be found in *The Pubic Interest* 64 (Summer 1981): 47–57.
27. Aaron Wildavsky, "The Annual Expenditure Increment," Working Papers on House Committee Organization and Operation (#96–321), Select Committee on Committees, Ninety–Third Congress (Washington, D.C.: U.S. Government Printing Office, 1973). A revised version, "The Annual Expenditure Increment—Or How Congress Can Regain Control of the Budget," can be found in *The Public Interest* 33 (Fall 1973): 84–108.
28. Allen Schick, *Congress and Money* (Washington, DC: The Urban Institute, 1980), p. 313.
29. Ibid., p. 571.
30. See Aaron Wildavsky, *How to Limit Government Spending* (Los Angeles and Berkeley: University of California Press, 1980).
31. See Louis Fisher, "In Dubious Battle? Congress and the Budget," *The Brookings Bulletin* 17 (Spring 1981): 6–10.

14

On the Balance of Budgetary Cultures

Aaron Wildavsky analyzes the budgetary process in America from the middle of the seventeenth century to the second decade of the twentieth century. He is struck by the differences between American national budgets and their European analogues. They have been consistently more balanced, the per capita revenue and expenditure ratio has been markedly lower, and the American budgetary process has stressed the budgetary power of the legislature to a far greater degree than is the case in the European cabinet system. Where European budgets have been unitary, with expenditures and revenues considered as one, American budgets have been fragmentary, with each agency submitting its own spending proposals and considering revenue sources separately. A unitary mechanism came to exist with the establishment of the Ways and Means Committee in the House of Representatives, but it has been subjected to frequent fragmentation since 1865. Wildavsky wonders why America has been so different.

An obvious explanation, of course, is that the United States of America was born in a revolution against a sovereign executive. Distrust of executive power tells us part of the story of American exceptionalism, but it does not tell us how the difference was translated into budgetary behavior. Wildavsky hypothesizes that American differences are a product of almost equal competition among three main cultures, namely, collectivism, individualism, and voluntarism. Their corresponding political regimes are, respectively, hierarchies, markets, and sects.

The winning side of the American Revolution was composed of three social orders: a weak social hierarchy that wanted to replace the English king with a native variety better suited to colonial conditions; emerging market men who wanted to control their own commerce; and the heirs of a continental republican tradition that stressed small, egalitarian, and voluntary associations.

The balanced budget at low levels, except in wartime, was the crucial compromise that allowed these three social orders to coexist. Unlike the signing of

277

the Declaration of Independence, the compromise was not made in a single day, nor was there a formal declaration. The informal understanding lasted for a century and a half, however. A new understanding was forged during the 1960s, and whether our generation can fashion a new consensus that will do as well in our time and last as long as the old one is being decided now.

What was this understanding? How was it verified and enforced? And what was in it for all concerned?

The Revolution was fought against the power of the English king. Even the Federalists, who joined social hierarchy and market forces to form the first independent American establishment, had their qualms about how strong the executive should be. They wanted political unity and economic order but on a minimal, not a maximal, basis. Republicans, first the social order and then the political party, originally known as Anti-Federalists, knew best what they were against: established churches, standing armies, and powerful executives. They were *life* on a smaller scale, and limitations on status and economic differences so as to permit people to manage their own affairs.

Left to their own devices, social hierarchies would have desired relatively high revenues and expenditures to support a stronger and more splendid central government. Because the market men would have to pay, they preferred a smaller central apparatus, except where spending and taxing provided direct aid. Together this establishment supported what were called internal improvements, namely subsidies for canals, harbors, and railroads.

But the establishment had to contend with the Republican belief in small, egalitarian collectives who threatened to withdraw consent to union unless the size and scope of the central government were severely limited. These egalitarians did not believe that government spending was good for the common man, the small farmer, and the artisan of their day. Government took from the people to support the establishment. Limiting, not expanding, central government was the hallmark of republicanism.

Governments that ran deficits might have been acceptable to the hierarchical social order as a necessary accompaniment to domestic grandeur. The "public interest" was their phrase. But continuous deficits were unacceptable to market forces, who feared financial instability, debasement of currency, and inflation. So market men would compromise to balance the budget. It was the egalitarian Republicans who insisted on lower levels of taxing and spending.

In the compromise that emerged, market men, the adherents of competitive individualism, won the opportunity to seek economic growth with government subsidy and internal improvement, and gained the stability that comes from knowing that spending will be limited by a willingness to increase revenues. Egalitarian republicans were able to place limits on central government. And the supporters of social hierarchy obtained a larger role for collective concerns, provided they were able to gather sufficient revenue. No order of society received all it sought, but all got assurances that they would not be subject to severe disadvantages in the compromise. The belief, widely espoused in the Jacksonian era, that equality of opportunity would lead to equality of result and that pure market relations would achieve sectarian objectives helped cement this cultural union.

Thus the doctrine of the balanced budget, a doctrine that became powerful over time because of the attendant negative impact should it be violated, was more than an economic theory. It meant, and, to some extent, still means, that things are all right. The balance referred to was not only between revenue and expenditure but between social orders. If the competing cultures that make up American life are in balance, meaning that they still accept the legitimacy of their uneasy alliance, all is indeed well in the New World.

*   *   *

"A successful financial system will conform to the political ideas which for the time being control society, and adjust itself to the political structure of the particular society to which it applies."—Henry Carter Adams, *The Science of Finance: All Investigation of Public Expenditures and Public Revenues.* New York: Henry Holt, 1899, p. 8.

I wish it were possible to obtain a single amendment to our constitution. I would be willing to depend on that alone for the reduction of the administration of our government to the genuine principles of it's [sic] constitution; I mean an additional article, taking from the federal government the power of borrowing. I now deny their power of making paper money or anything else a legal tender. I know that to pay all proper expenses within the year, would, in case of war, be hard on us. But not so hard as ten wars instead of one. For wars would be reduced in that proportion; besides that the State governments would be free to lend *their credit* in borrowing quotas. ...It is a singular phenomenon, that while our State governments are the very *best in the world,* without exception or comparison, our general government has, in the rapid course of 9 or 10 years, become more arbitrary, and has swallowed more of the public liberty than even that of England [Jefferson's emphasis]." —Jefferson to John Taylor, November 26, 1798. Paul Leicester Lord, ed., *The Works of Thomas Jefferson, Vol. VIII.* New York: G. P. Putnam's Sons, The Knickerbocker Press, 1904, p. 481.

"The habits of private life are continued in public; and we ought carefully to distinguish that economy which depends upon their institutions from that which is a natural result of their manners and customs."—Alexis de Tocqueville, *Democracy in America*, V. 1, p. 222.

From the middle of the seventeenth century to the second decade of the twentieth century, the period covered by this essay, America's difference from rather than its similarity to Europe's approach to a budgetary process is striking. The per capita revenue and expenditure ratio has been markedly lower in the United States. The process in America has historically stressed the budgetary power of the legislature. Europe has relied on the influence of the executive, in the form of a legislative committee called the cabinet. Where European budgets have been unitary, with expenditures and revenues considered as one, American budgets have been fragmentary, with each agency submitting its own spending proposals and considering revenue sources separately. A unitary mechanism existed with the establishment of the Congressional Ways and Means Committee. However, since 1865 it has been subjected to frequent fragmentation. Still, when viewed as an historic whole, American national budgets have been consistently more balanced than have European analogues. This most unideological of peoples practices more than it preaches. Why has America been so different?

Obvious explanations should not be ignored merely because they are familiar. The United States of America was born in a revolution against a sovereign executive. Therefore, no one should be surprised by the American distrust of executive authority. However, the threat of Indian and foreign attack and the need for the adoption of social and economic order necessitated the institution of a central government. The "Second American Revolution," the replacement of the Articles of Confederation with the Constitution, was devised to counter disorder by establishing a stronger central authority. Its radicalism consisted in a design for self-government rather than for economic and social equality, or "leveling," as they called it. Facilitating competition among elites instead of advocating their abolition, the constitutional debates and the Federalist papers reflected a distrust of the people being governed by mob rule as well as a paradoxical dependence upon the consent of those governed. The problem was to negotiate a balance between the suspicions inherent in big government and the specter of government by "mobocracy." Distrust of executive power tells us part of the story of American exceptionalism but not how that difference was translated into its budgetary behavior.

The framers of the Constitution feared that elected officials would compete for the support of the electorate by adopting measures to limit property rights. They had in mind the debasement of currency, they favored debtors over creditors and they feared a repetition of the days of Roman bread and circuses. Politicians did compete for popular favor, but why, for the longest time, did they reject large spending and heavy taxation?

Writing near the end of the nineteenth century, Lord James Bryce was one among many to say that Americans had been saved from their financial follies, presumably their failure to imitate Europeans, by the endowment of natural resources.[1] But how would Bryce explain today's suddenly oil-rich nations managing to raise their spending to empty a cornucopia of wealth? Thus, natural abundance alone does not explain why American governments raised only a fraction of the public funds that the wealth of their people might otherwise have dictated.

Perhaps it is not so much what America possessed but what it fortunately lacked. Louis Hartz has maintained that the absence of a hereditary hierarchy and feudal tradition has made America different.[2] But the question of the correlation between a weak hierarchy and a different pattern of budgeting remains. In *Democracy in America,* the magisterial interpretation of American politics, Alexis de Tocqueville saw a relation between the availability of land and the general equality of condition promoting a proclivity to voluntary association.[3] Presumably, the more Americans devoted themselves to private groups, the less they would want government, especially central government, to do things for them. Although this argument could not explain the continuing controversy over the role of government in regard to what were called "internal improvements," it suggested that there was a rival social order to challenge the prevailing hierarchies. How does a desire for equality interact with a desire for order, voluntary with involuntary organization?

If one asks the related contemporary question of why the United States has "lagged behind" European social democracies in expanding welfare provisions, the best answer comes from Anthony King: American values are opposed to large government.[4] American government does less because its people are opposed to doing more.

The same sort of question underlies the perennial debate over whether the United States, alone among Western industrial nations, does not have a strong socialist party.[5] Apparently, America has imbibed the values of a commercial nation, opposing free enterprise to governmental intervention, and has done well enough for business to stem protest. In the end, values seem to explain everything.

That could be the problem. These explanations resolve into new questions: Why are American values structured the way they are? If these values follow in a single, cohesive, and consistent direction, how can one explain the ubiquity of political conflict? The answer could perhaps rest in disagreements over values.

It would be a mistake, therefore, to assume that there is one dominant culture in one country at one time. Presuppositions concerning cultural uniformity lead to tortuous efforts to account for diverse behavior through a single set of values thought to be operative at the time. By abandoning uniformity and postulating diversity in cultures, and the shared values and the social orders they support, this essay hopefully will explain the discrepancies between European and American budgetary behavior in the mobilization and allocation of resources.

American exceptionalism is a product of a more equal competition among three main cultures, namely, collectivism, individualism, and voluntarism, whose corresponding political regimes are, respectively, hierarchy, markets, and sects. The special circumstances of American life have created conditions in which people pursuing these various cultures have been more evenly balanced than elsewhere. Americanism consists in the ability to pursue not the same vision but separate visions. What outcomes would result from conflict and cooperation among hierarchic social orders, decentralized market anarchies, and voluntary egalitarian sects? An answer to this question overwhelms the imagination. But if one can pinpoint the manifestation of the political regimes representing these cultures in the budgetary arena, one can come closer to understanding American differences.

Collectivism has been weaker in America than elsewhere, partly because its elites compete for popular favor. Competitive individualism has always been strongly encouraged. Voluntarism has waxed and waned in strength. In the budgeting sphere, to recall the basics, hierarchies prefer to follow forms, punctual tax collection, and spending to shore up the regime. Sects, by contrast, prefer no executive discretion, little spending on the regime, and revenues, when possible, collected from the more prosperous. Markets are indifferent to forms or discretion but insist on getting a return for their money, including that part which government collects. They prefer lower taxes and spending, except for supporting projects from which they benefit. Assuming that these three political regimes are relatively equal in strength and appeal, on what budgeting issues do they agree, and on which do they disagree?

In regard to the choice of budgeting style, sects prefer detail as a means of controlling extravagance and virtually demand a person-by-person, object-by-object description. Hierarchies favor funding by organizational level; they essentially mimic their own niches. Competitive individualists choose lump sum budgeting because they care only about outcomes. The result, if collectivists and individualists are in the majority, is likely to be a compromise between extreme and minute detail, for example, the use of line-item budgeting with lump sums reserved for emergencies when results matter. The unity of the budget is another issue, however, because voluntarists and collectivists oppose the external control a unified budget signifies, especially if it limits market transactions or individual liberty.

Because markets and sects prefer to keep government on a short and parsimonious leash, spending levels are low. Spending to enhance equality attracts sects, however, and markets favor spending to aid business. Hierarchies tend to prefer spending for its own sake inasmuch as each level seeks to spend to maintain its own position. Bargaining can result when the hierarchy offers to aid business or "the people" in return for support of governmental establishments.

What about revenues? All regimes would like someone else to pay for their privileges. Because no regime commands a majority at any given time, compromises are made in an attempt to keep taxes low. When circumstances permit—for example, when there is a surplus—government, business, and the populace share the proceeds. On the other hand, when circumstances dictate—during war, for example—taxes are raised to satisfy sects, debt is incurred to satisfy markets, and the government grows to satisfy hierarchies.

Why did the need for a balanced budget become almost a religion? Consider the answer to be that it is the one thing about which all three cultural tendencies could agree. Start with the voluntarists in a sectarian regime. Their humble posture, coupled with low spending, is their chosen style. Perennial outsiders, they are not likely to enjoy the largesse of government spending. Nor, believing as they do in equality, would they easily justify the imposition of taxes that distinguish among individuals. Tying spending directly to the pain of raising revenues, they insist on balanced budgets as a means to curtail establishment spending.

Adherents of markets emphasize credit and currency because without stable financial values their endless transactions cannot be carried out. Inflation is anathema to market adherents because it gives debtors advantages over creditors. Market people do not object to deficits in principle so long as they benefit from the borrowing and, therefore, must be concerned about its inflationary effects. They temper the desire to redistribute losses with the need for stability by agreeing that revenues should, as often as possible, cover expenditures. This practice limits the efforts of sects to please the populace (common in the state legislatures) and of hierarchies to dress up government in finery inappropriate for a commercial people. Left to their own devices, hierarchies would run deficits as each level spent to maintain its distinctive niche.

During the era of the Continental Congress, in which revenues were more often promised than paid, hierarchies agreed to limit spending in exchange for raising revenues. Because hierarchies agreed to raise sufficient revenue, markets and sects limited their need for government spending. Thus, the inability of any one regime to dominate the others led to a common-denominator consensus: the balanced budget. And, as follows from any boundary formation, violations became subject to penalties: unemployment, inflation, public immorality, private vice, and collective ruin.

So much for large-scale speculation. Let us see how the hypothesis of cultural diversity characterizes American budgetary behavior.

The Colonial Period

In the fifty to one hundred years after the first settlers arrived during the latter 1600s and early 1700s, there was no money. The first colonists were poor; gold and silver had not yet been discovered. The only currency in circulation was a motley mixture of Dutch, English, and later, Spanish coins. Prices, particularly in New England, might be specified in guilders, pistoles, pieces of eight, doubloons, rit-dollars, as well as pounds and shillings. Each colony valued the separate sets of coins differently, running the metal back and forth, as it were, so one kind of coin disappeared in one place to be succeeded for a time in another.[6] Understandably, the shortage of ready cash was a constant theme of financial complaints.

When coins did not suffice, which was most of the time, trade was conducted in barter. Various staple commodities were declared legal currency. Rice and tobacco in the South, and cattle, corn, and furs in New England, were used to pay bills. A college student might pay tuition with a cow or a goat. Lacking a better method, Dutch settlers began to use Indian shell beads, or "Wampampeake" currency, composed of white beads taken from conch shells and the more rare, and hence more valuable, black beads from mussel or clam shells. Taxes, labor, and court judgments were payable in wampum.[7] Inevitably, the ratio of two white to one black shell varied as much as the value of the currency and depreciated even more given charges levied by settlers or Indians that one or the other had dyed white shells black.[8]

In the absence of commercial banks (before the American Revolution there were none), credit was extended and commerce carried on by merchants. Merchants minted silver "pine-tree shillings," deliberately made twenty-two and a half times lighter than the English variety so they would be retained in the colonies rather than shipped abroad.[9] Other merchants acted as agents of exchange or issued letters of credit to Americans traveling abroad. It was a hit-or-miss business. Debt was undesirable because it was considered by many to be a form of immorality; indeed, the debtor laws were so severe that a hapless soul might find himself in prison without the ability to raise ready money for his release. The desire to experiment with various issues of paper money may well have sprung from the understandable need to facilitate trade and to mitigate the sanctions imposed on debtors.[10]

Another form of currency, treasury bills, were issued by colonies in anticipation of tax notes created to pay for wars or for general administration. These notes passed through so many hands and were of such uncertain value that the practice was finally halted in favor of floating loans in advance of tax collections.[11] Dependent as the colonists were on whatever credit they could internally muster, it is understandable that the English Bubble Act of 1719, forbidding bills of credit to be issued first in England and then in America, led by 1751 to considerable opposition.[12]

Shortage of specie was exacerbated by the wars against the French that occurred intermittently between 1730 and 1760. Taxes rose by as much as ten to twenty times their prewar rates,[13] and under the lash of necessity, several colonial legislatures issued "paper money" in the form of bills of credit that bore interest and required repayment in specie. So long as these bills were only a small portion of available currency, they held up, but eventually they depreciated from half to a tenth of their former value.[14]

Under massive popular pressure, many colonies began to issue paper money, much of which not only fluctuated but rapidly depreciated in value as the printing presses ran overtime. In response, moralistic tracts were written that stressed the desirability of limiting the amount of money in circulation as a bar to inflation. One of Benjamin Franklin's earliest papers was on this subject, though the warning was generally not as necessary in pacifist Pennsylvania, where Quakers steadfastly refused to issue paper money to pay for war.[15] Nonetheless, Franklin's support of British restrictions on paper money led to his only electoral defeat.[16]

Though government in colonial times was simple, frugal, and rudimentary, its start-up costs were considerable in relation to income, especially in regard to specie, or hard cash. Forts had to be constructed, courts established and supplied with personnel, roads built, and prisons established. And to these local needs for revenue were added those of the mother country, which occasionally tried to rule in fact as well as name.

Mercantilism held sway in England. The major purpose of the trade and navigation laws, and the customs and revenue services, was to provide an outlet for British manufacturers. At the end of the Seven Years War, the English navy was freed to form a "colonial squadron" in an effort to cut off unauthorized trade. Perhaps natural advantage would have won the trade for England anyway, but the prevailing economic doctrine was against such a trial.[17] Competition outside the mother country was not considered a virtue. The revenue realized was small and was designed to support the custom service rather than to raise funds.[18]

Within the colonies, types of taxes varied according to circumstances. The property tax dominated in New England. It included taxes on personal property, such as cattle and slaves, as well as on houses and land, assessed at current value multiplied by six. Rates were a penny to the pound of assessed valuation and varied from a high of sixteen times during King Phillip's war of 1676 to a low of half a rate. This tax weighed most heavily on farmers whose barns, cattle, and houses were difficult to hide. In an effort to shift the burden of taxation from farmers, a poll tax was instituted in which an individual was considered to be worth twenty pounds and was assessed at a rate of one penny per pound. The poll tax fluctuated according to the property tax. Because it placed particular hardship on the poor, the poll tax was later abandoned. There were exemptions to payment, of course, including the governor of the colony, schoolteachers, ministers, invalids, and students at Harvard College. Because the property and poll taxes were not directly related to income, there was also a "faculty" (or income or ability to earn) tax imposed on those who earned more than a given sum. This tax presumed, often with little evidence, that certain occupations could earn an anticipated salary.[19]

In the South one would not expect taxes on property, including land and slaves, or on income to be popular among the landholders. They preferred indirect taxes on exports and imports. Poll taxes were levied and usually were paid in pounds of tobacco or some other commodity.

The middle colonies, New York, New Jersey, and Maryland, used a combination of direct and indirect taxes. They added refinements of their own, including a graduated poll tax that levied the heaviest rates on apparently unpopular segments of the community, such as wig wearers, rich bachelors, and lawyers. Despite Quaker opposition, all of the colonies, at one time or another, indulged in lotteries to finance education: Dartmouth, Princeton, Harvard, and Yale all gained financial assistance from lotteries. Instead of forced labor on public projects, several colonies required that contributions in kind, such as tobacco, be paid for building a fort or as a fine in case one failed to attend church.[20]

Viewed outside of the contemporary context, colonial expenditures were as simple and bland as colonial taxation. Care of the poor, insane, sick, or otherwise indigent was a local responsibility. Public works were few and sparse. Highways were short and rough, and courthouses, though sometimes gilded with a handsome facade, were small. Judges were few and did not require much assistance. No colonial navy existed, and the army, except in the period of the great Indian wars and during the war with France for control of the North American continent, was composed of local militia. Legislatures met only for short periods of time and, if received, payments for service and attendance were in minimal amounts. The colonial executive departments were tiny, and officials were often paid by fees for services rather than from general revenues. The royal governors alone received substantial salaries.

Yet it was not the actual expenditures that mattered but the power relationships they signified. Why should the colonists be taxed to support governors who might flaunt their will and whom they did not appoint? Why should the home country pay for distant wars? Even the remnants of feudal dues, known as quit-rents and paid to government in return for land use, went to colonial treasuries. By 1762, the king refused to supply garrisons to those colonies who would not maintain them.[21]

The extraordinary effort of colonial legislatures to control executives by limiting their expenditures, the duration for which they could be paid, and the objects for which the money could be spent, gives this era its peculiar stamp. If the colonies belonged to England, and if the colonists were English subjects, then it was their duty to support royal governors. Because the colonists wanted British protection but not British rule, however, they freely used the English tradition of denying supply in order to force compliance with the legislative will. The commonplace view, so assiduously peddled by the colonists in the prerevolutionary period, that if the English king were only reasonable they would love him, is not supported by monetary or fiscal fact.

To say that royal governors were kept amenable to colonists' will does not do justice to their "Yankee" ingenuity in devising financial restraints.[22] Connecticut may have been extreme in making the salary of the governor and other important executives dependent upon semiannual appropriations, but it was a common practice to vote salaries annually. It might be thought that indirect taxes, excises, and import duties would be perpetual until changed, but these were often reenacted yearly. Royal governors were not permitted permanent sources of revenue.[23] Appropriations were specified by object and amount. Extremely long appropriation clauses prescribed exactly what could and could not be done. The requirement that all unexpended balances revert back to the treasury added insult to injury. It might be thought that once an appropriation was voted, the executive could proceed to spend the money for the purpose stipulated. Several colonies, however, elected treasurers independent of the colonial governors, which precluded management of his own finances. Other colonial legislatures insisted that no payment might be made except with their specific consent, a requirement which gave them control over the disbursement of public funds. And when an emergency arose that appeared to all to justify a special appropriation, colonial assemblies might well appoint a special commission accountable to them rather than to the governor. Colonial legislatures often segregated revenues by voting taxes for specific purposes, for example, the building of a fort, or of a lighthouse, or the salary of a governor. A clause would often be added stipulating that once these purposes had been accomplished the money could be spent for "no other use or purpose whatsoever."[24] Colonial assemblies frequently reduced the salary of royal officials. The assemblies stipulated the name of the person who was to do the work, making these officials legally accountable for all funds expended. Often these actions were accomplished without a specific legislative act. If the character of a government is known by its monetary policies, America was already "independent" in many respects.[25]

During the colonial period, the dimensions were understood: Royal governors and their supporters wanted a civil list of appointments and perquisites independent of the funds appropriated by legislatures, and the colonists wanted to create uncertainty, parsimony, and narrowness to keep royal governors amenable to the will of the colonies. To the English, it seemed only reasonable that the colonists should pay for the support of the royal government. The Stamp Act, duties on tea, and other tax impositions on the colonies were royal efforts to provide independent sources of income for their officials in America. Power, not money, was the issue. The American Revolution was fought over a revolutionary issue, the issue of who should rule in America. A contemporary of the period on the colonial government of New York commented,

It will be seen that the democratick branch of the colonial government had placed the governor, and almost every other office, in a state of dependence upon its votes and measures. Not a single shilling could be withdrawn from the treasury but by legislative consent. This was particularly galling to the lieutenant governor. It had stripped him of that executive patronage and influence which was deemed by him so essential to the support of his administration. In truth, it was a great step towards that independence which was afterward obtained.[26]

This brief background should help the modern reader to appreciate the colonists' insistence on legislative direction of fiscal policy. Their strategy for financing the Revolutionary War would not have been chosen by any contemporary European country, nor would it be recommended today. However, for the colonists it was entirely natural. A war for independence from a distant authority would be perverse, especially if it only replaced an English king with a new American hierarchy.

The First and Second American Revolutions

The Continental Congress was a temporary association of colonial assemblies gathered to fight a "temporary" war. Executive bodies, in addition to symbolizing the wrong kind of authority, suggested a future permanence that could not be envisioned by the colonial assembly. It could imagine what colonial governments had been, and it proceeded to behave in its new congressional form just as it had in the colonies. The Congress copied colonial assemblies by setting up committees, called boards, to direct foreign affairs and other essential activities, including finance. The fiscal committees, named the Board of Treasury and the Treasury Office of Accounts, were to act not directly but through colonial entities. The story is well known, a patchwork narrative of endless difficulties, embarrassments, ineptitudes, and contradictions, with only the final victory lending contour to its plot. If we rehearse this well-worn tradition, it would be not only to outline the weaknesses that the Constitutional Convention attempted to overcome but also to see in its methods a different and more decentralized mode of operation.

Fiscal policy during the Revolutionary War was inadequate and chaotic. The colonies in rebellion against the king differed in their devotion to the war, in their capabilities and suffering, and in their ability to figure out what they were expected to do. It is true that colonial militia, paid and supplied by colonial assemblies, conducted part of the fighting, but they did not assist the major army under the command of General George Washington.[27] As the Continental Congress began to demand larger contributions, colonial payments lagged further behind. Because neither payments in kind nor in coinage were adequate, the Continental Congress began to print paper. In a short time, the currency depreciated to almost nothing, leaving as its legacy only a phrase that survives as the epitome of worthlessness: "not worth a Continental."[28] In the doggerel of the time,

> A refugee captain lost two of his men;
> And ardently wishing to have them again,
> To the Major applied, on an exchange to fix,
> And requested to know if for two he'd tax six?
> Major Adams agreed, nor said a word more,
> And Paddy was order'd to fetch them ashore;
> Who cried out in surprise: "By Ja—s, my honey,
> Our men now depreciate as fast as our money."[29]

Soldiers were paid little and were often not paid on time. Officers were paid even less, on the supposition that they were independently wealthy. After several years of confusing policy, Robert Morris, a signer of the Declaration of Independence, was called in to restore financial order. A full-time executive rather than a part-time legislator was given the challenge. But even with his legendary ingenuity, Morris could not create something from nothing. At the end of a lengthy correspondence to Morris, General George Washington wrote,

> I must entreat you, if possible, to procure one month's pay in specie for the detachment which I have under my command. Part of the troops have not been paid anything for a long time past, and have upon several occasions shown marks of great discontent. The service they are going upon is disagreeable to the northern regiments; but I make no doubt that a douceur of a little hard money would put them in proper temper. If the whole sum cannot be obtained, a part of it will be better than none, as it may be distributed in proportion to the respective wants and claims of the men.[30]

Robert Morris replied,

> I have already advised Your Excellency of the unhappy situation of money matters, and very much doubt if it will be possible to pay the detachment a month's pay, as you wish. Therefore it will be best not to raise in them any expectation of that kind. Should it come unexpectedly, so much the better.[31]

Pressed from all sides, and sometimes subject to the anger of creditors and soldiers, Morris took the view that if he could not pay everyone he would pay no one at all.[32] As William Graham Sumner comments: "This reasoning shows that he had high qualifications for the Financier of the Revolution."[33] Under such circumstances, it was Morris's policy to get money from whatever sources he could and worry later about making payment. One of his tactics involved making a draft on Benjamin Franklin in Paris; he then cashed it and sent the paper for collection through Cuba and thence to Madrid, knowing that his private communications would reach Franklin weeks before the paper did. It was then "Poor Richard's" task to find an expedient way to raise money for payment of the bill when it did arrive. Of course, Morris was not thoughtful of Franklin's feelings, but then again, anyone with scruples would not have been suitable for the task. No doubt, as Grayson put it, Morris "told some grand lies," but that, in another writer's opinion, did not justify criticism by little men "none of whom would have been able to save a country when it was flat broke."[34] Morris later received his reward, however. Because of unfortunate speculation in a land transaction, he ended his days in a debtors' prison in Philadelphia. His one recorded solace was given by George Washington, who, upon hearing of the debacle, brought Morris supper and spent the night with him in prison.[35]

The Continental Congress lasted from 1775 to 1781, when it was replaced by the Articles of Confederation. The Articles spoke of a common treasury but left the taxing power in the hands of the individual states. Financial difficulty continued to plague the revolutionary forces. As debts multiplied, both during the war and in the years following, it became necessary for the states to print money to pay the debts incurred. Nonetheless, the debts incurred during the war remained unsatisfied. This situation was compounded by certain financial measures that made it difficult for states to trade abroad and with each other. Currency depreciated from state to state. The revolutionary elite wondered whether sufficient order could be maintained to keep the republic together.

That view may have been expressed by some, but it was not the only view. William Schultz and M. R. Caine have described an alternative view:

> The Colonials accepted the situation philosophically. Paper money they would and must have. If these were the evils of paper money, they would take the evil along with the good. As a Mr. Wise of Massachusetts wrote, in a pamphlet entitled *A Word of Comfort,* "Gentlemen! You must do by your Bills, as all Wise Men do by their Wives; Make the best of them."[36]

Far from condemning inflation, a writer in the *Pennsylvania Packet* gave his opinion that

> the natural unavoidable tax of depreciation is the most certain, expeditious, and equal tax that could be devised. Upon the scale which has lately existed, every possessor of money has paid a tax for it, in proportion to the time he held it. Like a hackney coach it must be paid for by the hour.[37]

Given time, a common market of currency and credit might have been created. No one will ever know, however, because the Constitutional Convention, without legal warrant under the Articles of Confederation, ended the experiment.

Then came a central government sufficiently strong to levy taxes on its own, giving it the potential to restore economic order.[38] Yet in 1789, the Constitution was still only a document with which the people had yet to have a practical experience. They had had over 200 years of experience being governed by England and of self-government under colonial assemblies. It is not surprising, therefore, that the practices and habits of mind gained in two centuries of day-to-day operations manifested themselves under the new rubric that was created as their chosen instrument of self-government. The framers realized that they had undertaken an experiment in self-rule that had little precedent. It was a then-prevailing tenet that governments evolved by practice of the common law rather than as a result of a willful act of self-creation. Yet it was, if we wish to explain American exceptionalism, not all new; it had a new structure, but it was composed of old practices. Nowhere was this interaction more evident than in the development of budgeting. Taxing and spending focused direct attention on how the general structure established by the Constitution was to be actually practiced. The import of the American story has been missed. The lack of a hierarchical European structure has been taken to mean no structure at all because the uniformity of practice indicated the lack of an operating ideology when it should have suggested the opposite. The significance of the commitment to budget balance is great, as is that of the rejection of a centralized executive, with its concomitant preference for decentralized, legislative forms of budgeting. There was an extraordinary combination of the absence of anything that could be called a central budget with a powerful, though informal, coordination of expenditure and revenue. This phenomenon needs neither criticism nor praise but understanding. The rise, at the beginning of the twentieth century, of a budgetary reform movement that was hostile toward past practices and structures (including the separation of powers in the Constitution) and monolithic by favoring executive domination has obscured a different way of budgetary life.

Understanding the present requires resurrecting the discarded ghost of budgets past. Therefore, in the following sections, we depart from a strict historical chronology to trace key questions of budgeting through time. The next section takes up the balance between expenditure and revenue.

Public Debt and Balanced Budgets

The history of American attitudes toward public debt may be translated into formulas for relating revenues to expenditures that are no less powerful for being simple. The first of these budgetary equations[39] is simplicity itself: revenues minus interest on the public debt equal allowable national government spending. The new Constitution provided ample taxing authority, including direct levies on individuals and internal excise taxes. In the debate over ratification, however, the proponents of the Constitution frequently insisted that the bulk of taxes be raised by custom duties and sale of public lands, with income and excise taxes reserved for emergencies. Despite Hamilton's major effort both to exert executive authority and simultaneously to give the government a sounder financial basis by invoking internal taxes,[40] the Jeffersonians soon reverted to their pretended version, in which tariffs predominated. Given the widespread agreement on balanced budgets and parsimony in government, as well as the desire to pay off the public debt, the first equation had appeal.

Life soon provided the circumstances that lawyers say alter cases. During war the second equation prevailed: revenues, this time including internal taxes, equal ordinary civilian expenditures minus wartime debt. When surpluses appeared or the attractiveness of internal improvements proved irresistible, or both, a third equation operated: revenues in surplus minus interest on debt, minus ordinary spending, minus internal improvements equal central government spending. It was only with the revolution in fiscal thought following the Great Depression of the 1930s that the fourth equation, sometimes called a full-employment surplus, took center stage. The idea was to balance not the budget but the economy at full employment. The fourth equation stipulates that revenues plus a deficit sufficient to secure full employment equals spending. The formulation of a fifth equation is under discussion today.

The first American Constitution reacted against the Articles of Confederation. A major motivation behind the new governmental structure was to provide the national government with sufficient powers to levy taxes (without the direct concurrence of the states) so that national credit might be placed on a firm foundation. In the first month after President George Washington took office and before a treasury department existed, laws were enacted establishing customs duties and providing for their collection.[41] In his magisterial reports on public credit of 1790 and 1795, Alexander Hamilton argued the importance of consolidating state debts by adding them to the national debt and arranging to fund them with revenues provided for that specific purpose. This was hard for his agrarian, small-farmer Jeffersonian opponents to accept. Much of the debt had been severely discounted and was owned by speculators who stood to gain far more than the original holders. Additionally, there was no way to effect even rough equanimity of burden in states who, had they done more during the revolutionary period, would be owed less. Yet the idea of public faith and sound credit proved as difficult to resist as the related idea that funding the debt would help balance the budget each year. Each generation was, therefore, encouraged to pay its own costs.[42] The problems Hamilton's argument created for his agrarian opponents were well placed and succinctly stated by John Taylor of Carolina:

> We moderns; we enlightened Americans; we who have abolished hierarchy and title; and we who are submitting to be taxed . . . without being deluded or terrified

by the promise of heaven, the denunciation of hell . . . or superstition. A spell is put on our understandings by the words "public faith and national credit."[43]

Yet there was more to the argument than a magic charm. In a classic case of bargaining, Hamilton arranged the transfer of the nation's capital from New York to Washington, D.C., which was nearer Virginia and the South, in exchange for votes to pass the bill concerning assumption of debt.[44] Critical discussion of the subject usually ends here, but such an ending is inappropriate. Without a general value congruence on the virtue of a balanced budget, this political exchange would not have been feasible. Moreover, the attack by the Republican party on the powers of the executive branch has not been considered. The agrarian, egalitarian Republicans did agree to assume state debts. Using the same skill as those who sought to incorporate institutional safeguards through the Constitution, however, the Republicans filled in the Constitutional interstices with articles designed to limit the executive branch's use of whatever spending powers it gained through an assumption of debt. The Republicans relied on their own financial formulas more than they did on those promulgated by the federalist position.

President Thomas Jefferson (1801-1808) promoted a budgetary belief corresponding with his conviction that the soil of liberty had to be nurtured in every generation with the blood of martyrs. Thinking it wrong for one generation to bind the next by its debts, Jefferson believed that, when incurred, debts should be paid within twenty years. For Jefferson, economy meant frugality and parsimony. Favoring the lowly style and the lingua humis popular at the time, Jefferson viewed economy and debt payment as necessities for a moral life. "I place economy among the first and most important of republican virtues," he wrote, "and public debt as the greatest of the dangers to be feared."[45] Though he believed that "the earth belongs always to the living generation," and therefore favored rapid retirement of the public debt, Jefferson would rather cut spending than raise taxes. "I am for government rigorously frugal and simple," Jefferson wrote, "applying all the possible savings of the public revenue to the discharge of the national debt."[46]

Jefferson, however, gave enough importance to a balanced budget to propose enshrining the concept in the Constitution. For him, as for other anti-Federalists, it was the Republican form of government that was at stake. Looking back to political philosopher James Harrington and to the Whig "party of the country" in England, Jefferson viewed debt and its holders as the equivalent of the place in Parliament of the king, who corrupted government by financial interests and hence exerted executive control.[47]

Observe that Jefferson's rejection of debt was not merely abstract but depended on a certain historical context: a central government led by its executive power trying to introduce new inequalities or maintain old ones. State governments, thought to be free from this corrupting influence, could presumably assume as much debt as desired.

Life was good in early America. Despite the repeal of internal taxes in the first year of Jefferson's administration and the $11 million spent to acquire the Louisiana Territory, the increase in American commerce enabled both substantial repayments on the debt and an increase in Treasury reserves. Part of the impetus that drove Jefferson and Gallatin to retire the debt was surely the reduction of this "moral cankor," but they also believed that erasing the debt would free the remaining revenues for public purposes. The conflicts between those favoring economy for its own sake and those wishing better education or other internal improvements could be mitigated by including expenditures under the mantle of the balanced budget.[48]

The War of 1812 upset budgetary expectations for two reasons: It was expensive, and it disrupted commerce and thereby reduced income. Initially, the war was to be strictly financed by debt, but by 1813 millions of dollars in internal taxes were voted, as were rate increases on tariffs. The net result was a substantial increase in debt. Taxes were willingly paid in view of the urgency and proximity of war, but there were substantial misgivings about the debt incurred.[49] Following Jefferson's lead, President James Madison (1809-1817) wanted his administration "to liberate the public resources by an honorable discharge of the public debt." Similarly, James Monroe (1817-1824) and John Quincy Adams (1825-1829) wanted to reduce debt to free customs revenues.[50] The ideal of a balanced budget took on increasingly moralistic overtones. John Quincy Adams considered its achievement "among the maxims of political economy," and his Secretary of the Treasury called debt reduction "amongst the highest duties of a nation" because it showed that a government is a prompt payer.[51] Debt reduction was a good thing either in and of itself or as a prelude to incurring still more debt. Debt reduction could mean both less and more spending.

By the time of President Andrew Jackson (1829-1836), debt reduction had become a patriotic duty. Realizing that the remaining debt might be retired during his administration, Jackson waxed lyric: "We shall then exhibit the rare example of a great nation, abounding in all the means of happiness and security, altogether free from debt." American exceptionality was publicly proclaimed when Secretary of the Treasury Levi Woodbury heralded the extinction of the debt as an "unprecedented spectacle . . . presented to the world."[52]

Then, from within the wellsprings of abundance, the specter of a corresponding evil surfaced: "the unnecessary accumulation of public revenue," as Andrew Jackson called it, or more simply, a surplus. Why should this cornucopia be an embarrassment? Because, as President Martin Van Buren (1837-1841) remarked, governments would be "constantly exposed to great deficiencies or excesses, with all their attended embarrassments." In his last annual message,

Van Buren argued that the surplus "would foster national extravagance" and would thus encourage rapid accumulation of a larger and more onerous debt. His theory was that if a government does not have revenues, it cannot spend them. Once a surplus existed, it would be too tempting to resist spending and a vicious cycle of increasing expenditures would begin.[53] As depression brought debt, President John Tyler (1841-1845) railed against owing money, maintaining, as did his successor James K. Polk (1845-1849), that debt reduction was a source of strength among the nations of the world. Warning against the errors occasioned by the War of 1812, in particular the excessive and unnecessary expenses, Polk argued that war was an additional reason for economy in all ordinary expenditure.[54]

These presidents did not believe government spending would encourage redistribution of wealth from the rich to the poor. "Melancholy is the condition of that people," President Polk wrote, "whose government can be sustained only by a system which periodically transfers large amounts from the labors of the many to the coffers of the few."[55] For these men, as for the citizens they governed, debt was equated with privilege. Between 1849 and 1861, when the Civil War began, every national government had pledged itself both to apply surpluses to extinction of the debt and to reduce revenues to the level of spending. Beyond this minimum, President James Buchanan (1857-1861) would only allow expenditures clearly warranted by the Constitution, such as increases in naval and coastal defenses.[56]

Faith in the balanced budget ideal was strengthened by an economic theory that negatively tied wages to debt. As Secretary of the Treasury Robert J. Walker claimed in 1838: "Wages can only be increased in any nation, in the aggregate, by augmenting capital, the fund out of which wages are paid....The destruction or diminution of capital, by destroying or reducing the fund from which labor is paid must reduce wages." This wage/fund argument had the added value of suggesting that the wage earner would be hurt by any effort to go into debt to improve his lot.[57] During the recession of 1837 and 1838, when efforts were made to increase federal spending in order to alleviate suffering, President Van Buren invoked the sagacity of the Founding Fathers, who "wisely judged that the less government interferes with private pursuits the better for the general prosperity."[58] The economy would improve by reducing the deficit, not by building railroads or canals. President Buchanan blamed the financial panic and recession of 1857 and 1858 on "the habit of extravagant spending."[59]

The Civil War of 1861 to 1865 marked the first break in consensus on debt reduction. The necessity for balanced budgets remained the norm but the growth of presidential discretion and the rise of industrial expansion left the role of debt open to argument. Abraham Lincoln (1861—1865) thought that citizens "cannot be much oppressed by a debt which they owe to themselves." His theory, followed by President Rutherford B. Hayes a decade later (1877-1881), was to effect a wider distribution of the debt among citizens. Postulating that the debt might be paid over time, President Ulysses S. Grant (1869-1877) asserted that the capacity to pay grew with the wealth of the nation. Rather than raising taxes to pay the debt over a shorter period, he suggested a cut in taxes to increase wealth and thereby provide greater subsequent revenues.[60] During a time of expansion the desire for internal improvements seemed compatible with fiscal prudence.

Expressing the prevailing sentiment, Grant's Secretary to the Treasury, George S. Boutwell, claimed in 1870 that "a public debt is a public evil, especially injurious to working people." Having inherited a debt of some two and a half billion dollars, President Andrew Johnson (1865-1869) considered debt a burden on the economy that should be paid off within twenty years. Despite the considerable increase in population and wealth, Johnson was startled to learn that expenditures during his term would total around $1.6 billion, only slightly less than the entire amount for the period from 1789 to 1861. He feared that per capita expenditure would reach nearly $10. The expenditure before the war had been held to $9 per person. He responded by urging retrenchment.[61] These were days during which spending, and the revenues supporting it, could not be too low.

President Grover Cleveland (1885-1889) believed that withdrawing capital from the people and transferring it to government imperiled prosperity. His words were a last stand against the spending boom that followed:

> When we consider that the theory of our institutions guarantees to every citizen the full enjoyment of all the fruits of his industry and enterprise, with only such deduction as may be his share toward the careful and economical maintenance of the government which protects him, it is plain that the exaction of more than this is indefensible extortion and a culpable betrayal of American fairness and justice. This wrong inflicted upon those who bear the burden of national taxation, like other wrongs, multiplies a brood of evil consequences. The public Treasury, which should only exist as a conduit conveying the peoples tribute to its legitimate objects of expenditure, becomes a hoarding place for money needlessly withdrawn from trade and the people's use, thus crippling our national energies.[62]

Viewing debt as something a people owes itself, to be judged not as an inherent evil but relative to a country's ability to pay, is not far from the idea that the size of the deficit matters less than the government's, and through it the people's, return on monies expended. The presidents from 1898 to 1920 were all opposed to unbalanced budgets. But their twentieth-century successors, imbued with the progressive gospel of efficiency, were more inclined to stress the duality of spending. For this new breed of president, efficient organization, and "value for money," as the English say today, mattered more than parsimony.[63] The American people, Woodrow Wilson said, "are not jealous of the amount their Government costs if they are sure that they get what they need and desire for the outlay, that the money is being spent for objects of which they approve, and that it is being applied with good business sense and management."[64]

Supporting this development of professional interest in efficiency and the new civil service movement's concomitant stress on neutral competence and expertise was a homiletic literature urging thrift. Mr. Micawber's advice to David Copperfield in King's Bench prison that spending just below income is happiness while spending just above it is misery was endlessly repeated. Thriftiness was synonymous with morality and success.

These vague rumblings of fiscal prudence, both against the growing debt and for a balanced budget, reasserted themselves with a vengeance in the 1920s. World War I had been largely fought on borrowed money. From 1914 to 1918, the government's role in directing economic activity expanded enormously. There was a sudden public concern that the profligate habits of wartime would carry over into peacetime civilian life. The Victory Liberty Loan Act of 1919 established a sinking fund to reduce the debt, which was cut by a third—from $24 to $16 billion—by the end of the 1920s. Wilson's Secretary of the Treasury, Carter Glass, pointed out the "grave danger that the extraordinary success of the Treasury in financing the stupendous war expenditures may lead to a riot of public expenditures after the war, the consequences of which could only be disastrous." His successor under President Harding (1921-1923), David F. Huston, similarly observed that "we have demobilized many groups, but we have not demobilized those whose gaze is concentrated on the Treasury."[65]

The idea that government should function like a business, that "our public household," like a successful private enterprise, should be operated under a "rigid and yet sane economy" was a leitmotif of the 1920s. Whereas in past decades decrease of the public debt was said to reduce the influence of its foreign holders, President Calvin Coolidge (1923-1928) argued that low taxes and spending would give the American people "that contentment and peace of mind which will go far to render them immune from any envious inclination toward other countries." Competition over markets would subside if Americans were prosperous at home.[66] Coolidge contended that "economy reaches everywhere. It carries a blessing to everybody." Whereas "the result of economic dissipation to a nation is always moral decay," Coolidge believed that "economy is idealism in its most practical form."[67] The substance of this practical idealism was probably less important than the spirit it conveyed.

This economic mood could and did get more mawkish. Speaking at the tenth regular meeting of the Business Organization of the Government, the second head of the Bureau of the Budget, Director Lord, exclaimed, "We still follow you, Mr. President, singing the old and tried battle song, economy with efficiency, one and inseparable. May we continue to sing it until in a noble paean of praise it heralds the day when taxes cease to be burdensome and serve what is a grateful expression of our appreciation of the numberless privileges and boundless blessings we enjoy in this most favored Nation of the earth."[68] Director Lord accordingly founded various clubs to hold expenditures down, such as the Two-percent Personnel Club in order to cut personnel spending in that amount per year and a Correspondence Club to save money on messages. He also established the Loyal Order of Woodpeckers, "whose persistent tapping away at waste will make cheerful music in government offices and workshops during the coming year."[69]

Then came the market crash of 1929, followed by the Depression of the 1930s. The Depression marked both an end to the primacy of the balanced budget and a beginning of the variable expenditure as an instrument of economic stabilization. The great budgetary equation had been fundamentally reoriented. The emphasis shifted from matching spending and revenue at the lowest possible level to manipulation of the difference between them. The Employment Act of 1946 signaled a new equation focusing federal policy on the goal of full employment, with deficits and surpluses left to vary in its wake. Spending and owing, instead of being the great enemies of economy, had become its greatest friends. There was also the tradition of internal improvements to which supporters of higher spending could turn for historical justification of their position.

Internal Improvements

The subject of internal improvements may be taken broadly to include any sort of governmental subsidy for any purpose whatsoever, and not just those subsidies for roads and canals that gave the controversy its historical name. Advocates of markets might generally wish lower taxes and spending, but they always stood ready to accept subsidies that would diffuse the costs of sustaining commerce over a range of taxpayers. Adherents of hierarchy are generally willing to undertake expenditures that will add to national unity and help maintain order throughout the nation. Egalitarians would be opposed to internal improvements, seeing in them unjustified advantages for those in government who would occupy places of profit and those in society who already had more than their share of wealth and privilege. Americans who straddled the line between equity and hierarchy, and who viewed internal improvement as a means of assisting small farmers scattered throughout the vast extent of the nation, would be convicted. They would resolve this conflict by adhering first and foremost to the doctrine of a balanced budget, believing that when that was achieved they might spend the surplus to benefit the general lot of citizens. Given this rough division of forces, it could be expected that over time there would be more rather than less subsidy. And, as the nation industrialized, giving market adherents greater prominence, internal improvements would turn out to be even a better thing.

With 30 percent of the federal budget devoted to interest payments on the national debt and 55 percent given over to the army and navy, and with the nation still recovering from the war, the administrations of George Washington and John Adams resorted to long-term loans to cover current deficits. In that situation no room for internal improvements existed. The Republicans under Jefferson engaged in a policy of retrenchment, practically eliminated the navy, slimmed down the army, and reduced the rest. The Republicans also cut internal taxes but left tariffs intact to create a surplus.[70] By 1805, with commerce improved and the end of the public debt in sight, Jefferson hoped that "the revenue thereby liberated may . . . be applied, *in time of peace, to* rivers, canals, roads, arts, manufacturers, education and the other great objects within each State." Undecided on the constitutional validity of such spending, Jefferson recommended that there be a constitutional amendment to remove doubt on the subject. Gallatin, his Secretary of the Treasury, had already made room for building the Cumberland Road and National Pike. The funds came from the sale of public lands in Ohio, which was then still a territory.[71] At the end of Jefferson's administration, Gallatin prepared a major report on public works calling for a $20 million program of canal and highway construction.[72]

Except for tariffs, which were already firmly ensconced because industry in America called for protection against Europe, Jefferson's administration did not otherwise attempt to act on the economy. Though its abandonment of old Republican principles concerning internal improvements caused considerable conflict within the party, these departures were made good by a strict constitutionalism, concern for states' rights, and meticulous circumscription of the role of executive officials. Older Republicans, such as John Randolph and John Taylor, were absolutely opposed to these new federal commitments to internal improvements. But new Republicans, such as John Calhoun, John Quincy Adams, and later, Henry Clay, were in favor of liberal spending for canals and roads. Whatever the decline of partisanship in the "era of good feelings," extending from the presidencies of Monroe and John Quincy Adams (1817-1828), the consensus did not extend to internal improvements.

Criticized for adopting Monroe's proposed plan for internal improvements, President John Quincy Adams avidly sought appropriations for rivers, harbors, lighthouses, beacons, piers, and most of all, roads. Adams' major effort had been to use the surplus to provide "a permanent and regular system . . . of . . . internal improvements" so that "the surface of the whole Union would have been checkered with railroads and canals."[73] During his presidency there were set up a House Committee on Roads and Canals, a Civil Engineer Corps inside the Army Engineers; grants of public lands were routinely made to new states to encourage them to build roads and canals, and "Rivers and Harbors" appro-

priations were made. The (in)famous "Pork Barrel" legislation had its beginning in which it was alleged, with good reason, that congressmen dipped their
hands to get goodies for their districts, much as the boys at the country store
did around a barrel of real pork.[74]

What was to stop this bucolic movement for internal improvements from
continuing? This answer rested in President Andrew Jackson (1828-1836),
whose forces had fought internal improvements in Congress. "Old Hickory"
stopped them in their tracks. Jackson maintained himself in office by dethron-
ing "King Caucus," the method of presidential nomination by senatorial caucus, in favor of a more egalitarian and popular national nominating convention. I mention this only to show that the same voluntaristic impulses that led
to the one—opposition to federal support or subsidy of internal improvement—
also led to the other—the replacement of an oligarchical by a more egalitarian
mode of presidential nomination. Because Jacksonians believed that interest
payment on the national debt meant a redistribution of income from the poor
to rich, the fund from which wages were drawn was depressed by such payments and the capital released from government spending into private hands
would increase productivity and therefore wages, their disapproval of internal
improvements was to them part of their public policy in favor of the ordinary
citizen. Favoring the common man, in those days, meant favoring individual
and not governmental enterprise.[75]

The same strictures that applied to federal debt did not apply with equal
force to the states. On the contrary, if egalitarians viewed state governments as
enhancing equality by virtue of popular control, then they might also be encouraged to help the citizenry by all manner of activities. Louis Hartz has
shown that laissez-faire was hardly the prevailing practice in Pennsylvania
before the Civil War.[76] When the states warmed up to their task after the demise
of the Second Bank of the United States, they borrowed more from 1835 to
1838 than the total federal deficit from 1789 to 1838. The debt was devoted to
canal and railroad construction and to capital for chartering state banks.[77]

Support for and opposition to internal improvements waxed and waned for
the thirty years before the Civil War. Congressional advocates like Henry Clay
produced one bill after another. What would stop "a disreputable scramble for
public money," President Polk asked while vetoing a rivers and harbors bill, if
all that were left were congressional discretion as to the fitness of things? Why,
internal improvements were "capable of indefinite enlargement and sufficient
to swallow up as many millions annually as could be extracted from the foreign commerce of the country." Allied with a protective tariff that brought in
ever-larger sums, Polk believed that "the operation and necessary effect of the
whole system would encourage large and extravagant expenditures, and thereby
. . . increase the public patronage, and maintain a rich and splendid government at the expense of a taxed and impoverished people."[78] Acquiring Texas or

another large expanse of territory was another matter, properly a part of the nation's "manifest destiny." Even so, many of the promises made to get Texas into the Union, promises in the way of Federal largesse, remained unfulfilled.[79]

If it was money that mattered to Polk, it was public morality about which Presidents Pierce and Buchanan cared. They rejected internal improvements on the grounds that these were unconstitutional because they usurped state functions. They saw internal improvement as a means by which the general government would aggrandize itself at the expense of states.[80] For other leading men of the day, however, from Daniel Webster to John Calhoun and President Millard Fillmore the great issue was, as it had been to Jefferson, the growth of the nation. They believed that although the work might be done locally, it had a larger general or national importance. Although no one would ever say that they wanted to encroach on the right of any single state, it was a case of a big brother helping a smaller one so as, as Fillmore put it, to "strengthen the ties which bind us together as a people."[81]

Needless to say, in that day as today, the learned scribes were on both sides of the situation. It was not Adam Smith's *Wealth of Nations* or Ricardo's *Principles of Political Economy* but, rather, Jean-Baptiste Say's *A Treatise on Political Economy*, which appeared in 1803, that became popular in the United States. Louis Kimmel, whose brilliant book on federal debt I have often cited, believes that "a factor in Say's favor was that he avoided Smith's distinction between 'productive' and 'unproductive' employment. Neither professors of moral philosophy nor the clergy had been quite willing to accept an exposition into the moral science of political economy that classified them as unproductive." Say did agree with Adam Smith, however, on the crucial consideration that consumption of wealth by government, although it might be necessary, was justified only to the extent that it brought in returns of equivalent value. The doctrine of opportunity costs, the value of the object is what has to be given up to acquire it, here finds an early statement. And so does a notion of cost-benefit analysis: "The whole skill of government," Say says, ". . . consists in a continual and judicious comparison of the sacrifice about to be incurred, with the expected benefits to the community."[82] A native book, Henry Vethake's *The Principles of Political Economy,* objected to debt financing because it led to less care in the spending of public money. But so long as government funds were used for productive purposes, he thought such spending was as good as if the money had been left in private hands.[83] All in all, it does not appear that the writings of learned men exerted much influence one way or the other on the debate about internal improvements.

Compared to European countries, spending in the United States stood practically still, barely keeping up with the increase in population. Nevertheless, the federal government did do some things outside of its limited sphere. As early as 1796, collectors of revenue assisted in the enforcement of state quarantine laws. Medical care for disabled and sick seamen was instituted in 1798, eventually leading to the establishment of the United States Public Health Service. Small numbers of agricultural statistics were collected and free seeds distributed. Statistics on commerce and lifesaving stations on the Atlantic coast were established. Moving onto larger matters, there were subsidies to carriers of ocean mail and railroads.[84] The mail subsidies were justified by a parallel policy adopted in Great Britain for the purpose of encouraging steamships that could be readily converted to naval use.[85] From the 1830s through the 1850s, despite presidential opposition, substantial subsidies were made available to a variety of railroads, either by way of subscription to their stock or by deeding over to them large amounts of public land. States rights were preserved. The money was given to states which then passed it on to finance the construction of railroads. The justification was that a nation was being built.[86] Yet by European standards or even by absolute standards, the amounts were small. Support for agriculture hardly amounted to $5,000 by 1860.[87]

There was regulation. *Nile's Register* reported in 1830 that 1,500 people had died from steamboat explosions. Boilers blew up with such regularity that it eventually caused scandal and led to the establishment of federal inspection. The same was also true of mass importation of foreign drugs; questions as to the prevalence of impurities led to investigation and then regulation.[88]

Major developments were occurring in the states, where combinations of private and public funding led to the development of canals and railroads. The first and most famous was the New York Erie Canal, which, despite all prognostications to the contrary, returned handsome profits on its multimillion dollar investment. The boom in canal building was on, and many states followed suit. In the 1820s and 1830s the State of Virginia floated bonds to build a number of canals and railroads, and though only one railroad survived the Civil War, Virginia kept paying the debt, which was finally paid off in 1966.[89] A typical example was the Central Ohio Railroad, chartered in 1847, whose management found it difficult to get people to subscribe. The vendors made stump speeches throughout the territory, indulged in newspaper and pamphlet publications, went door to door with only indifferent success. The deficit was eventually made up by subscriptions from counties and towns, with some state money contributed. A more enterprising company went to London and borrowed on State of Maryland bonds. Less savory, though equally enterprising, were the railroads that issued paper script worth so little that workers sometimes rioted. Unfulfilled subscriptions might be used as collateral for still new loans.[90] By the early 1840s, things were so bad that seven states defaulted in failing to pay the interest on their debt. This was called repudiation, though within a few years all states had made good on their defaults. The specter of repudiation led English bards to remonstrate in the manner of the Reverend Sidney Smith:

Yankee Doodle borrows cash,
Yankee Doodle spends it,
And then he snaps his fingers at
The jolly flat who lends it.
Ask him when he means to pay,
He shows no hesitation,
But says he'll take the shortest way
And that's Repudiation!

Yankee vows that every State
Is free and independent:
And if they paid each other's debts,
There'd never be an end on't.

They keep distinct till "settling" comes,
And then throughout the nation
They all become "United States"
To preach Repudiation! . . .

And what does freedom mean, if not
To whip our slaves at pleasure
And borrow money when you can,
To pay it at your leisure?[91]

For the federal government, however, the era before the Civil War remained a time of tiny government. Between 1800 and 1860, as Table 14.1 shows, federal expenditures rose from near $11 to $63 million. More than half were military expenditures. The general category of "Civil and miscellaneous" included a substantial amount for the postal deficit, thus covering everything except defense, pensions, Indians, and interest on the debt. Kimmel is correct in his conclusion "that federal expenditures made little or no contribution to the level of living. Only a minor portion of Civil and miscellaneous expenditures were for developmental purposes."[92]

The Civil War changed all that. The government grew from tiny to small. It promoted the interests of businessmen and farmers, sometimes aiding railroads and at other times intervening to regulate railroads in the interests of farmers. Beginning with the Morrill Act of 1862, which gave huge land grants to states for the purpose of establishing agricultural and mechanical universities, a variety of measures were adopted to aid education. Not unlike Thomas Jefferson, post-Civil War presidents generally regarded education as an exception to whatever strictures they laid upon unnecessary expenditures. And as the nation was settled and the frontier neared its end, the beginnings of a movement to set aside land for conservation purposes appeared. But it is not in these modest departures from the strict doctrine of minimum states'

Table 14.1.

Federal Expenditures, Fiscal Years 1800, 1825, 1850, and 1960[a]
(in millions of dollars)

	1800	1825	1850	1860
Civil and miscellaneous	1.3	2.7	14.9	28.0[b]
War Department	2.6	3.7	9.4	16.4
Navy Department	3.4	3.1	7.9	11.5
Indians	—	0.7	1.6	2.9
Pensions	0.1	1.3	1.9	1.1
Interest	3.4	4.4	3.8	3.2
	$10.8	$15.9	$39.5	$63.1[b]

[a]*Annual Report of the Secretary of the Treasury on the State of the Finances for the Fiscal Year Ended June 30, 1934*, pp. 302-303.

[b]Includes postal deficit of $9.9 million.[93]

rights that one can find the sources of budgetary conflict or the seeds of future spending.

Money may or may not be the root of all evil. But the availability of substantial surpluses in the post-Civil War period proved a greater temptation than most private interests and public officials were able to withstand. No one can say whether it was the change in national opinion attendant to the swift pace of the industrial revolution, the change in public morality signified by the term "robber barons" applied to the new industrialists whose business scruples and public behavior were less than exemplary, or the huge revenues generated by the growing protective tariff or the attendant changes in the process of budgeting that mattered most. Suffice it to say that soon enough even the $3 billion Civil War debt became readily manageable and that higher tariffs still produced substantial surpluses.

It would be difficult to overemphasize the part played by high tariffs in the public policy of the Republican Party. The tariff, and the surpluses it generated, enabled Republican governments to do several things simultaneously: It allowed subsidized domestic manufacturing, provided "infrastructure" for industry, paid off a substantial part of the Civil War debt, used debt payments to strengthen central banking, discouraged efforts to introduce progressive income taxation, and generally cemented an alliance between a stronger central government and business enterprise. But I cannot follow that path here.

Repeating the litanies of past presidents, Grover Cleveland (1885-1889) voiced the fears that growing surpluses would "tempt extravagance" and that public extravagance "begets extravagance among the people."[94] Cleveland's predecessor, President Chester A. Arthur (1881-1884), who, in 1882, experienced a congressional override of his veto of the Rivers and Harbors Act, also condemned surpluses on the grounds that they corrupted public morality and inexorably contributed to rising expenditures.[95] Whether as cause or reflection of the temptations provided by having money to spend without having to raise taxes, changes in the congressional appropriations process facilitated the spread and extent of internal improvements.

The issue of internal improvements experienced a change of perspective as a result of the Depression of the 1930s, when they were seen as a positive aid to increasing employment. The soup line was added to the pork barrel. The earlier notion of internal improvements as a means of increasing national harmony by extending communications was replaced by a belief in social cohesion as a result of putting people back to work. The era of entitlements that bound people to government by giving them rights to its revenues was yet to come.

In the budgetary sphere, hierarchies prefer to follow forms, punctual tax collection, and spending to shore up the regime. Sects, by contrast, prefer no executive discretion, little spending on the regime, and revenues collected from the more prosperous. Markets are indifferent to forms or discretion but insist on getting a return for their money, including the part that government collects. They prefer lower taxes and spending, except for supporting projects from which they benefit. The special circumstances of American life have created conditions in which people pursuing these various cultures have been more evenly balanced than elsewhere.

In regard to the choice of budgeting style, collectivists favor funding by organizational level, individualists typically choose lump sums (because they care only about outcomes), and voluntarists prefer detail as a means of controlling extravagance. Voluntarists demand a person-by-person, object-by-object description. If collectivists and individualists are in the majority, the result is likely to be a line-item budget with lump sums reserved for emergencies when results matter. The unity of the budget is another matter, however, inasmuch as collectivists and voluntarists oppose the external control a unified budget signifies.

In regard to spending levels, both individualists and voluntarists want to keep the levels low because they prefer to keep government on a short and parsimonious leash. Spending to enhance equality does attract voluntarists, however, and individualists favor spending to aid business. Collectivists tend to prefer spending for its own sake because each level of the hierarchy seeks to spend to maintain its own position. Bargaining results when the hierarchy offers to aid business or "the people" in return for support of governmental establishments.

In regard to revenues, all regimes would like someone else to pay for their privileges. Since no regime commands a majority at any given time, compromises are made in an attempt to keep taxes low. When there is a surplus, government, business, and the populace share the proceeds. When circumstances are trying—during war, for example— taxes are raised to satisfy sects, debt is incurred to satisfy markets, and the government grows to satisfy hierarchies.

The need for a balanced budget became almost a religion in American society because it is the one thing about which all three cultures can agree. Because voluntarists in a sectarian regime are perennial outsiders, they are not likely to enjoy the largesse of government spending. A humble posture with low spending is their chosen style. Believing as they do in equality, they could not easily justify the imposition of taxes that distinguish among individuals. Tying spending directly to the pain of raising revenues, they insist on balanced budgets as a means to curtail establishment spending.

Individualist adherents of markets emphasize credit and currency because without stable financial values their endless transactions cannot be carried out. Inflation is anathema to them because it gives debtors advantages over creditors. Market people do not object to deficits in principle as long as they benefit from the borrowing. They must therefore be concerned about inflationary effects. They temper the desire to redistribute losses with the need for stability by agreeing that revenues should cover expenditures. This practice limits the efforts of sects to please the populace (common in state legislatures) and of hierarchies to dress up government in finery inappropriate for a commercial people.

Left to their own devices, hierarchies would run deficits as each level of the hierarchy spent to maintain its distinctive niche. But since markets and sects limit their need for government spending, hierarchies typically seek to limit spending also, in exchange for agreement on raising sufficient revenue. The inability of any one regime to dominate the others led to a common-denominator consensus: the balanced budget. As follows from any boundary formation, violations became subject to penalties—unemployment, inflation, public immorality, private vice, and collective ruin.

Notes

1.   James "Lord" Bryce, *The American Commonwealth* (London: Macmillan, 1891), p. 188.
2.   Louis Hartz, *The Liberal Tradition in America* (New York: Harcourt, Brace, 1955).
3.   Alexis de Tocqueville, *Democracy in America* (New York: Alfred A. Knopf, Vintage Books, 1945).
4.   Anthony King, "Ideas, Institutions and the Policies of Governments: A Comparative Analysis: Part 111," *The British Journal of Political Science* 3 (October 1973): 409-423.
5.   Seymour Martin Lipset, "Why No Socialism in the United States?" in *Sources of Contemporary Radicalism,* eds. Seweryn Bialer and Sophia Sluzar (Boulder, CO: Westview Press, 1977), pp. 31-149.

6. William J. Shultz and M. R. Caine, *Financial Development of the United States* (New York: Prentice-Hall, 1937), pp. 7-9. There was ingenuity. Lacking small change, the colonists cut Spanish dollars into quarters, eighths, and sixteenths, a phenomenon known as "sharp" change or cut money.
7. Ibid., p. 10.
8. Margaret G. Myers, *A Financial History of the United States* (New York and London: Columbia University Press, 1970), p. 3; and Davis R. Dewey, *Financial History of the United States* (New York: Longmans, Green, 1939), pp. 18-19.
9. Shultz and Caine, *Financial Development of the United States*, p. 9.
10. Dewey, *Financial History of the United States*, p. 8.
11. Charles Bullock, "The Finances of the United States from 1775-1789 with Special Reference to the Budget," *Bulletin of the University of Wisconsin,* Vol. I (1894-1896) (Madison: University of Wisconsin Press, 1897), p. 225.
12. Myers, *Financial History of the United States*, p. 11.
13. Gary B. Nash, *The Urban Crucible: Social Change, Political Consciousness and the Origins of the American Revolution* (Cambridge: Yale University Press, 1979), pp. 60-70.
14. Ibid., pp. 225-253.
15. Franklin's argument was so effective his printing company got the contract for putting out the paper money. The money Franklin left in his will to aid industrious and honest mechanics was due in large part to his recognition of the difficulty ordinary people faced in amassing any amount of capital in the absence of a plentiful sound currency (Myers, *Financial History of the United States*, p. 10).
16. Dewey, *Financial History of the United States*, pp. 23-30.
17. Shultz and Caine, *Financial Development*, p. 23.
18. Dewey, *Financial History of the United States*, pp. 9-10.
19. Myers, *Financial History of the United States*, pp. 15-16; and Dewey, *Financial History of the United States*, pp. 11-12.
20. Myers, in ibid., pp. 17-18; and Dewey, in ibid., p. 17.
21. Shultz and Caine, *Financial Development*, p. 15.
22. See Robert C. Tucker and David C. Hendrickson, *The Fall of the First British Empire: Origins of the War of American Independence* (Baltimore, MD: Johns Hopkins University Press, 1982), pp. 152-159, 174-175, 406-410.
23. Bullock, "Finances of the U.S.," pp. 217, 225.
24. Ibid., pp. 216-219.
25. Ibid., pp. 219-221.
26. Ibid., p. 218.
27. Shultz and Caine, *Financial Development of the United States*, pp. 60-61.
28. Myers, *Financial History of the United States*, pp. 30-31; and Bullock, "Finances of the U.S.", pp. 214-215, 257.
29. Shultz and Caine, *Financial Development of the United States*, p. 69.
30. William Graham Sumner, *The Financier and the Finances of the American Revolution* (New York: Dodd, Mead, 1891), pp. 301-302.
31. Ibid., pp. 302-303.
32. Theodore J. Grayson, *Leaders and Periods of American Finance* (New York: John Wiley and Sons, 1932). pp. 36-37.
33. Sumner, *Financier and the Finances*, p. 301.
34. Grayson, *Leaders and Periods*, p. 34.
35. Ibid., pp. 44-45.
36. Shultz and Caine, *Financial Development of the United States*, pp. 37-38.

37. Albert S. Bolles, *The Financial History of the United States 1774-1789* (New York: D. Appleton, 1979), p. 201.
38. Bullock, "Finances of the U.S.," pp. 115-120.
39. See Samuel P. Huntington, *The Common Defense* (New York: Columbia University Press, 1969); and Patrick Crecine et al., "Presidential Management of Budgetary and Fiscal Policymaking," *Political Science Quarterly* 95 (Fall 1980): 395-425, for contemporary versions during the administrations of Harry S. Truman and Dwight D. Eisenhower.
40. Dall W. Forsythe, *Taxation and Political Change in the Young Nation 1781-1833* (New York: Columbia University Press, 1977), p. 38.
41. Lewis Kimmel, *Federal Budget and Fiscal Policy 1789-1958* (Washington, DC: Brookings Institution, 1959), p. 8.
42. Ibid., p. 9.
43. Forsythe, *Taxation and Political Change*, p. 31.
44. Ibid., pp. 28-29.
45. Kimmel, *Federal Budget and Fiscal Policy*, p. 14.
46. Ibid.
47. I am indebted to James Savage's dissertation ("Balanced Budgets and American Politics") on the balanced budget idea for elaboration of this point. All serious students of the subject should read his book from Cornell University Press.
48. Kimmel, *Federal Budget and Fiscal Policy*, pp. 14-16.
49. Ibid., pp. 27-28; and Forsythe, *Taxation and Political Change*, p. 60.
50. Kimmel, *Federal Budget and Fiscal Policy*, pp. 16-17.
51. Ibid., pp. 17-18.
52. Ibid., pp. 19-21.
53. Ibid., pp. 21-22.
54. Ibid., p. 28.
55. Ibid., p. 23.
56. Ibid., p. 24.
57. Ibid., pp. 24-25.
58. Ibid., pp. 25 26.
59. Ibid., pp. 26-27.
60. Ibid., pp. 65-69.
61. Ibid., pp. 71-73.
62. Ibid., pp. 71-73.
63. Ibid., pp. 84-85.
64. Ibid., pp. 87-88.
65. Ibid., p. 88.
66. Ibid., p. 96.
67. Ibid., pp. 95-96.
68. Ibid., p. 96.
69. Ibid., p. 97.
70. Shultz and Caine, *Financial Development of the United States*, pp. 134-135.
71. Myers, *Financial History of the United States*, pp. 106- 108.
72. Shultz and Caine, *Financial Development of the United States*, pp. 137-140.
73. Leonard D. White, *The Jeffersonians: A Study in Administrative History 1801-1829* (New York: Macmillan, 1951), p. 483.
74. Myers, *Financial History of the United States*, pp. 108-109.
75. Kimmel, *Federal Budget and Fiscal Policy*, p. 19; and White, *Jeffersonians*, p. 483.

76. Louis Hartz, *Economic Policy and Democratic Thought: Pennsylvania 1776-1860* (Chicago, IL: Quadrangle Books, 1968).
77. See Henry C. Adams, *Public Debts: An Essay in the Science of Finance* (New York: D. Appleton, 1887), p. 321; and B. U. Ratchford, *American State Debts* (Durham, NC: Duke University Press, 1941), pp. 77-83. Chapter 3, "Colonial America to the Civil War," of James Savage's dissertation is an indispensable guide to the intricacies of this subject.
78. Kimmel, *Federal Budget and Fiscal Policy*, pp. 31-32.
79. Ibid., p. 33.
80. Ibid., pp. 34-35.
81. Ibid., p. 34.
82. Ibid., p. 41.
83. Ibid., p. 52.
84. Leonard D. White, *The Jacksonians: A Study in Administrative History 1829-1861* (New York: Macmillan, 1954), p. 438.
85. Ibid., pp. 450-451.
86. Ibid., p. 451.
87. Ibid., p. 442.
88. Ibid., pp. 450-451.
89. Myers, *Financial History of the United States*, p. 116.
90. Ibid., pp. 115-116.
91. Shultz and Caine, *Financial Development of the United States*, pp. 235-236; see also Myers, *Financial History of the United States*, p. 109.
92. Kimmel, *Federal Budget and Fiscal Policy*, p. 57.
93. Ibid.
94. Ibid., pp. 71-72.
95. Ibid., pp. 70-71.

Part 3

Budgeting and Governing

15

Securing Budgetary Convergence within the European Community without Central Direction

The most general statement of problems of social life involves a divergence between individual and collective rationality. The problem is never just one of good will, the problem is always to make good will worthwhile. The problem of budgeting may be stated as one in which it has to be worthwhile for everyone to sacrifice for expenditure control in order for it to be worthwhile for anyone. What usually happens at ministerial and subcabinet meetings is that whoever offers to sacrifice their program, interest and reputation finds that the expenditure cuts they have made are absorbed by the other spending interests, thereby accomplishing two things at once: their reputations are ruined and the national interest is not served. In order to secure effective expenditure control it is necessary to create rules under which it is worthwhile for everyone to contribute to a common interest if and when they recognize that interest.

My idea is to devise a set of norms and rules of procedures that would facilitate economic convergence within an expanded European Community over a considerable period of time. The first consideration is that command and control methods, though minimally essential, cannot perform this task. It is not possible for me to imagine that a European Community, let us say of eighteen nations, could issue, to use the old tsarist term, *ukases* telling the member nations what sort of tax or expenditure they should have in one area after another. Command and control also violate an essential rule of all of our experiences, in that central controllers are very far away and the spending departments are very close at hand, so that if it is a struggle over who knows the most about local conditions the central controllers will lose. I take it, therefore, that while a reserve power might be retained to do what the Maastricht Protocol says about placing sanctions on nations who deviate from their responsibilities for deficit limitation, if we use this tactic very often, the Community would disintegrate, the threat being much better than the use. We ought not wish to interfere with member nations in regard to particular matters. Instead there should be a series of norms and procedures which, if adopted by member states, and reinforced by mutual education as well as self-interest over considerable periods, would lead to desirable outcomes most of the time. Thus the need for self-defeating central measures would be obviated.

I should add that I am a great supporter of the European Community on the grounds of world pluralism. I do not think it is desirable for the United States to be the only hegemonic world power, albeit the most pacific that has existed in human memory. Given what we know about human proclivities, it is desirable that there should be several major powers around the world and Europe should be one of them. I am also a supporter of the radical project of modest limitations in national sovereignty. It is desirable that Europe should carry on this great experiment while we in America have the privilege of watching.

Now I have to explain that expenditure control is the most important thing rather than the alternative, which is revenue enhancement. For one thing, the smaller the number of items one tries to control the greater the chances of success. If one places the control over budget balance rather than either revenue or expenditure, the difficulties multiply.[1] One has both to control expenditure and to control revenue, when it is very difficult to control either. The possibilities for fudging, for end runs around every rule we develop, on the general proposition well attested to in human experience that people will find a way around almost any rule, suggest to me that one should seek to create, maintain and educate people in the smallest number of rules possible. This will be much easier if either an expenditure or revenue limit is adopted. My second reason is that for most members of the EC as well as for most modern capitalist democracies, revenues are already quite high. Most social democracies have found high income tax rates self-defeating. So I have sought out the rules that would be effective in most of the nations now and will be necessary in all of them in the next twenty years. I also think that the major impetus to unbalanced budgets has come from the rapid rise in expenditure, a rise exceeding the growth in national product, rather than shortfalls in revenue. If we go back to that ancient and much-abused subject, poor Mr. Wagner's law, having long since forgotten whatever it is he said, if he actually said it, but reinterpreting it for our purposes to mean that state activity keeps increasing as a proportion of GNP, we see that it has been true for over a century, with the partial exception of the 1980s. And we do not yet know whether the 1980s will prove an exception in a sense that the rise was halted, but that in the next century spending will continue to grow. That question has not yet definitively been answered. I stress expenditure control, moreover, because if one looks at the rationales given for the applicability of Wagner's law, for the law of increasing state activity, they are laughable. Why, after all, have expenditures grown over the last hundred years? Well, it is said, because our country is so large that we need considerable infrastructure, or because our country is so small, people hang all over each other's necks we need many social workers to separate them. Ah, yes, they say, expenditure is rising because our population is growing old, and that has its logic. Ah, but another voice says, expenditure is growing because our population is very young. I did a piece on the logic of public sector growth in which I try to show that all such explanations are contradicted by the exact obverse.[2] What this indicates is a tremendous desire in Europe's social democracies to spend for egalitarian purposes, for unmet needs, as they are called. If there were not unfortunate effect of high levels of borrowing over time, I believe these nations would all follow Belgium. Indeed, they would do more than Belgium. They would multiply their debt many times over, because they believe that it is so desirable to spend money on old people and young people and big spaces and small spaces. There is hardly any rationale for increasing spending that is not being used. Indeed, progressivism, leftism, egalitarianism, basically means more spending for whatever is defined as social welfare, to which we now add environmental purposes. I see these factors as much more powerful than a desire to tax one's citizens. Indeed, the tax decisions are often painful and lag behind the spending decisions, which is one reason for big deficits. Do we believe that the big problem for most of these nations is that for political reasons the government decides to tax too little or that, given the enormous rise in expenditures, governments find it difficult to raise revenues to keep them going? In any event, I have taken my position, which is that expenditure control is the way to control deficits. My idea is to start with what exists, namely the Maastricht norm—deficits should not grow beyond 3 percent of GNP. I take no position on whether this is the best that could be devised. It is a human product. I do not myself see any other set of norms that are obviously much better and I would join with those who say that these norms are not final. They could perhaps be altered, although I think they should be altered, if at all, only once, because a large part of the benefits of what I will talk about would come from teaching them to ourselves and coming to believe them ourselves.

To the Maastricht norm, I would like to add just one other, a more specific norm that I believe will accomplish the purpose. This norm is that *outlays are not to grow faster than the growth of gross domestic product.* They are measured in a very straightforward way, or at least as straightforward as human ingenuity will allow. One takes last year's outlays, (outturn, as the British call it), and multiplies by the percentage increase, or decrease, in the GDP. If you started with a hundred billion ecus in outlays and you add 3 percent next year you could spend 103 billion ecus. If, however, you had a decline in GDP of 3 percent, you could spend only 97 billion. Now, when I spoke to the Commission's group on finance, they raised the question, which I will now answer for you, and that is whether a main defect of this norm would be that one cannot therefore engage in countercyclical economic activity. I think this is what we would call a "false arrest." First of all, I am not the one to blame. You should blame the first Maastricht norm, because what that norm tells you is that if you have a deficit of above 3 percent of GDP you must consider reducing that deficit your primary economic goal. Where then is economic management? One could argue over it, but I have also thought back to various countries' experiences and there are other reasons. First of all, fiscal policy, in the sense of countercyclical activity, is becoming extremely rare. In the U.S., which I studied in a book written with Joseph White of the Brookings Institution, called *The Deficit and the Public Interest,* we show that there has been a virtual abandonment of any idea of fiscal policy. When was the last time the government sized its deficits so as to manage the economy? No, governments are driven by their deficits. Monetary policy—interest-rate and money supply setting by central banks—have become the key instruments of economic policy. The Keynesian approach has steadily declined in importance. Why? Because I think it is fundamentally fallacious. It is fallacious, I think economically, which is controversial, but it is also fallacious politically, which is not at all controversial and understood by everyone. So I will take the easy part first. It is unfortunate politically because it upsets the great budgetary norms of the past, which told us that deficits were bad and therefore high spending was bad. What did Lord Keynes tell us? Spending under certain circumstances is good. You should cut your taxes, you should raise your spending, you should increase your deficits. And that would help moderate economic swings. Keynes, who was an English Brahmin, thought that very clever people dedicated only to the public interest would decide these matters. As a person with long experience in politics, I am still not clear why he assumed this. He believed that governments would actually follow his advice, that is, they would increase spending and lower taxes when the economy was slow, but when the economy was overheated, as the economists say, they would then cut spending and increase taxes. But, of course, in the political arena, this was greeted with immense cheer; at long last there were decision rules that politicians could understand, and talk about as if they were knowledgeable. There was a period when the Tony Crosslands of the world talked about economics as if there was a macroeconomics and they knew what they were doing. But in their practice they followed the first rule, but rarely the second. So that when they ought to have increased spending they often increased it over the longer term. But when they ought to have cut they only decreased it over the short term or not at all. The result was greatly enhanced spending.

Now for the more controversial part. It has been assumed, it certainly was assumed in the economic courses I took in college and graduate school, that there was something called the multiplier: that when you tax people, and put that money to work by the government, that it had certain positive effects. I think the whole enterprise is flawed. I doubt very much that there are multipliers, or that we know that there are, I doubt very much the exercises on which this is based. I do not think that the variations in governments spending and tax policies have the effects that are credited to them.

In any event I take it that the whole point of the Maastricht norm is to rule out countercyclical activities beyond a certain level of deficits. Blame the EC, the Maastricht norm, not me, for burying fiscal policy. What my norm does is to provide a line of defense. The task is to defend that line so that governmental expenses will not grow beyond the rate of growth of the economy. The growth norm has to be backed up by a number of rules without which I believe it would be either ineffective or much less effective. You will note, by the way, as I did in the previous days' discussions, that a number of the mechanisms adopted in Denmark and Britain as well as in other countries, are very close to what I am suggesting here. They did not take it from me and I did take it from them, so I think there might be reason in experience for this convergence.

My first rule is that *the overall ceiling is determined by the previous year's spending times the percentage increase of the GDP. My second rule is that subceilings on the above principle should be established on major traditional spending accounts.* The idea of subceilings is absolutely critical. If you simply try to defend a national spending ceiling as such, you would never know who is responsible for what. And it would be impossible to observe discipline. Therefore, it is important to elucidate this consideration. If you have too many spending accounts to control you'll fail. If you only have one you'll fail; it is in between that you need to go. In the United States, there are traditionally thirteen major spending accounts (defense is 050). And it is these accounts that I recommend. There are certain warnings: do not invent new accounting rules. It is not that I believe the existing ones are wonderful, or that we understand them, or that there might not be others that are better (I would like to see an accounting Newton arise who would explain to us the differential effects of different types of accounting rules). But you wish to be effective in this life and not in the next one. If you fiddle with the accounting rules, then I think the whole thing will collapse. Best is to find some series of accounts whose numbers are certified in various accounting decisions where there is as much certainty as these matters will allow. And there is as much tradition behind them as possible.

The third rule—I shall come back to the second in a moment, because they have to be read together—is the PAYASUGO rule, which was earlier known as the offset procedure. It has actually been followed in the United States Senate but not in the House of Representatives, and the differential consequences are extremely instructive. What the PAYASUGO rule says is that within your subaccount you may do whatever you damn please that the ministers can agree on.

But if you wish to exceed that amount then you must get some other account, and its occupants, either to agree on a revenue increase of some kind, or to cut their own spending. Naturally, this is not easy to do, but at least everybody will understand that it is mutual sacrifice that is called upon here.

What the PAYASUGO rule does, when taken together with subceilings, is alter the fundamental rules of rationality in budgeting. It makes collective sacrifices worthwhile. It means that the occupants of one account and their beneficiaries cannot reach into the different accounts in order to make up whatever they need. Mutual consent and mutual sacrifice are the rule and order of the day. It is this combination of the first three rules that I believe will restore rationality to expenditure budget. By rationality, by the way, I mean what economists mean by the doctrine which I consider the most important doctrine in economics, the doctrine of opportunity costs: that something is worth what you have to give up for it. This is, of course, budgeting, and budgeting is a political process, which means that the trade-offs in the end are made by top-level political decision-makers in processes of bargaining. But by conducting the bargaining within these rules we know that either they are accepting the allocation, as they come out of the formula (which is the second norm I have proposed, i.e., that outlays are not to grow faster than Gross Domestic Product), or explicit trade-offs have to be made. I believe this is as much rationality as one could expect or get from any form of government.

Moreover, this type of rationality should work to overcome one of the most unfortunate splits in society, unfortunate in the sense that it leads to bad consequences. I refer to one so obvious and so well known that it may not come to your mind right away: the conflict between producers and the redistributors. Not long ago I did some work on the American Catholic Bishops' pastoral letter on the economy. To my astonishment they did not say one word about the production of wealth. Wealth came from some process with which they did not have to concern themselves. To them, economics was all about the virtues of redistribution, their so-called "preferential option" to the poor. One might well be interested in redistribution, whether among nations or within them, but one also has to be interested in where those resources will come from and therefore be interested in production. I foresee, if these budget rules were believed in and therefore enforced over a period of years, different political coalitions form.

When I studied the relation between the Treasury and the Department in the United Kingdom, they had a lovely phrase which says that every Minister defends his or her own corner. And they tried many devices in order to overcome this difficulty. There were committees of nonspending Ministers. There were morality sessions in which the prime minister gave his lectures about the common good. But none of these prevailed. Under the rules that we are talking about here, however, it should become in the interest of those who care about redistribution to secure greater production. Let me put it more forcefully. If the only way to get greater redistribution is through enhanced production, then I foresee much more interesting dialogue leading to cooperation. I have in my lifetime, although not now, served on three boards of directors. And I am not enamored of the current discussion which tells them to be social workers concerned about everything except what they know about. Instead, I hope that we will hear from stockholders who will say: Why do you not make more economic decisions so there can be greater tax collections so that there can be greater redistribution to protect the environment, or old people, or the homeless or whoever? It's very important in our society that we try to forge a connection between redistributors and producers.

PAYASUGO also reverses completely the old idea of budgeting as budgeting by addition. The interest groups and politicians who support these programs, see themselves as supporting good things. They do not and have never seen themselves as supporting bad things like taking resources from other people. But here I had evidence in United States Senate experience: the defense interest is looking in the welfare budget, the welfare people are looking in the defense budget. In other words, instead of every minister defending only his or her corner, they are now looking into other people's dark corners. They think that's the way for them to grow. Interest groups, particularly the old people's lobby, complain bitterly, that it's not right, that it's immoral to have them come up to Congress and say who are they are going to take the money from. How could you ask such a thing? Their constituents are worthy; they are blameless, they are pure, and they should not be sullied by the political business of where the money is going to come from. These rules would force them to answer that question.

A fourth rule: no inflation premium. Subceilings for the coming year are established by the prior year's outlay, period. When I studied the British system they had what I called volume budgeting: spenders were promised whatever it took to carry out last year's policy at this year's prices. Why am I concerned about dragging up this old dirt? Because in the U.S. we are still doing what the Brits long ago abandoned and for good reason, that is, we have something called the current service budget which means that a program gets what it got last year times inflation. The idea is to provide the same volume of services. Alan Schick, a distinguished scholar in budgeting in the U.S. has written an excellent book about the consequences of embracing inflation. The discussion should go quite differently. Is our problem that governments spend too little? Or is it that they spend too much? If we think it's that they spend too much, we do not wish the finance ministry chasing the spenders. We wish the spenders to have to come to the finance ministers. We wish the conversation to be something like this: the finance ministry says, well, there's, hopefully, only 3 percent inflation; explain to us why you have not achieved an efficiency gain of this amount, rather than the Treasury having to claw back what it had automatically given by formula. I do not say this rule is impartial. It is designed to help the central controllers. So I must now explain why I think it's desirable to help central control.

With some partial exceptions in the 1980s, for the last 100 years central controllers always lose. Oh, they sometimes win for a year or two. But even when they are beautiful or handsome, when they are strong, when they do everything right, over time they lose. Why? One reason is that there are so few of them, and so much more of the other people on the spending side. They lose also because the spenders feel their gains much more powerfully, as our literature shows, than those who are taxed feel their losses. That is to say, almost any program can be financed by a few pennies here and there. It's only when you add them together that they cause difficulties. One could not compare a group like the National Taxpayers Union in the U.S., of which I am a member, to the various spending lobbies. There are so many more of the other. The NTU is comparatively so weak. So I think that when you look at the picture as a whole, spending interests are much more powerful than saving interests. Therefore, we have seriously to consider as political economists how we can alter the rules so as to restore some balance between spending and savings.

My idea, which is embodied in the first four rules, is to throw spending interests into conflict. I do not ever see, whatever we say, making finance ministers, budget directors, powerful enough by themselves. We have much experience in the world in the last 100 years which argues to the contrary. But if we can use some of the power spending interests have to offset the power of other spending interests, maybe we can get somewhere. You will see, therefore, that the interest in one spending category may be opposed to the interest of others, that in order for one to get more for its side it will have to generate the onus of raising taxes or get some other spending department to accept reductions. I do not believe this is impossible. One of the ways in which we safeguard the preferences of our citizens is by entrusting them to governmental departments in some part, expecting that agriculture ministries will defend their corners and labor ministries others. I do not think we want to tell everybody to defend somebody else's business. One of my favorite quotations comes from John C. Calhoun's ancient but still relevant, *Disquisition on Government,* in which, in a most eloquent way, he says that, if it were the case that every person should look out for everybody else's interest, about which they know very little, there would be such confusion in the world as to who wanted what that governments would have to pass laws introducing selfishness in order to make the world work. We do not want Spending Ministers to pursue only their interest. On the one hand we want to make it feasible for them to sacrifice when they feel that it is either necessary or desirable. And on the other we want to make it obvious to them that they cannot have a great deal more than they are getting without taking others into account. One may well ask, how this was done in the past. There was agreement on major implicit budgetary norms. One was annularity. I live to see the day when one of your countries will decide on a two-year budget cycle instead of one year, and thus give your poor budget officers a little relief.

Another norm was comprehensiveness, which is a big problem in many places. I like the norm attributed to county budget officers in the U.S., which is to protect the general fund. In California we did not do this, so we have horrendous deficits, which are still with us. In addition to the norm of balancing, there was understanding that revenues would not rise very fast. Now if revenues did not rise very fast and people believed that terrible things would happen if the budget became unbalanced, if you busted the budget, if your expenditures increased greatly, then you would be taking it out of the hide of other departments. Therefore, there came to be a common interest in keeping down demands of the others as well as your own. Keynesianism destroyed this whole understanding. So you could look at my norms and rules as an effort to replace by design what was built up by the accretion of understandings over long periods of time.

Now I wish to introduce a fifth rule which perhaps has not occurred to you. You may think either that it's such a wonderful idea, you are sorry you did not think of it, or you think it's so dumb that you understand exactly why. I call it quasi-entitlements. Government is given authority to vary entitlement spending 5 percent a year. In my youth a young man put his arm around his girlfriend and said: darling, you are one in a million. Now, under my rule he has to say: darling, you are only one in a 950,000. The reason for this is that the burden of sacrifice between the citizen and the government has become unbalanced. I view government and society as an immense centipede—you know these insects with enormous numbers of legs; the idea used to be that the government helps the citizen and the citizen helps sustain government. But now, if you look at the rules that have evolved over time, government sustains citizens, but citizens do not do very much to sustain government. Government upholds all those feet, but who upholds government? Let me give you an example. Thirty years ago there were no cost of living increases written into legislation. You did not have written entitlement provisions against inflation. You did not have indexing for inflation. The result of that was that the value of these expenditures for citizens were eroded, and that gave the government greater discretion. So then politicians could come back and vote tax increases. So on one hand the value of expenditures voted was diminished, but also there was bracket creep, which has just the right raspy sound in English, which meant that inflation would put people into higher tax brackets, but the value of what they could buy was diminished. In the U.S. that gave the government 1.6 times the amount of income for every percentage increase in the price level.

Notice that the rules of the game were established so as to protect the government. They got more revenue from inflation and they had less expenditures. But now we index against inflation. Now in many countries like my own we index tax brackets. The result is to take away the leeway from the government. I have a special interest in this position, because I am concerned about the viability of democratic government in the Western world given the enormous amount of criticism they face. Especially unfortunate is the criticism that suggests, sometimes truthfully but often not, that civil servants and elected officials are beholden to what are called "special interests." Of course, those interests are special to those who love them. Just as our children are to those who have them, every interest group is special to somebody. Accusations of special interest is just a way of cursing out your opponent. Yet the level of such complaints through the media has become immense. Another image is that politicians are like pool-balls: The interest groups have these big sticks and they knock the civil servants and the politicians into their pockets. Therefore I have been thinking not only about how to hold elected officials responsible, but about how to give them discretion so that their responsibility is more worthwhile: with galloping incrementalism, with entitlements threatening to squeeze out other concerns, politicians are often excoriated. But they do not have the resources available to at least fail for what they attempted to do. Notice now that if you do not have an inflation premium, that gives several percent more a year for the government to allocate up or down, and if you have quasi-entitlements, then you have up to 5 percent. I figure that would give a government in a year something like 5 percent, maybe 7 percent to allocate. That's big money. That's probably as much as the governments would try to do in any particular year. Interest groups cannot allocate this discretionary money. Only the government through its committees can do so. I believe these rules would make governments much more important than interest groups and better still it would make governments appear to the public to be more important than interest groups.

Finally, I have adopted from Van Hagen and others our longtime experience, which he has now demonstrated to us, that governmental provisions matter. So as my last rule I put simply governmental responsibility—*budgets should be voted up or down as a whole.* I didn't want to burden the rules with various particularities, but the greater the control that the central authorities have over the budget, the better the chances are of expenditure control. It is by no means certain that every government will be dedicated to expenditure control. If a central government is not so dedicated, I cannot think of any kinds of rules, other than punishment at the polls, that would be appropriate for this purpose.

Now I will take a moment to give you an analogy to a condition in the U.S. It appears to some people that there could be lower deficits if the president of our country had what is called an item veto. Maybe, but I am very doubtful.

Why? First of all there is a very important distinction that needs to be made, even perhaps by your central controllers, between the right to veto a particular item of appropriation of spending, and the right to diminish it. First we thought that maybe, from state government experience, an item veto increases the power of governors and therefore decreases spending. But more refined analysis shows that an item veto is generally weak. But a diminishing item veto is very strong. Oftentimes if you have to choose between everything or nothing, then you have to choose everything. If you can choose 70 percent or 80 percent of everything, you are better off. There are real defects in an item veto. It means that legislators often vote anything they feel like because it's the governors' job to stop this. We see in your parliaments that this avoidance of responsibility is not desirable. Moreover, let us suppose you are one of those people (I know many of them) who love spending, and who think there are so many unmet needs that cry out for attention that it's a crying shame that we are sitting here today doing nothing about it. And you are faced with an item veto. What would you do? One possibility is that you would form a larger instead of a smaller coalition. In the past you needed a coalition just large enough to get your expenditure through. Under the new system you'll need one in the U.S. that would gather a two-third majority. So that means you have to promise even more. Thus, it's quite possible that an item veto would be met with such large "logrolls," as we call them, such large bargaining coalitions, that you would get much higher spending. It's also possible that a president, perhaps Clinton, would love spending even more, and use an item veto to cut defense next to nothing, in order to get support for spending proposals. Nevertheless, I think that both democratic governments and spending control would be furthered by giving the central government powers to have the budget voted up/down as a whole. I just want everyone to realize that there are circumstances in which this would be counterproductive.

In conclusion I wish to stress that these are meant to be ideas that would go into a white or a green paper: that would go out from the Commission to the member countries for discussion about them. I assume right away that you know more about your circumstances than I possibly could. Therefore you may want to amend or eliminate or substitute certain rules for others. But I believe that if some such set of rules were adopted, especially the first norm, outlays not to grow faster than GDP, together with the subceilings and the PAYASUGO principle, that they would increase effective budget control over considerable periods of time in those countries whose governments adopted it. You would believe in them and teach them to your colleagues and they would teach it to their colleagues and therefore there would be some sense of professional pride in maintaining these norms. I give again an American example. During the first years of the Reagan administration the spending estimates of the Office of Management and Budget were wildly off. I came across a number of instances in which people from the Congressional Budget Office, from the House Budget Committee, from the Appropriation Committees, would greet Office of Management and Budget estimators and ask them, what dreams they were putting down instead of numbers. Nobody likes to be thought of as a poor professional. I do not mean to give this factor an enormous importance, but I did notice an increasing professionalism, a greater realm of agreement over time, over what would count as an expenditure and what would not, and a closer correspondence between the estimate and the reality.

Now I do not want to give up a certain point. It may well be that instead of relying on five-year expenditure estimates we could have a simpler rule: Outlays for the next fiscal year will be exactly what they were the year before. This would result in less fooling around, less time wasted and more accuracy. If professionals see that some such set norms and rules make sense, then over time they will have greater force among those who work on these matters. Therefore violations would be more likely to be caught at the source and the authorities, already overburdened and under attack, will not have to act as forcefully or as frequently.

Notes

1. Aaron Wildavsky, *How to Limit Government Spending* (Los Angeles/Berkeley: University of California Press, 1980).
2. Aaron Wildavsky, "The Logic of Public Sector Growth," in *State and Market,* ed. Jan-Erik Lane (London: Sage Publications, Ltd., 1985), pp. 231-270.

16

If You Can't Budget, How Can You Govern?

Budgeting has become the great issue of our time. Members of the House and the Senate spend as much time on taxing and spending as they do on all other matters put together. Not that they love budgeting; in fact they have grown to hate it. They spend endless amounts of time to discover that they no longer agree. What is it they disagree about? Nothing much, really: how much revenue should be raised, who should pay, how much should be spent and on what.

To some it appears that the great issue is the federal deficit. But the deficit hides its political significance from us. It appears that people are concerned solely about the size of the gap between spending and revenue. The real issue is different: what kind of government are we going to have, and therefore what kind of people are we going to be? Will we balance the budget at much higher levels of revenue and expenditure, or will we balance it at much lower levels of revenue and expenditure? The Democratic Party now has as its dominant faction liberals whose main purpose in achieving power in government is to do good deeds with public money. The main purpose of the major faction of the Republican Party is to assure a limited government; that is, their idea of a good deed is to let taxpayers spend their own money. These conceptions are fundamentally at odds.

Equality

Politicians like Hubert Humphrey and Henry Jackson—liberal Democrats who want a substantial welfare state and a substantial defense effort—no longer exist. Now defense policy is considered a domestic issue. Republicans look at it as an index of determination to support our institutions, as a sign of patriotism. Democrats look at it as a question of equality; more for defense means less for social welfare.[1] I recall Representative Barney Frank of Massachusetts

325

saying the defense budget was immoral. To call it too big is one thing (so we compromise on a little bit less or more), but immoral—you don t have much room to go from there. Walter Fauntroy from Washington, D.C., said it would be unconscionable to provide so many billions for national defense while there was one homeless person in the United States; clearly he assumed that defense was not defending the people, just as Republicans no longer necessarily consider welfare programs part of the general welfare.

Americans are able to agree on the desirability of equality precisely because we all mean something different by it. Some believe in equality before the law so that different people can follow their different gender, income, class, or other destiny. Other people believe in equality of opportunity so that people can be different from each other and end up with more or less than others depending on their luck or talents. Still others believe in greater equality of results to reduce the power differences between men and women, blacks and whites, parents and children, and even animals and people. How could social movements that have transformed the lives of all Americans, like feminism and civil rights, fail to have an impact on the major priority-making machine of the public sector, the government budget?

Between Democrats and Republicans there is a big divide, with Republicans sticking to equality before the law and equal opportunity and Democrats moving more and more toward more equal results. Republicans talk about opportunity, about how wonderful the United States is because it enables people to be different; Democrats talk about how most people are left out of power—women, poor people, racial minorities, gays, the elderly. Only a few fat cats are left in. It is these fundamental differences about how people ought to live with one another—to secure more equal opportunity or more equal outcomes—that create irresolvable conflicts over budgeting.

Dissensus

In the last twenty years as a sign of dissensus (or fundamental disagreement) every relationship in budgeting has been radically transformed. From the early 1920s to the 1970s the starting point for consideration of the budget was the president's proposal. Today the phrase used to describe the president's budget when it gets to Congress is "dead on arrival."

Even more significant is the concept called the budgetary base. The past pattern of agreement maintained funding for programs at a level approximating what they got the year before. Instead of fighting the past over again in each year's budget, budgeters focused on incremental changes. Nowadays budgeters not only disagree on where the budget ought to go, they disagree on where it ought to start. Is the budgetary base what an agency spent last year? Maybe. Is it the current services budget (last year plus an inflation allowance)?

Possibly. Is it the president's budget message? Unlikely. Is it the first Senate budget resolution? Perhaps. Is it the House budget resolution? Is it the first of a series of conference reports? Could be. Is it a continuing resolution, a new and exotic art form, which accommodates dissensus by providing for different levels of funding depending on how far along (subcommittee, committee, floor, conference) a bill has moved? Or is it the omnibus continuing resolution, that wrap-all package that puts everything together in a single bill? It is not easy for a president to veto the government. In recent years all of the above have been used by some of the participants some of the time as the budgetary base. None of the above has been used by most of the participants most of the time as the agreed budgetary base.

Disagreement about the base occurs not because Congress or the president is foolish or because they try to fool the people. These differences are driven by policy preferences: the starting point for additions or cuts helps determine how much will go to defense or welfare or other programs about which the participants differ. Public officials disagree about policy not because they cannot agree on the budget; they cannot agree on the budget because they are fundamentally at odds over policy.

The problem is not that our legislators are dumber than we are or that they lack good will. Any one of them alone could make a terrific budget. The problem is that legislators together cannot agree on a good budget.

Gramm-Rudman-Hollings (GRH) is more than a sign of dissensus; it also tells us what our politicians can agree about. It calls for cumulative proportionate cuts to reduce the deficit. Three types of programs are not subject to the dreaded sequestration (reduction of budget authority): major entitlements, poor people's programs, and veterans' programs. What can be cut fully is (1) defense and (2) general government. Consequently more than half the spending budget is outside GRH. Obviously entitlements are now the nation's number one priority whereas defense and the federal establishment are last. Our politicians can agree not to savage the poor (a good thing), not to harm huge numbers of voters (an expected thing), and to threaten each other with doing damage to government (a bad thing if one is supposed to govern).

The deficit-reducing provisions of GRH are deliberately unintelligent because the alternative, agreeing on an intelligent budget, is something that can't be achieved. Every year for the last eight years we have heard about the coalition of moderates that believes in budget balance, budget rationality, and budget intelligence. We keep hearing about them, but we never see them winning votes. Moderates do not win because they are outnumbered.

The disappearance of the annual budget made on time and followed for a whole year is caused by dissensus over public policy. Liberals want higher progressive taxes, lower defense spending, and more welfare programs. Conservatives want the opposite. Because the budgeters do not agree, they wait until the last moment only to discover that they are no better able to work out their differences at the end than they were at the beginning. Dissensus is now so deep that it extends beyond the issues of the day to the norms of proper action that used to guide and constrain budgetary behavior.

Norms

Once upon a time budgeters agreed on the old norms of balance, comprehensiveness, and annual review. Balance meant not only that revenue would be within hailing distance of expenditures (except for times of war and depression) but also that everyone acknowledged a limit on acceptable taxation so that they knew what total spending could add up to. Because they agreed on an acceptable range for total spending, they also knew that a lot more for one program meant a lot less for another. In other words, the participants in budgeting—agencies, appropriations committees, interest groups, politicians—all knew they were in this together. If one agency or program tried to break the bank, that money would be taken out of the hide of the others; therefore they exerted mutual discipline on one another. Now they don't. So what?

You do not stop the growth of budgets by turning people down. That is hopeless. There are so many of them and so few budget controllers. The rise of spending is stopped by inhibiting people's desire to ask in the first place. If kids choose to importune all the time, parents can rarely turn them down. But if through some parental magic they have persuaded their children not to ask, then there is no need to turn them down.

Comprehensiveness died because we can no longer tell the value of different expenditures. In the old days most of the talk was about appropriations. Now appropriations are around 40 percent of the budget. Most of the money is in entitlements. The structure of the budget reveals the dilemma. Roughly 47 percent is in social welfare programs, legally mandated payments to individuals. Defense is 28 percent. With interest on the debt at 14 percent, that totals 89 percent. The rest, that bloodless category, is called nondefense discretionary. There are many types of spending, moreover, that barely existed in the early 1960s. Today over a trillion dollars in loans and loan guarantees is outstanding. These expenditures do not appear as one trillion dollars in the budget; only defaults, which are only three or four billion, appear in the budget. There are off-budget corporations. There are hundreds of billions of dollars in tax preferences. There is a marvelous institution called the Federal Financing Bank, which is capable of changing tens of billions of dollars from on- to off-budget. Thus it is impossible to say how much is being spent. What is the value of a loan versus a loan guarantee versus money for an off-budget corporation versus several hundred billion dollars in tax preferences, like fringe benefits or various subsidies for housing? The desire to spend from different spigots (I haven t mentioned imposing costs on the private sector through regulation) has overwhelmed the old budget process.

Historically, the United States has never made a formal decision on how much revenue it should raise or how much it should spend. The norms of balance and comprehensiveness served as informal safeguards. A lot of trouble was avoided by not voting on matters that might become contentious, such as how much should be taxed and spent. According to the Budget Act of 1974, all that was changed. From the new budget resolutions came decisions on the total amount of taxing and spending. There is only one problem: although everybody agrees legislators should stand up and be counted, nobody agrees on what they ought to stand up for. That is the basic reason the budget has not been passed on time in the last fifteen years.

Deficits

Delay is one thing; huge deficits are another. One would think that if you had disagreements there would be just stalemate. What happened?

President Reagan thought of budgets as political instruments. As he saw it, Democrats were using spending to create constituents. As they addicted these constituents to federal largesse, they got more votes. Tax and spend and elect was their accomplishment; Reagan feared if this went on for too long the public would dominate the private sector. To prevent this Reagan brought in his children's allowance theory, namely, that the way to stop spending was not to issue endless admonitions but to cut down on the allowance. If you took the tax money away, Congress wouldn't have it to spend. Believing the budget was about political economy, not just economic economy, the president radically reversed the conventional wisdom, which held that spending had to be cut before taxes could be lowered.

The reverse happened. Income tax rates were cut 23 percent over three years. But, of course, it didn't happen exactly the way Reagan thought. What he wanted was prosperity to show that increasing economic incentives worked. What he got (the result of the Federal Reserve's efforts to stop stagflation) was recession.

Reagan had two choices. One was to give up everything he believed in, to do exactly what Mondale would have done, that is, to raise taxes, thereby erasing differences between Democrats and Republicans. Instead Reagan accepted large deficits in preference to the alternative of strengthening the Democratic Party and its egalitarian vision of the United States.

In considering the components of the deficit, we cannot know whether, if income tax rates had gone up, the economy might have slowed down, leading to a still worse situation. We do know that higher defense spending contributed to the deficit. But that ended by 1984. Since then defense budget authority (the right to spend into the future) has declined substantially. What does contribute to the size of the deficit? When the Federal Reserve slammed on the monetary brake in 1981-82, the resulting recession not only caused spending to go up and revenue to go down, which increased the deficit, but it also pushed prices down a lot faster than anyone had thought possible. This severely reduced bracket creep, which raised the deficit still further.

A good half of the deficit is caused by the lasting effects of the recession of 1981-82. When one adopts a version of what the British call the public sector borrowing requirement (in the United States that means including state surpluses), the deficit that matters for economic purposes declines. Adjusting for inflation makes the deficit go down further.

When one considers that economic data fail to support the notion that large deficits are necessarily harmful, one wonders why Democrats reversed their longstanding liking for deficits. This rationale is more important than a desire to remind Republicans of their previous opposition to deficits.

Consider the Law of Political Compound Interest: interest on the debt drives out future Democratic programs. A large deficit does two things: it works as the only powerful instrument to keep spending down that we have had in half a century, and it drives out future Democratic programs. Ask also, in the older tradition of institutional political economy, to whom is the debt owed? It's owed to the constituents of the Republican Party. If the deficit didn't exist, on whom would the money be spent? On the constituents of the Democratic Party.

The Law of Political Compound Interest accounts for the Democratic born-again commitment to budget balance. What the party would like, especially its mainstream liberal faction, is to raise taxes substantially from the richest segment of the population to support larger social programs. There is nothing new in this. But then President Reagan cut them off at the pass again. If he could wed much lower tax rates to much lower tax preferences, he could make it difficult for Democrats to raise income taxes. Any time the Democrats say they want to raise taxes, they will be accused of breaking their compact (lower preferences for lower rates) with the people. Yet without new money, the Democratic Party may self-destruct.

Realignment

Liberals cannot live with perpetual cuts in social programs. The devotion of Democrats to reducing inequalities through governmental action is now so great that they will not be able to tolerate doing less. Therefore, their main need is for money. Where is that money going to come from? Before Jimmy Carter's time the government took something like 18 percent of GNP in revenues. Jimmy Carter took that figure to 20 percent. And he also left the nation a present: there were built-in tax increases—bracket creep through inflation,

Social Security, and windfall taxes on energy—amounting to about 4 percent of GNP. Left alone, the tax code would have produced about 22 percent of GNP in revenues. What Reagan did was not to lower the tax take but to bring it back to traditional levels. Reagan took away the increment that Democrats would have used to fund their programs.

That is why I believe the value-added tax or some related consumption tax will be the next great issue of our time. [2] A value-added tax is a turnover tax, a sales tax at different stages of production. It is a giant revenue raiser. Experience from Europe is uniform: in no country has the value-added tax replaced the income tax. In every country that adopted the value-added tax the proportion of GNP spent by the government has gone way up. Thus the question of whether the United States will remain capitalist or go semisocialist will be decided on the question of the value-added tax. And with the nature of the regime will go the character of the party system.

If the Democrats don't get their money, I believe they will split. Left liberals will form their own party so that they can at least advocate what they would like, even if they can't get the government to do it.

Economic individualists support the Republican Party because it brings limited government. But if Republicans move toward higher taxes, individualists in the party will see no reason to support it. Then they might well form their own libertarian party.

Reform

With budgeting becoming equivalent to governing, while dissensus makes it difficult to do either, the aims of recent budgetary reforms come into clearer focus. The balanced-budget amendment, which limits federal spending to the last year times the increase in GNP, aims to restore by formal action what was previously accomplished by the informal workings of budgetary norms. A formula provides the limits that hitherto welled up spontaneously as balance, comprehensiveness, and annual review. Consensus is to be restored by altering the formal rules of the game. [3]

The amendment encapsulates a macro and a micro political theory. The macro theory expresses a political preference: the public sector should not expand into the private sector. This philosophy is supported by the provision that spending cannot exceed the percentage growth in national income. The micro theory seeks to create incentives for limiting expenditure by making it in the interest of program advocates to restrain their demands. Imposing a global limit means that increases for one program or agency above the percentage increase in national income have to be accompanied by equivalent decreases in others. Budgeting by addition, in which program costs are piled on top of each other to be paid for by tax increases or debt, would be replaced by budgeting by subtraction, in which desired increases would have to compete within the limits of economic growth.

The grand purpose of constitutional revenue and expenditure limitation is to increase cooperation in society and conflict in government. As things stand, program advocates within government have every incentive to raise their spending income while reducing their internal differences. How? By increasing their total share of national income at the expense of the private sector. Why fight among their public selves if private persons will pay? Thus conflict is transferred from government to society.[4]

Once limits were enacted, however, the amendment's advocates believe that the direction of incentives would reverse: there would be increasing cooperation in society and rising conflict in government. Citizens would have a common interest in growth, whereas the sectors of policy—housing, welfare, environment, defense—would plunge into conflict. This change in the pattern of perceiving interests would come about because society would be united in increasing productivity and government would be divided over the relative shares of each sector within a fixed limit. Organizations interested in income redistribution to favor poorer people would come to understand that the greater the increase in real national income, the more there will be for government to spend on their purposes. Instead of acting as if it didn't matter where the money came from, they would have to consider how they might contribute to enhanced productivity. Management and labor, majority and minorities, would be thinking about common objectives, about how to get more out of one another rather than about how to take more from the other.

Until now the arguments on both sides have been hypothetical. The opposing view goes from the ridiculous—the Constitution contains no economic provisions (try reading it and stop after ten such provisions), or there will be a runaway convention creating a wholly new, radically revised Constitution (imagine economic libertarians and social conservatives agreeing beyond the preamble)[5]—to the unanswerable: people will find ways around every provision. These arguments come from people who in other contexts pride themselves on the punctilious observation of constitutional dictates.

Fortunately, a lesser known provision of GRH involves a real-life test of the theory behind the amendment. For the last two years the Senate has operated under GRH's offset provisions. Essentially this means that within every large appropriations account any effort to increase spending must be accompanied by either a spending cut or a revenue increase elsewhere, subject to a 60 percent vote against a point of order prohibiting the proposed increase. This provision results in far fewer proposed increases because of the difficulty of finding offsets. Friends of one kind of spending keep other spending down by refusing to provide offsets. Defense contractors scrutinize welfare spending while its defenders examine the military budget. Spending interests guard each other.[6]

Governing

The lateness, confusion, and obfuscation surrounding the budget; the pro-liferation of gimmicks designed to hide increases; the failure to agree on sub-stantial deficit reduction measures; the experience of budget, budget, budget, apparently to little purpose—all these have limited the capacity of Congress and the president to govern the nation. This is the view not only of external critics of Congress but also (and more importantly) of leading members. The resignation from the Senate of Democrat Lawton Chiles, chair of its Budget Committee, is but one of many such signs of the times.

Yet experience under the Senate offset provision (the liberal majority in the House has so far refused to adopt it) offers hope for demonstrating Congress's ability to govern. If Congress refuses to support the amendment, it could still rescue its self-respect by using the offset provision to demonstrate a capacity to govern.

Once both houses, by legislation or by rule, adopt offset provisions, elected officials will not only govern but be seen by themselves and observers to be governing. They will face fewer demands because demanding increases will cease to be an unalloyed good. The costs not only for the deficit, and hence future programs, but for other desired expenditures will immedi-ately be apparent. Demands will be countered by other spending interests that are thereby threatened with loss. Soon enough there will be fewer impor-tuners around. Instead, the special interests will have to go to the politicians because they are the only ones who can make the hard trade-offs in which X, Y, and Z give something to support A, B, and C. The genuine mediating skill of politicians will become apparent as soon as resource addition, for which no help is needed, gives way to resource subtraction, for which political media-tion is essential.

It is said that the growth of government has led to inflated currency and inflated expectations. Certainly it has led to inflated rhetoric. What we have not realized is that getting government to grow and grow inflates political capital as well. The first few generations of politicians who practice budgeting by addition get inflated reputations. After a few decades have passed, however, politicians are disparaged either because they (1) give in to special interests or (2) fail to give in. For politicians, at least, this is ultimately a losing game.

For the federal government, ultimately is now. Those who disagree about taxing and spending may still wish to see the political vocation valued in our democracy. But if politicians are to be important, they must be concerned with more than giving away and giving in.

Trends

One obvious trend for the future is a gradual but pronounced growth of government. As government grows so will the Democratic Party, expanding its semipermanent majority in the House to the Senate and winning the presidency more often. Another trend would be maintenance of a smaller government. Republicans would be able to compete not only for the presidency and the Senate, as they do now, but for the House as well.

For either of these trends to take place, the general public would have to change its voting patterns. Realignment on ideological grounds, so far restricted to the South, would have to expand to the rest of the nation. Suppose, however, that the people continue to give inconsistent results, on the one hand, while their elected officials, on the other, show signs of deep dissensus? Then politicians will have to decide whether their capacity to govern is more important to them than their differing ideologies. My crystal ball clouds over, but so far ideology appears to be winning.

Notes

This paper is a much revised version of my Dillon Lecture at the University of South Dakota, April 9,1987.
1. See Aaron Wildavsky, "No War Without Dictatorship, No Peace Without Democracy: Foreign Policy as Domestic Politics," *Social Philosophy & Policy* 3, no. 1 (Autumn 1985): 176-91. Also in Ellen Frankel Paul et al., eds., *Nuclear Rights/ Nuclear Wrongs* (Oxford: Blackwell, 1986).
2. See Aaron Wildavsky, "The Unanticipated Consequences of the 1984 Presidential Election," *Tax Notes* 24, no. 2 (July 9, 1984): 193-200.
3. My reasons for believing that the item veto will be inefficacious in overcoming ideological dissensus are found in Aaron Wildavsky, "Item Veto without a Global Spending Limit: Locking the Treasury after the Dollars Have Fled," *Notre Dame Journal of Law, Ethics and Public Policy* 1, no. 2 (1985): 165-76. For a powerful argument that the federal budget, unlike that in most states, does not lend itself to the item veto, see Louis Fisher and Neal Devins, "How Successfully Can the States' Item Veto Be Transferred to the President?" *Georgetown Law Journal* 75, no. 1 (October 1986): 159-97.
4. I recapitulate here my argument in *How to Limit Government Spending* (Berkeley and Los Angeles: University of California Press, 1980).
5. See Aaron Wildavsky, "The Runaway Convention or Proving a Preposterous Negative" (Paper prepared for the Taxpayers' Foundation, 1983), pamphlet ISBN 0911415-10-5.
6. For a fuller account, see Aaron Wildavsky, *The New Politics of the Budgetary Process* (Glenview, IL: Scott, Foresman; Boston: Little Brown & Co., 1987).

Postscript

Aaron Wildavsky, Cultural Theory, and Budgeting

Brendon Swedlow

In the 1980s Aaron Wildavsky revisited his old friend budgeting in the company of a recent acquaintance called "cultural theory,"[1] to which he had been introduced by British anthropologist Mary Douglas.[2] For a chance encounter, this one was pretty consequential: "It changed his life."[3] It also surprised those who knew him primarily through his early budgetary writings. The same man who brought politics and incremental theory to the study of the budgetary process now arrived in the company of individualists, egalitarians, hierarchs, and fatalists. This postscript surveys Aaron's efforts to apply cultural theory to budgeting, suggests how the theory might be extended to budgetary topics Aaron had previously analyzed in other terms, tries to answer criticism, and offers some illustrations of how this cultural approach might improve future budgetary theorizing. I am writing from the perspective of a student who came to study budgeting with Aaron and ended up learning about cultural theory and using it in my own work.[4] Like Aaron, I hope to suggest the utility of this approach for studying budgeting.

What is Cultural Theory?

Cultural theory is fundamentally an organizational theory—or, more dynamically, "a theory of organizing and disorganizing"[5]—and consequently should be of interest to those who study public administration and budgeting. It is "cultural" because it takes from cultural studies the observation that culture defines social environments where everything makes sense to the people

335

in them but often makes very little sense to those traveling among them. Not only languages, but also ways of seeing and thinking differ, which is why we experience "culture shock" as tourists. Cultural theory retains these connotations of culture because it predicts that social organizations will be accompanied by a lot of ideological baggage. Like cultures, organizations are self-contained, self-satisfied, self-justifying, and self-perpetuating because the people in them hold beliefs and values that permit their organizations to function. But cultural theory drops the historically contingent aspects of culture, so that instead of speaking of British and American cultures (for example), cultural theorists speak of hierarchical and individualistic cultures. This abstract conception of culture allows useful comparisons to be made among social organizations as large as nations or as small as families—whether ancient, primitive, or modern—as to the degree to which they are hierarchical, individualistic, egalitarian, or fatalistic.

Douglas and Wildavsky make the extent of individual autonomy and the extent of collectivization in society into independent dimensions rather than poles on a continuum, as is customary. This conceptual shift allows analysts to account for four rather than two patterns of social relations. People in *individualistic* and *fatalistic* social relations *are not* part of a collective undertaking, but individualists retain their autonomy, while fatalists do not. People in *egalitarian* and *hierarchical* social relations, meanwhile, *are* part of a collective undertaking, but egalitarians retain much more of their autonomy than hierarchs. Hierarchical social relations are highly structured, with everyone and everything having his, her, and its place. Individualistic social relations, by contrast, are highly fluid, and subject to individual choice. Fatalistic social relations, meanwhile, are tenuous and unreliable, driven by the "whim and caprice" of others. Egalitarian social relations retain their autonomy by giving all members an equal voice in and thus the power to veto collective decisions.

Government represents a type of collective action, which leaves fatalists indifferent and repels individualists, but attracts egalitarians and hierarchs. The federal government, and its budgetary process in particular, has characteristics of centralization, expertise, and comprehensiveness that make it the natural home of hierarchs. Egalitarians also like the collective, communitarian, public qualities of government, but they do not like centralization, large bureaucracies, and decision making driven by experts. Thus they have reasons to be attracted to federal budgeting and reasons to dislike it. Individualists, by contrast, generally prefer a small public and large private sphere, where they can move about freely, and have the greatest scope to arrange their lives as they choose. Their self-regarding, self-seeking behavior can of course have perverse consequences when it comes into contact with the public sphere, producing a "tragedy of the commons," as they catch a "free ride," contributing less than they extract.[6] The strength of the egalitarian and particularly the individualistic way of life during much of this country's history, one could argue, registered itself not so much in the federal budgetary process as in keeping the federal government an inconsequential player in national life.[7]

The Beginning of a Journey: Revisiting Budgeting with Cultural Theory

As Aaron tells it, his methods have always been anthropological; it was a theory of culture that his early analyses lacked. As examples of his "fieldwork in anthropology" he lists a number of his early budgetary books, in which he and others tried to "get inside" participants' "skins" and "recreate a world recognizable to the budgeters in the United States, Britain, the City of Oakland, California, and a variety of poor countries." Yet, he notes, "Despite the heavy emphasis upon the texture of relationships among the actors, these are not works of cultural theory. The most explicitly ethnographic of these books, *The Private Government of Public Money*, should serve to bring out the contrast I have in mind. The chapter titles – "Kinship and Culture," "The Nuclear Family," "Village Life in Civil Service Society"—bespeak an explicit anthropological interest. We do try to penetrate to the rules by which the Treasury, departments, and ministers regulate their interaction. But the book contains no cultural theory; that is, it does not attempt to locate the form(s) of social organization involved and the consequences for budgeting of one form versus another; therefore it does not systematically relate the behavior of the participants to their larger way of life."[8] He cites *A History of Taxation and Expenditure in the Western World* (with Carolyn Webber) as an attempt to do so.[9]

"A Cultural Theory of Budgeting" is a good introduction to the theory in a budgeting context since Aaron's aim in this piece was "to bring together various strands of thought about cultures and budgets." He revisits "the standard topics of the subject," expecting to discover the effects of four "political regimes" composed of cultural alliances in the kinds of results striven for in the budgeting process and in the type of auditing that is done to ascertain these results. He analyzes different forms of budgeting, from the ongoing line-item budgeting to the unsuccessfully enacted zero-based budgeting and planning-programming budgeting systems, finding that each serves the interests of distinct social orders. He claims that the budgetary base means different things to these different orders, and will be sanctified, attacked, or allowed to dissolve, depending on which cultural type dominates the process. He predicts the different levels of revenue and expenditure that will be associated with different regimes; that these regimes will favor different rates of economic growth; that there will be regime differences in agreement on totals and items within the budgetary base; that budgetary procedures will vary among regimes in their flexibility; and that responsibility will be assigned by distinct criteria depending on which regime dominates the process.[10]

In Aaron's most comprehensive theoretical statement—reproduced here as chapter 8—culture becomes one of several variables which when combined in different configurations produce the variation Aaron found in budgetary processes and outcomes when he studied rich and poor countries and budgeting in American cities and states. A political jurisdiction's wealth, the certainty of its control over revenue and expenditure, its size, growth rate and political structure all interacted with its political culture to produce the distinct outcomes he observed. As he presented it, the first two variables, wealth and certainty, could account for budgeting behavior in all but the rich and uncertain countries, which puzzle, Aaron notes, was the spur to his introducing political culture into the analysis.[11]

The Private Government of Public Money[12] is also a fascinating book to revisit for those who may be interested in applying cultural theory to budgeting. Its richness of detail and its constant illuminating analysis of British budgeting's "nested complexes," as Aaron's co-author Hugh Heclo might now put it, is a good testing ground for cultural theory. How much of the detail and dynamics are captured by the theory? And how much, if at all, can the theory add to our understanding of a story that is already so well told? Aaron supplies a partial answer to these questions. Had he and Heclo been able systematically to relate their budgeters' behaviors to the theory's subcultures,

> we should have understood earlier than we did... that "volume" budgeting, guaranteeing a specified level of activity, by safeguarding departments against inflation, eased internal relations within the expenditure community at the expense of Treasury control, whereas budgeting by "cash limits" in nominal currency, which compels departments to absorb price increases, places considerable strain on those relationships. Volume budgeting belongs to a hierarchical culture in which adjusting internal relationships is paramount, whereas cash limits, which imposes fixed limits on resources, belongs to an individualist culture that establishes opportunity costs (the value of a good is what you have to give up to get it) as the leading rule of resource allocation.[13]

Trips not Taken but Worth Making

Unfortunately, Aaron did not revisit all of his earlier budgeting anthropology with the benefit of his later theoretical insights. Had he taken a few more of these trips, we would have a more complete answer to what "cultural theory" might contribute to the study of budgeting and there might be more continuity between his earlier and later budgetary theorizing. Like *The Private Government of Public Money*, *The Politics of the Budgetary Process* is great political anthropology because it tries "to penetrate the rules by which [budgetary actors] regulate their interaction." But it is not a work of cultural theory because it "does not systematically relate the behavior of the participants to their larger way of life." Had Aaron revisited the roles, rules, and norms of this "classical" American budgeting with cultural theory, it is likely that he would have seen it as a cultural hybrid. It was not as centralized as the top-down, synoptic, "program budgeting" of the Defense Department then being held up as a model for federal budgeting to emulate. Nor did the fragmentation of power in American national government permit a single budgetary actor to impose its priorities on the budget the way the Cabinet of the ruling party in Britain could impose its will on the Parliament. Rather, American budgeting reflected the individualism of American life, and it was this individualism in the form of incrementalism that Aaron defended against various proposals for centralizing budgetary control.

The "shared tradition [of 'government by discussion'] has taken different institutional forms in the two countries," Heclo writes in comparing individualistic and hierarchical cultural influences on American and British institutions. "These forms express and reinforce different conceptions of the way authority is constituted, and they sanction different norms of appropriate conduct in exercising that authority. Budgeting processes, as well as relations between politicians and bureaucrats more generally, are embedded in these differing constructions."[14] Washington careers "are handcrafted by political entrepreneurs who carve out their own personal niches" and are uninterested in becoming part of "an executive team," while Whitehall careers are made by "pleasing peers and superiors."[15] Consequently, high-level administrative positions in Washington are filled "by a passing parade of presidential appointees and their aides, people who have few shared stakes and whose 'real' careers lie outside government," while "Whitehall bureaucrats... see themselves as officers of the Crown... exercising guardianship over a larger public interest than the comings and goings of party governments."[16]

Nevertheless, the American budgetary process in the post-World War II era was confined to a village of beltway insiders, who had very well defined roles and norms of behavior associated with those roles. As Allen Schick notes, this too was the private government of public money.[17] Agency requests may have originated with the demands of their clientele, but they were always requests for increases, which were reduced by "guardians" of the federal purse in the House, and increased again by Senate committees acting as "appellate courts." Significantly, the net result of this ritualized interaction was almost always an increase over the agency's prior appropriation, but a lesser increase than the agency had requested. These well-defined roles and norms were made possible by the insular nature of the budgetary world, and the insularity of the budgetary process was preserved because most constituency demands were channeled through the agencies and because there was an acceptance of steady, incremental budgetary growth. In other words, these politics of the budgetary process share many features of the more hierarchical budgetary environments found in Britain and in the American Defense Department.

This is not simply to posit a hierarchical continuum or merely quantitative differences, however. In cultural theory there are two dimensions that define social environments, including hierarchical ones. One dimension measures the extent of collectivization and the other the extent of individual autonomy. Hierarchical social environments are strongly collectivized and offer little individual autonomy. Hierarchical budgeting is minimally a process for itself, and budgetary actors have clearly defined and delimited roles to play in that process. Decreasing collectivization or increasing individual autonomy produces a qualitative shift at some point: not just a weaker form of hierarchical organization, but a new pattern entirely. If collectivization remains strong but autonomy of group members increases, an egalitarian pattern of social relationships results. Whereas, if collectivization weakens and autonomy of group members increases, an individualistic cultural pattern emerges. Finally, if the extent of collectivization and individual autonomy both weaken, fatalism follows. All three processes distinguished the new politics of the American budgetary process from the old. A somewhat hierarchical budgetary process gave way to a more egalitarian budgetary process, and then to a struggle between individualistic and egalitarian cultural elements that increased fatalism among budgetary actors.

Both Schick and Aaron note that the budgetary process of the 1970s was distinguished by the presence of more outside actors.[18] In fact, what had happened may better be characterized as the growth of an egalitarian budgetary community alongside the old mostly hierarchical one. Budgetary actors now included Democrats who represented the previously underrepresented constituencies (such as blacks, women, labor, consumers, poor and handicapped people, and environmentalists) in Congress, federal judges who interpreted the new welfare, health, safety, and environmental legislation to the benefit of these constituencies, and members of the public who by their behavior or innate characteristics met legislative and judicial criteria that entitled them to government money. Authorizing committees increasingly "appropriated" money in the form of entitlements, particularly since, as Aaron put it, "the norms of participatory democracy had their way in Congress" too, power being dispersed from committee to subcommittee chairs, controlled by the Democratic caucus and flush with increased staff.[19] The old budgetary community centered on appropriations committees persisted, but was responsible for a smaller and smaller portion of total outlays. The net result of these changes was a larger public and a smaller private sphere and a redistribution of public resources from richer to poorer constituencies, or exactly what one would expect from egalitarians.

These budgetary changes provoked a reaction from the individualistic, entrepreneurial, and business interests in society, predominantly represented by the Republican Party. The size, growth, and equalizing aims of government became an issue as these cultural elements reacted to the activist state of President Johnson's Great Society programs. Various attempts to control spending growth by reforming the budgetary process followed. These were largely unsuccessful until a Republican president with predominantly individualistic leanings was elected. Ronald Reagan cut the taxes of his individualistic business constituency, and raised defense spending for his hierarchical constituency, but was unable to cut the spending of the egalitarian Democratic constituency to the same degree, resulting in ballooning deficits. The cultural dissensus that led to lesser rates of taxation than expenditure generated a sense of budgetary fatalism as elites became immobilized like deer caught in the headlights of an oncoming train.

Had Aaron revisited not only budgeting in Whitehall and Washington with cultural theory, but also budgeting in poor countries, we would have gotten an even fuller sense of the contribution his new approach could make to parsimonious yet nuanced, comprehensive explanation of budgetary processes and outcomes. He and Naomi Caiden found that poverty compounds uncertainties, leading to the constant remaking of budgets.[20] In poor countries, budgetary actors never know how much money they will get, nor even how much they have. They consequently hoard appropriations and attempt to create their own revenue sources, generating further uncertainties for other budgetary actors. In this social environment, resignation to poverty becomes an entirely rational response to existing poverty and uncertainty, and these are exactly the elements that define a fatalistic cultural environment in cultural theory.[21] Nor is budgetary fatalism confined to poor countries. "As uncertainty is joined to poverty, we find the characteristic budgetary behavior of poor countries appearing in [] American cities."[22]

Cultural theory gave Aaron a parsimonious and exhaustive way to characterize the institutions and ideologies of the wider political systems in which budgeting was embedded. His incremental theory of budgeting relied on the idea that human cognitive and organizational capacities (or, rather, incapacities) constrain or bound rationality. His typology of budgetary processes was also based on the idea that budgeting behavior was constrained by the environmental factors of wealth and certainty, which, while they may have been the product of culture historically or epiphenomenally, were largely beyond the control of present actors. His cultural theory of budgeting too drew on the idea that rationality and human behavior are constrained or bounded, yet here the boundaries were imposed not by cognitive limits or environmental factors, but by culture. The effect of Aaron's theoretical journey was progressively to multiply limits on budgetary behavior, narrowing the range of behaviors that might be expected within these boundaries, and thereby increasing our chances of predicting these behaviors. With culture, Aaron introduced the idea of "plural rationalities,"[23] in which human behavior was constrained by different patterns of social relations and by the institutions that were the manifestations of these relations, as well as by purposive, goal-directed behavior aimed at maximizing the values that were functional for these different patterns of social relations. Knowing a little about cognitive limits, or environmental factors, or types of social organization, or political ideologies, allowed Aaron to know a lot about budgetary processes and outcomes. Not coincidentally, knowing a lot by knowing a little was also his definition of good theory.

The Problems and Promise of this Cultural
Approach to Studying Budgeting

"Why do we not simply admit it [?]," Aaron's one-time co-author Heclo wonders. "[T]he general tendency is for all our conventional interpretive 'models'—whether Rational Choice, Cultural Theory, Functionalism, Stages of Economic Growth, or any other—to collapse under scrutiny toward a recognition of open, situational, historical contingency." Heclo thinks that we should instead analyze budgeting, indeed, all politics, as "Complex Adaptive Systems" composed of "nested complexes of ideas, interests, and institutions that are ongoing, mutually shaping interactions of an indeterminate, evolutionary nature."[24] Heclo claims that "we do not know and cannot know where we are going in such systems. Political and economic competition is a learning process through which capabilities are created and destroyed in individuals, groups, and institutions. But given bounded rationality, actors' capabilities develop in idiosyncratic and historically dependent ways."[25] If these criticisms are directed at cultural theory, they miss their mark, for cultural theorists do not try to predict which individuals, groups, or institutions are going to ascend or decline as the result of cooperation, coalition, competition, and conflict.

Budgeting as Complex Adaptive System and Cultural Type

Cultural theorists do claim, however, that individuals, groups, and institutions can usefully be characterized as being of four types, a claim frequently greeted with incredulity. The "buzzing, blooming variety" of the world appears all too manifest to sustain it, and the burden of proof would quite naturally seem to lie with those who argue for human similarities rather than differences. But social scientists might do well to remember that similarity and difference are social constructs, and that the claim that institutions, ideas, and interests are endlessly varied and idiosyncratic is also a generalization. In fact, the insistence on differences is as much a generalization as the insistence on similarities. Consequently, the burden of sustaining these generalizations is equally shared by all that make them. Cultural theorists merely claim that their construction of the social world as composed of four cultural types is a generalization that will allow them to understand and predict more about social life than those whose generalization about social life is that it is infinitely varied and only comprehensible in its particular, historically contingent configurations.

How might this claim be tested? Doesn't constructivism lead to relativism, where every construct is as valid as the next? While it may be true that our generalizations never confront reality directly but rather are "tested" through measures and methods which are the constructs of social scientists, that doesn't mean there isn't a distinction between subject and object. It just means that we can't be very sure about where our constructions leave off and external realities begin to intrude. Moreover, while our observations may always be several parts projection, and the most we can hope for is inter-subjective agreement, saying something is so doesn't make it so. All constructs are not created equal. While none may be falsifiable in a positivistic sense, some constructs will get a better purchase on external realities, on objects beyond the subject, than other constructs. And while the extent of the "fit" between a construct and external realities is always subject to social agreement and dispute, those whose constructs get the better purchase on their social, political, and physical environment will be more successful in interacting with that environment than those whose "stipulated worlds" are comparatively at odds with their "actual worlds."[26]

Knowing a lot about budgeting in Britain, as Heclo certainly does, doesn't help him to know anything about budgeting in Japan or France. Knowing nothing about budgeting in Britain, Japan, or France, but having some hypotheses about how budgeting might be organized in an hierarchical political environment, a cultural theorist, on the other hand, will be able to make some intelligent guesses about budgeting in all of those places. This comparison also defines the limits of generalization in cultural theory. There are important differences, for example, in the way these predominantly hierarchical countries handle conflict in their budgetary processes, by Aaron's own account. "The *containment* (or fortress or even 'Maginot line') *style* practiced in France is an attempt to keep conflict within bounds by arbitrating disputes at many levels up the hierarchy. The Japanese, whose smaller number of levels is accompanied by an emphasis on proportionality, have an *avoidance style*. No one has to be told he is wrong; all share equally in the benefits or the miseries because proportional rewards (usually comparable increases) are granted at each level. The British follow an *absorption style*. Working with a high degree of trust and a few levels of decision, the British accommodate conflict through anticipatory adjustment. No one is expected to deny differences, but these are carried on within the overall expectation that each actor will work out his position so as to take account of the vital interests of others. That they should be able to settle is usually more important than the substance of the agreement. That is what it means to carry on Her Majesty's Government."[27]

Only repeated comparison with other budgetary processes can sort out the historically contingent from the socially invariant. Cultural theory offers a very useful framework within which to pursue such comparisons, because, as Alexander George might say, this framework permits "structured, focused comparison."[28] Instead of comparing budgetary processes willy nilly, from country to country, to states, to cities, using Heclo's nominal, "natural" categories, we can make comparisons within theoretically derived types. Thus, when Heclo complains "that time can give even the same word different meanings, so that egalitarian or individualist labels signify something different at the end of the century than they did at its beginning,"[29] he merely affirms, as David Collier and James E. Mahon, Jr. point out in their revisitation of Giovanni Sartori's work on concept formation, that "the challenge of achieving the virtue of conceptual traveling without committing the vice of conceptual stretching remains very much with us today."[30]

"We are not saying that egalitarianism in twentieth-century China looks exactly the same as it does in seventeenth-century England, or that competitive individualism among the Igbo is no different than it is among Americans," Richard Ellis reminds us. "In this respect, egalitarianism and individualism are no different from any other terms designed to cross large stretches of time and space, whether capitalism, socialism, liberalism, feudalism, bourgeois, modernity, tradition, charisma, authority, government, class, or revolution. One cannot extend the set to which one applies a term without decreasing the properties that define that term."[31] It is exactly this process of reducing the properties that define a cultural type by successive structured, focused comparisons within that type, or within combinations of the same types, that will help further define and delimit the generalizations that are possible with the theory. Categorizing budgetary processes in Britain, France, and Japan as hierarchical, for example, allows the analyst to isolate their commonalties and differences, with the commonalties being those features that are really universal in hierarchical cultural environments, and the differences being those features of these environments that require some other kind of explanation.

It is important to remember that the properties which define a type and the type itself are constructed by social scientists, and can also be deconstructed and reconstructed in the pursuit of generalizations that are really generally applicable. It is also important to remember that cultural theory has the virtue of its defects. The promise and not just the problems of Aaron's cultural approach are suggested by his use of these subcultures to characterize the political coalitions that constitute American political parties, allowing him to analyze the politics of a 400-year history in the same terms: the individualistic market men and egalitarian sectarians who rebelled against English hierarchy;

the Federalists who replaced the English as domestic advocates of social hierarchy, who occasionally formed an establishment with individualistic business types, who were opposed by the egalitarian Anti-Federalists and then Republicans. And Aaron describes current Republicans as having the same coalition of social conservatives and individualists as the former Federalists, while in the Democratic Party southern social conservatives have steadily been displaced by the now dominant egalitarians. Aaron thus provides a consistent independent variable in accounting for budgetary practices from colonial to contemporary times.[32]

Moreover, these concepts not only travel through time but within time to different places. An example of Aaron's use of cultural concepts for cross-sectional rather than longitudinal analysis can be found in his argument that the uncertainty of budgeting in wealthy nations is caused by the rise of egalitarianism. In the European social democracies, uncertainty is the result of egalitarians' simultaneous demands for more redistribution and attacks on the authority of the larger, bureaucratic governments that try to achieve it, while in the United States uncertainty is the product of individualists resisting the rise of egalitarianism. Aaron uses this same dynamic, with an additional cultural twist, to explain the growth of government as well as the particular expenditures that have increased the most. In all countries it is redistributive welfare spending that accelerated most quickly, reflecting egalitarian preferences. In Europe, where notions of hierarchical community are stronger than individualistic impulses, central governments have assisted egalitarians in achieving their objectives. In America, hierarchy is only a necessary evil, leaving stronger individualists to deny (under Ronald Reagan) egalitarians the revenue for the welfare state without being able to rein in spending to the same degree.[33]

Explaining Budgetary Change

Recalling his and Aaron's work together, Heclo notes that "eventually one could describe that there was an old politics of the budgetary process and a new, a traditional political system in Washington and Whitehall and a new. But what were the ligatures of development by which the old became the new? When political change happened, what was happening?"[34] Saying that many of these changes can be characterized in terms of the waxing and waning presence and strength of the various cultural types in our governmental institutions doesn't explain why or how these cultural or any other changes occur. Cultural theorists say cultural change is the result of conscious choice among ways of life, and that the reason people choose one way of life over another is because its predictions about human nature and the environment appear to be more accurate than those of their own way of life. Heclo thinks "these sensible observations do not really come to grips with the contingent, unfolding quality of what happens in the real world."[35]

A more complex theory of theory of change relying on cultural analysis would need to account for at least the following types of change. First, there is the inter-penetration of cultural types, which creates the possibility of surreptitious institutional and value changes. As Nelson Polsby has described it, governmental and nongovernmental institutions in Washington are staffed by layers of personnel who arrived with each new presidential administration, so that people of different ages also tend to have different political commitments.[36] As administrations of different parties come to town this must variously disrupt and create political alignments and policy potentials between the old-timers and the newcomers. A second possibility for cultural change exists in the instrumental use of organizations and policies of one cultural type by those with antagonistic cultural commitments. Egalitarians and individualists have each used the centralized authority and power of the federal government to pursue objectives that were hostile to the social and political if not the governmental hierarchical establishment: egalitarians to redistribute resources and to open the establishment to disenfranchised outsiders, and individualists, under Ronald Reagan, to dismantle government. The hierarchical establishment, meanwhile, fights back by enveloping its cultural antagonists: creating a place for individualism and a place for egalitarianism, to keep them in their place.

Third, reforms will be adopted that appear to serve certain values while in practice others are advantaged. For example, program budgeting appealed to market-types because it forced programs to compete for funding, but the real effect of this reform as practiced was to strengthen centralized authority. The point of these examples is that cultural inter-penetration creates instabilities and potentials that become pathways for cultural change. Fourth, so does the phenomenon of gaps opening up between a pattern of social relations and the values by which people in those relations justify them to each other. If corporate executives tout free markets while increasingly accepting governmental subsidies, something—either their values or their social relations—has got to give.

Toward a Grander Budget Theory[37]

The late Marcia Lynn Whicker outlines Aaron's contributions to budgetary theory, notes that it "seems greedy" to ask for more, and then goes on to list six aspects of budgeting a "full-blown" or "grander budget theory" could be expected to encompass.[38]

A Typology of Possible Budgetary Process Reforms

Whicker implies that knowing the general characteristics of proposed reforms, thus allowing their grouping as types, may create an independent variable simple enough to be used in a budgetary theory predicting different types of impacts. Thinking through the precepts of cultural theory, I am led to view proposed changes in the budgetary process as proposed changes in social relationships, within and between government and society. Perhaps these changes will be positive-sum, so that everyone affected gets more of the kind of social relations that they like. Perhaps they are redistributive, so that some get more of their preference, while others get less. At any rate, the theory posits that these relations will take four forms, so that we, like the people involved, know what the possibilities are and who the likely winners and losers are. The typology of budgetary process reforms the theory thus offers is first a typology of ways of life.

A Redistributive Measure of Political Outcomes

If Whicker is right that the "guts of politics is redistribution" and that, therefore, "the guts of any basic political and budget theory must be about redistribution,"[39] then measuring redistribution would consist of determining, in cultural terms, who did and did not gain from particular reforms or appropriations. This would require tracking such changes from their initial consequences for Congress and the Presidency, to their effects on the administering agencies and states, to their impact on societal organizations and individual citizens. The fact that such changes probably would not just benefit or harm one way of life, but two or more in some proportion, complicates this analysis, but provides a basis for aggregating the effects of hundreds of individual spending categories and programs.

Greater Attention to Measuring the Redistributive Component of Various Political Ideologies and Partisan Philosophies

Whicker claims that "[i]deologies, filtered through political parties, drive politics and budgets;"[40] that "[b]udgets are by definition redistributional, and different ideologies favor different budget outcomes for this reason"[41]; and that these conditions "would allow the eventual theorizing that if the system, or key parts of it, is controlled by actors of X ideology, then Y redistributive outcomes will emerge."[42] Only now, with cultural theory, we can say what the Xs and Ys might be: those who most value liberty, equality, or order will try to produce budgets that respectively increase, decrease, or maintain power differentials among people.[43] In fact, with cultural theory, many more budgetary predictions are possible, since ideology includes not only values but also beliefs about human nature, the environment, and the economy, and since redistributive outcomes will affect the extent of not only individual autonomy but also collectivization in social relationships. Thus, cultural theory provides a basis for predicting which political actors are most likely to form coalitions, which parts of the system they will probably try to control, and how they will probably try to shape budgetary processes and outcomes to favor their way of life.

Specification of Linkages between Adoption of Specific Budget Reforms and Specific Redistributional Aspects

The next step in building better budgetary theory, according to Whicker, should be to produce specific hypotheses regarding the relationships between her two independent variables of (1) budget process reform and (2) ideology or partisanship and her dependent variable of (3) redistributive outcomes. As an example of a simple bivariate hypothesis, she suggests that "executive-enhancing reforms [might] produce greater redistributive impacts than congressionally enhancing reforms."[44] As examples of her more complex multivariate hypotheses, she posits that "when Republicans control the White House, executive-enhancing reforms will diminish economic equality. Or conversely, when Democrats control the White House, executive-enhancing reforms will promote economic equality."[45] Here she is of course using "redistribution" in the egalitarian sense.

Since the Republican and Democratic parties are currently composed of coalitions of at least two cultures,[46] and since we can deduce how the various cultures value economic equality, we can predict that only particular kinds of Republican and Democratic presidents will diminish, maintain, or promote that equality. A predominantly individualistic Ronald Reagan Republican will diminish economic equality by letting free men in free markets accumulate all the wealth that they can. A hierarchical George Herbert Walker Bush Republican, however, is more likely to maintain economic inequities than to increase or decrease them. A predominantly egalitarian Bill Clinton Democrat is the only one in this group who would try to promote economic equality (because of his 1960s Yale law school socialization), but when cross-pressured he is easily mistaken for a Republican due to his roots in the socially hierarchical south.[47]

Some Attention to the "Feedback Loop" in a Budget Theory

Whicker notes that "budgetary outcomes contribute to the formation of new arrays of political ideologies which, in turn, contribute to demand for different budget reforms in order to attain different political outcomes. How this feedback occurs, resulting in political realignments, needs to be explored."[48] Cultural theorists' theory of change can be transposed to budgeting to characterize a "feedback loop" in which budgetary outcomes advance the policies of some ways of life over others, leading to a test of those policies, their vindication or invalidation, and either increased or decreased spending on them. Thus, Lyndon Johnson's Great Society initiatives were victories for egalitarians who believed that government should do more to help the poor, uneducated, and disenfranchised develop the capacities to participate in and enjoy the benefits of mainstream, middle-class society. These programs, and their funding, came under attack in the Reagan years in part because they were not able to demonstrate sufficient success in moving people out of poverty, culminating in Bill Clinton's campaign and legislation to "end welfare as we know it." Other times, it is the perceived success rather than failure of a policy that leads to decreased government spending in a particular area. Against heavy Democratic opposition, Ronald Reagan pursued a policy of "peace through strength," ratcheting up defense expenditures and thereby contributing to the collapse of the Soviet system, resulting in drastic cutbacks in American defense expenditures, and much talk about how to spend the so-called "peace dividend."

Examination of the Implications of Budget Outcomes for Economic Growth

"A full budget theory would take both economic conditions and perceptions of economic conditions by budget actors into account," Whicker thinks.[49] More generally, it is not only the economic, but also the political, demographic, and environmental contexts, among others, that need to be accounted for by the sort of predictive budgetary theory she would like to see. While cultural theory cannot predict these causes of government spending and taxation, such conditions and events have no meanings except those given to them by people having different cultural commitments. Perceptions, as Whicker says, are very important. With respect to economic growth, for example, analysts and ideologues will not only debate the extent to which the economy is growing and who is benefiting from that growth, but whether growth itself is a good thing. Cultural theorists predict that different subcultures will have different ideas about how to make ends meet, because they perceive natural resources and human needs differently. Individualists, for example, think that there is no limit to economic growth, since there are no limits to human wants that human ingenuity, the ultimate renewable resource, cannot satisfy. Egalitarians, meanwhile, think that economic growth is constrained by natural resources, which are finite, which is all well and good because humans uncorrupted by "consumer capitalism" have very simple needs anyway. Hierarchs, for their part, believe in sustainable economic development, where the rate and type of growth, and control and allocation of resources, human and natural, are within the purview of the state, and its experts and authorities.

Similarly, political, demographic, and environmental factors don't become factors or influences on the budget until people of differing cultural commitments decide to make them factors or influences. The decision to go to war, even against Hitler, is not inevitable. Initially, Roosevelt was only able to get the American public to acquiesce in a "lend-lease" program, in which Britain was supposed to give back our tanks and planes when it was done with them! Likewise, just because the population is aging doesn't mean this fact has to have any bearing on the federal budget, as proposals to privatize Social Security indicate. The existence and extent of various alleged environmental problems is also highly contested, underscoring the fact that budgetary outlays in these areas are the result of political decisions, not "acts of God."

A Normative Theory of Budgeting?

"We should not shrink" from attempting to develop a normative theory of budgeting despite the difficulty, Whicker concludes, although she does not set this as one of the tasks of a grander budget theory.[50] As Aaron specified the problem, "a normative theory of budgeting would be a comprehensive and specific political theory detailing what the government's activities ought to be at a particular time."[51] He derided such a theory as utopian and totalitarian, but did observe that "adherence to different normative theories is quite common."[52] He also acknowledged that there is no neutral position from which to criticize cultural practices, including budgeting. Every critique of a normative position is made from some other normative position. Aaron's individualism was usually stronger than his hierarchical tendencies, and this was the normative position from which he criticized the centralizing proposals of management science types.

Moreover, every system of budgeting is normative in the sense that it promotes some values over others. Normative theories of budgeting are omnipresent rather than rare. One cannot budget without them, because the question of who gets to make allocative decisions has to be answered with some principle, and those allocations have to serve some values. American budgeting is no different. Our fragmented, accessible institutions reflect the strength of individualism and egalitarianism in our society. Our normative theory is that budgets should reflect the preferences of ways of life in proportion to their political representatives' relative presence and power in our government institutions. Our constitutional democratic theory of budgeting is the American answer to V.O. Key's question: "On what basis shall it be decided to allocate X dollars to activity A instead of activity B?"[53]

The dominance of any cultural type would mean the dominance of a particular normative theory of budgeting. But not all ways of life, if dominant, would prefer a centralized itemization and expenditure of societal resources. This kind of budgeting is most likely to be the result of societal dominance by hierarchical ways of life, as in Britain, France, and Japan, or in the extreme, the former Soviet Union. If individualists were dominant they probably would prefer non-centralized, fragmented budgeting: perhaps Articles of Confederation[54] or state budgeting, or at the extreme, with no states, just personal, family, or firm budgeting. Egalitarians, if dominant, might be satisfied with budgeting by referendum, as in California voting on bond issues or property taxes, or with New England Town Hall or some other form of community budgeting that permitted as many people to participate in these decisions as possible. Fatalists, given the uncertainty endemic to their relationships, if dominant would resign themselves to some form of repetitive, every-person-and-agency-for-themselves budgeting.

With His Work, with Us Still

Aaron Wildavsky put some forty books on our library shelves and hundreds of articles in our journals. Among these studies were many in the anthropological tradition of Clifford Geertz: close analyses, rich in detail, with modest if any theory. If we want to find out about presidential elections over the last thirty years,[55] implementation of federal policies in Oakland,[56] the leadership of Moses,[57] contemporary environmental science in policy-making,[58] or budgeting in America, Britain, France, Japan and poor countries,[59] among many other topics, we can go to those shelves (or often the ones at home) and Aaron will tell us what we need to know. Most will remember him for these studies of particular things in particular places at particular times. And for founding Berkeley's school of public policy, and for the kind of person he was, among many other memories. But even with this incredible scholarly and personal legacy, what Aaron most want to be remembered for was developing and refining an analytical and interpretive tool that others could pick up and use in their own work. Cultural theory, with all its warts, and all of its unanswered questions,[60] was, in his view, his most important work, and his most valuable legacy. It is with this work, this living legacy, that he is still with us, and wanted to be with us.

People have to know who gets to do what with and to whom under what circumstances in order to live together. The resulting regularities in behavior and patterns in relationships allow the possibility of social science. At the same time, the apparent variation in the way people solve the problems of social organization militates against forming generalizations about human behavior. As social scientists, one of our special tasks should be to construct concepts and theories that make some of these idiosyncratic, varied behaviors and practices comparable. Similarities and differences, the categories of human experience, are always imposed; we just have to distinguish between our constructs and those of the people we are studying. Like those we seek to understand, we are a meaning-creating community or series of communities. We share some concepts and theories, but we also have many specialized vocabularies and grammars. Cultural theory is an attempt to create a durable, universal language for social scientists, which can be used as an interpretive framework, an analytical tool, and a source of hypotheses.

It certainly is easier and safer to believe that no general theory of budgeting, much less of other aspects of social life, is possible. Indeed, Aaron was more aware of the difficulties than most, since he had spent a lifetime studying an incredibly broad array of social phenomena in as much detail as those narrowly specialized on these phenomena. No starry-eyed optimist, he had chosen, he said, "to break his bones on the rocky shoals of general social theory." He agreed with Heclo that "the results of generations of intellectual endeavor are clear. No one knows how to reduce the interactions of thought and action to any formulae existing outside the contingencies of historical time."[61] But just because something hasn't been done, he might have said, doesn't mean it can't be done, nor that we should stop trying to do it. No one has yet found a cure for cancer either, but that doesn't mean we have stopped trying. Aaron was aware of the criticism—"this man is dangerous, confused, incomprehensible, or, let us face it, incompetent," was his paraphrase—but he also believed that "if you listen to too much of what is now acceptable, you will never do (or think) anything different."[62]

"The reader cannot take existing theory for granted," Aaron counseled. "Rather his task is to make theory out of disparate and disconnected material. This is a formidable task, which is one reason there is so little readily available for the taking. Theory cannot just be picked up; it has to be searched for, chiseled, shaped, pounded, reorganized, and reoriented. Creating coherence out of existing bits of theory is like getting an inside straight in poker."[63]

In case you missed it, that was a clear invitation to pull up a seat at the table and build on the hand he has dealt us!

Notes

Many thanks to Naomi Caiden, Richard Coughlin, Margarita Decierdo, Mary Douglas, Richard Ellis, Richard Gunther, Chandra Hunter, Charles Lockhart, Rob Pirro, James Savage, Allen Schick, Percy Tannenbaum, Michael Thompson, Marcia Whicker, and Joe White for their many helpful comments on an earlier draft of this postscript.

1.   Michael Thompson, Richard Ellis, and Aaron Wildavsky, *Cultural Theory* (Boulder, CO: Westview Press, 1990).
2.   Mary Douglas, *Purity and Danger: An Analysis of Concepts of Pollution and Taboo* (London: Routledge & Kegan Paul, 1966); Mary Douglas, *Natural Symbols: Explorations in Cosmology* (London: Barrie & Rockliff, 1970); Mary Douglas, "Cultural Bias," in Mary Douglas, ed., *In the Active Voice* (London: Routledge & Kegan Paul, 1982); Mary Douglas, ed., *Essays in the Sociology of Perception*

(London: Routledge & Kegan Paul, 1982); and Mary Douglas and Aaron Wildavsky, *Risk and Culture: An Essay on the Selection of Environmental and Technological Dangers* (Berkeley: University of California Press, 1983).

3. "Having a general theory gave him an intellectual purchase that he previously lacked and provided a vantage point from which he could contribute insightfully to a broad range of issues," continue Charles Lockhart and Richard M. Coughlin in their foreword to Aaron Wildavsky, *Culture and Social Theory*, Sun-Ki Chai and Brendon Swedlow, eds. (New Brunswick, NJ: Transaction Publishers, 1998) ix.

4. Brendon Swedlow and Aaron Wildavsky, "Is Egalitarianism Really on the Rise?," in Aaron Wildavsky, *The Rise of Radical Egalitarianism* (Washington, DC: American University Press, 1991); Brendon Swedlow, "Cultural Influences on Policies Concerning Mental Illness," in *Politics, Policy & Culture*, Dennis J.Coyle and Richard J. Ellis, eds.(Boulder, CO: Westview Press, 1994); and Brendon Swedlow, *Scientists, Spotted Owls, and Forests: Policymakers in the Pacific Northwest* (Ph.D. Dissertation, University of California, Berkeley, forthcoming).

5. Michael Thompson, *Inherent Relationality: An Anti-Dualist Approach to Institutions*, Report 9608 (Bergen, Norway: LOS Centre, 1996): 46. For current attempts to relate cultural theory to the literature on organizations, see H. Edward Flentje, "State Administration in Cultural Context," in *Handbook of State Administration*, John J. Gargan, ed. (New York: Marcel Decker, 2000); Christopher Hood, *The Art of the State* (New York: Clarendon Press, 1998); Dennis J. Coyle, "A Cultural Theory of Organizations," in *Culture Matters: Essays in Honor of Aaron Wildavsky*, Richard J. Ellis and Michael Thompson, eds. (Boulder, CO: Westview Press, 1997): 59-78; for Aaron's own efforts to apply cultural theory in analyzing organizations, see Aaron Wildavsky, "Administration Without Hierarchy? Bureaucracy without Authority?," in *Public Administration: The State of the Discipline*, Naomi B. Lynn and Aaron Wildavsky, eds. (Chatham, NJ: Chatham House, 1990): xiii-xix; Aaron Wildavsky, *Federalism and Political Culture*, David Schleicher and Brendon Swedlow, eds. (New Brunswick, NJ: Transaction Publishers, 1998); and Aaron Wildavsky, *Applying Cultural Theory*, Brendon Swedlow, ed. (New Brunswick, NJ: Transaction Publishers, forthcoming). Of related interest are Mary Douglas, *How Institutions Think* (Syracuse, NY: Syracuse University Press, 1986); and particularly Alan Page Fiske, *Structures of Social Life: The Four Elementary Forms of Human Relations* (New York: The Free Press, 1991), which develops a typology of social relations— communal sharing, authority ranking, equality matching, and market pricing— very similar to Douglas and Wildavsky's, and relates this to analogous typological efforts in many other kinds of literatures.

6. Garrett Hardin, "The Tragedy of the Commons," *Science* 162, (December 13, 1968): 1234-48; Aaron thought that "free-riding" only occurred in egalitarian social environments; see Aaron Wildavsky, "Indispensable Framework or Just Another Ideology? Prisoner's Dilemma as an Antihierarchical Game," *Rationality and Society* 4, 1 (January 1992): 8-23; and Jesse Malkin and Aaron Wildavsky, "Why the Traditional Distinction between Public and Private Goods Should be Abandoned," *Journal of Theoretical Politics* 3, 4 (1991): 355-78; both of these articles are also reprinted in *Culture and Social Theory*.

7. Aaron assumed that contention among these cultural types would always register in federal budgetary processes and outcomes. His assumption is probably increasingly realistic since the New Deal, but is less realistic a starting point prior to

World War I, and particularly prior to the Civil War, when the federal government only grew, in Aaron's words, from "tiny to small."

8.   Aaron Wildavsky, "From Political Economy to Political Culture, Or Why I Like Cultural Analysis," in Aaron Wildavsky, *Applying Cultural Theory*, Brendon Swedlow, ed. (New Brunswick, NJ: Transaction Publishers, forthcoming).
9.   Carolyn Weber and Aaron Wildavsky, *A History of Taxation and Spending in the Western World* (New York: Simon and Schuster, 1986).
10. Aaron Wildavsky, "A Cultural Theory of Budgeting," *International Journal of Public Administration*, 11, 6 (1988): 651-77.
11. Aaron Wildavksy,"Toward a Comparative Theory of Budgetary Processes," *Budgeting: A Comparative Theory of Budgetary Processes*, revised 2nd edition (New Brunswick, NJ: Transaction Publishers, 1986); reprinted as chapter 8 of this volume.
12. Hugh Heclo and Aaron Wildavsky, *The Private Government of Public Money*, 2nd edition (London: Macmillan, 1981).
13. *Applying Cultural Theory*.
14. Hugh Heclo, "Naturalistic Inquiry in Washington and Whitehall," *Public Budgeting & Finance* 14,1 (Spring 1994): 59.
15. Idem.
16. Ibid, 60.
17. Allen Schick,"From the Old Politics of Budgeting to the New," *Public Budgeting & Finance* 14,1 (Spring 1994): 135-6.
18. Idem and Aaron Wildavsky, *The New Politics of the Budgetary Process* (Glenview, Illinois: Scott, Foresman & Company, 1988): xvi.
19. *The New Politics of the Budgetary Process*, 192.
20. Naomi Caiden and Aaron Wildavsky, *Planning and Budgeting in Poor Countries* (New York: John Wiley & Sons, 1974; New Brunswick, NJ: Transaction Publishers, 1980).
21. For uses of cultural theory to understand the causes of poverty, see the analysis of Edward Banfield's *The Moral Basis of a Backward Society* [(New York: Free Press, 1958)] in *Cultural Theory*, 223-27; Michael Thompson and Aaron Wildavsky, "A Poverty of Distinction: From Economic Homogeneity to Cultural Heterogeneity in the Classification of Poor People," *Policy Sciences* 19 (1986): 163-99; Gotfried Engbersen, et al., *Cultures of Unemployment: A Comparative Look at Long-Term Unemployment and Urban Poverty* (Boulder, CO: Westview Press, 1993); Richard J. Ellis, "The Social Construction of Slavery," *Politics, Policy, & Culture*, 117-35; and Brendon Swedlow, "Culture and Poverty: The Rios Family Revisited," (typescript 1992).
22. *Planning and Budgeting in Poor Countries*, 95-96.
23. Charles Lockhart, "Cultural Change and Rational Decisions," Comparative Political Studies 33 (forthcoming April 2000); Charles Lockhart and Richard M. Coughlin, "Building Better Comparative Social Theory Through Alternative Conceptions of Rationality," *Western Political Quarterly* 45 (September 1992): 793-809. See also Aaron Wildavsky, "Why Self-Interest Means Less Outside of a Social Context: Cultural Contributions to a Theory of Rational Choices," *Journal of Theoretical Politics* 6, 2 (1994): 131-59; and Aaron Wildavsky, "Can Norms Rescue Self-Interest or Macro Explanation be Joined to Micro Explanation?," *Critical Review* 5, 3 (Spring 1991): 301-23. Aaron's articles also appear in *Culture and Social Theory*.
24. "Naturalistic Inquiry in Washington and Whitehall," 64.
25. Ibid, 65.

26. For more on the confrontation between "stipulated worlds" and "actual worlds" see *Cultural Theory*, 69-81.

27. *Budgeting: A Comparative Theory of Budgetary Processes*, 21; and Chapter 8 of this volume.

28. Alexander L. George and Timothy J. McKeown, "Case Studies and Theories of Organizational Decision-Making," *Advances in Information Processing in Organizations* 2: 21-58.

29. "Naturalistic Inquiry in Washington and Whitehall," 62.

30. David Collier and James E. Mahon, Jr., "Conceptual 'Stretching' Revisited: Adapting Categories in Comparative Analysis," *American Political Science Review* 87, 4 (December, 1993): 845; and Giovanni Sartori, "Concept Misformation in Comparative Politics," *American Political Science Review* 64 (1970): 1033-53; Giovanni Sartori, "Guidelines for Concept Analysis," in *Social Science Concepts: A Systematic Analysis*, Giovanni Sartori, ed. (Beverly Hills, CA: Sage, 1984).

31. Richard Ellis,"The Case for Cultural Theory: Reply to Friedman," *Critical Review* 7, 1 (1993): 101.

32. Aaron Wildavsky, "On the Balance of Budgetary Cultures," in *A Centennial History of the American Administrative State* (New York: Free Press, 1987): 379-413; and chapter 14 in this volume.

33. Aaron Wildavsky, "A Cultural Theory of Expenditure Growth and (Un)balanced Budgets, Journal of Public Economics, 28 (1985): 349-57; and chapter 12 in this volume.

34. "Naturalistic Inquiry in Washington and Whitehall," 62. For answers to Heclo's question in contexts most relevant to budgeting see Sun-Ki Chai and Aaron Wildavsky, "Cultural Change, Party Ideology, and Voting Stability," in *Culture and Social Theory*, 299-316; and John W. Houghton, *Culture and Currency: Cultural Bias in Monetary Theory and Policy* (Boulder, CO: Westview Press, 1991). See also Aaron Wildavsky, "Change in Political Culture," *Politics* 20, 2 (November 1985): 95-102; Daniel Polisar and Aaron Wildavsky, "From Individual to System Blame in the Law of Torts," *Journal of Policy History* 1, 2 (1989): 129-55; and Richard Ellis and Aaron Wildavsky, "A Cultural Analysis of the Role of Abolitionists in the Coming of the Civil War," *Comparative Studies in History and Society* 32, 1 (January 1990): 89-116. These three articles will be reprinted in *Applying Cultural Theory*. For additional examples of cultural analysis of historical change see Charles Lockhart, "Cultural Change and Rational Decisions;" and Dean C. Hammer, "Cultural Theory and Historical Change: The Development of Town and Church in Puritan New England," *Politics, Policy & Culture*, 137-56. See also Jeffrey Friedman, "Accounting for Political Preferences: Cultural Theory vs. Cultural History," *Critical Review* (Spring 1991): 325-51; Richard Ellis, "The Case for Cultural Theory: Reply to Friedman," 81-128; Jeffrey Friedman, "Cultural Theory as Individualistic Ideology: Rejoinder to Ellis," *Critical Review* 7, 1 (1993): 129-58.

35. "Naturalistic Inquiry in Washington and Whitehall," 62.

36. Nelson W. Polsby, "The Washington Community, 1960-1980," *The New Congress*, Thomas E. Mann and Norman J. Ornstein, eds. (Washington, D.C.: American Enterprise Institute).

37. This sectional heading and the six enumerated headings under it are taken from Marcia Lynn Whicker, "An Academician's Response: Toward a Grander Budget Theory," *Public Administration Review* 52, 6 (November/December, 1992): 601-603. Whicker was responding to Wildavsky's self-assessment of his early work on the budgetary process; Aaron Wildavsky, "Political Implications of Budget

Reform: A Retrospective," *Public Administration Review* 52, 6 (November/December, 1992): 594-99.
38. "An Academician's Response: Toward a Grander Budget Theory," 602.
39. Idem.
40. Idem.
41. Idem.
42. Idem.
43. "Toward a Comparative Theory of Budgetary Processes," 8; reproduced here as chapter 8.
44. "An Academician's Response: Toward a Grander Budget Theory," 603.
45. Idem.
46. "The Republican party of today," Aaron wrote in the late 1980s, "is something like two-thirds market to one-third hierarchical (some would say 55-45). Its internal conflict is between hierarchs whose overriding consideration is social stability and the market forces that want to expand the private and contract the public sectors. Because he takes a hierarchical, collectivist view of defense and a free-market, individualist view of domestic policy, President Ronald Reagan encapsulates these conflicts within his own administration. The Democratic party is divided in a different direction, between its hierarchical and egalitarian wings. Once the restraint of budget balance was removed they came together in support of the welfare state. With the hierarchical elements returning to support of higher defense and lower domestic spending in an effort to re-establish a social and financial equilibrium, the Democratic coalition is in danger of splitting." Aaron Wildavsky, "The Political Economy of Efficiency has not Changed but the World has and so have I," *Public Budgeting and Financial Management* 1, 1 (1989): 43-54. For an analysis of American political parties as shifting cultural coalitions, see Aaron Wildavsky, "Are American Political Parties Pretty Much the Same as they Used to Be in the 1950s, only a Little Different, or are they Radically Different? A Review Essay," *Journal of Policy History* 4, 2 (1992): 228-47 (this essay also appears in *Applying Cultural Theory*); Aaron Wildavsky, "The Internal Transformation of the American Political Parties: Democratic Activists are Increasingly Egalitarian, Republicans Individualist and Hierarchical," and "The Turtle Theory, Or Why has the Democratic Party Lost Five out of the Last Six Presidential Elections, Yet Retained Strong Control of the House, Won Majorities in the Senate, and Kept Three-Fifths of State Houses and Most Governorships?" in *The Rise of Radical Egalitarianism*. See also Nelson W. Polsby and Aaron Wildavsky, *Presidential Elections*, seventh edition (New York: Free Press, 1988); and Sun-Ki Chai and Aaron Wildavsky, "Cultural Change, Party Ideology and Electoral Outcomes," in *Culture and Social Theory*.
47. For a cultural analysis of the Reagan and Bush presidencies, see Aaron Wildavsky, *The Beleaguered Presidency* (New Brunswick, NJ: Transaction Publishers, 1991); for the Bush presidency see also Kerry Mullins and Aaron Wildavsky, "The Procedural Presidency of George Bush," *Society* (January/February 1991): 49-59; for the Clinton presidency see Aaron Wildavsky, "At Once Too Strong and Too Weak: President Clinton and the Dilemma of Egalitarian Leadership," *Presidential Studies Quarterly* 23, 3 (1993): 437-44. This article is also reprinted in *Applying Cultural Theory*. For a cultural analysis of early American presidencies, see Richard Ellis and Aaron Wildavsky, "Greatness Revisited: Evaluating the Performance of Early American Presidents in Terms of Cultural Dilemmas," *Presidential Studies Quarterly* 21, 1 (Winter 1991): 15-34; and Richard Ellis and Aaron Wildavsky,

Dilemmas of Presidential Leadership from Washington through Lincoln (New Brunswick, NJ: Transaction Publishers, 1989).

48. "An Academician's Response: Toward a Grander Budget Theory," 603.
49. Idem.
50. Idem. For an attempt to find a normative theory in cultural theory, see Charles Lockhart and Gregg Franzwa, "Cultural Theory and the Problem of Moral Relativism," *Politics, Policy & Culture*, 175-89.
51. "Political Implications of Budget Reform: A Retrospective," 595.
52. Idem.
53. As quoted in Ibid, 408. See also V.O. Key, Jr., "The Lack of a Budgetary Theory," *The American Political Science Review* 34 (December 1940): 1137-40.
54. To better visualize this alternative, see Aaron Wildavsky, "What if the United States were Still Governed Under the Articles of Confederation? Noncentralized versus Federal Systems," in *Federalism and Political Culture*, 83-134.
55. Nelson W. Polsby and Aaron Wildavsky, *Presidential Elections*.
56. Jeffrey Pressman and Aaron Wildavsky, *Implementation: How Great Expectations in Washington are Dashed in Oakland, Or Why It's Amazing that Federal Programs Work at All* (Berkeley: University of California Press, 1973).
57. Aaron Wildavsky, *The Nursing Father: Moses as a Political Leader* (Birmingham: University of Alabama Press, 1984. See also Aaron Wildavsky, *Assimilation versus Separation: Joseph the Administrator and the Politics of Religion in Biblical Israel* (New Brunswick, NJ: Transaction Publishers, 1993).
58. Aaron Wildavsky, *But Is It True? A Citizen's Guide to Environmental Health and Safety Issues* (Cambridge: Harvard University Press, 1995).
59. Aaron Wildavsky, *Budgeting: A Comparative Theory of Budgetary Processes*.
60. See the last chapter of *Cultural Theory*, "Hard Questions, Soft Answers," 261-75. See also Per Selle, "Culture and the Study of Politics," *Scandinavian Political Studies* 14, 2 (1991): 97-124; Aaron Wildavsky, "What Other Theory Would Be Expected to Answer Such Profound Questions? A Reply to Per Selle's Critique of *Cultural Theory*," *Scandinavian Political Studies* 14, 4 (1991): 355-61; and Per Selle, "It Must Have Something to do with Logic," 361-64.
61. "Naturalistic Inquiry in Washington and Whitehall," 63.
62. Aaron Wildavsky, *Craftways: On the Organization of Scholarly Work* (New Brunswick, NJ: Transaction Publishers, 1989), 152.
63. Ibid, 29.

Index

defined, 179
differences and variability in, 186–87
narrowly focused conflict over, 270
purposes, 3–5, 139–40, 179–81
similarities and constants in, 185
in turbulent times, 235–37
variables in, 185–91
Budgeting: A Comparative Theory of Budgetary Processes (Wildavsky), xvi
Budgeting and Accounting Act of 1921, 101
budgeting change, explaining, 345–46
Budgeting in Comparative Perspective (Wildavsky), xv
budget(s)
  as distributive document, 241–42
  imperfect, and negligent guardians, 113–15
  last year's, 115–16
  nature of, 179–81
  as political instruments, 329
  traditional, 4–5
  voted up or down as a whole, 322
Bureau of the Budget. *See* Budget Bureau
bureaucracy, 151
  as self-generating, 153, 167
bureaucratic conspiracy, 151, 152
bureaucratic inertia, 3, 10, 139. *See also* inertia
bureaucratization *vs.* representation, 124–25
bureaucrats, 167
  rewarding and punishing of, 151, 166
  voting by, 153, 167
bureaus *vs.* departments, 102. *See also* agencies

cabinet committees, 223–26
cabinet government, 223, 224
Cabinets, Canadian, 238
Caine, M. R., 290
calculations, budgetary, 74, 76, 181. *See also* incremental calculation
  making them manageable, 123
Calhoun, John C., 320
"camel's nose," tactic of, 142
Canada, 216–18, 228–30
  experience with spending limits, 228–29

Canadian Cabinets, 238
Canadian Policy and Expenditure Management system, 226
capitalism, 164–65, 267, 281. *See also* private enterprise
"caps," 146, 232
Carter, Jimmy, 330
Cathings, Waddill, 265
ceilings, 125, 149, 220, 222, 224, 229, 272, 273, 317. *See also* spending limits
central budget unit, 235
centralization, 38
change(s)
  quick and last-minute, 146–47
  resistance to, 3, 53. *See also* inertia; personnel
Christensen, Jorgen Gronngard, 234
civil servants, 153
Civil War, 262–63, 295, 303
Cleveland, Grover, 263, 296, 304
collectivism and collectivization, 194, 282, 305, 340
colonial period, 283–88
command and control methods, 313
committees
  having multiple, 123–24
  revitalizing old ones *vs.* creating new ones, 124
competition, 54, 255, 280, 281, 297
competitive individualism, 255, 260, 270, 278, 282, 344
"compound republic," theory of, 169
comprehensive analysis/approach, 79–80. *See also under* incremental calculation/budgeting
comprehensiveness, 79–80, 83, 242, 246
  escape routes from, 240–41
  horizontal and vertical, 9, 143
  ideology of, 100–101
  loss of, 239, 241, 243
  norm of, 193, 240, 244, 321, 328, 329
conflict, 138, 144, 270
  between finance and planning over expenditures, 119
  increase in, 106
  programming for, 101–5
confusion, 203
Congress, 78–79, 87–88, 218, 229. *See also* Continental Congress; *specific topics*

confidence in appropriations process, 111, 138, 139
conflict within. *See* conflict
delegation of power, 107
guidelines and implications for, 232
lessons from other countries for,
122–23
knowledge needed by, 105
legitimacy, xv
need to regain control of budget,
131–32
pluralism, 124
use of appropriations power, 90–93
Congress and Money (Schick), 271
Congressional Budget and Impoundment Control Act. *See* Budget Reform
Act of 1974
Congressional Budget Office (CBO),
139, 158, 273
congressional choice, criteria for, 125
congressional environment, characteristics of, 123–24
congressional guardianship of treasury.
See guardianship
congressional power of the purse, 113–
15
congressional realities, 123–25
Congressional Ways and Means Committee. *See* Ways and Means Committee
congressmen
providing representation *vs.* bureaucratization, 124
who vote for high spending, 113
conservatism, 3
conservatives, fiscal, 100
constant *vs.* minus-sum games, 206
Constitution, 72, 261, 280, 290–92
constitutional amendment(s), 158, 159,
229, 238, 299, 331, 333. *See also* Senate Joint Resolution 58
feasibility, 230
rationale for, 153–57, 230
to remedy "discovered faults" in
political arrangements, 270–71
types of, 218, 230
constitutional revenue and expenditure
limitation, purpose of, 332
constructivism, 342–43
consumption, unnecessary excessive, 152

consumption tax, 331
containment style, 192, 343
Continental Congress, 288–90
contingency analysis, 32
contingency funds, 227–28
control, 16, 78, 115, 142, 314
decline in, 242, 243
regaining, 131–32
spending limits and, 232
types of, 12–13, 145
central, 245, 313, 322, 323
legal, 146
"remote," 147
and uncontrollability, 5, 220, 271
control departments, 242
control methods, command and, 313
controllers, budget, 117–19, 313
Coolidge, Calvin, 297
coordination, 80–82, 97, 151, 220, 272
cost-benefit analysis, 22–23, 34, 36, 37,
66, 126
advantages, 28, 29
economic and political assumptions
underlying, 23–25
limitations in the utility of, 25–27
mixed results of, 27–29
purpose, 22–23
Council of Economic Advisors (CEA),
93, 135
countries. *See* nations
Crecine, John, 136
credit. *See also* loans
national, 292–93
credit outstanding, federal and federally
assisted, 148–50
"crisis" strategies, 87
cultural approach to studying budgeting,
337–38
problems and promise of, 342–46
cultural diversity, hypothesis of
and the colonial period, 283–88
cultural hypothesis, 195
cultural theory, xviii, xxii, 335
extended to other budgetary topics,
338–42. *See also specific topics*
nature of, xvii, 335–37, 352
"Cultural Theory of Budgeting, A"
(Wildavsky), xviii, 337
cultural types, 342–45
inter-penetration of, 346

sectarianism in America and Europe,
253, 256
sectarians, xvii, 195–97, 251, 255, 256.
See also egalitarian regimes/collectives
self-regulation, 251
Senate Appropriations Committee, 75,
77, 78, 83, 97, 129. *See also* appropriations committees
Senate Budget Committee, 273
Senate Joint Resolution 58 (S. J. Res.
58), 163, 218, 274
seniority system, 100
sequestration, 327
sertice sote, 116
Shooshan, Harry, 61
simplification *vs.* mystification, 125
Smith, Adam, 301
Smith, Sidney, 302–3
Smithies, Arthur, 39, 93
social constructivism, 342–43
Social Development Committee, 223
social environments, dimensions that
define, 340
social welfare and social programs, 315,
325, 328. *See also* government programs; internal improvements; welfare
growth of, 165
Soil Conservation Service (SCS), 28
Soviet industrial firms, 89
special interests. *See under* interests
specialization, 77, 124
spend, penalties for failing to, 134
spending
public, 157–59
trends in, 148–49
uncontrollable, as percentage of
federal budget, 273
spending agencies, 130
spending habit, kicking the, 156–57
spending increases, 220–22, 227
trading them for reductions in later years, 226
spending limits, 149, 156, 159, 163, 175,
222, 244. *See also* constitutional
amendment(s)
alternatives to, 159
Canada's experience with, 228–29
change from micro-control to
macro-limits, 216
criticisms of and problems with,
227, 274

desire for, 163
emergence of, 238
erosion of, 245
getting around, 157
governments' failure to abide by
their own, 228
implementation, 227
purposes, 225
self-enforcing, 230
Spinoza, Benedict de, 72
Spring Preview, 136
status quo, 95
Steiner, G. A., 38
strategic information, increasing the
availability of, 101–3
strategic planning, 67–68, 76
defined, 49
strategic political information, 103–4
"Structural Budget Margin," 15–16
subceilings, 317–19, 349
subcultures, 338, 344
subordination, 194
subsidies, 156
sunset laws, 158
supplemental appropriations, 96, 137
surplus. *See under* deficit(s)
system *vs.* partisan *vs.* policy politics, 38, 42
systems analysis, 29–34, 38. *See also*
program budgeting
vs. policy analysis, 49–50
systems studies, 47

tax, individual income, 314, 329, 330
amount of and increases in per-
capita personal income and, 267,
268
tax expenditures, 13, 145–46, 155–56,
224, 239
tax indexing, 217, 322
tax rates, 118, 157, 191, 329, 330
and the economy, 316
increasing, 113, 269, 330–31
tax subsidies, 13
taxation, 238, 293, 294, 315, 331
during colonial period, 285–86
limits on, 244
taxes
"earmarked," 243
"reverse," 157